Converging Economic Policy, Corporate Strategy, and Technology for Emerging Economies

Erum Shaikh
Shaheed Benazir Bhutto University, Sanghar Campus, Pakistan

Abdul Samad Dahri
Shaheed Benazir Bhutto University, Pakistan

IGI Global
Scientific Publishing
Publishing Tomorrow's Research Today

Vice President of Editorial | Melissa Wagner
Managing Editor of Acquisitions | Mikaela Felty
Managing Editor of Book Development | Jocelynn Hessler
Production Manager | Mike Brehm
Cover Design | Phillip Shickler

Published in the United States of America by
IGI Global Scientific Publishing
701 East Chocolate Avenue
Hershey, PA, 17033, USA
Tel: 717-533-8845
Fax: 717-533-8661
Website: https://www.igi-global.com E-mail: cust@igi-global.com

Library of Congress Cataloging-in-Publication Data

Names: Shaikh, Erum, 1988- editor. | Dahri, Abdul Samad, 1987- editor.
Title: Converging economic policy, corporate strategy, and technology for emerging economies / [edited by] Erum Shaikh, Abdul Dahri.
Description: Hershey, PA : IGI Global Scientific Publishing, [2025] | Includes bibliographical references and index. | Summary: "This area of study focuses on how technology is transforming the industrial and service sectors in emerging markets. It explores the significant effects on economic landscapes of the strategies, innovations, and problems that characterize the integration of technology into these essential sectors"-- Provided by publisher.
Identifiers: LCCN 2024054550 (print) | LCCN 2024054551 (ebook) | ISBN 9798369357231 (hardcover) | ISBN 9798369357248 (paperback) | ISBN 9798369357255 (ebook)
Subjects: LCSH: Technological innovations--Economic aspects--Developing countries. | Strategic planning--Developing countries. | Developing countries--Economic policy.
Classification: LCC HC59.72.T4 C66 2025 (print) | LCC HC59.72.T4 (ebook) | DDC 338/.064091724--dc23/eng/20250123
LC record available at https://lccn.loc.gov/2024054550
LC ebook record available at https://lccn.loc.gov/2024054551

British Cataloguing in Publication Data
A Cataloguing in Publication record for this book is available from the British Library.

Table of Contents

Detailed Table of Contents

This study is one of the descriptive studies written to highlight the importance and use of Blue Ocean Strategies. Previous research that indicates the use and significance of Blue Ocean Strategies is very few. Hence, there is a need for a thorough study that may make readers understand the importance and role of Blue Ocean Strategies in the performance of the firm. Hence, this study is designed to foster the understanding that may foster research and better policymaking. Therefore, the significance of this study has multiple folds and may be found to be fruitful for numerous stakeholders.

This research explores the synergistic relationship between economic policy, corporate strategy, and technological advancements in fostering sustainable growth in emerging economies. As these nations face unique challenges, such as infrastructural gaps, resource constraints, and rapidly evolving global markets, the alignment of policy frameworks, corporate objectives, and technological innovation becomes crucial. This study analyzes how cohesive economic policies can incentivize corporate strategies that leverage technology for competitive advantage, driving productivity and inclusive growth. It also highlights the role of government regulations in creating an ecosystem conducive to innovation and entrepreneurship. By examining case studies of emerging markets, this paper offers insights into optimizing resource allocation, fostering technological adoption, and aligning corporate strategies with long-term development goals. The findings suggest that a unified, integrative approach is essential for unlocking the full potential of emerging economies in the global marketplace.

The chapter investigates advancements within the service sector, particularly focusing on leveraging technology to enhance client experiences. It comprehensively analyzes a spectrum of technological innovations, encompassing virtual reality, automation, artificial intelligence, and the Internet of Things, elucidating their profound impact on service provision across diverse industries. The chapter incorporates a structured class exercise aimed at fostering creative problem-solving for service delivery, promoting critical thinking, innovation, and a deeper understanding of technology's pivotal role in shaping service ecosystems. It also serves real-world case study featuring Zomato, an Indian-based online food ordering and delivery company, which serves to illuminate the practical challenges and intricacies inherent in implementing state-of-the-art service delivery methodologies. By meticulously dissecting this case study, the chapter offers invaluable insights into the hurdles of client adoption, internal organizational resistance, and the intricacies of technological integration.

This chapter deeply explores the production sector's complex dynamics, emphasizing the revolutionary effects of manufacturing technology breakthroughs. This chapter explains how automation, additive manufacturing, and the Internet of Things (IoT) revolutionize production processes, increase efficiency, and improve supply chain operations. It does this by exploring these technologies in detail. The unique contributions of each technology are that automation enhances productivity and consistency while lowering costs and minimizing human error; additive manufacturing, or 3D printing, allows for mass customization, decreases waste, and speeds up prototyping; and IoT enables real-time monitoring, predictive maintenance, and supply chain optimization. These technologies are propelling the development of smart factories and Industry 4.0, leading to highly efficient, flexible, and responsive production systems. A practical experience that simulates the establishment of an intelligent factory enhances students' comprehension of Industry 4.0 technology and in digitalized environment.

Foreword

In the dynamic landscape of emerging economies, the interplay between economic policy, corporate strategy, and technological advancement is reshaping pathways to sustainable growth and global competitiveness. As these regions strive to achieve stability and innovation, the convergence of these three critical elements becomes a cornerstone for progress.

Converging Economic Policy, Corporate Strategy, and Technology for Emerging Economies offers a timely and comprehensive exploration of these interconnected forces. This volume brings together a diverse array of perspectives from academics, policymakers, and industry experts, providing an insightful synthesis of how strategic decisions and policies can foster innovation, economic resilience, and social progress. The chapters address real-world challenges and propose practical frameworks for leveraging technology to drive corporate success and economic development.

As the world witnesses rapid technological shifts, the insights contained in this book underscore the importance of adaptive strategies and forward-thinking policies. Readers will find valuable analyses of issues such as the digital economy, corporate governance, and policy frameworks that support sustainable innovation. The discussions herein are not only academically robust but also pragmatically focused, offering guidance for leaders and decision-makers working to navigate the complexities of emerging markets.

This volume is an essential contribution to the discourse on sustainable development and strategic growth in a technology-driven world. It provides a roadmap for aligning policy, strategy, and technology to unlock the full potential of emerging economies.

I commend the editor for curating such a thought-provoking collection and the contributors for their scholarly contributions. I am confident that this book will catalyze further research, dialogue, and innovation.

Muhammad Nawaz Tunio
University of Sufism and Modern Sciences, Bhitshah, Sindh, Pakistan.

Preface

In the rapidly evolving landscape of emerging economies, the intersection of economic policy, corporate strategy, and technology is reshaping industries and driving global transformation. The historical development and current dynamics of technology in these markets offer valuable insights into how technology impacts not just companies and communities, but entire international marketplaces. As editors, we have carefully curated this volume to shed light on the profound effects of this convergence, providing a comprehensive exploration of the challenges, advancements, and strategies that define how technology is integrated into key sectors.

This book explores the dynamic interplay between the service and production sectors of emerging markets and the ever-expanding role of technology. It serves as a thorough guide for readers, taking them through the intricate tactics, obstacles, and breakthroughs that shape the adoption of technology within these critical industries. Through this exploration, we uncover how technological innovations influence economic environments, transforming industrial and service sectors in profound and sometimes unexpected ways.

The central theme of this work lies at the nexus of economic policy, corporate strategy, and technological transformation. The strategies employed by companies within these sectors not only impact industry dynamics but ripple out to affect the socioeconomic fabric of these regions, influencing employment, innovation, and overall quality of life. This book offers insights into the consequences of these shifts, both within emerging markets and on the global stage.

Organized into twelve insightful segments, the book covers diverse topics, from historical underpinnings and market entry strategies to the evolving role of digital infrastructure and advancements in service delivery. Each chapter delves into specific aspects of the technology-driven revolution, offering readers a nuanced understanding of how technology drives transformation in the heart of emerging economies. The culmination of this investigation reveals key strategies, inventions, and collaborations that have contributed to the growth and success of businesses and economies alike.

Our goal with this publication is to provide a roadmap for those seeking a deeper understanding of how technology shapes economic landscapes, focusing on the strategies and innovations that empower businesses and communities in emerging markets. Whether you're a business professional, an entrepreneur, an academic, a policymaker, or a technology enthusiast, this book offers valuable insights into the unique dynamics of these markets and how technology is facilitating their growth.

We hope that this book serves as an invaluable resource for business professionals, executives, entrepreneurs, academics, policy makers, investors, technology enthusiasts, and global development practitioners alike. By offering a comprehensive understanding of the role technology plays in transforming emerging economies, we aim to foster further innovation, collaboration, and development in this dynamic and ever-changing field.

ORGANIZATION OF THE BOOK

Chapter 1: A Computational Bibliometric Analysis of Systematic Review of Herding Behavior in Financial Markets

This chapter offers a comprehensive examination of investor herding behavior in both developed and emerging stock markets. Drawing from the Scopus database, it surveys 85 empirical and descriptive research papers spanning from 1980 to 2022. The study employs bibliometric analysis using VOSviewer to identify key trends, highly cited authors like Demirer R. and Kaminsky, and four distinct research clusters. By analyzing the connections between authors, countries, and publications, the chapter sheds light on the current state of literature and identifies potential research opportunities. The findings are valuable for researchers aiming to explore herding behavior and its effects on stock market dynamics.

Chapter 2: Decision to Determine the Optimal Firm's Capital Structure: A Systematic Literature Review

This chapter explores various theories on capital structure to understand how companies make financing decisions. Beginning with the foundational Modigliani and Miller (1958) theory, it critically examines other theories such as trade-off theory, pecking order theory, and market timing theory. These theories attempt to explain how firms balance debt and equity financing in response to information asymmetry. Despite these advancements, the question of why some firms prefer debt while others opt for equity remains unresolved. The chapter contributes to ongoing debates, particularly in light of the market timing theory and its implications for corporate financial strategies.

Chapter 3: Examining the Sector-Specific Ramifications of Initial Public Offering (IPO) Underpricing in the Indian Stock Market

Focusing on the phenomenon of IPO underpricing in India, this chapter investigates its impact on the Nifty 50 index, distinguishing between industrial, financial, and service sectors. Using Market Adjusted Abnormal Returns (MAAR) and Ordinary Least Squares (OLS) regression models, the study identifies key factors influencing IPO underpricing, including market returns, listing gains, oversubscription, issue price, and issue size. The chapter finds significant underpricing across all sectors, offering valuable insights for investors navigating IPOs and their initial returns, especially during periods of market fluctuation such as the pandemic.

Chapter 4: Blue Ocean Strategies and Firm Performance: Exploring the Ideas and Concepts in the New Normal

This chapter introduces Blue Ocean Strategies as a critical approach to firm performance in today's competitive landscape. The study emphasizes the role of innovation and differentiation in creating new market spaces, particularly in the context of the "new normal" post-pandemic economy. It argues for the strategic importance of moving away from saturated markets (the "red ocean") and innovating in ways that create uncontested market space. The findings underscore the need for organizations to rethink their strategic directions to remain competitive and resilient in changing global markets.

Chapter 5: Optimizing Economic Growth: A Unified Approach to Corporate Strategy, and Technological Advancements in Emerging Economies

This chapter explores how the intersection of economic policy, corporate strategy, and technological advancements can drive sustainable growth in emerging economies. Given the unique challenges faced by these countries, such as infrastructure gaps and resource constraints, the study advocates for cohesive policy frameworks that incentivize technological innovation and strategic corporate goals. The chapter emphasizes the role of government regulations in fostering an ecosystem conducive to entrepreneurship and innovation, ultimately positioning emerging markets for global competitiveness. Case studies further illustrate the benefits of a unified approach to economic development.

Chapter 6: Designing the Future of Service in Technology-Driven Innovation: Service Delivery Revolutionizing

Focusing on the service sector, this chapter highlights how technology is revolutionizing service delivery. It explores innovations such as virtual reality, artificial intelligence, automation, and the Internet of Things, demonstrating their transformative potential across various industries. Through a structured class exercise and a real-world case study of Zomato, the chapter illustrates the challenges and intricacies of integrating advanced service delivery methodologies. It offers valuable insights into the complexities of client adoption, organizational resistance, and technological integration, providing practical solutions for service-based companies.

Chapter 7: Production Sector Dynamics Technological Advances in Manufacturing and Production: Technological Advancement in the Modern Era

This chapter delves into the transformative impact of technology on the manufacturing and production sectors. It discusses automation, additive manufacturing (3D printing), and the Internet of Things (IoT) as key enablers of productivity, flexibility, and efficiency in modern production systems. These technologies are driving the evolution of smart factories and Industry 4.0. The chapter also includes a hands-on experience simulating the setup of an intelligent factory, helping readers understand how digitalization and technological advances are reshaping the manufacturing landscape.

Chapter 8: OpenStreetMap Empowering Digital Infrastructure for Emerging Markets

OpenStreetMap (OSM) presents a unique opportunity for emerging markets to develop cost-effective, scalable, and community-driven digital infrastructure. This chapter examines the benefits of OSM, including local knowledge utilization and integration with digital services, and how it empowers local entrepreneurs and communities. Despite its potential, challenges such as limited internet access and low digital literacy can hinder effective use. The chapter proposes solutions such as offline tools, community initiatives, and continuous training to overcome these barriers and ensure the sustainable growth of digital infrastructure in emerging markets.

Chapter 9: Catalyzing Growth: Charting a Path to 50 Lakh New Job Openings in India's IT and Software Sector Over the Upcoming Two Years

This chapter explores how India's Information Technology (IT) and Software sector can generate 50 lakh new job opportunities within the next two years. It identifies key drivers such as digital transformation, emerging technologies, and government initiatives that will help achieve this ambitious target. The chapter emphasizes the importance of skill development, innovation, and regulatory reforms in fostering job creation. Beyond economic growth, the findings suggest that this job creation initiative will enhance technological advancement and innovation, while addressing unemployment challenges in India.

Chapter 10: Discrimination, Gender, and Immigration: European Social Survey Investigation

This chapter investigates the ethnic and gender disparities between self-identified ethnic minorities and the majority populations across Western Europe. Using data from the European Social Survey, it highlights how factors like family background and socioeconomic status contribute to the persistent ethnic gaps in education, employment, and income. The study underscores the limited intergenerational mobility for ethnic minorities, particularly those from migrant backgrounds, and how these gaps cannot be fully explained by individual education levels alone. The chapter provides critical insights into the structural barriers that hinder social mobility for ethnic minorities in Europe.

Chapter 11: Artificial Intelligence and Its Implications for Cattle and Buffalo Farming

The last chapter seeks to make readers understand the role of AI in cattle farming. Previously studies on this topic were scarce and did not contain all the possible benefits of smart-cattle farming. Therefore, this study is developed through consulting multiple studies to reflect vividly on benefits that AI may provide to cattle farmers. Hence, this study is highly significant for researchers, scholars, and academicians who as this study is not only beneficial for improvement of knowledge and conduction of further studies but may also aid better business practices and policy making associated with the use of AI in cattle farming. However, this is a generic form of study which is developed for better understanding and improvement of research activities rather than to reflect outcomes inferentially. Hence, further work that may add to one's understanding must be conducted through focusing on the gist of this study.

CONCLUSION

In conclusion, the chapters within this edited reference book collectively illuminate the diverse and intricate dynamics that shape the landscape of business, technology, and economic policy. By exploring a wide range of topics—ranging from the psychological underpinnings of investor behavior in financial markets to the transformative power of technology in service delivery and manufacturing, this compilation offers both theoretical insights and practical applications. The integration of cutting-edge research on capital structure, IPO underpricing, and the optimization of corporate strategies for emerging economies further enriches the conversation, providing a global perspective on the challenges and opportunities faced by contemporary businesses. As we navigate the evolving "new normal," the inclusion of blue ocean strategies and technological innovations demonstrates a forward-thinking approach to sustainable growth and competitive advantage.

Moreover, chapters focused on the role of OpenStreetMap in empowering emerging markets and the ambitious goals of India's IT sector reflect the pivotal role of digital infrastructure and innovation in driving economic development and job creation. The research on social disparities and migration underscores the importance of understanding societal complexities in shaping inclusive policies for growth. Together, these contributions offer invaluable insights for researchers, practitioners, and policymakers seeking to understand and address the complexities of the modern business environment.

We hope this book will serve as an essential resource for advancing research and practice, offering critical perspectives and actionable solutions to the challenges of today's rapidly changing world. The collective work presented here not only deepens our understanding of each subject but also underscores the interconnectedness of the various factors influencing contemporary business, technology, and economic growth.

Acknowledgement

We would like to express our deep gratitude to everyone who contributed to the realization of this edited volume, *Converging Economic Policy, Corporate Strategy, and Technology for Emerging Economies.*

First and foremost, our sincere thanks go to the chapter contributors for sharing their insightful research and expertise. Their dedication and scholarly rigor have enriched this book, making it a meaningful resource for both academics and practitioners.

We extend Our appreciation to the team at IGI Global for their continuous support, professional guidance, and commitment throughout the editorial process. Their efforts in ensuring the quality and timely publication of this work have been invaluable.

We are also grateful to Our colleagues, and peers for their encouragement, constructive feedback, and thought-provoking discussions that shaped the direction of this book.

Finally, a heartfelt thanks to our family and friends for their unwavering support and understanding throughout this journey. Their patience and belief in our work have been a constant source of motivation.

This book is a testament to collective effort, and we hope it will inspire further research and strategic initiatives that drive sustainable growth in emerging economies.

Editors:

Erum Shaikh
Abdul Samad Dahri

Introduction

The historical development and current dynamics of technology in emerging economies offer a profound insight into a multidisciplinary field that bridges economic policy, corporate strategy, and technological innovation. This convergence clarifies the far-reaching ramifications of these intersections, illuminating the transformative effects on companies, communities, and international marketplaces. The interplay of these forces defines how technology shapes the industrial and service landscapes in emerging markets, reflecting both the opportunities and challenges that lie ahead.

This book, *Converging Economic Policy, Corporate Strategy, and Technology for Emerging Economies,* serves as a comprehensive exploration of the dynamic relationship between emerging markets' service and production sectors and the transformative potential of technology. By delving into the strategies, obstacles, and innovations shaping these crucial industries, the book aims to provide readers with a thorough understanding of how technology integrates into these sectors and influences economic ecosystems.

At its core, the study of this intersection emphasizes the significant effects of technology on economic landscapes. The strategies, innovations, and challenges discussed throughout this volume highlight the essential role of technology in driving transformation in the industrial and service sectors. This integration impacts not only industry dynamics but also extends into the socioeconomic fabric of emerging economies, influencing employment, innovation, and overall societal well-being.

The book is organized into eleven insightful chapters, each focusing on a unique aspect of the technology-driven revolution. Beginning with an overarching overview, it transitions through historical underpinnings, market entry strategies, advancements in service delivery, production sector dynamics, and the pivotal role of digital infrastructure. This structure ensures a logical progression that builds a holistic understanding of the subject matter.

This investigation lies at the nexus of economic policy, corporate strategy, and technological development. It delves into the strategies adopted by corporations and policymakers, shedding light on the consequences that ripple far beyond industry dynamics. By addressing the socioeconomic implications of technological integration, this book highlights its impact on innovation, employment, and the broader well-being of communities in emerging markets.

Essentially functioning as a roadmap, this publication provides a comprehensive understanding of how technology drives transformation at the heart of emerging markets. It unveils the strategies, innovations, and collaborative endeavors that propel businesses and economies forward, offering invaluable insights to a diverse range of stakeholders.

TARGET AUDIENCE

This book is designed to cater to a diverse audience, each with a vested interest in understanding the dynamics of technology in emerging markets. The key audiences include:

1. **Business Professionals and Executives:** Individuals in managerial or executive roles within technology-enabled service and production sectors in emerging markets, seeking insights into industry trends and strategies.
2. **Entrepreneurs and Start-Up Founders:** Aspiring and established entrepreneurs looking to leverage technology for success in the service and production sectors of emerging markets.
3. **Academics and Researchers:** Scholars and researchers examining the dynamics, challenges, and opportunities within technology-driven sectors in emerging markets.
4. **Policy Makers and Government Officials:** Professionals responsible for formulating policies on technology, innovation, and economic development, aiming for a nuanced understanding of these topics.
5. **Investors and Financiers:** Individuals or organizations exploring investment opportunities within the technology-driven service and production sectors, seeking data-driven insights for informed decision-making.
6. **Technology Enthusiasts:** Passionate individuals eager to explore the intersection of technology and business, particularly within the context of emerging markets.
7. **Consultants and Advisers:** Business consultants and advisers working with companies in the technology-enabled service and production sectors, looking for best practices and industry trends.
8. **Students and Educators:** Learners and educators in business, technology, or economics seeking a resource to deepen their understanding of technology-driven transformation in emerging markets.

9. **Industry Associations and Trade Groups:** Organizations representing businesses in the service and production sectors, using the insights in this book to support their members and advocate for industry interests.
10. **Global Development Practitioners:** Professionals engaged in global development initiatives who wish to comprehend the role of technology in shaping economic development in emerging markets.

The convergence of economic policy, corporate strategy, and technology is reshaping the industrial and service sectors of emerging economies. By examining this transformation through a multidisciplinary lens, this book provides a comprehensive guide for navigating the challenges and harnessing the opportunities presented by technological integration. It invites readers to explore the strategies, innovations, and collaborative efforts that are driving progress, ensuring that stakeholders across various sectors can contribute to and benefit from the ongoing technological revolution in emerging markets.

Chapter 1
A Computational Bibliometric Analysis of Systematic Review of Herding Behaviour in Financial Markets

Mohsen Brahmi
https://orcid.org/0000-0002-0995-0761
University of Sfax, Tunisia

Deepika Krishnan
https://orcid.org/0000-0002-1471-6953
Symbiosis International University, India

K. Archana
Sambhram Academy of Management Studies, India

ABSTRACT

The purpose of this paper is to provide a complete understanding on investors herd behavior in both developed and emerging nations' stock markets. In this regard a survey is betrothed from Scopus database from month 1980 to month 2022 which consist of 85 empirical and descriptive research papers from the total of 135 full published documents. Systematic Literature Review and bibliometric scrutiny have been done with the help of VOSviewer. The finding of the study through Systematic Literature Review was that Demirer. R was the highly cited author followed by Kaminsky. Four clusters with different themes were identified through Bibliometric analysis. It also revealed the degree of connection among authors, countries, and

DOI: 10.4018/979-8-3693-5723-1.ch001

publications. This study would help prospective researchers gain meaningful insight into the contemporary state of the prevailing literature and conduct a qualitative review of the literature, and would also provide insight into the research profile and opportunities that can be conducted regarding herd behavior in the stock market.

INTRODUCTION

In the realm of financial markets, one prevalent and widely recognized phenomenon is herd behavior. It arises because of spontaneous cognitive processes, where individuals react to signals from the actions of others. This behavior is commonly observed among both institutional and individual investors and is often identified as a significant driver behind periods of heightened volatility and market instability (Ng et al, 2022; Hasanet al, 2023; Ahn et al, 2024). Scharfstein and Stein (1990) conducted a comprehensive examination of herd behavior across different time periods, countries, financial crises, and financial markets. According to Bikhchandani et al., (1992), herding occurs when an individual's actions or decisions are more influenced by the actions of others in the market than by their private information. It manifests as investors blindly following their peers due to a deep-seated desire to conform to the market consensus, sometimes setting aside their own convictions (Devonow and Welch, 1996).

Christie and Huang (1995) provided a more precise definition of herding behavior, describing it as investors forsaking their own judgments and instead relying on the collective actions of the market (Missaoui, Brahmi and Rajeb, 2022), even when their perspectives conflict with prevailing market forecasts in their investment decisions. However, despite the commonly held belief that herding behavior is prevalent in financial markets, the available empirical evidence does not unequivocally support this notion, as highlighted by Welch (2000).The concept of herding was initially conceptualized as "reciprocal mocking," leading to a convergence of actions, as articulated by Hirshleifer and Teoh (2003). Herd behavior among market participants can be driven by various factors, including the acquisition of information from prior market participants' actions, reactions to the emergence of significant information (Mohsen and Sonia 2013), a desire among experts to protect their reputations, or the pursuit of potential rewards by following the crowd (Ahmad& Wu, 2022; Youssef,2022; Ah Mand et al, 2023). Sometimes, investors may also engage in herd behavior due to irrational decision-making (Spyrou, 2013). Yang (2011) suggests that the accuracy of costly private indicators and the methods used to extract signals can influence investors' propensity for herd behavior. Nonetheless, some economists argue that herd behavior can create deceptive situations in financial markets and contribute to price instability (Choijilet al, 2022; Mavruk, 2022; Yousaf &Yarovaya, 2022; Jiang et al, 2022; Youssef& Waked, 2022; Gavrilakis& Floros, 2023; Ghorbel et al, 2023, Li et al, 2023; Filip &Pochea, 2023; Vieito et al, 2023).

In the existing body of literature, a substantial portion of research has concentrated on investigating the presence of herd behavior in stock markets, yet there has been relatively limited focus on conducting comprehensive literature reviews. This will be assessed through the Following hypotheses:

(a) The scarcity of comprehensive literature reviews on herd behavior within financial markets implies an overlooked research domain, necessitating further in-depth investigations to advance our comprehension of this phenomenon.
(b) The analysis of published works on Investor Herd Behavior in Stock Markets from 1980 to 2022, through the combination of Systematic Literature Review Analysis and Bibliometric Analysis, will reveal significant patterns, trends, and gaps in the existing research landscape, contributing to a comprehensive understanding of this phenomenon.

Consequently, there is a distinct need for both bibliometric analysis and an exhaustive review of the existing literature. Thus, the primary aim of this article is to conduct a systematic literature review that consolidates and offers a concise overview of the extensive research on herd behavior. Additionally, this article endeavours to undertake a thorough bibliometric analysis, summarizing an extensive array of bibliometric data to provide insights into the current state of herd behavior in stock markets.This paper contributes significantly to this field of study in several ways. It commences by providing a summary of the quantity of publications and citations, which can serve as a valuable resource for aspiring researchers contemplating previous studies. Furthermore, it delves into an in-depth exploration of the most prominent nations, authors, publications, and articles in this domain. Finally, the research offers insights into co-authorship networks, shedding light on how nations collaborate in the creation of scholarly articles. The conclusions drawn from this study will be instrumental in aiding researchers in identifying promising areas for future research endeavors.

The study comprises four primary sections. The initial section primarily centres on providing an overview and establishing the study's framework. The subsequent section delves into the selection criteria, analytical tools, and the range of databases employed for conducting literature reviews. Following this, the third section encompasses bibliometric and descriptive analyses. Lastly, the concluding section offers insights and suggestions for further research.

REVIEW OF LITERATURE

Despite the multitude of articles on herding behavior in the stock market, limited research has delved into the underlying factors driving this behavior. Up to the end of 2018, discussions within tier 1, 2, and 3 journals have been extensive regarding research on herding behavior in capital markets. Over time, there has been a diversification of research methods and contexts in herding behavior studies (Mohsen and *al.* 2018). However, our comprehension of herding behavior remains constrained, and empirical evidence of herding behavior in the stock market remains inconclusive. Furthermore, Cipriani and Guarino (2005) argue that the theory does not entirely explain herd behavior in capital markets, necessitating a comprehensive literature review to gather and assess all pertinent research on herding behavior across various markets.

Komalasari et al. (2021) conducted both a bibliometric analysis and a Systematic Literature Review to offer researchers a comprehensive overview of study outcomes, research trends, and influential works in the realm of herding behavior. They employed co-occurrence of research keywords analysis on 279 papers retrieved from the Scopus database, culminating in the creation of a knowledge structure for herding in capital markets. Spyrou (2013) undertook a literature review focused on herding behavior in financial markets, providing empirical evidence on this phenomenon. However, unresolved issues and areas lacking definitive evidence were highlighted in the discussion.

Haghani et al. (2019) systematically reviewed the terms "panic," "irrationality," and "herding" in an integrated manner, drawing from peer-reviewed journal articles to encompass definitions, supporting and opposing evidence, and underlying theories. Campenhout and Verhestraeten (2010) conducted a literature review on the herding behavior of financial analysts. Their review delved into the occurrence, significance, and implications of this behavior, along with an overview of analysts' incentives and characteristics that influence its manifestation, while also presenting empirical evidence.

Marietza et al. (2021) provided an overview of the broader bibliometric literature related to the term and concept of herding behavior in capital markets. Chojil et al. (2022) analyzed 30 years' worth of scholarly research on financial market herd behavior, utilizing the Web of Science database to collect bibliographic data and employing bibliometric approaches for visualizing similarities. Their findings underscored a substantial increase in research on herd behavior since the subprime crisis.

It is important to note that systematic literature reviews and bibliometric analysis in this research area are currently limited and inconclusive, indicating a significant need and scope for conducting further research in this domain. This paper aims to investigate articles published in peer-reviewed and freely accessible journals pertaining to Investors' Herd Behavior in Stock Markets between 1980 and 2022, offering a detailed analysis of the existing literature.

RESEARCH DESIGN

This study employs a combination of bibliometric analysis and a systematic literature review to analyse the data. The data were sourced from the Scopus Database. Various combinations of keywords, including "investors," "stock market," "herding behavior," and "financial markets," were used to search for articles related to herding behavior. The search criteria were restricted to articles in English, at the final publication stage, and from journal sources. The identified articles were then extracted following predefined inclusion criteria and saved in CSV files within an Excel sheet.

For the purposes of this study, the VOS viewer software was selected due to its ability to simplify the visualization of extensive bibliometric maps. The software offers convenient features for resizing and zooming in on these maps. The descriptive analysis provides insights into the year-by-year publication trends of the articles, along with identifying the most influential journals and authors in the field.The data saved in CSV format within Excel sheets were utilized to generate graphs and tables for the Systematic Literature Review. In the second phase, the study delves into bibliometric analysis, encompassing bibliometric coupling, cluster formation analysis, and citation analysis. Visualizations were created using data from Excel and the VOS viewer software.Figure 1 presents an overview of the study's research framework.

1 Selection Criteria

The articles selected for this study were specifically chosen for the purpose of review. Inclusion criteria comprised articles published exclusively in English-language, peer-reviewed journals that were accessible in open access formats. The study deliberately excluded conference papers, books, and conference proceedings as potential sources. These criteria were applied to ensure the quality and relevance of the articles included in the Systematic Literature Review and bibliometric analysis. In total, 85 articles were incorporated in this study, as detailed in Table 1which represent the Count of Articles.

Figure 1. Research Outline of the study (Authors)

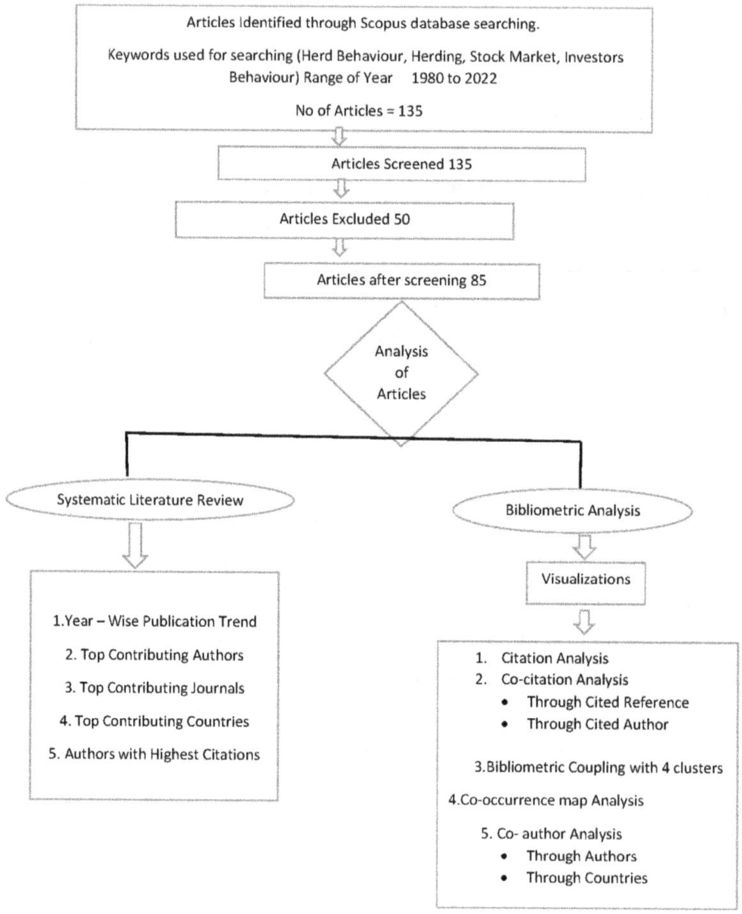

Table 1. Count of articles

Receptacles	Articles
Academia Revista Latinoamericana de Administracion	1
Advanced Science Letters	1
African Finance Journal	1
Afro-Asian Journal of Finance and Accounting	1
Applied Economics	1
Asia Pacific Business Review	1

continued on following page

Table 1. Continued

Receptacles	Articles
Brazilian Business Review	1
Chinese Economy	1
Cogent Economics and Finance	1
Computational Economics	1
Contemporary Economics	1
Emerging Markets Finance and Trade	3
Emerging Markets Review	1
Empirical Economics	1
Energy Economics	1
Estudios de Economia Aplicada	1
European Research Studies Journal	1
Finance Research Letters	1
Gadjah Mada International Journal of Business	1
IEEE Transactions on Systems, Man, and Cybernetics: Systems	1
Information Systems and e-Business Management	1
International Journal for Equity in Health	1
International Journal of Approximate Reasoning	1
International Journal of Emerging Markets	1
International Journal of Engineering and Technology(UAE)	1
International Journal of Finance and Economics	1
International Journal of Financial Studies	1
International Journal of Information Technology and Decision Making	1
International Journal of Innovation, Creativity and Change	1
International Journal of Islamic and Middle Eastern Finance and Management	1
International Review of Economics and Finance	1
International Review of Financial Analysis	4
Investment Management and Financial Innovations	1
Journal of Advances in Management Research	1
Journal of Applied Accounting Research	1
Journal of Applied Business Research	1
Journal of Asian Finance, Economics and Business	4
Journal of Asset Management	1
Journal of Banking and Finance	4
Journal of Behavioral Finance	2

continued on following page

Table 1. Continued

Receptacles	Articles
Journal of Economic Behavior and Organization	1
Journal of Economics and Finance	2
Journal of Empirical Finance	3
Journal of International Financial Markets, Institutions and Money	2
Journal of International Money and Finance	1
Journal of Multinational Financial Management	2
Journal of Sustainable Finance and Investment	1
Journal of the Asia Pacific Economy	1
Managerial Finance	2
New Journal of Physics	1
Pacific Basin Finance Journal	4
Physica A: Statistical Mechanics and its Applications	1
Psychologia	1
Qualitative Research in Financial Markets	1
Research in International Business and Finance	1
Review of Accounting and Finance	1
Review of Behavioral Finance	2
Review of Quantitative Finance and Accounting	1
Revista de Contabilidad-Spanish Accounting Review	1
Romanian Journal of Economic Forecasting	1
South Asian Journal of Business Studies	1
Sustainability (Switzerland)	1
Wireless Communications and Mobile Computing	1

Source: Scopus Database computed by Authors

2 DESCRIPTIVE ANALYSES

2.1 Year-wise Publication Trend of the both empirical and conceptual papers in Herding in stock market from 1980 to 2022

A year-by-year chart illustrates the number of articles published each year, dating back to 1999. While articles have been consistently published since then, a notable surge occurred in 2013, as depicted in Figure 2. The chart clearly demonstrates a fluctuating trend, with a decrease in the number of papers published in 2014, followed by a subsequent rise in 2015, gradually increasing the overall publication count. Remarkably, the year 2020 witnessed a substantial surge in the number of articles published compared to previous years. The trendline depicted in the chart unmistakably indicates a rising trajectory in this research area, signifying ample opportunities for further investigation. .

Figure 2. Year-wise publication trend (Scopus database computed by Authors)

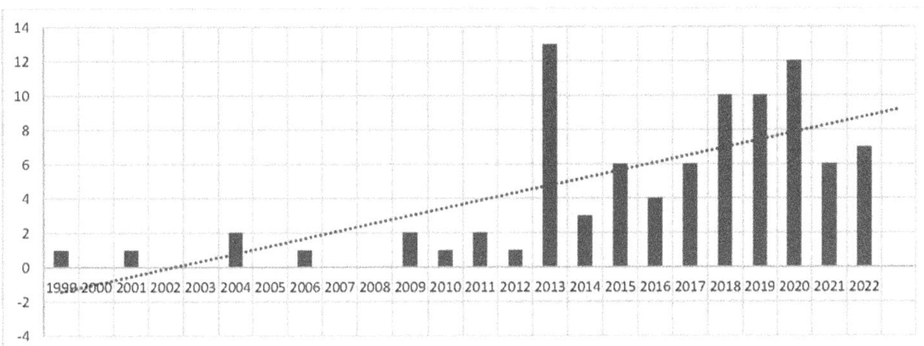

2.2 List of Journals with Highest Number of Publications.

Table 2 provides a list of the prominent journals that have made significant contributions to this area of study. Leading the list are four journals, each with four publications: International Review of Financial Analysis, Journal of Asian Finance, Economics and Business, Journal of Banking and Finance, and Pacific Basin Finance Journal. Following closely are two journals, Emerging Markets Finance and Trade, and Journal of Empirical Finance, each with three publications. Additionally, the Journal of Behavioural Finance, Journal of Economics and Finance, Journal of International Financial Markets, Institutions and Money, and Journal of Multinational Financial Management have two publications each, further highlighting their substantial contributions to this field of research.

Table 2. Top contributing journals

Journals	Count of papers
International Review of Financial Analysis	4
Journal of Asian Finance, Economics and Business	4
Journal of Banking and Finance	4
Pacific Basin Finance Journal	4
Emerging Markets Finance and Trade	3
Journal of Empirical Finance	3
Journal of Behavioral Finance	2
Journal of Economics and Finance	2
Journal of International Financial Markets, Institutions and Money	2
Journal of Multinational Financial Management	2

Source: Scopus database computed by Authors

2.3 Top Contributing Authors

The foremost author in this list is Demirer, R, who has contributed four articles and amassed an impressive 271 citations. Following closely are several authors, each with two articles to their name. Bohl, M. T, has garnered 72 citations, while Klein, A. C, has received 70 citations, and Lai, R. N, has accumulated 61 citations. Additionally, authors Srivastava, M, Shi, Y, Fang, H, and Alhaj-Yaseen, Y. S, also have two articles each. However, their citation counts are comparatively lower, likely due to the recency of their published papers. Figure 3 provides a comprehensive list of these authors with the highest number of publications, along with their corresponding citation counts.

Figure 3. Top contributing authors (Scopus database computed by Authors)

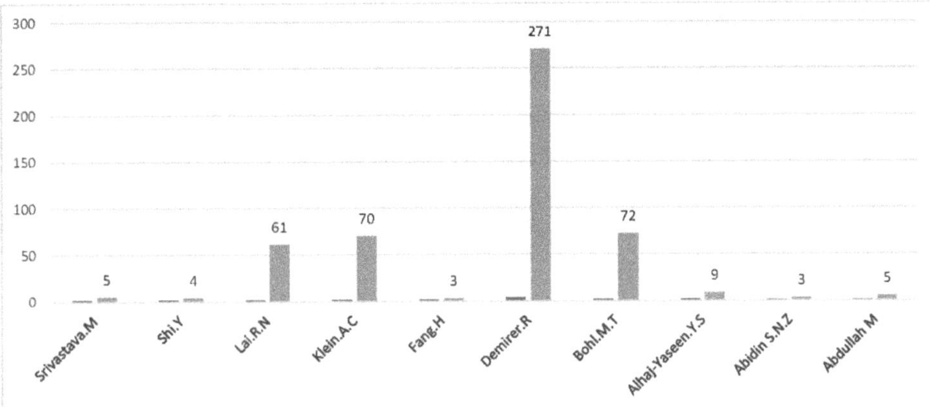

2.4 Authors with Highest Number of Citations

Table 3 presents a list of highly cited authors in the field. At the top of the list is Demirer, R, with the highest number of citations, totalling 271. Demirer's research covers a wide range of markets, including emerging markets, developing countries' stock markets, international stock markets, and currency markets, all examining investor herding behavior.Following closely are Kaminsky, G. L, and Schmukler, S. L, with a total of 209 citations. Their work delves into investor herding behavior during various financial crises in different markets. Gleason, K. C, Mathur, I, and Peterson, M. A, are next on the list with a combined total of 141 citations. Chen, C. D, and Kutan, A. M, have received 129 citations for their contributions. Lastly, Galariotis, E. C, and Rong, W, have garnered 111 citations for their respective research endeavours. These authors have made significant contributions to the understanding of herding behavior in various financial markets.

Table 3. Authors with high citations

Authors	**Citations**
Demirer R.	271
Kaminsky G.L.	209
Schmukler S. L	209
Gleason K.C	141
Mathur I.	141

continued on following page

Table 3. Continued

Authors	Citations
Peterson M.A.	141
Chen C. D	129
Kutan A.M	129
Galariotis E.C	111
Rong W	111

Source: Scopus database computed by Authors

2.5 Top Contributing Countries with Citations

The United States of America have contributed more when compared to other countries with 21 documents and 944 citations. China stands second with 14 documents; its citations are low compared to United Kingdom with 8 documents, France and Germany with 5 documents and Greece with 4 documents.

Table 4. Top contributing countries

Countries	Documents	Citations
United States	21	944
China	14	145
United Kingdom	8	393
Taiwan	6	95
France	5	170
Germany	5	207
Greece	4	151
Turkey	4	134
Hongkong	3	123
Israel	3	120

Source: Scopus database computed by Authors

BIBLIOMETRIC ANALYSIS (WITH VOSVIEWER)

Bibliometric analysis serves as a measurable technique for evaluating and comprehending the current state of research within a specific academic domain. This approach is well-supported by scholars such as Dzikowski (2018), Small (1973), and

Garfield et al. (1964). Compared to traditional methods, bibliometric analysis offers a competitive edge. Traditional methods lack the capacity to consider the evolutionary aspects of research, as they rely on individual manuscript selection and shape the examination based on predefined criteria, as noted by Kajikawa et al. (2007).

One valuable application of bibliometric analysis is its ability to identify the most cited papers in each area of research. To accomplish this, bibliometric analysis is often conducted using data from the Scopus database. Various techniques can be employed to determine the number of published documents and citations. Citation analysis, for instance, can be carried out to extract insights on citations. The software VOSviewer is frequently utilized for this purpose, facilitating the visualization and analysis of citation data.

3.1 Citation Analysis

Citation analysis operates on the foundational premise that authors routinely reference works pertinent to their field, with citations serving as a metric of impact. This perspective is well-supported by scholars such as Dzikowski (2018) and Van Raan (2003). The number of citations garnered by an article is often regarded as a gauge of its popularity, and it signifies its level of recognition and significance in the field, as emphasized by Ding and Cronin (2011).Table 5 provides an overview of the documents within this research domain that have received a substantial number of citations. Among the 85 documents examined, only 18 met the minimum threshold for citation count, with merely 10 papers achieving a notably high number of citations, as displayed in Table 5. These highly cited papers are noteworthy for their impact and influence within the domain.

Table 5. List of top ten papers based on citations

Title of the paper	Journal name	Author name	Citations
What triggers market jitters? A chronicle of the Asian crisis	Journal of International Money and Finance	Kaminsky G.L., Schmukler S.L.	209
Analysis of intraday herding behavior among the sector ETFs	Journal of Empirical Finance	Gleason K.C., Mathur I., Peterson M.A.	141
Do investors herd in emerging stock markets? Evidence from the Taiwanese market	Journal of Economic Behavior and Organization	Demirer R., Kutan A.M., Chen C.-D.	129
Herding on fundamental information: A comparative study	Journal of Banking and Finance	Galariotis E.C., Rong W., Spyrou S.I.	111

continued on following page

Table 5. Continued

Title of the paper	Journal name	Author name	Citations
Investor herds and regime-switching: Evidence from Gulf Arab stock markets	Journal of International Financial Markets, Institutions and Money	Balcilar M., Demirer R., Hammoudeh S.	97
Herding and information-based trading	Journal of Empirical Finance	Zhou R.T., Lai R.N.	91
Firm specific and macro herding by professional and amateur investors and their effects on market volatility	Journal of Banking and Finance	Venezia I., Nashikkar A., Shapira Z.	75
Causes and consequences of short-term institutional herding	Journal of Banking and Finance	Kremer S., Nautz D.	73
Individual and institutional herding and the impact on stock returns: Evidence from Taiwan stock market	International Review of Financial Analysis	Hsieh S.-F.	66
Investor herding during financial crisis: A clinical study of the Jakarta Stock Exchange	Pacific Basin Finance Journal	Bowe M., Domuta D.	62

Source: Scopus database computed by Authors

From Table 5, the research paper titled, "What triggers market jitters? A chronicle of the Asian crisis" received the maximum citations of 209.Followed by Analysis of intraday herding behavior among the sector ETFs by Gleason K.C., Mathur I., Peterson M.A. and A clinical investigation of the Jakarta Stock Exchange by Bowe M. and Domuta D. received the fewest citations of 62.

3.2 Co - Citation Analysis

Co-citation analysis serves as a valuable method for assessing the strength of citations, examining how frequently specific articles are cited together, thereby forming clusters indicative of typical research themes. This approach is supported by scholars such as Marshakova (1973) and Small (1973). The primary objective of co-citation analysis is to reveal the connections that exist among research themes, researchers, and keywords, as highlighted by Pilkington and Liston-Heyes (1999).

In co-citation analysis, sets of papers are referenced in conjunction with the source articles, indicating their thematic associations. For instance, when both articles are cited together, it suggests that they belong to the same subject domain. To perform co-citation analysis using VOSviewer, one selects "cited reference" and "cited authors" as the items of analysis, often imposing a predetermined minimum citation count as a requirement for inclusion in the analysis. This method offers valuable insights into the interrelationships among research themes, authors, and sources.

Figure 4. Co-citation Analysis by selecting cited references (Scopus database computed by Authors)

Figure 4 displays a total of 3,320 cited references, and among them, 29 references have garnered at least five citations, meeting the specified requirement. Each of these 29 items is connected to a network of references, creating a comprehensive network that links all the depicted items. The figure effectively illustrates the connections between these items and highlights areas within the citation network characterized by high density, thereby confirming the existence of these research aspects.

In Figure 5, co-citation analysis is presented in relation to the cited authors. Out of the 3,571 authors considered, 48 authors have reached a significant threshold, with each of them accumulating a minimum of twenty citations. This signifies that every author depicted in the figure has received at least twenty citations. The co-citation analysis of authors has resulted in a map featuring four distinct clusters, representing the 48 authors featured in the study. At the forefront of this network, Hirshleifer, D, leads with 88 citations, followed closely by Shleifer, A, with 81 citations, and Demirer, R, with 76 references. These findings offer valuable insights into the prominence and influence of these authors within the field of study.

3.3 Bibliographic Coupling (Data Clustering)

To cluster the data effectively, the VOSviewer software is employed. This process involves selecting a Scopus file from the database and generating a map based on bibliographic information. In this analysis, the unit of analysis chosen is "documents," and the type of analysis applied is bibliographic coupling. Bibliographic coupling serves to identify potential connections between two works and reveals their association with a common theme or subject.

Figure 6 illustrates the diverse clusters obtained through this analysis. This figure offers the advantage of providing a visual representation of authors who share similar research profiles or cite similar sources of literature. By combining authors with comparable study profiles or who reference similar sources, this figure facilitates a graphical mapping of these authors, as emphasized by Torrijo and Giner (2022).

Figure 5. Co-citation through cited authors (Scopus database computed by Authors)

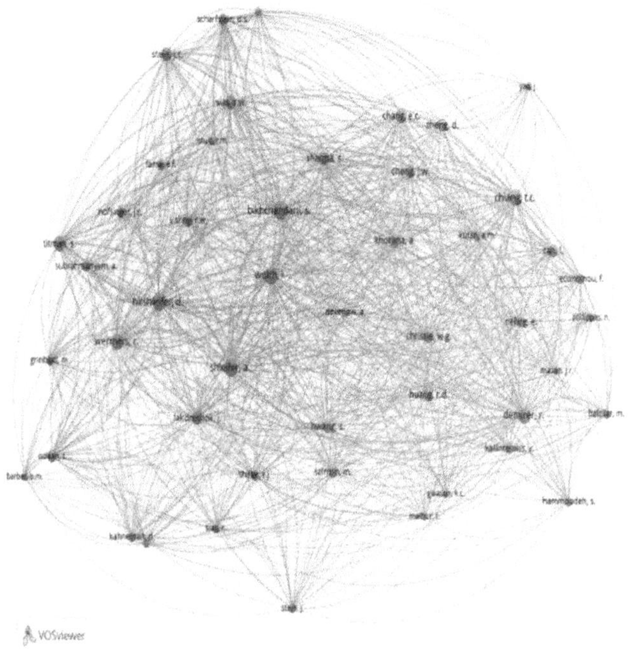

The articles have been organized into clusters based on the degree of relatedness between research topics, making clustering a valuable approach for identifying distinct facets of current themes within the literature. In this visualization, the size of each circle corresponds to the number of citations received by a particular paper. Out of the total of 85 articles, 34 articles are interconnected and have formed three distinct clusters. To distinguish between these groupings, different colors have been employed, and the size of each circle indicates the number of citations received by the respective article. This visual representation effectively highlights the relationships and importance of these articles within their respective clusters.

- *Examination of Clusters Formed*

Utilizing VOSviewer, bibliographic coupling plays a pivotal role in the formation of clusters. Bibliographic coupling comes into play when authors of two separate papers cite the same third paper, thereby establishing a bibliographic connection between them (Mohsen and al., 2024). The degree of connection intensifies with the increasing number of shared bibliographic references, as elucidated by Kessler (1963).

Figure 6 visually represents the clusters of articles formed through bibliometric coupling. The thickness of the lines connecting authors within these clusters indicates a significant degree of connectivity, suggesting that these authors share comparable or even overlapping research interests, as noted by Torrijo and Giner (2022).

Cluster I, highlighted in red, is one of the largest clusters, encompassing 15 articles and amassing a total of 1,094 citations. This cluster primarily centers on the herding behavior of institutional investors during periods of extreme market conditions and financial crises, with a focus on information asymmetry. Notably, this cluster includes highly cited articles authored by Kaminsky, G. L (1999) with 209 citations and a link strength of 14, Gleason, K. C (2004) with 141 citations and a link strength of 128, and Galariotis, E. C (2015) with 111 citations and a link strength of 300. These articles serve as key references in this research area.

Figure 6. Image of document clusters connected to one another (Scopus database computed by Authors)

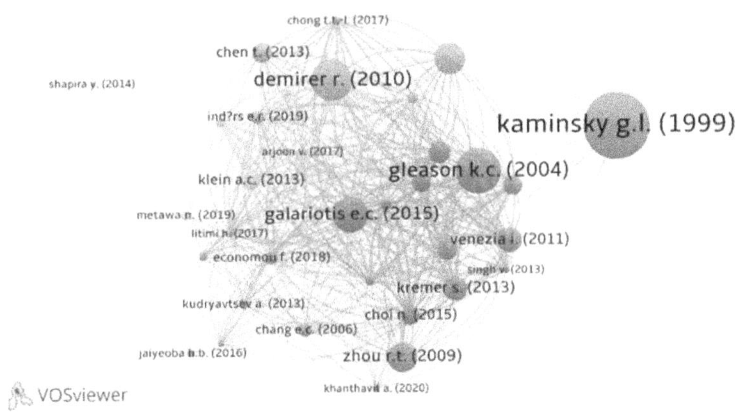

Cluster II, highlighted in green, consists of seven articles that have received a total of 402 citations. The primary theme of this cluster revolves around herding behavior observed in emerging and frontier markets (Mohsen and *al.* 2023). Among the highly cited articles within this cluster are Demirer, R (2010) with 129 citations and a link strength of 237, Balcilar, M (2013) with 97 citations and a link strength of 211, and Chen, T (2013) with 60 citations and a link strength of 111.

Cluster III, marked in blue, comprises seven articles with a combined total of 191 citations. This cluster focuses on the impact of idiosyncratic volatility on the herding behavior of investors in the market. Prominent articles in this cluster include Chang, E. C (2006) with 39 citations and a link strength of 57, and Economou, F (2018) with 39 citations and a link strength of 212.

Cluster IV, represented in yellow, encompasses five articles. This cluster delves into the analysis of time-variations in herding behavior among investors in the market, as well as the relationship between sentiments and herding behavior. Key articles in this cluster include Klein, A. C (2013) with 56 citations and a link strength of 230, and Metawa, N (2019) with 31 citations and a link strength of 89.

Table 6 provides a comprehensive list of the most cited documents within each cluster. In total, this research yields four distinct clusters, with fifteen authors in the first cluster, seven in the second cluster, seven in the third cluster, and five in the fourth cluster. These authors represent the most cited and influential researchers in the field of herding behavior, along with the respective publication years of their contributions.

Table 6. Highly cited document of each cluster

Cluster 1	Cluster 2	Cluster 3	Cluster 4
Bowe M (2004)	Arjoon.V (2017)	Chang. E.C (2006)	Humayun Kabir .M (2018)
Choi. N (2015)	Balcilar. M (2013)	Economou F (2018)	Klein A. C (2013)
Dang H.V (2016)	Balcilar .M (2017)	Jaiyeoba H.B (2016)	Metawa. N (2019)
Galariotis E.C (2015)	Chen. T (2013)	Kudryavtsev. A (2013)	Shapriya Y (2014)
Gleason K.C (2004)	Chong T. T (2017)	Litimi. H (2017)	Simoes Vieira E.F (2015)
Goodfellow C (2009)	Demirer. R (2010)	Shantha. K.V. A (2019)	
Hsiehs- F (2013)	Indirs. E.R (2019)	Vo.X. V (2019)	
Kaminsky. G.L (1999)			
Khanthavit. A (2020)			
Kremer S (2013)			
Luo. B (2013)			
Singh. V (2013)			
Venezia. I (2011)			
Zheng. D (2015)			
Zhou. R. T (2009)			

Source: Scopus database computed by Authors

Figure 7. Cluster of sources of documents (Scopus database computed by Authors)

Cluster of sources of documents is showed in Figure 7. 32 journals met the thresholds and divided under four groups.14 journals in Cluster I which is highlighted in red. There are nine journals in Cluster II which is portrayed in green. Four journals are in the cluster IV, which is yellow, and five are in the cluster III, which is blue. These groups are created based on the degree of resemblance between the published papers.

The clusters of bases and the number of documents were discussed in Table 7.Each cluster in the table has a theme that is determined by the article's nature. The top two journals in each cluster were picked up by seeing the number of published documents and their links.

Table 7. Cluster of sources with number of documents.

Clusters	Journals	No of Documents	Links	Link Strength
Cluster -I	Journal of Banking and Finance	4	123	995
	International Review of Financial Analysis	3	94	752
Cluster - II	Journal of Behavioural Finance	2	54	274
	Journal of Economic Behavior and Organization	1	31	237
Cluster - III	Pacific Basin Finance Journal	2	54	147
	Applied Economics	1	31	212

continued on following page

Table 7. Continued

Clusters	Journals	No of Documents	Links	Link Strength
Cluster - IV	Pacific Basin Finance Journal	1	31	230
	Journal of International Financial Markets, Institutions and Money	1	31	293

Source: Scopus database computed by Authors.

In Cluster I, the Journal of Banking and Finance emerges as the most prominent contributor with four articles, fostering 123 connections with other articles and amassing a substantial linkage strength of 995. Following closely is the International Review of Financial Analysis, which boasts three documents, 94 links, and a link strength of 752.Cluster II is characterized by the Journal of Behavioral Finance as the major contributor, featuring two documents that establish 54 connections and a link strength of 274. Additionally, the Journal of Economic Behavior and Organization contributes one document with 31 links and a link strength of 237.Within Cluster III, the Pacific Basin Finance Journal stands out with the maximum contribution, offering two documents that create 54 links and a link strength of 147. Additionally, Applied Economics contributes one document, featuring 31 links and a link strength of 212.In Cluster IV, both the Pacific Basin Finance Journal and the Journal of International Financial Markets, Institutions, and Money have made contributions, each presenting one document. These journals facilitate 31 links each, with link strengths of 230 and 293, respectively.

3.4 Co-Occurrence Map Analysis

As per the methodology outlined by Su and Lee (2010), this analysis aims to identify frequently occurring keywords in the selected articles. To accomplish this, VOSviewer is employed to generate a co-occurrence map, highlighting the most commonly used keywords or phrases within these articles. The process involves creating a map using the specified bibliographic data from VOSviewer and subsequently reading the information contained in the bibliographic database file.

From the bibliographic database file, terms are extracted utilizing the "all-keywords" option, considering both the Scopus file and the requisite text file. The counting approach chosen for this analysis is the entire counting approach, ensuring a comprehensive assessment of keyword frequency. To streamline the analysis, a minimum threshold for the number of appearances of a keyword is set. Consequently, 53 out of the 357 keywords, each with at least two occurrences, meet this threshold and are included in the analysis. These 53 keywords are selected based on their total connection power, ensuring a focused examination of the most influential search terms.

Figure 8. Image of network visualization map of keyword occurrences, created using VOSviewer (Scopus database computed by Authors)

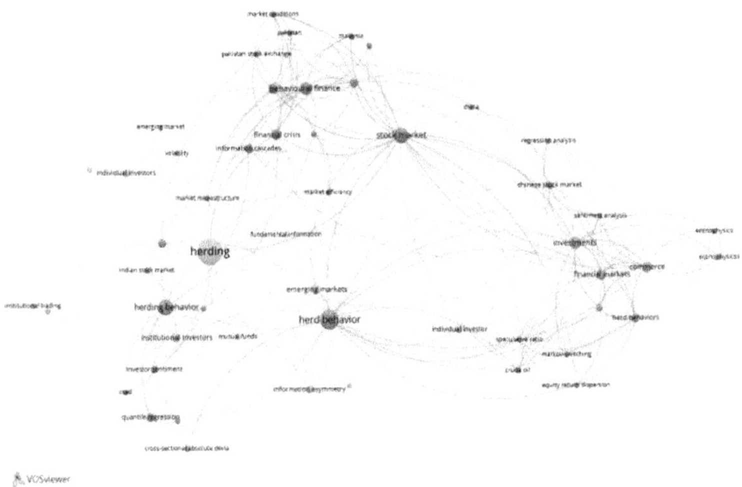

Figure 8 depicts the 53 keywords that were used more frequently in the articles. The keyword Herding has occurred 37 times in the selected articles, Stock Market has occurred 12 times, investments 8 times, herding behaviour has occurred 20 times, financial markets has occurred 6 times, Investor Sentiments has occurred 5 times, Market condition and market efficiency has occurred 4 times. The interrelationships between the words are also evident in the generated image. The analyzed objects are represented by the map's nodes, which grow in size with frequency.

3.4.1 Co-Authorship Analysis

The associated authors or countries are referred to as the nodes in this analysis. The degree of co-authorship can be determined by how many distinct co-authors an author has over the course of a certain amount of time. By choosing "make a map based on bibliographic data" option from the VOSviewer menu a co-authorship map can be obtained. Next step chooses the" read data from the bibliographic database's file" and the necessary Scopus file. Under the full counting method, select the type of analysis as co-authorship and authors as a unit of analysis After that, select the number of authors and the necessary threshold.121 of the 205 authors encounter the criteria when their number of papers was listed as one and their least number of citations was listed as five. Figure 9 demonstrates the clusters.

Figure 9. Authors' clusters linked with the articles (Scopus database computed by Authors)

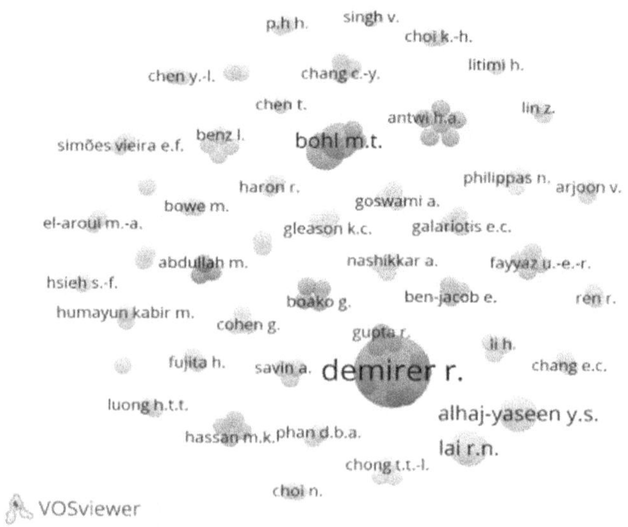

The Authors' cluster related with the documents are depicted in Figure 9. Only ten of the 121 authors chosen have a connection to one another, and the remaining authors do not have any connections to one another. The map depicts the various authors who collaborated on a single paper with other co-authors.Figure 10 shows the level of scientific collaboration and communication between them, as well as the most prolific nations, to reveal the co-authorships by country. (Merigó et al. 2018). Out of 39 countries only 37 meet the condition of minimum 1 article with two citations. Out of 39, only 14 countries were associated to each other with one publication. Largest nodes are the most influential countries like United States, United Kingdom and to lesser extent China, Germany and Greece. It can be understood that the USA has considerably cooperated with China and United Kingdom and, to a lesser extent, with south Africa, Turkey and France among others.

Figure 10. Co-authorship network of author associated countries (Scopus database computed by Authors)

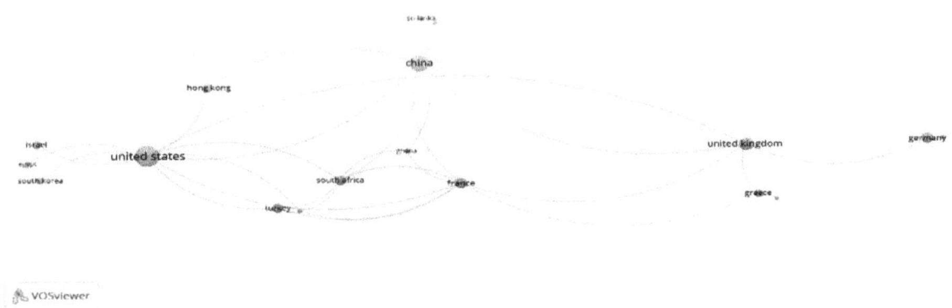

CONCLUSION AND FUTURE RESEARCH DIRECTIONS

This paper endeavours to contribute significantly to the field of herding behavior research by conducting a comprehensive bibliometric analysis and Systematic Literature Review. The primary objective is to offer both a precise focus and a panoramic view of the research landscape in this domain. The analyses conducted herein serve multiple purposes, including identifying leading journals that publish articles related to herding behavior, recognizing prominent authors and their citation counts, exploring journal associations, and conducting analyses such as citation, co-citation, and cluster formation.

By employing a bibliographic database sourced from the highly influential Scopus core collection, this study delivers its findings. It is worth noting that pivotal theoretical groundwork was laid in 1992 by Banerjee, Bikhchandani et al., and Welch, initiating the development of this research area. Nevertheless, the empirical research conducted thus far often falls short of conclusively establishing the presence of herding behavior in the stock market, leading to relatively underdeveloped research themes.

In pursuit of a more thorough understanding of stock market herding behavior, this study undertakes both bibliometric analysis and systematic literature review. The results of the bibliometric analysis underscore the pivotal role played by top finance journals in advancing herding behavior research, including notable publications such as the Journal of Banking and Finance, International Review of Financial Analysis, Journal of Behavioral Finance, and Pacific Basin Finance Journal.

Certain academics have made remarkable contributions to the analysis of stock market herding behavior. Notably, Demirer. R stands out as the most highly cited author, with a focus on emerging markets, closely followed by Kaminsky, who authored the influential article titled "What triggers market jitters? A chronicle of the Asian crisis." These findings suggest that both Demirer and Kaminsky hold paramount significance in the realm of stock market herding behavior research.

Furthermore, the analysis of 85 papers within the literature provides insights into the organization of knowledge concerning stock market herding behavior. It becomes apparent that much of the research relies on secondary data to identify and primarily examine the presence or absence of herding behavior. Yet, factors contributing to herding, the extent of herding, and the various types of herding observed in the market remain underexplored dimensions. The market data used to capture herding phenomena are often considered imprecise, as they do not adequately reflect investors' efforts to emulate the investment decisions of others.In conclusion, the study highlights the need for the development of a comprehensive research model capable of encompassing all facets of herding behavior. While this presents a significant challenge, it also opens up a multitude of opportunities for future research in this field.

REFERENCES

Ah Mand, A., Janor, H., Abdul Rahim, R., & Sarmidi, T. (2023). Herding behavior and stock market conditions. *PSU Research Review*, 7(2), 105–116. DOI: 10.1108/PRR-10-2020-0033

Ahmad, M., & Wu, Q. (2022). Does herding behavior matter in investment management and perceived market efficiency? Evidence from an emerging market. *Management Decision*, 60(8), 2148–2173. DOI: 10.1108/MD-07-2020-0867

Ahmed, F., & Karira, D. (2019). Empirical analysis of Herd Behavior in Pakistan Stock exchange. *Estudios de Economía Aplicada*, 37(1), 147–169. DOI: 10.25115/eea.v37i1.2582

Ahn, K., Cong, L., Jang, H., & Kim, D. S. (2024). Business cycle and herding behavior in stock returns: Theory and evidence. *Financial Innovation*, 10(1), 6. DOI: 10.1186/s40854-023-00540-z

Akbar, U. S., Oad Rajput, S. K., & Bhutto, N. A. (2019). Do investors herd with industries or markets? Evidence from Pakistan stock exchange. *Cogent Economics & Finance*, 7(1), 1698089. DOI: 10.1080/23322039.2019.1698089

Alhaj-Yaseen, Y. S., & Ladd, D. (2019). Which sentiments do US investors follow when trading ADRs? *Journal of Economics and Finance*, 43(3), 506–527. DOI: 10.1007/s12197-018-9452-z

Alhaj-Yaseen, Y. S., & Yau, S. K. (2018). Herding tendency among investors with heterogeneous information: Evidence from China's equity markets. *Journal of Multinational Financial Management*, 47, 60–75. DOI: 10.1016/j.mulfin.2018.11.001

Ansari, A., & Ansari, V. A. (2021). Do investors herd in emerging economies? Evidence from the Indian equity market. *Managerial Finance. Vol. 47 No. 7, pp.* 951-974. https://doi.org/DOI: 10.1108/MF-06-2020-0331

Aparisi T, S., & Ribes Giner, G. (2022). Entrepreneurial leadership factors: a bibliometric analysis for the 2000-2020 period.https://doi.org/DOI: 10.5295/cdg.211456sa

Arjoon, V., & Bhatnagar, C. S. (2017). Dynamic herding analysis in a frontier market. *Research in International Business and Finance*, 42, 496–508. DOI: 10.1016/j.ribaf.2017.01.006

Asante Antwi, H. (2022). Mitigating the destructive outcome of negative environmental stock market behaviours on environmental health security in China. *Journal of Sustainable Finance & Investment*, 12(3), 870–885. DOI: 10.1080/20430795.2020.1809291

Balcilar, M., Demirer, R., & Hammoudeh, S. (2013). Investor herds and regime-switching: Evidence from Gulf Arab stock markets. *Journal of International Financial Markets, Institutions and Money*, 23, 295–321. DOI: 10.1016/j.intfin.2012.09.007

Balcılar, M., Demirer, R., & Ulussever, T. (2017). Does speculation in the oil market drive investor herding in emerging stock markets? *Energy Economics*, 65, 50–63. DOI: 10.1016/j.eneco.2017.04.031

Beer, F., Hamdi, B., & Zouaoui, M. (2018). Investors' sentiment and accruals anomaly: European evidence. *Journal of Applied Accounting Research*, 19(4), 500–517. DOI: 10.1108/JAAR-03-2017-0043

Belgacem, A., & Lahiani, A. (2013). Herding behavior around US macroeconomic announcements. [JABR]. *Journal of Applied Business Research*, 29(5), 1401–1410. DOI: 10.19030/jabr.v29i5.8022

Benz, L., Jacob, A., Paulus, S., & Wilkens, M. (2020). Herds on green meadows: The decarbonization of institutional portfolios. *Journal of Asset Management*, 21(1), 13–31. DOI: 10.1057/s41260-019-00147-z

Bharti, B., & Kumar, A. (2020). Herding in fast moving consumer group sector: Equity market asymmetry and crisis. *The Journal of Asian Finance. Economics and Business*, 7(9), 39–49. DOI: 10.13106/jafeb.2020.vol7.no9.039

Bhattacharya, A. K. (2001). The Asian financial crisis and Malaysian capital controls. *Asia Pacific Business Review*, 7(3), 181–193. DOI: 10.1080/713999106

Bikhchandani, S., Hirshleifer, D., & Welch, I. (1992). A theory of fads, fashion, custom, and cultural change as informational cascades. *Journal of Political Economy*, 100(5), 992–1026. DOI: 10.1086/261849

Boako, G., Tiwari, A. K., Ibrahim, M., & Ji, Q. (2019). Analysing dynamic dependence between gold and stock returns: Evidence using stochastic and full-range tail dependence copula models. *Finance Research Letters*, 31. Advance online publication. DOI: 10.1016/j.frl.2018.12.008

Bohl, M. T., Klein, A. C., & Siklos, P. L. (2014). Short-selling bans and institutional investors' herding behaviour: Evidence from the global financial crisis. *International Review of Financial Analysis*, 33, 262–269. DOI: 10.1016/j.irfa.2014.03.004

Bowe, M., & Domuta, D. (2004). Investor herding during financial crisis: A clinical study of the Jakarta Stock Exchange. *Pacific-Basin Finance Journal*, 12(4), 387–418. DOI: 10.1016/j.pacfin.2003.09.003

Cakan, E., Demirer, R., Gupta, R., & Marfatia, H. A. (2019). Oil speculation and herding behavior in emerging stock markets. *Journal of Economics and Finance*, 43(1), 44–56. DOI: 10.1007/s12197-018-9427-0

Chang, C. L., McAleer, M., & Wang, Y. A. (2020). Herding behaviour in energy stock markets during the Global Financial Crisis, SARS, and ongoing COVID-19. *Renewable & Sustainable Energy Reviews*, 134, 110349. DOI: 10.1016/j.rser.2020.110349 PMID: 34234619

Chang, C. Y., Chen, H. L., & Jiang, Z. R. (2012). Portfolio performance in relation to herding behavior in the Taiwan stock market. *Emerging Markets Finance and Trade, 48*(sup2), 82-104.https://doi.org/DOI: 10.2753/REE1540-496X48S205

Chang, E. C., & Dong, S. (2006). Idiosyncratic volatility, fundamentals, and institutional herding: Evidence from the Japanese stock market. *Pacific-Basin Finance Journal*, 14(2), 135–154. DOI: 10.1016/j.pacfin.2005.09.001

Chen, T. (2013). Do investors herd in global stock markets? *Journal of Behavioral Finance*, 14(3), 230–239. DOI: 10.1080/15427560.2013.819804

Chin, A. L. L., & Shahzad, A. (2018). Are the Effects of Age Still Relevant in Predicting Malaysian Investors' Risk-Taking Behavior in Stock Market?. *International Journal of Engineering & Technology, 7*(3.21), 238-242.

Choi, K. H., & Yoon, S. M. (2020). Investor sentiment and herding behavior in the Korean stock market. *International Journal of Financial Studies*, 8(2), 34. DOI: 10.3390/ijfs8020034

Choi, N., & Skiba, H. (2015). Institutional herding in international markets. *Journal of Banking & Finance*, 55, 246–259. DOI: 10.1016/j.jbankfin.2015.02.002

Choijil, E., Méndez, C. E., Wong, W. K., Vieito, J. P., & Batmunkh, M. U. (2022). Thirty years of herd behavior in financial markets: A bibliometric analysis. *Research in International Business and Finance*, 59, 101506. DOI: 10.1016/j.ribaf.2021.101506

Chong, T. T. L., Liu, X., & Zhu, C. (2017). What explains herd behavior in the Chinese stock market? *Journal of Behavioral Finance*, 18(4), 448–456. DOI: 10.1080/15427560.2017.1365365

Christie, W. G., & Huang, R. D. (1995). Following the pied piper: Do individual returns herd around the market? *Financial Analysts Journal*, 51(4), 31–37. DOI: 10.2469/faj.v51.n4.1918

Chung, C. Y., & Wang, K. (2016). Short-term trading by individual investors in the Korean stock market. *Journal of the Asia Pacific Economy*, 21(4), 599–611. DOI: 10.1080/13547860.2016.1187798

Dalgıç, N., Ekinci, C., & Ersan, O. (2021). Daily and intraday herding within different types of investors in Borsa Istanbul. *Emerging Markets Finance & Trade*, 57(6), 1793–1810. DOI: 10.1080/1540496X.2019.1641082

Dang, H. V., & Lin, M. (2016). Herd mentality in the stock market: On the role of idiosyncratic participants with heterogeneous information. *International Review of Financial Analysis*, 48, 247–260. DOI: 10.1016/j.irfa.2016.10.005

Danrimi, M. L., Abdullah, M., & Alfan, E. (2018). Investors' herding practice: Do IFRS and national economic culture matter? *Managerial Finance*, 44(9), 1117–1133. DOI: 10.1108/MF-08-2017-0311

Demirer, R., Kutan, A. M., & Chen, C. D. (2010). Do investors herd in emerging stock markets?: Evidence from the Taiwanese market. *Journal of Economic Behavior & Organization*, 76(2), 283–295. DOI: 10.1016/j.jebo.2010.06.013

Devenow, A., & Welch, I. (1996). Rational herding in financial economics. *European Economic Review*, 40(3-5), 603–615. DOI: 10.1016/0014-2921(95)00073-9

Ding, Y., & Cronin, B. (2011). Popular and/or prestigious? Measures of scholarly esteem. *Information Processing & Management*, 47(1), 80–96. DOI: 10.1016/j.ipm.2010.01.002

Donthu, N., Kumar, S., Mukherjee, D., Pandey, N., & Lim, W. M. (2021). How to conduct a bibliometric analysis: An overview and guidelines. *Journal of Business Research*, 133, 285–296. DOI: 10.1016/j.jbusres.2021.04.070

Dzikowski, P. (2018). A bibliometric analysis of born global firms. *Journal of Business Research*, 85, 281–294. DOI: 10.1016/j.jbusres.2017.12.054

Economou, F., Hassapis, C., & Philippas, N. (2018). Investors' fear and herding in the stock market. *Applied Economics*, 50(34-35), 3654–3663. DOI: 10.1080/00036846.2018.1436145

Eduardus Tandelilin, S., Hartono, J., & Hanafi, M. M. (2013). Detecting the existence of herding behavior in intraday data: Evidence from the Indonesia stock exchange. *Gadjah Mada International Journal of Business*, 15(1), 27–44. DOI: 10.22146/gamaijb.5399

Fang, H., Lu, Y. C., & Yang, T. Y. (2013). The decomposition and causes of securities dealers' cascades in the Taiwan stock market. *Investment management and financial innovations*, (10, Iss. 3), 30-39.

Fang, H., Lu, Y. C., Yau, H. Y., & Lee, Y. H. (2013). Stock Characteristics Herded by Foreign Investors with Higher Abnormal Returns in the Taiwan Stock Market. *Romanian Journal of Economic Forecasting*, 16(4), 232–245.

Filip, A. M., & Pochea, M. M. (2023). Intentional and spurious herding behavior: A sentiment driven analysis. *Journal of Behavioral and Experimental Finance*, 38, 100810. DOI: 10.1016/j.jbef.2023.100810

Galariotis, E. C., Rong, W., & Spyrou, S. I. (2015). Herding on fundamental information: A comparative study. *Journal of Banking & Finance*, 50, 589–598. DOI: 10.1016/j.jbankfin.2014.03.014

Garfield, E., Sher, I. H., & Torpie, R. J. (1964). *The use of citation data in writing the history of science*. Institute for Scientific Information Inc Philadelphia PA. DOI: 10.21236/AD0466578

Gaviria-Marin, M., Merigo, J. M., & Popa, S. (2018). Twenty years of the Journal of Knowledge Management: A bibliometric analysis. *Journal of Knowledge Management*, 22(8), 1655–1687. DOI: 10.1108/JKM-10-2017-0497

Gavrilakis, N., & Floros, C. (2023). ESG performance, herding behavior and stock market returns: Evidence from Europe. *Operations Research*, 23(1), 3. DOI: 10.1007/s12351-023-00745-1

Ghorbel, A., Snene, Y., & Frikha, W. (2023). Does herding behavior explain the contagion of the COVID-19 crisis? *Review of Behavioral Finance*, 15(6), 889–915. DOI: 10.1108/RBF-12-2021-0263

Gleason, K. C., Mathur, I., & Peterson, M. A. (2004). Analysis of intraday herding behavior among the sector ETFs. *Journal of Empirical Finance*, 11(5), 681–694. DOI: 10.1016/j.jempfin.2003.06.003

Goodfellow, C., Bohl, M. T., & Gebka, B. (2009). Together we invest? Individual and institutional investors' trading behaviour in Poland. *International Review of Financial Analysis*, 18(4), 212–221. DOI: 10.1016/j.irfa.2009.03.002

Gupta, S., & Shrivastava, M. (2021). Herding and loss aversion in stock markets: Mediating role of fear of missing out (FOMO) in retail investors. *International Journal of Emerging Markets*, 17(7), 1720–1737. DOI: 10.1108/IJOEM-08-2020-0933

Haghani, M., Cristiani, E., Bode, N. W., Boltes, M., & Corbetta, A. (2019). Panic, irrationality, and herding: Three ambiguous terms in crowd dynamics research. *Journal of Advanced Transportation*, 2019, 1–58. Advance online publication. DOI: 10.1155/2019/9267643

Haritha, P. H., & Uchil, R. (2019). Impact of investor sentiment on decision-making in Indian stock market: An empirical analysis. *Journal of Advances in Management Research*, 17(1), 66–83. DOI: 10.1108/JAMR-03-2019-0041

Hasan, I., Tunaru, R., & Vioto, D. (2023). Herding behavior and systemic risk in global stock markets. *Journal of Empirical Finance*, 73, 107–133. DOI: 10.1016/j.jempfin.2023.05.004

Hasana, M. F., & Al-Dahanb, N. S. (2019). The herding effect of domestic investors on foreign investors: Evidence from the Iraq stock exchange. *International Journal of Innovation. Creativity and Change*, 10(6), 234–245.

Hirshleifer, D., & Hong Teoh, S. (2003). Herd behaviour and cascading in capital markets: A review and synthesis. *European Financial Management*, 9(1), 25–66. DOI: 10.1111/1468-036X.00207

Hsieh, S. F. (2013). Individual and institutional herding and the impact on stock returns: Evidence from Taiwan stock market. *International Review of Financial Analysis, 29*, 175-188. https://doi.org/DOI: 10.1016/j.irfa.2013.01.003

Hulland, J., & Houston, M. B. (2020). Why systematic review papers and meta-analyses matter: An introduction to the special issue on generalizations in marketing. *Journal of the Academy of Marketing Science*, 48(3), 351–359. DOI: 10.1007/s11747-020-00721-7

Indārs, E. R., Savin, A., & Lublóy, Á. (2019). Herding behaviour in an emerging market: Evidence from the Moscow Exchange. *Emerging Markets Review*, 38, 468–487. DOI: 10.1016/j.ememar.2018.12.002

Jaiyeoba, H. B., & Haron, R. (2016). A qualitative inquiry into the investment decision behaviour of the Malaysian stock market investors. *Qualitative Research in Financial Markets*, 8(3), 246–267. DOI: 10.1108/QRFM-07-2015-0027

Jalal, R. N. U. D., Sargiacomo, M., Sahar, N. U., & Fayyaz, U. E. (2020). Herding behavior and cryptocurrency: Market asymmetries, inter-dependency and intra-dependency. *The Journal of Asian Finance. Economics and Business*, 7(7), 27–34. DOI: 10.13106/jafeb.2020.vol7.no7.027

Jiang, R., Wen, C., Zhang, R., & Cui, Y. (2022). Investor's herding behavior in Asian equity markets during COVID-19 period. *Pacific-Basin Finance Journal*, 73, 101771. DOI: 10.1016/j.pacfin.2022.101771

Kabir, M. H., & Shakur, S. (2018). Regime-dependent herding behavior in Asian and Latin American stock markets. *Pacific-Basin Finance Journal*, 47, 60–78. DOI: 10.1016/j.pacfin.2017.12.002

Kajikawa, Y., Ohno, J., Takeda, Y., Matsushima, K., & Komiyama, H. (2007). Creating an academic landscape of sustainability science: An analysis of the citation network. *Sustainability Science*, 2(2), 221–231. DOI: 10.1007/s11625-007-0027-8

Kamil, K. H., & Abidin, S. N. Z. (2017). Does herd behavior exist among investors of Shariah-compliant equities in Malaysia? *Advanced Science Letters*, 23(5), 4968–4972. DOI: 10.1166/asl.2017.8978

Kaminsky, G. L., & Schmukler, S. L. (1999). What triggers market jitters?: A chronicle of the Asian crisis. *Journal of International Money and Finance*, 18(4), 537–560. DOI: 10.1016/S0261-5606(99)00015-7

Kanojia, S., Singh, D., & Goswami, A. (2020). Impact of herding on the returns in the Indian stock market: An empirical study. *Review of Behavioral Finance*, 14(1), 115–129. DOI: 10.1108/RBF-01-2020-0017

Kashif, M., Palwishah, R., Ahmed, R. R., Vveinhardt, J., & Streimikiene, D. (2021). Do investors herd? An examination of Pakistan stock exchange. *International Journal of Finance & Economics*, 26(2), 2090–2105. DOI: 10.1002/ijfe.1895

Kessler, M. M. (1963). Bibliographic coupling between scientific papers. *American Documentation*, 14(1), 10–25. DOI: 10.1002/asi.5090140103

Khanthavit, A. (2020). Foreign investors' abnormal trading behavior in the time of COVID-19. *The Journal of Asian Finance. Economics and Business*, 7(9), 63–74. DOI: 10.13106/jafeb.2020.vol7.no9.063

Kiran, F., & Khan, N. U. (2016, August). The Herding Behavior on Pakistan Stock Exchange. In *4th International Conference on Advances in Management, Economics and Social Science-MES* (pp. 18-19). DOI: 10.15224/978-1-63248-103-0-81

Klein, A. C. (2013). Time-variations in herding behavior: Evidence from a Markov switching SUR model. *Journal of International Financial Markets, Institutions and Money*, 26, 291–304. DOI: 10.1016/j.intfin.2013.06.006

Ko, Y. C., & Fujita, H. (2018). Evidential probability of signals on a price herd prediction: Case study on solar energy companies. *International Journal of Approximate Reasoning*, 92, 255–269. DOI: 10.1016/j.ijar.2017.10.015

Komalasari, P. T., Asri, M., Purwanto, B. M., &Setiyono, B. (2021). Herding behaviour in the capital market: What do we know and what is next?. *Management Review Quarterly*, 1-43.https://doi.org/DOI: 10.1007/s11301-021-00212-1

Kremer, S., & Nautz, D. (2013). Causes and consequences of short-term institutional herding. *Journal of Banking & Finance*, 37(5), 1676–1686. DOI: 10.1016/j.jbankfin.2012.12.006

Krichene, H., & El-Aroui, M. A. (2018). Agent-based simulation and microstructure modeling of immature stock markets. *Computational Economics*, 51(3), 493–511. DOI: 10.1007/s10614-016-9615-y

Kudryavtsev, A., Cohen, G., & Hon-Snir, S. (2013). 'Rational'or'Intuitive': Are behavioral biases correlated across stock market investors?. *Contemporary economics, 7*(2), 31-53.

Kumar, A., Paul, J., & Unnithan, A. B. (2020). 'Masstige'marketing: A review, synthesis and research agenda. *Journal of Business Research*, 113, 384–398. DOI: 10.1016/j.jbusres.2019.09.030

Kumar, N. K., & Yadav, A. S. (2022). A Systematic Literature Review and Bibliometric Analysis on Mobile Payments. *Vision (Basel)*, 09722629221104190. Advance online publication. DOI: 10.1177/09722629221104

Lai, R. N., & Zhang, Y. (2020). Spillover and profitability of intraday herding on cross-listed stocks. *Chinese Economy*, 53(1), 25–61. DOI: 10.1080/10971475.2019.1625244

Lavin, J. F., & Magner, N. S. (2014). Herding in the mutual fund industry: Evidence from Chile. *Academia (Caracas)*, 27(1), 10–29. DOI: 10.1108/ARLA-09-2013-0137

Li, T., Chen, H., Liu, W., Yu, G., & Yu, Y. (2023). Understanding the role of social media sentiment in identifying irrational herding behavior in the stock market. *International Review of Economics & Finance*, 87, 163–179. DOI: 10.1016/j.iref.2023.04.016

Litimi, H. (2017). Herd behavior in the French stock market. *Review of Accounting and Finance*, 16(4), 497–515. DOI: 10.1108/RAF-11-2016-0188

Lulin, Z., Antwi, H. A., Wang, W., Yiranbon, E., Marfo, E. O., & Acheampong, P. (2016). The effect of herd formation among healthcare investors on health sector growth in China. *International Journal for Equity in Health*, 15(1), 1–15. DOI: 10.1186/s12939-016-0393-x PMID: 27436298

Luo, B., & Lin, Z. (2013). A decision tree model for herd behavior and empirical evidence from the online P2P lending market. *Information Systems and e-Business Management*, 11(1), 141–160. DOI: 10.1007/s10257-011-0182-4

Luu, Q. T., & Luong, H. T. T.LUU. (2020). Herding behavior in emerging and frontier stock markets during pandemic influenza panics. *The Journal of Asian Finance. Economics and Business*, 7(9), 147–158. DOI: 10.13106/jafeb.2020.vol7.no9.147

Madaan, V., & Shrivastava, M. (2020). FIIs herding in energy sector of Indian stock market. *South Asian Journal of Business Studies*, 11(2), 174–194. DOI: 10.1108/SAJBS-02-2020-0033

Mahmud, S. F., & Tiniç, M. (2018). Herding in Chinese stock markets: A nonparametric approach. *Empirical Economics*, 55(2), 679–711. DOI: 10.1007/s00181-017-1281-y

Marabelli, M., & Newell, S. (2014). Knowing, power and materiality: A critical review and reconceptualization of absorptive capacity. *International Journal of Management Reviews*, 16(4), 479–499. DOI: 10.1111/ijmr.12031

Marietza, F., Nurazi, R., & Santi, F. (2021). Bibliometric Analysis Of Herding Behavior In Times Of Crisis. *arXiv preprint arXiv:2106.13598*.https://doi.org//arXiv.2106.13598DOI: 10.48550

Marshakova, I. V. (1973). System of document connections based on references. *Nauchno-TekhnicheskayaInformatsiya Seriya 2-Informatsionnye Protsessy I Sistemy*, (6), 3-8.

Mavruk, T. (2022). Analysis of herding behavior in individual investor portfolios using machine learning algorithms. *Research in International Business and Finance*, 62, 101740. DOI: 10.1016/j.ribaf.2022.101740

Mengist, W., Soromessa, T., & Legese, G. (2020). Method for conducting Systematic Literature Reviewand meta-analysis for environmental science research. *MethodsX*, 7, 100777. DOI: 10.1016/j.mex.2019.100777 PMID: 31993339

Metawa, N., Hassan, M. K., Metawa, S., & Safa, M. F. (2018). Impact of behavioral factors on investors' financial decisions: Case of the Egyptian stock market. *International Journal of Islamic and Middle Eastern Finance and Management*, 12(1), 30–55. DOI: 10.1108/IMEFM-12-2017-0333

Missaoui, I., Brahmi, M., & Rajeb, J. B. (2022). Ownership structure management and its effect on dividend policy in the Tunisian stock exchange enterprises: An empirical study. *International Journal of Technology Transfer and Commercialisation*, 1(1), 83–96. http://www.inderscience.com/storage/f171021139684125.pdf. DOI: 10.1504/IJTTC.2022.123084

Mohsen, B., Bruna, B., Karambir, S. D., Luca, E., & Anna, P. (2024). From manure to megawatts: Navigating the sustainable innovation solution through biogas production from livestock waste for harnessing green energy for green economy. *Heliyon*, 10(14), e34504. https://www.sciencedirect.com/science/article/pii/S240584402410535X. DOI: 10.1016/j.heliyon.2024.e34504

Mohsen B., Espisoto L., Anna A., Karabir S D., Shruti A, Arun K G., & Loan N. (2023). The Role of Greener Innovations in Promoting Financial Inclusion to Achieve Carbon Neutrality: An Integrative Review, *Economies*, Vol. 11(7), 1-18. RePEc:gam:jecomi:v:11:y:2023:i:7:p:194-:d:1196091

Mohsen, B., Ibtissem, M., & Jaleleddine Ben, R. (2018). Quantitative relationship between corruption ad development of the Tunisian stock market. *Public and Municipal Finance*, 7(2), 39–47. DOI: 10.21511/pmf.07(2).2018.04

Mohsen, B., & Sonia, Z. (2013). Efficiency of monetary policy approach and activist rules, *Journal of Economics and Management,* Vol. (3), 7-17, Published by University of Defense in Brno. https://www.anakan.cz/soubory/kisdis/riv-anakan-2013-14.pdf#page=21

Ng, S. H., Zhuang, Z., Toh, M. Y., Ong, T. S., & Teh, B. H. (2022). Exploring herding behavior in an innovative-oriented stock market: Evidence from ChiNext. *Journal of Applied Econometrics*, 25(1), 523–542. DOI: 10.1080/15140326.2022.2050992

Niyitegeka, O., & Tewari, D. D. (2015). Short and long-term dynamics of herd behaviour at the Johannesburg stock exchange. *African Finance Journal*, 17(2), 84–103.

Palmatier, R. W., Houston, M. B., & Hulland, J. (2018). Review articles: Purpose, process, and structure. *Journal of the Academy of Marketing Science*, 46(1), 1–5. DOI: 10.1007/s11747-017-0563-4

Pilkington, A., & Liston-Heyes, C. (1999). Is production and operations management a discipline? A citation/co-citation study. *International Journal of Operations & Production Management*, 19(1), 7–20. DOI: 10.1108/01443579910244188

Ren, R., & Wu, D. (2018). An innovative sentiment analysis to measure herd behavior. *IEEE Transactions on Systems, Man, and Cybernetics. Systems*, 50(10), 3841–3851. DOI: 10.1109/TSMC.2018.2864942

Scharfstein, D. S., & Stein, J. C. (1990). Herd behavior and investment. *The American Economic Review*, •••, 465–479.

Shantha, K. V. A. (2019). Individual investors' learning behavior and its impact on their herd bias: An integrated analysis in the context of stock trading. *Sustainability (Basel)*, 11(5), 1448. DOI: 10.3390/su11051448

Shapira, Y., Berman, Y., & Ben-Jacob, E. (2014). Modelling the short-term herding behaviour of stock markets. *New Journal of Physics*, 16(5), 053040. DOI: 10.1088/1367-2630/16/5/053040

Shi, Y., Zheng, Y., Guo, K., & Ren, X. (2022). Relationship between herd behavior and Chinese stock market fluctuations during a bullish period based on complex networks. *International Journal of Information Technology & Decision Making*, 21(01), 405–421. DOI: 10.1142/S0219622021400010

Shrotryia, V. K., & Kalra, H. (2020). Herding and BRICS markets: A study of distribution tails. *Review of Behavioral Finance*, 14(1), 91–114. DOI: 10.1108/RBF-04-2020-0086

Signorelli, P. F. C. L., Camilo-da-Silva, E., & Barbedo, C. H. D. S. (2021). An Examination of Herding Behavior in the Brazilian Equity Market. *BBR.Brazilian Business Review*, 18(3), 236–254. DOI: 10.15728/bbr.2021.18.3.1

Singh, V. (2013). Did institutions herd during the internet bubble? *Review of Quantitative Finance and Accounting*, 41(3), 513–534. DOI: 10.1007/s11156-012-0320-1

Small, H. (1973). Co-citation in the scientific literature: A new measure of the relationship between two documents. *Journal of the American Society for Information Science*, 24(4), 265–269. DOI: 10.1002/asi.4630240406

Snyder, H. (2019). Literature review as a research methodology: An overview and guidelines. *Journal of Business Research*, 104, 333–339. DOI: 10.1016/j.jbusres.2019.07.039

Spyrou, S. (2013). Herding in financial markets: A review of the literature. *Review of Behavioral Finance*, 5(2), 175–194. DOI: 10.1108/RBF-02-2013-0009

Su, H. N., & Lee, P. C. (2010). Mapping knowledge structure by keyword co-occurrence: A first look at journal papers in Technology Foresight. *Scientometrics*, 85(1), 65–79. DOI: 10.1007/s11192-010-0259-8

Theriou, N. G., Mlekanis, G., & Maditinos, D. (2011). Herding by mutual fund managers in the Athens Stock Exchange. *European Research Studies*, 14(4), 131–154. DOI: 10.35808/ersj/339

Van Campenhout, G., & Verhestraeten, J. F. (2010). Herding behavior among financial analysts: A literature review.Hub Research Paper 2010/39 November 2010.

Van Raan, A. (2003). The use of bibliometric analysis in research performance assessment and monitoring of interdisciplinary scientific developments. *TATuP-Zeitschrift für Technikfolgenabschätzung in Theorie und Praxis*, 12(1), 20–29. DOI: 10.14512/tatup.12.1.20

Venezia, I., Nashikkar, A., & Shapira, Z. (2011). Firm specific and macro herding by professional and amateur investors and their effects on market volatility. *Journal of Banking & Finance*, 35(7), 1599–1609. DOI: 10.1016/j.jbankfin.2010.11.015

Vieira, E. F. S., & Pereira, M. S. V. (2015). Herding behaviour and sentiment: Evidence in a small European market. *Revista de Contabilidad*, 18(1), 78–86. DOI: 10.1016/j.rcsar.2014.06.003

Vieito, J. P., Espinosa, C., Wong, W. K., Batmunkh, M. U., Choijil, E., & Hussien, M. (2023). Herding behavior in integrated financial markets: the case of MILA. *International Journal of Emerging Markets*. https://doi.org/DOI: 10.1108/IJOEM-08-2021-1202

Vo, X. V., & Phan, D. B. A. (2019). Herd behavior and idiosyncratic volatility in a frontier market. *Pacific-Basin Finance Journal*, 53, 321–330. DOI: 10.1016/j.pacfin.2018.10.005

Wang, C. S., Tang, H. W., & Chen, R. C. (2017). Does IPO subscription demand affect investor herd behavior in Taiwan? *International Review of Economics & Finance*, 51, 258–272. DOI: 10.1016/j.iref.2017.06.004

Welch, I. (2000). Herding among security analysts. *Journal of Financial Economics*, 58(3), 369–396. DOI: 10.1016/S0304-405X(00)00076-3

Xie, J., Wang, J., & Yang, L. (2018). Reference group perspective on individual investors'herdbehavior: The effects of self-esteem and trait anxiety. *Psychologia*, 61(1), 1–25. DOI: 10.2117/psysoc.2019-A003

Yang, W., Yang, C., Yang, B., & Feng, G. (2022). Time-Varying Research on Investors' Trading Psychology Rational and Irrational Market Sentiment Based on the Perspective of 5G Networks and Information Economics. *Wireless Communications and Mobile Computing*, 23(2), 675–689. DOI: 10.1155/2022/3594213

Yang, W. R. (2011). Herding with costly information and signal extraction. *International Review of Economics & Finance*, 20(4), 624–632. DOI: 10.1016/j.iref.2010.12.004

Yang, W. R., & Chen, Y. L. (2015). The response of dynamic herd behavior to domestic and us market factors: Evidence from the greater China stock markets. *Emerging Markets Finance and Trade, 51*(sup1), S18-S41.https://doi.org/DOI: 10.1080/1540496X.2014.998884

Yousaf, I., & Yarovaya, L. (2022). Herding behavior in conventional cryptocurrency market, non-fungible tokens, and DeFi assets. *Finance Research Letters*, 50, 103299. DOI: 10.1016/j.frl.2022.103299

Youssef, M. (2022). What drives herding behavior in the cryptocurrency market? *Journal of Behavioral Finance*, 23(2), 230–239. DOI: 10.1080/15427560.2020.1867142

Youssef, M., & Waked, S. S. (2022). Herding behavior in the cryptocurrency market during COVID-19 pandemic: The role of media coverage. *The North American Journal of Economics and Finance*, 62, 101752. DOI: 10.1016/j.najef.2022.101752

Zheng, D., Li, H., & Zhu, X. (2015). Herding behavior in institutional investors: Evidence from China's stock market. *Journal of Multinational Financial Management*, 32, 59–76. DOI: 10.1016/j.mulfin.2015.09.001

Zheng, Z., Tang, K., Liu, Y., & Guo, J. M. (2021). Gender and herding. *Journal of Empirical Finance*, 64, 379–400. DOI: 10.1016/j.jempfin.2021.10.005

Zhong, L. X., Xu, W. J., Ren, F., & Shi, Y. D. (2013). Coupled effects of market impact and asymmetric sensitivity in financial markets. *Physica A*, 392(9), 2139–2149. DOI: 10.1016/j.physa.2013.01.030

Zhou, R. T., & Lai, R. N. (2009). Herding and information-based trading. *Journal of Empirical Finance*, 16(3), 388–393. DOI: 10.1016/j.jempfin.2009.01.004

Chapter 2
Decision to Determine the Optimal Firm's Capital Structure: A Systematic Literature Review

Ibtissem Missaoui
https://orcid.org/0000-0002-1548-9094
University of Sousse, Tunisia

Mohsen Brahmi
https://orcid.org/0000-0002-0995-0761
University of Sfax, Tunisia

ABSTRACT

This chapter aims to study several theories of capital structure in finance literature to help illuminate how companies make decisions about their capital structure. Starting with the Modigliani and Miller (1958) capital structure irrelevance theory, the review scrutinizes various theories such as trade-off theory, pecking order theory and market timing theory. These theories explain how companies balance the benefits and costs of debt and equity financing, as well as how they prioritize financing options based on information asymmetry. Nevertheless, there is still a lack of complete explanation for why some companies choose debt whereas others prefer equity under different conditions. The market timing theory introduced by Baker and Wurgler (2002) suggests that companies' capital structure decisions are affected by their past attempts to time the equity market. The predictions of these theories sometimes conflict with each other, leaving Myers (1984)question of "How companies choose their capital structure?" still unanswered after 32 years.

DOI: 10.4018/979-8-3693-5723-1.ch002

INTRODUCTION

Corporate or business operates in a financial environment that offers specific tools and resources to manage risk and optimize financial performance. These challenges help to clarify the purpose of the financial capital structure, taking into account both opportunities and barriers created by financial landscape. "Capital structure" is a crucial topic to have attention of researchers since many years. It refers to the mix of funding sources utilized to finance the company's investments and operations(Abeywardhana 2017). The main sources of funds mentioned in the literature are debt and equity. The cost of equity is defined as the required return on total assets without considering the firm's capital structure, and specifically, without taking into account the impact of financing investments with debt. Given the independence between the determinants of this environment, it is essential to define the concept of the financial system in order to indicate all the instruments, institutions, markets, and modes of regulation that address the realization of financial operations in a universal economic space as well as local. Each financial system, in such a country, has aspects of specific but generally sustainable organizations. This is implied by the concept of the financial structure of capital. It represents one of the most debated concepts in corporate finance (de Jong, Kabir, and Nguyen 2008; Aggarwal and Padhan 2017; Abeywardhana 2017). It emerged as the distribution of financial debts and equity. This has always given rise to reflections and several controversies since the work of founders (Modigliani and Miller 1958).Many researchers have conducted studies on the main elements of capital structure in order to understand the concept of an optimal capital structure. This is generally defined as one that minimizes the company's cost of capital and maximizes its overall value. Companies are constantly seeking out the most cost-effective sources of financing available. As previous research has shown, the financial structure of a company and its financing decisions vary from country to country and are closely tied to the level of economic development in each nation. The decision-making process regarding optimal capital structure is a major concern for most companies, presenting a significant challenge for financial management. The problems of financing and finding appropriate financing terms for businesses is a subject of ongoing debates in both political and economic circles.

Indeed, the emergence of financing problems, following the failures of banking systems, significantly hampers the activities of companies in the world. The decision to determine a firm's capital structure is crucial in corporate finance (Fama and French 2002). Therefore, the main objective of this chapter is to provide a theoretical analysis that explains the foundational principles of capital structure and various strategic financing tools. Selecting the optimal capital structure is a complex challenge in financial theory (Bui, Nguyen, and Pham 2023).Therefore, our chapter is dedicated to exploring the financial structure of capital to contribute to the advancement of theoretical frameworks. The organization of this chapter is as follows: Section 1 examines critical literature on capital structure, while Section 2 presents the key theories of capital structure.

1. FINANCIAL STRUCTURE OF CAPITAL: CRITICAL ANALYSIS OF THE THEORETICAL LITERATURE

1.1 The Origins of the Capital Structure

Capital structure is a subject that has engaged many controversies, with three main approaches being the classical approach, the neoclassical approach, and the multifaceted or modern approach. The classical approach is based on the accounting principle of financial leverage. It shows the presence of a break-even point for the profitability of the company which asserts the existence of two zones. On the one hand, debt presents a progressive advantage for the shareholder, i.e. a positive financial leverage effect. On the other hand, debt represents a progressive disadvantage for shareholders. Empirically, this approach has been widely criticized due to its highly accounting nature and lack of theoretical foundation (Levi and Welch 2017). The neoclassical approach was born through the work of Modigliani and Miller (1958), who state that the choice of a company's financing structure does not affect its value. Therefore, the cost of capital is entirely independent of the financial structure. More than 50 years have passed since the groundbreaking work of Modigliani and Miller (1958), the importance of capital structure as well as the question of how to finance investments remains inconclusive. Several assumptions have been established by the Modigliani and Miller (1958)theorem. They assume that markets are perfect:

- Absence of frictions, transaction costs, default risk, or taxation,
- Investors and clients can borrow at the same interest rate.

Modigliani and Miller (1958 et 1963) introduced two key propositions. In a tax-free world, company's capital structure does not impact its value, leading to no optimal mix between debt and equity. However, this proposition was later revised in 1963. In a world with taxes, a leveraged company holds a higher value compared to an unleveraged one. This valuation difference is attributed to the tax savings obtained from deducting interest on debt. The goal of the neo-classical approach is to maximize company value through utilizing maximum debt. The modern theory of the firm, developed in the mid-1970s, aims to challenge and improve upon the assumptions of Modigliani and Miller's model. It delves into strategic behaviors within companies, considering private information and conflicts of interest among stakeholders.

Over time, there have been numerous empirical studies conducted on the optimal financing mix and capital structure of companies (Tailab 2014; Harris and Raviv 1991). Tailab (2014) stated that capital structure has always been a difficult subject to study since the research conducted by Modigliani and Miller. There have been various explanations provided for the concept of capital (Levi and Welch 2017), which has long been recognized as a crucial resource for any company. Capital is typically classified into two main categories: equity and debt. Equity is generated when companies issue ownership rights (shares) to raise funds for their operations and investments, while debt involves companies borrowing money and repaying it with interest within a specified time frame. Different researchers have offered various definitions of the financial structure of a company's capital. Brealey and Myers (1991)define capital structure as the combination of debt, equity, or hybrid securities issued by the company.

Schlosser (1989) described capital structure as the part of debt in the total capital of companies. Robert and Lemma (1988)considered capital structure as the selection between internal and external financial instruments for companies. Bistrova, Lace, and Peleckienė (2011)noted that capital structure influences both the profitability and risk of the company. According to the definitions of previous researchers, capital structure can be described “the combination of sources of funds a firm utilizes” (debt, preferred stock, and common stock). The portion of debt that the company uses to fund its assets is referred to as leverage, with a high proportion of debt in a company’s capital structure having a significant leverage effect. Conversely, a company without debt is considered unleveraged. Benito (2003)defines capital structure as a mix of long-term permanent financing for the company, represented by preferred stock, debt, and common stock. All firms consider the capital structure as important decisions. The decision is vital not only because of the necessity to maximize returns for investors but also because of its impact on a company's ability to manage its competitive environment and financing commitment (Simerly and Mingfang 2000). Abeywardhana (2017)argues that: “Capital structure or financial leverage decision should be examined regarding how debt and equity mix in the firm's capital structure influence its market value.

The debt-to-equity mix of the firm can have important implications for the value of the firm and the cost of capital”. Aggarwal and Padhan (2017)emphasize the importance of capital structure for company, highlighting the importance of maximizing firm returns. Črnigoj and Mramor (2014)argue that modern capital structure theory can explain the differences in capital structure in mature market economies and financing decisions in emerging markets. Batten and Vo (2015)suggest that these differences could be explained by similarities in institutional, regulatory, and cultural structures among developed countries, contrasting the distinct legal and institutional structures prevalent in emerging markets. Bui, Nguyen, and Pham (2023)defines capital structure as the proportional mix of debt and equity used to finance a company in the long term, encompassing debt, preferred stock, and common stock. Berger and Bonaccorsi di Patti (2006)suggest that most studies examine the impact of capital structure on company performance. They do not consider the reverse impact of performance on capital structure. Therefore, the decision regarding capital structure is crucial for any organization. It holds an important place in financial management studies (Abeywardhana 2017). It is crucial due to its close that connection to a company's ability the meet the needs of its stakeholders.

1.2 Capital Structure Choices: Principles of Finance

Studies on the choice of a company's the financial structure is numerous. Leary and Roberts (2014) assume that the choice of capital structure is one of the major issues in corporate finance. Various theories have been emerged to explain why companies choose their capital structure, taking into account the costs and benefits linked with debt and equity financing. The theories suggest that companies choose their capital structure based on attributes that determine the various costs and benefits related to debt and equity financing. Many researchers have introduced market frictions to provide rational explanations for adjustments in firms' debt levels, leading to the development of three main theories: the trade-off theory, the pecking order theory, and the market timing theory (Cole, 2013). Priorto 1958, the traditional capital structure theory, known as the Naïf theory, was based on the concept of the weighted average cost of capital (WACC). According to this theory, companies use debt to reduce their weighted average cost of capital (WACC),as it is considered less costly than equity.

The ground-breaking research of Modigliani and Miller (1958)established the foundations of capital structure theory by determining that financial leverage does not impact a company's market value. Subsequent studies by Myers (1984)further delved into capital structure decision-making. Following the publication of Modigliani and Miller's framework, modern financial structure theory emerged, emphasizing the irrelevance of capital structure on a company's securities value. However, Modigliani and Miller (1958) also found that in a tax-free world, a company's value and cost of capital remain unaffected by capital structure choice. In contrast, considering corporate taxes, they concluded in 1963 that a company's market value can increase and its overall cost of capital decrease when interest deduction is tax-deductible.

Since the publication of Modigliani and Miller (1958), many economists and financial experts have studied a number of relevant leverage theories to explain the variation in debt ratios between companies. The arbitrage theory has explained the relevance of debt with the existence of taxes and bankruptcy costs (DeAngelo and Masulis 1980). The general result of this theory is that the combination of leverage cost and debt tax benefits produces an optimal capital structure. The pecking order theory is another important theory in the study of capital structure that explains the relevance of debt and the optimal capital structure. This theory was developed by Steward Myers in 1984 in his paper, "Capital structure of the Puzzle". Myers (1984)describes two sides of the capital structure issue, called the static trade-off theory and the pecking order theory.

The static trade-off theory argues that the choice of capital structure can be explained by the trade-off between the benefits and costs of debt versus equity. The assumption of the pecking order theory suggests that the debt ratio is not well defined and the company has a preferred order of financing. According to Myers (1984), companies prefer to finance their investments first with retained earnings, secondly with debt, and as a last resort, with external funds. The reason for this ranking is justified by the fact that internal funds are considered "cheaper". External debt is ranked next as it is cheaper and has fewer restrictions compared to issuing stocks. Issuing stocks is considered "the most expensive" and risky as it may lead to potential loss of control over the company. Another important theory is called the agency theory. It was developed by the works of Jensen and Meckling (1976). This theory considered debt as a major factor can be create the conflict between proprietors and directors. Jensen and Meckling (1976)established that, due to the increasing agency costs between equity holders and debt holders, there would be an optimal combination of external debt and equity to decrease agency charges.

Furthermore, Ross (1977)emphasizes the signaling theory of capital structure which indicates that company managers have privileged information. Managers issue more debt if the future prospects are positive because they are willing to incur higher bankruptcy risk and other relevant debt costs. Similarly, Al-Zoubi et al. (2018) show that corporate decisions regarding capital structure determine a persistent and cyclical evolution of the debt effect.

2. CAPITAL STRUCTURE THEORIES

2.1 Modigliani and Miller Hypothesis (1958, 1963)

According to the theories regarding the financial structure of capital, Modigliani and Miller (1958)explain that there are certain conditions under which multiple financial decisions are irrelevant. They suggest a set of assumptions within the framework of a perfect financial market with the absence of bankruptcy costs and information asymmetry. Jiang and Peng (2011) add that the absence of a conflict of interest between shareholders and managers allows economic agents to lend or borrow at a fixed rate and without limitation. The proposition of Modigliani and Miller (1958) provides a basis for analyzing how financing decisions can create or destroy the market value of a company. They emphasize that the firm has a particular set of expected cash flows. When the firm chooses a certain proportion of debt and equity to finance its assets, the company's debt has no effect on the market value of the company (Frank and Goyal, 2007). Furthermore, Modigliani and Miller (1958) state that financing strategies can be made independently of shareholder preferences as long as they do not have an effect on the company's value. The financial structure of the capital inapplicable can be demonstrated under a range of circumstances. There are two propositions of the inapplicable capital structure.

The first proposition in the article by Modigliani and Miller (1958)entitled "The Cost of capital, Corporation Finance and The Theory of Investment". They state that: "the market value of any firm is independent of its capital structure and is given by capitalizing its expected return at the rate (...) appropriate to its class". This proposition suggests that in a perfect market the value of a firm depends on its operating profit and the level of investment risk. Therefore, the value of the firm is not linked to its capital structure. Changing the financing structure and risk management will not affect the value of the company if the capital market is perfect. In other words, even if two companies have different financial structures, these two companies belonging to the same risk class must have the same value on the market. In fact, this model establishes that the financing choices of the company do not provide any signal to investors about the financial position of the company. In this case, the investor has no interest in valuing the two companies differently since they provide him with a similar income. He will invest more in the debt-ridden firm. Furthermore, he will sell the shares of the non-debt-ridden firm. This operation is continued until the values of the two firms are similar (Belghiti, 2006).

According to the second type of capital structure, (Modigliani and Miller, 1961) concluded that "given a firm's investment policy, the dividend payout it chooses to follow will affect neither the current price of its shares nor the total return to its shareholders". In a world characterized by a perfect market, the choice of capital structure and dividend policy decisions does not have an impact on the value of the company. Investment decisions are not dependent on financing strategies. Additionally, corporate finance has examined these results and created theories based on the existence of market imperfections. The article by Modigliani and Miller (1958)underwent rigorous research to determine if it is a theoretical or empirical issue. This study confirmed that the Modigliani and Miller (1958)theorem describes shortcomings under various circumstances such as the presence of taxes, transaction costs, bankruptcy costs, agency conflicts, etc.

In 1963, Modigliani and Miller made some modifications to their initial contribution from 1958. They implemented two corrective proposals regarding the assumptions of the absence of tax and bankruptcy costs. The theoretical literature has two fundamental aspects in which the presence of tax has an impact on the company's capital structure. The first approach is based on the deductibility of corporate debt tax (Modigliani and Miller 1963). The second approach studied the impact of taxation. Therefore, Modigliani and Miller (1963)state that the value of the company increases with the increase in debt. In a world with taxes, the value of a debt-ridden firm is higher than that of a debt-free firm. The added value of a debt-ridden firm is equal to the discounted sum of tax savings due to the deductibility of interest on debt. Indeed, the interest generated by tax deductibility is considered as a deductible expense. Therefore, after paying the interest, the company will benefit from tax savings. This tax advantage leads the company to maximize its debt in order to maximize the company's value. Jensen (1986) stated that debt can reduce agency costs.

Agency costs come into play when managers choose to invest cash flow at a rate generally lower than the cost of capital. However, Frank and Goyal (2007) argue that the impact of agency conflicts on capital structure has not been fully explained. DeAngelo and Masulis (1980)emphasize that tax considerations are independent of the level of firm indebtedness, which reduces the positive effect of tax deductibility of interest expenses on the value of the company. They point out that the tax rate decreases in SMEs and the use of debt leads to the deductibility of tax expenses. On their part, Modigliani and Miller (1963)show that there is no cost of bankruptcy for the company. Therefore, investors then seek to reduce the debt of their companies in order to reduce the risk of bankruptcy. In the 1970s, economists argue that the financial capital structure resulting from a balance of two major forces. De Angelo and Masulis (1980)present Miller's proposition (1977) in a more realistic context. They show that taking into account taxation other than interest on debt pour generates an optimal non-zero level of debt even in equilibrium.

2.2 Recent Theoretical Development

For a long time, the financial structure of capital has remained a central theme in the field of corporate finance. Concurrently, the issue of corporate financial behavior continues to attract attention in recent theoretical and experimental (Kayhan and Titman 2004; Frank and Goyal 2007; Adedeji 1998; Baker and Wurgler 2002). These studies have high lighted that the tests conducted primarily revolve around financing decisions, with a particular emphasis on three main theoretical areas:

- The Trade-off Theory (Kayhan and Titman 2007; Nicodano and Regis 2019)
- The Pecking Order Theory (Myers and Majluf 1984)
- The Market Timing Theory (Baker and Wurgler 2002; Mahajan and Tartaroglu 2008).

2.2.1 The Trade-Off Theory

The trade-off theory is one of the most important and oldest theories of capital structure. This theory was suggested by Myers (1984), who emphasized a balance between the tax savings resulting from debt and bankruptcy costs. It is related to the theory of Modigliani and Miller (1963), who focus on optimal capital structure. Modigliani and Miller (1963) find that the tax deductibility advantage of interest expenses positively influences the value of a leveraged firm. The optimal financial structure is one where a company is primarily financed by debt. However, the relevance of this theory has been criticized due to the existence of bankruptcy costs that can arise from excessive debt.

The concept of the trade-off theory is inspired by an arbitrage between tax benefits and bankruptcy costs. Under the assumption of no financial distress, proponents of this theory believe that bankruptcy costs associated with debt, when combined with the tax advantages of debt, allow a company to theoretically determine a target debt ratio. The optimal financial structure results from the trade-off between tax savings and bankruptcy costs, which is reflected in the equalization of additional profits related to the deductibility of financial expenses and the marginal costs of bankruptcy associated with increased debt. The trade-off theory suggests that the tax advantages of debt financing, as outlined by Modigliani and Miller, must be considered in relation to the potential costs of financial distress and agency costs within a company (Nicodano and Regis 2019).

Essentially, the optimal level of debt is achieved by balancing the benefits of interest payments with the drawbacks of issuing securities (Abeywardhana 2017). Benito (2003)argue that companies following the trade-off theory should aim for a target capital structure that minimizes market imperfections costs and maximizes overall company value. According to the theory, a company's ideal debt ratio is determined by the trade-off between the advantages and disadvantages of borrowing (Myers 1984). Debt financing offers the benefit of tax-deductible interest expenses, resulting in reduced overall financing costs for the company. However, excessive debt increases financial risk, potentially resulting in bankruptcy and subsequent explicit (such as legal and liquidation costs) or implicit costs (like loss of customers, trust, and reputation) (Molay, 2005).

Myers (2001) proposes that a company should borrow up to the point where the marginal value of additional debt tax savings is equalized by the present value of possible financial distress costs. Financial distress involves the costs associated with bankruptcy or reorganization, as well as agency costs that occur when the company's solvency is in doubt. DeAngelo and Masulis (1980) introduced other non-debt tax-deductible expenses, such as "depreciation and provisions," which diminish the benefits of tax-deductible interest expenses on the company's value, making debt less appealing for firms. Harris and Raviv (1991) argue that bankruptcy laws and creditor rights specific to each country are embedded in debt contracts, serving to discipline managers and restrict corporate debt levels. Ardalan (2018) has established the presence of an optimal capital structure for businesses. Various factors utilized in the trade-off theory to elucidate company financial behavior have been corroborated by several empirical studies, such as those conducted by Frank and Goyal (2009) and Campbell and Rogers (2018).

2.2.2 Pecking Order theory

The literature on capital structure focuses on the theory of hierarchical financing which was introduced by Donaldson (1961)and modified by Myers and Majluf (1984). They argue that equity is a less preferred means of financing. They specify that companies prioritize their sources of funding based on the cost of financing. Firms prefer to raise capital as a last resort for financing. Internal funds are used first. When these funds are exhausted, debt is issued, and when it is not reasonable to issue more debt, equity will be issued. This line of research aims to establish a ranking between different sources of funding: self-financing, debt, and equity issuance Mefteh-Wali and Rigobert (2013) imply that self-financing is defined as the operation that allows a company to fund its investments without resorting to external financing. It therefore finances itself with the profits generated by its activity. However, debt is the classic borrowing solution. Companies with financing needs turn to financial institutions to borrow. They opt for short-term debt given its importance compared to long-term debt and bond debt. Equity issuance comes last as it is riskier than debt. Debt is seen by potential shareholders as an unfavorable signal that leads to a decrease in the company's value and therefore an increase in the cost of capital.

This theory is based on the concept of information asymmetry between managers and investors (Myers and Majluf 1984). Companies choose sources of financing with less information asymmetry. This is explained by the fact that borrowing costs rise with this metric. Therefore, companies rely first on retained earnings since they are the best means of financing, which are difficult to affect by information asymmetry (Abeywardhana 2017). In the second place, debt is used because there is low information asymmetry due to fixed commitments acting as an effective control device. Finally, new equity issuances are only used as a last resort. Therefore, there is no “optimal” relationship between debt and equity under the explanation of the pecking order theory. Lemmon and Zender (2010)argue that this theory is also compatible with shareholder wealth maximization as it aims to minimize the increase in financing costs.

The pecking order theory of financing may be based on adverse selection considerations or other factors. There appear to be two common devices that underlie the pecking order theory. The first device is the linearity of the company's objective function. While the second is based on the simplicity of the model. Companies should issue equity when they experience high stock valuations for two reasons. On the one hand, the costs of the firm's information asymmetry are expected to be low when stocks are overvalued. On the other hand, firms have higher growth opportunities that lead them to finance their financing needs with equity in order to maintain their debt capacity in the future (Rajan and Zingales 1995). According to Ebel Ezeoha (2008)managers try to cover their financing needs according to the pecking order financing theory. This means that firms use sources of financing in order: equity, short-term borrowing, long-term borrowing, and finally issuing new stocks.

In a context characterized by information asymmetry, Myers (1984)suggest that conflicting interests among stakeholders can result in a prioritization of financing schemes. They developed a theory known as the hierarchy of financing theory to address these issues. According to Myers (1984), a financial model can be viewed as a strategic game between owners and managers. Managers aim to maximize shareholder wealth, while fund providers seek to minimize risks. This dynamic creates a link between investment and financing decisions, forming the basis of the hierarchy of financing theory. This theory considers informational asymmetries and signaling problems to propose a structure that addresses conflicts of interest and promotes efficient decision-making.

The pecking order financing theory has come under criticism for its fundamental arguments and suggestions. Adedeji (1998)concludes that the pecking order financing theory suggests that only internal fund scarcity motivates companies to raise external funds. This is because it disregards other theories and the influence of institutional factors that could impact the company's choice of financing instruments, such as interest rates, borrower-lender relationships, and government interventions. Myers (1984) posits that information cost and adverse selection problem induces companies to follow the behavior of pecking order financing theory. However, Baskin (1989)counter that transaction and information costs are not the only factors that could discourage the use of external financing in general and equity in particular. However, Myers (1984) argues that companies' trust in internally generated funds is correlated with other factors such as ownership and control separation.

Fazzari, Hubbard, and Petersen (1988)indicate the major sources of cost hierarchy that lead companies to follow the theory of the pecking order, such as transaction costs, agency costs, and information asymmetry costs. Fama and French (2005)also show that:"... financing with equity is not a last resort, and asymmetric information problems are not the sole (or perhaps even an important) determinant of capital structure as suggested by the pecking order theory". In fact, the explanations obtained from the study by Fama and French (2005)require that a high level of new shares be issued by less indebted companies that normally have less risky debt capacity. This argument is contradicted by the pecking order financing theory. Halov and Heider (2011) suggest that the pecking order financing theory is based on the misevaluation of shares caused solely by the lack of knowledge of the value of investments. However, when investors do not know the level of risk of these investments, debt will also be misvalued. They conclude that taking into account information asymmetry regarding both value and risk transforms the logic of adverse selection into a theory of debt and equity issuance. The theory of hierarchical order is clarified through Figure 1 cited below:

Figure 1. Illustration of the theory of pecking order

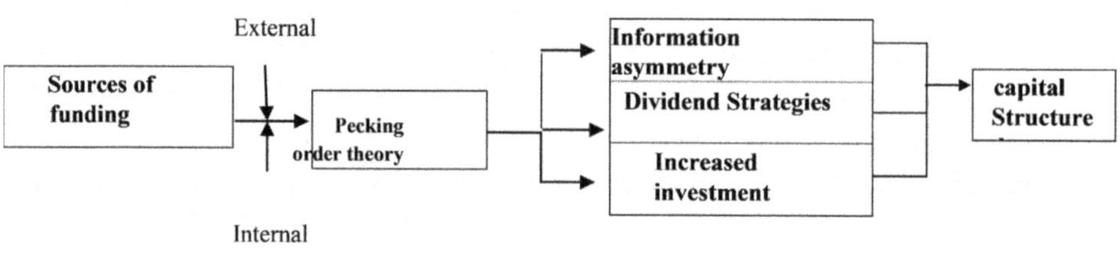

2.2.3 Market Timing theory of capital structure (MTT)

The emergence of a recent theoretical framework addressed by the work of Baker and Wurgler (2002)known as the "Market Timing Theory of Capital Structure". This approach involves arbitrage on a net asset value, meaning making a profit from a potential price difference. This theory, which is part of behavioral finance, ignores the existence of a target debt ratio. There are two fundamental strategies in the Market Timing theory. The first one concerns "Equity Market Timing", while the second one concerns "Debt Market Timing". The differences between these two aspects of Market Timing lie in the type of information used. Indeed, the first one is based on obtaining private or internal information, while the second one is based on publicly disclosed information.

The Market Timing theory suggests that companies issue shares when stock prices are high, and buy them back when stock prices are falling. The funding behavior recommended by this theory has been empirically proven by (Baker and Wurgler 2002). They assert the importance of taking into account factors from the theoretical framework of Market Timing to overcome the shortcomings of the two reference frameworks, namely the theory of hierarchical order and the compromise theory. Baker and Wurgler (2002)establish that the choice of the current financial structure depends on market conditions and the opportunistic attitude of financial managers. Therefore, it would be advisable to issue shares when prices are high, while borrowing and repurchasing shares when prices are low. The Market Timing theory has questioned the implications of the two theories: pecking order theory and trade-off theory.

These previous theories of financial structure assume that agents enjoy absolute rationality and are supposed to perfectly predict the future. The Market Timing theory is mainly based on the market timing effect on capital structure. Fama and French (2005)assume that the variable that greatest measures Timing behavior is manifested by the weighted average of the historical market-to-book ratios. In the behavior of Timing, two versions have been exposed. The first version establishes that economic agents are rational. The first one assumes that the costs of adverse selection change over time. Whereas, the second one suggests that economic agents are irrational and that companies sell stocks when stock prices are high and buy them back when stock prices are low. Market Timing theory refers to the financial market environment in order to better clarify the financial structure of companies. Therefore, the choice of financing modes depends on market conditions. In cases where the stock market climate is adequate, it would be appropriate for a firm to proceed with capital increases. In other words, investor optimism is reflected when stock prices are rising. In cases where pessimism dominates the behavior of the stock market, the firm will therefore be interested in buying back its stocks or taking on debt.

However, the "Market Timing" theory predicts that executives have the ability to identify periods in which the cost of issuing stocks is low following a strong valuation of the stocks by the market. They issue stocks based on the relative cost of debt and equity, which varies over time. The main issue decisions have permanent effects on the financing structure. The financial structure observed at date t is the result of past decisions. Therefore, companies prefer to issue shares when the cost of shares is low and decide to take on debt when the cost of shares is high. Thus, the theory of "Market Timing" also shows a long-term decrease in stock performance for firms that have chosen to issue shares. Therefore, managers prefer to introduce the firm when economic performance is abnormally high. Then, after the issuance of shares, the value of the company is reduced. Becker and Wurgler (2002) approve that the capital structure is the mechanical consequence of the continuous desire to "time" the market.

Figure 2. Illustration of capital structure theory

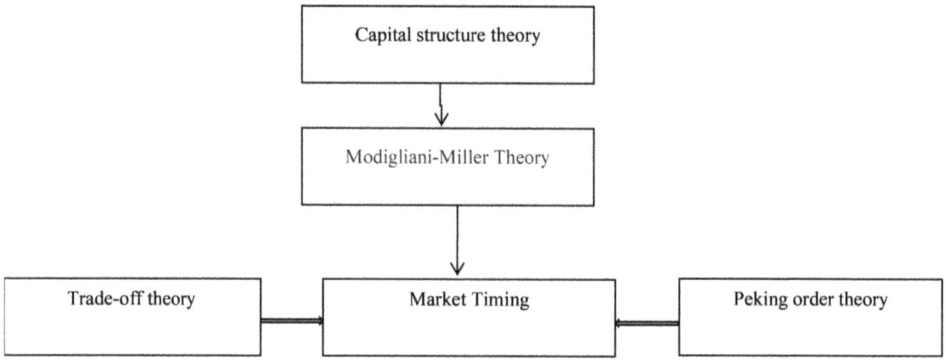

CONCLUSION

In this chapter, we have presented the theoretical foundations of various theories of the financial structure of capital. Indeed, the traditional theory asserts that leverage and financial risk determine an optimal financial structure that reduces the weighted average cost of capital. On the contrary, Modigliani and Miller (1958) argue that the financial structure is arbitrary due to the independence between the financing choices and firm's value. We have noticed that the results of research on capital structure decisions are criticisms that thus develop the interest to attribute to this crucial research field. These results are based on the assumption of perfect capital markets. Through their analysis of taxation, Modigliani and Miller (1963) explain that firms can potentially reduce their taxable income by deducting financial expenses. This deductibility can be viewed as a form of subsidy approved by the state to the firms with debt. This observation states that companies have the potential to generate value by improving their financial structure. However, Miller (1977) when considering individual taxation. In this case, Miller (1977)establishes that at the equilibrium of the bond market, the value of a leveraged company is equal to that of a debt-free company.

By considering the specificities of each tax system, several empirical studies have refuted Miller's model and have shown that, despite taking into account income tax for investors, debt remains advantageous for firms. As a result, the focus has on understood what limits companies' borrowing. The trade-off theory confirms that due to bankruptcy costs, debt is not unlimited. There is an optimal financial structure that results from a trade-off between tax savings connected to the deductibility of interest expenses and the costs of a potential bankruptcy. The tax deductibility of debt interest is challenged by the existence of non-monetary advantages not related to debt (DeAngelo and Masulis 1980). Mostly, the conclusions of research studies do not lean towards favoring debt.

We have noticed that the treatment of the financial structure concept of capital has gained significant interest in the works of (Parsons and Titman 2007; Frank and Goyal 2007). The strategies for choosing capital structure remain a financial behavior issue and continue to be a current topic that attracts the attention of numerous research studies. Additionally, we have observed that according to the "Trade-off" theory, the optimal capital structure of a firm depends on its liquidity, bankruptcy costs, and credit risk. As a result, a wide range of theoretical literature on the cost of capital has been debated. Firstly, the theoretical context of determining the cost of capital for companies with the WACC and the Capital Asset Pricing Model (CAPM) has been discussed. Furthermore, the main areas of application of the cost of capital in financial management - capital allocation and capital structure, as well as measures of return and value-based management - have been addressed. This prompted us to take an interest in the issue of the required rate of return by the investor (cost of capital), which is the general theme of this thesis. After defining the concept of cost of capital and reviewing the financial literature on the subject, we noticed the emergence of new financial theories emphasizing the need to establish a set of prerequisites for financial and institutional development.

REFERENCES

Abeywardhana, D. K. Y. (2017). 'Capital Structure Theory: An Overview', *Accounting and Finance Research*, 6.

Adedeji, A. (1998). Does the Pecking Order Hypothesis Explain the Dividend Payout Ratios of Firms in the UK? *Journal of Business Finance & Accounting*, 25(9-10), 9–10. DOI: 10.1111/1468-5957.00230

Aggarwal, D., & Padhan, P. C. (2017). Impact of Capital Structure on Firm Value: Evidence from Indian Hospitality Industry. *Theoretical Economics Letters*, 07(4), 982–1000. DOI: 10.4236/tel.2017.74067

Baker, M., & Wurgler, J. (2002). Market Timing and Capital Structure. *The Journal of Finance*, 57(1), 1–32. DOI: 10.1111/1540-6261.00414

Baskin, J. (1989). An Empirical Investigation of the Pecking Order Hypothesis. *Financial Management*, 18(1), 18. DOI: 10.2307/3665695

Batten, J. A., & Vo, X. V. (2015). Foreign ownership in emerging stock markets. *Journal of Multinational Financial Management*, 32-33, 15–24. DOI: 10.1016/j.mulfin.2015.05.001

Benito, A. (2003). 'The capital structure decisions of firms: is there a pecking order?', *Working Papers 0310, Banco de España.*

Berger, A. N., & Bonaccorsi di Patti, E. (2006). Capital structure and firm performance: A new approach to testing agency theory and an application to the banking industry. *Journal of Banking & Finance*, 30(4), 1065–1102. DOI: 10.1016/j.jbankfin.2005.05.015

Bistrova, J., Lace, N., & Peleckienė, V. (2011). The Influence of Capital Structure on Baltic Corporate Performance / Kapitalo StruktŪra Baltijos ĮmonĖse. *Journal of Business Economics and Management*, 12(4), 655–669. DOI: 10.3846/16111699.2011.599414

Brealey, R. A., & Myers, S. C. (1991). *Principles of Corporate Finance* (4th ed.). McGraw-Hill.

Bui, Thi Ngoc, Xuan Hung Nguyen, and Kieu Trang Pham. (2023). 'The Effect of Capital Structure on Firm Value: A Study of Companies Listed on the Vietnamese Stock Market', *International Journal of Financial Studies*, 11.

Črnigoj, M., & Mramor, D. (2014). Determinants of Capital Structure in Emerging European Economies: Evidence from Slovenian Firms. *Emerging Markets Finance & Trade*, 45(1), 72–89. DOI: 10.2753/REE1540-496X450105

de Jong, A., Kabir, R., & Nguyen, T. (2008). 'Capital structure around the world: The roles of firm- and country-specific determinants', *Journal of Banking &amp. Finance*, 32, 1954–1969.

DeAngelo, H., & Masulis, R. W. (1980). ' Optimal Capital Structure under Corporate and Personal Taxation. '. *Journal of Financial Economics*, 8(1), 3–29. DOI: 10.1016/0304-405X(80)90019-7

Donaldson, G. (1961). ' Corporate Debt Capacity: A Study of Corporate Debt Policy and the Determination of Corporate Debt Capacity. ', *Division of Research, Graduate School of Business Administration, Harvard University. Boston.*

Ezeoha, E. (2008). Firm size and corporate financial-leverage choice in a developing economy. *The Journal of Risk Finance*, 9(4), 351–364. DOI: 10.1108/15265940810895016

Fama, E. F., & French, K. R. (2002). Testing Trade-Off and Pecking Order Predictions about Dividends and Debt. *Review of Financial Studies*, 15(1), 1–33. DOI: 10.1093/rfs/15.1.1

Fama, E. F., & French, K. R. (2005). Financing decisions: Who issues stock? *Journal of Financial Economics*, 76(3), 549–582. DOI: 10.1016/j.jfineco.2004.10.003

Fazzari, S., Hubbard, R. G., Petersen, B., Blinder, A. S., & Poterba, J. M. (1988). Financing Constraints and Corporate Investment. *Brookings Papers on Economic Activity*, 19(1), 141–206. DOI: 10.2307/2534426

Frank, Murray Z., and Vidhan K. Goyal. (2007). ' Trade-Off and Pecking Order Theories of Debt '.

Halov, N., & Heider, F. (2011). ' Capital Structure, Risk and Asymmetric Information '. *The Quarterly Journal of Finance*, 1(4), 767–809. DOI: 10.1142/S2010139211000171

Harris, M., & Raviv, A. (1991). ' The Theory of Capital Structure'. *The Journal of Finance*, 46(1), 297–355. DOI: 10.1111/j.1540-6261.1991.tb03753.x

Jensen, M. C., & Meckling, W. H. (1976). Theory of the Firm: Managerial Behavior, Agency Costs and Ownership Structure. *Journal of Financial Economics*, 3(4), 3. DOI: 10.1016/0304-405X(76)90026-X

Kayhan, A., & Titman, S. (2004). ' Firms' Histories and Their Capital Structures ', *NBER Working Paper No. w10526, Available atSSRN:*https://ssrn.com/abstract=552889 DOI: 10.2139/ssrn.552144

Kayhan, A., & Titman, S. (2007). Firms' histories and their capital structures. *Journal of Financial Economics*, 83(1), 1–32. DOI: 10.1016/j.jfineco.2005.10.007

Lemmon, M. L., & Zender, J. F. (2010). Debt Capacity and Tests of Capital Structure Theories. *Journal of Financial and Quantitative Analysis*, 45(5), 1161–1187. DOI: 10.1017/S0022109010000499

Levi, Y., & Welch, I. (2017). Best Practice for Cost-of-Capital Estimates. *Journal of Financial and Quantitative Analysis*, 52(2), 427–463. DOI: 10.1017/S0022109017000114

Mahajan, A., & Tartaroglu, S. (2008). Equity market timing and capital structure: International evidence. *Journal of Banking & Finance*, 32(5), 754–766. DOI: 10.1016/j.jbankfin.2007.05.007

Mefteh-Wali, Salma, and Marie-Josèphe Rigobert. (2013). 'Les facteurs déterminants de l'endettement en devises des entreprises françaises', *Revue Finance ContrÃ´le StratÃ©gie*, 16: 31-47.

Miller, M. H. (1977). Debt and Taxes. *The Journal of Finance*, •••, 261–275.

Modigliani, F., & Miller, M. (1958). ' The Cost of Capital, Corporation Finance and the Theory of Investment. '. *The American Economic Review*, 48, 261–297.

Modigliani, F., & Miller, M. H. (1963). Corporate income taxes and the cost of capital: A correction. *The American Economic Review*, 53(3), 433–443.

Myers, S. C. (1984). The Capital Structure Puzzle. *The Journal of Finance*, 39(3), 574–592. DOI: 10.1111/j.1540-6261.1984.tb03646.x

Myers, S. C., & Majluf, N. S. (1984). Corporate financing and investment decisions when firms have information that investors do not have. *Journal of Financial Economics*, 13(2), 187–221. DOI: 10.1016/0304-405X(84)90023-0

Nicodano, G., & Regis, L. (2019). A trade-off theory of ownership and capital structure. *Journal of Financial Economics*, 131(3), 715–735. DOI: 10.1016/j.jfineco.2018.09.001

Parsons, Christopher A., and Sheridan Titman. (2007). 'Capital Structure and Corporate Strategy '.

Rajan, R. G., & Zingales, L. (1995). ' What Do We Know about Capital Structure? Some Evidence from International Data', *Journal of Finance. American Finance Association*, 50, 1421–1460.

Robert, A. (1988). Bankruptcy and Agency Costs: Their Significance to the Theory of Optimal Capital Structure. *Journal of Financial and Quantitative Analysis*, 23(1), 27–38. DOI: 10.2307/2331022

Ross, S. A. (1977). The Determination of Financial Structure: The Incentive-Signalling Approach. *The Bell Journal of Economics*, 8(1), 8. DOI: 10.2307/3003485

Simerly, R. L., & Li, M. (2000). Environmental dynamism, capital structure and performance: A theoretical integration and an empirical test. *Strategic Management Journal*, 21(1), 31–49. DOI: 10.1002/(SICI)1097-0266(200001)21:1<31::AID-SMJ76>3.0.CO;2-T

Tailab, Mohamed. (2014). 'The Effect of Capital Structure on Profitability of Energy American Firms ', *International Journal of Business and Management Invention* 3.

Chapter 3

Examining the Sector-Specific Ramifications of Initial Public Offering (IPO) Underpricing in the Indian Stock Market

Deepika Krishnan
https://orcid.org/0000-0002-1471-6953
Symbiosis International University, India

Mohsen Brahmi
https://orcid.org/0000-0002-0995-0761
FEM, University of Sfax, Tunisia

K. Archana
Sambhram Academy of Management Studies, India

ABSTRACT

This study delves into the phenomenon of IPO (Initial Public Offerings) under-pricing in India and its implications on Nifty 50 index, both pre-pandemic and during the pandemic, with a specific focus on categorizing IPOs into three sectors: industrial, financial, and service. To analyse this, we employed the Market Adjusted Abnormal Return (MAAR) and Ordinary Least Squares Regression (OLS) model, which allowed us to investigate how market return, listing gain, oversubscription, issue price, and issue size impact IPO under-pricing and its subsequent effect on the Nifty 50 index. The results obtained through the OLS analysis revealed that, except for market index return, all the aforementioned factors exerted a significant

DOI: 10.4018/979-8-3693-5723-1.ch003

influence on IPO under-pricing. Furthermore, we conducted t-tests to assess Market Adjusted Abnormal Return. This analysis revealed a significant degree of under-pricing in IPOs of industrial, financial, and service sectors.These findings serve as valuable insights for investors seeking to navigate the complexities of IPOs and their initial returns.

INTRODUCTION

IPO pricing, a nuanced and crucial aspect of financial markets, has been extensively examined in academic literature. Recent studies highlight the phenomenon of IPO underpricing, where the market price on the first trading day surpasses the initial offering price, and its diverse impacts on long-term stock performance and investor risk, particularly within the context of Nifty stock prices (Das et al., 2016; Manjunath et al., 2020; Kumar & Sahoo, 2021).The findings suggest that underpriced IPOs exhibit varying long-term outcomes, influencing the performance dynamics of Nifty stocks. Some IPOs, after initial underpricing, maintain positive performance trajectories, while others may face subsequent post-IPO price fluctuations affecting the Nifty index and investor risk (Brav et al., 2002; Chang et al., 2014; Lowry et al., 2017).As noted by Ljungqvist et al. (2003), the market perceives underpricing as a positive indicator, suggesting high demand and positive sentiment for a newly listed stock. This positive perception often translates into increased demand and associated risk for IPO shares, leading to an initial surge in stock prices, as discussed by Honjo (2021).

However, the cautionary note from Thomadakis (2012) emphasizes the need for investors to consider the long-term performance, associated risks and fundamentals of the company beyond the initial underpricing-induced gains. While underpricing indeed signals market enthusiasm, its impact on stock prices is dynamic, with the short-term positive effects requiring careful evaluation against the backdrop of sustained performance.Top of FormThis underpricing strategy continues to play a pivotal role in shaping the functioning of IPO markets globally. In the specific context of India, where this phenomenon is evident, recent research by Chatterjee et al., (2022) underscores that a substantial portion of IPOs (76 per cent) in the primary market were underpriced, highlighting the prevalence of undervalued IPOs. This will have an influence on risk averse investor. Since risk-averse investors might be attracted to underpriced IPOs due to the potential for immediate gains on the first trading day.

Indian IPOs adopt various pricing mechanisms, including the fixed price method, book building process, and the anchor investor mechanism, depending on company preference and regulatory requirements (SEBI, 2021).Investors engaging in underpriced IPOs often experience immediate positive returns on the first trading day, impacting the broader Nifty stock prices (Anand & Singh, 2019). However, the long-term performance of such IPOs may exhibit a more nuanced picture, as demonstrated by recent research by Wang & Wang (2021) within the Nifty context, emphasizing the importance of considering broader market dynamics in understanding IPO underpricing effects.While the existing literature provides valuable insights, recent research continues to shed light on the nuanced impacts of underpriced Initial Public Offerings (IPOs) on returns (Sundarasen et al., 2017; Wasiuzzaman et al., 2018; Rathnayake et al., 2019).But Rathnayake et al., (2019) delve into the contemporary dynamics, suggesting that underpricing remains a prevalent strategy to attract investor attention, leading to positive initial returns. As investors who are Risk-taker might embrace underpriced IPOs for their potential high returns, accepting the inherent risks and fluctuations. However, the research emphasizes the need for investors to consider the evolving market conditions and company-specific factors, as recent underpriced IPOs have shown varying patterns of long-term performance. This aligns with the findings of Gupta et al. (2023), who explore the influence of market sentiment and economic factors on the post-IPO returns of underpriced stocks. The nuanced insights from these recent studies underscore the importance of a comprehensive understanding of underpricing dynamics, acknowledging both short-term gains and potential long-term variations in returns.

The phenomenon of IPO underpricing has garnered significant attention during the COVID-19 pandemic, marked by the unprecedented challenges introduced by the global health crisis (Dong & Huang, 2022; Baig & Chen, 2022). In a study conducted by Füllbrunn et al., (2020), the authors delve into the intricate dynamics of IPO underpricing amidst the pandemic, navigating through economic disruptions and heightened market volatility. Meanwhile, Bajo & Raimondo (2017) contribute to this discourse by investigating the role of investor sentiment during, different market risk scenarios, the pandemic and its impact on shaping IPO underpricing. Their findings offer valuable insights into the influence of market sentiment fluctuations on the initial returns of IPOs. The overall sentiments by the investors under different risk categories balance their approach, weighing both short-term gains and long-term stability, and diversifying their portfolio to mitigate risks.

Furthermore, Bhuyan et al. (2021) provide a nuanced exploration of the consequences of IPO underpricing on specific industries, focusing on the manufacturing sector in Indonesia. Their study reveals both positive and negative implications on financial metrics such as return on assets and return on equity, emphasizing the importance of conducting industry-specific analyses to comprehend the multifaceted outcomes of underpricing (Luigi et *al.* 2021). The exploration of IPO performance in India has been equally compelling, with research aiming to unravel the complexities influencing post-listing outcomes (Zou et al., 2020; Deng et al., 2023; Payne et al., 2023) delves into the factors influencing IPO performance, emphasizing the role of institutional ownership and industry-specific conditions in determining post-listing stock returns. Similarly, Arora & Singh (2019) investigate the impact of underwriters on IPO performance, offering nuanced insights into the factors that influence investor response and subsequent market behavior. These studies collectively contribute to a comprehensive understanding of the multifaceted factors shaping both IPO underpricing and performance in the Indian market, providing valuable perspectives for various stakeholders.

The existing body of literature demonstrates that IPO underpricing is a common phenomenon.However, it is worth noting that there is currently no study specifically examining IPO underpricing in a sector-wise manner. This would involve categorizing these IPOs into industry sectors such as industrial, finance, and services, and then analyzing their short-term post-listing performance, especially in the context of the COVID-19 pandemic. Understanding these sector-wise dynamics is crucial because, although investors of different risk type may initially experience positive abnormal returns on the first day of trading due to underpricing, the subsequent performance in the aftermarket for these firms often diminishes. This study also adds to the existing body of knowledge on IPO underpricing by examining how IPO firms perform shortly after going public, with a specific focus on the period during the COVID-19 pandemic. The research aims to compare this short-term post-listing performance with data from the pre-pandemic era, offering insights into the impact of the unprecedented global health crisis on IPO dynamics. Exploring these implications on a sector-specific level could provide valuable insights for investors navigating the post-listing phase.

The subsequent sections of the study proceed to detail the hypotheses, data sources and methodology employed in the research process. This section outlines how the data was collected, organized, and analysed to derive meaningful insights. The subsequent sections will unveil the results obtained through the research process, offering a detailed discussion of these findings. This discussion provides a platform to analyse and interpret the results within the context of the research objectives and hypotheses.Finally, the study will conclude by summarizing the key findings, discussing their implications, and potentially suggesting avenues for further research in the field of IPO pricing under uncertainty.

2. LITERATURE REVIEW AND HYPOTHESES

Research on Indian Initial Public Offerings (IPOs) holds a central position in financial literature, with a specific focus on comprehending both IPO underpricing and overall performance within the Indian market(Chandler et al., 2019; Dambra et al., 2018; Helbing, 2019; Engelen et al., 2020. Considering this research design, the study formulates hypothesis to further advance our understanding of the implications of the pandemic on IPO outcomes.

Hypothesis 1: IPOs that were underpriced on their listing day during both the COVID-19 pandemic and the pre-COVID period will exhibit statistically significant positive Market Adjusted Abnormal Returns (MAAR) over a specified post-listing time frame, indicating that underpricing serves as a signal of strong future performance in the stock market. The Market adjusted abnormal returns are Zero.

Additionally, we hypothesize that IPOs with a higher level of over-subscription will demonstrate greater MAAR, reflecting increased investor interest and confidence in these offerings. But recently, Facebook's IPO was highly anticipated, but it faced challenges in providing substantial rewards to investors initially. The company's stock price fell shortly and created a risky environment after the IPO due to concerns about its mobile strategy and valuation. While numerous studies have explored underpricing in various contexts in India, the specific dynamics of the IPO market during a pandemic have become a unique area of inquiry (Killins, 2019; Teti & Montefusco, 2022; Liu et al., 2023). Recent empirical evidence suggests that the primary market in India displayed remarkable resilience during the pandemic, potentially due to IPOs being undervalued, attracting investors investors of different risk type seeking rapid returns. Datar and Mao (2006) introduced the idea that issuers might intentionally undervalue IPOs to encourage a broader base of subscribers. To shed light on this intriguing scenario, our study delved into the performance and underpricing of 502 IPOs on their listing day, both in the pre-pandemic and intra-pandemic periods in India. We categorized these IPOs into industry sectors, including industrial, finance, and services.

Hypothesis 2(a): Higher issue prices will be associated with lower levels of underpricing in IPOs during both the COVID and pre-COVID periods. This hypothesis suggests an inverse relationship between the issue price and underpricing.

Hypothesis 2(b): Larger issue sizes will be correlated with lower levels of underpricing in IPOs during both the COVID and pre-COVID periods. This hypothesis proposes that larger IPOs may attract more sophisticated investors, reducing underpricing.

Hypothesis 2(c): Higher subscription levels, indicating strong investor demand, will lead to lower levels of underpricing in IPOs during both the COVID and pre-COVID periods. This hypothesis suggests that oversubscribed IPOs will experience reduced underpricing.

Hypothesis 2(d): The overall performance of the market, as measured by a relevant market index, will influence underpricing in IPOs. During the COVID period, underpricing may be affected by market volatility, leading to higher levels of underpricing.

Hypothesis 2(e): The performance of the Nifty 50 index, a benchmark for Indian stock markets, will impact underpricing in IPOs in India during both the COVID and pre-COVID periods. A strong Nifty 50 performance may correlate with lower levels of underpricing

The set of hypotheses (2a-2e) put forth in this study offers a comprehensive exploration of various factors influencing underpricing in IPOs during both the COVID and pre-COVID periods. Hypothesis 2a and 2b propose an inverse relationship between issue prices and underpricing, and larger issue sizes and underpricing, respectively. These hypotheses align with conventional wisdom, suggesting that higher issue prices and larger offerings may mitigate underpricing by attracting more sophisticated investors under different risk horizon.. Hypothesis 2c delves into the role of oversubscription as an indicator of strong investor demand, positing that oversubscribed IPOs may experience lower levels of underpricing. The study thus recognizes the potential impact of market sentiment on underpricing dynamics. Additionally, Hypothesis 2d considers the broader market scenario, suggesting that during the COVID period, market volatility may contribute to higher levels of underpricing in IPOs. Finally, Hypothesis 2e introduces the influence of the Nifty 50 index on IPO underpricing, proposing that a robust Nifty 50 performance may be associated with lower underpricing levels. These hypotheses collectively underscore the multifaceted nature of underpricing determinants, encompassing both micro and macroeconomic factors, and contribute to a nuanced understanding of IPO dynamics in varying market conditions.

3. RESEARCH METHODOLOGY

3.1 Data

The study comprises data from 502 Indian IPOs and daily closing price of Nifty 50 index, sourced from the Centre for Monitoring the Indian Economy (CMIE). These IPOs were categorized into their respective sectors, such as industrial, financial, and service sectors, using the Standard Industrial Classification (SIC) codes. To gauge the sector-wise performance of these IPOs, the study relied on the difference between the offer price and the closing price on the day of listing. The data encompass IPOs issued between January 2010 and December 2023. The study period is further divided into two segments: the pre-COVID period (January 2010 to December 2019) and the COVID period (January 2020 to December 2023).

3.2 Method

a. Return on security: It is calculated to know the return of the IPO shares on listing day. Michaely and Shaw (1994), Lowry and Shu (2002), and Lowry and Murphy (2007) have used this formula to know the under-pricing of IPOs. Ri = (Pi-Po) / po. Here, Ri = Return on security on listing day, Pi = Closing price of the security on listing day, Po = Offer price of the security.
b. Market return on the listing day: It is intended as the benchmark index return on the closing value of Nifty. (Shah, S. N. and Mehta, D. H.; 2015). Mi = (Ii – Io) / Io. Here, Mi = Market return on listing day, Ii = Closing index at listing day, Io = Closing index at offer day.

3.2.1. Market Adjusted Abnormal Return (MAAR)

The calculation of an IPO's Market Adjusted Abnormal Return involves dividing the change in price from the issue price by the concurrent change in the overall market level. In simpler terms, it compares the difference between the IPO price and the market change from the IPO issuance to the listing. Therefore, MAAR serves as a metric capturing how well an IPO has performed in comparison to the overall market performance during that period. Building on the insights of Fama (1970) and Fama and French (1993), the adjustment for market movements allows abnormal returns to provide information about a stock's performance beyond what can be attributed to general market trends. To know the degree of under-pricing of IPOs, market adjusted abnormal return for the IPOs are premeditated by using this formula:

$$MAAR =[(1+Ri) / (1+Mi) – 1)] * 100$$

3.2.2. Ordinary Least Square Model (OLS)

OLS is used to analyse the effect of factors like Listing Gain, Market index return, Issue price, Issue Size and oversubscription on Under-pricing of IPOs. This method makes it easier to comprehend the extent to which these independent variables influence IPO under-pricing.

$$Y1i = \alpha + \beta 1X1 + \beta 2X2 + \beta 3X3 +......+ i$$

$$Log\ Ri = \alpha + \beta 1log\ MR +\beta 2log\ LG + \beta 3log\ IP+ \beta 4log\ IS+ \beta 5logOS + i$$

Log Ri = Under-pricing of security, β1log MR = Market Index Return, β2log LG = Listing gain, β3log IP = Issue price, β4log IS = Issue size, β5logOS = Over subscription and i = Constant

Table 1. Shapiro–Wilk test for normality

	Pre covid (January10-December 19) p-value			During Covid (January20– December 23) p-value		
	Industrial	**Service**	**Finance**	**Industrial**	**Service**	**Finance**
Market return	.995	.054	.913	.996	.078	.402
Listing Gain	1.000	1.000	.994	.228	.955	.510
Issue price	.804	.222	.825	.882	.683	.272
Issue Size	1.00	.288	.149	.200	.063	.561
Over Subscription	.090	.509	.132	.345	.593	.140
Under pricing	.139	.200	1.000	.376	.917	.158
Nifty 50	.090	.286	.835	.890	.989	.256

Note. Normality test for the variables.

Determining the data distribution of variables is a pivotal step in selecting an appropriate statistical procedure, particularly when utilizing secondary data in research. In this study, the Shapiro-Wilk test was executed, and the results presented in Table 1 indicate no evidence of anomalies. This statistical assessment, supplemented by a visual examination of the variables' histograms, guided the decision to employ parametric tests for subsequent analyses. This comprehensive approach ensures a robust foundation for the chosen analytical methods, aligning with established practices in statistical research (Shapiro & Wilk, 1965).Furthermore, the decision to use parametric tests after verifying the normality of the data aligns with the assumptions underlying these tests, enhancing the reliability and validity of the study's findings. It is crucial to consider the potential impact of data distribution on the appropriateness of statistical procedures, and the chosen methodology reflects a careful consideration of this aspect in the research design.

4. RESULTS AND DISCUSSION

The study includes a detailed summary of each variable under investigation, along with an examination of their co-movement through descriptive statistics. Descriptive statistics, such as mean, minimum, maximum, and standard deviation, were computed for various variables including Market Return, Listing Gain, Issue

Price, Issue Size, and Over-subscription of the IPOs across the three sectors, both during and before the COVID-19 pandemic.

Table 2 presents inferential statistics for these variables. In the Industrial Sector, the mean Market Return was relatively high before the COVID-19 pandemic, with a minimum return of 1.03, maximum return of 1.15, and a standard deviation of 0.029. These figures indicate a strong performance of the secondary market in the period preceding the pandemic, characterized by high average returns. Negative skewness and kurtosis values suggest a negatively skewed and asymmetric data distribution, which is platykurtic.Similarly, in the Service Sector, the average Market Index Return was high before the pandemic, with a minimum return of 1.00 and a maximum return of 1.09, along with a standard deviation of 0.015. This also points to a robust performance of the secondary market before the pandemic (Mazur et al., 2021; Fasanya& Akinwale, 2022). The data exhibited negative skewness, indicating an absence of positive skewness.

The positive kurtosis value suggests a leptokurtic distribution with data asymmetry. In the Financial Sector, the lower mean Market Index Return before the pandemic, with a minimum value of 0.92 and a maximum value of 0.99, accompanied by a standard deviation of 0.018, suggests a period of relatively higher average market returns during the COVID-19 period. Positive skewness values indicating a positively skewed data distribution suggest that there may be more occurrences of returns on the higher end, potentially signifying positive market sentiment. Additionally, the leptokurtic distributions implied by kurtosis values suggest increased volatility in returns during the pandemic, pointing to a more pronounced variability in market performance.The implication of standard deviation is that it measures the degree of variability or dispersion of returns from the mean. In this context, a higher standard deviation during the COVID-19 period indicates increased market volatility, reflecting the greater extent of fluctuations in returns (Mohsen et *al.,* 2024). This heightened volatility can be both an opportunity and a risk for investors, as it may present potential for higher returns but also increases the likelihood of larger market swings(Black, 1986).In the Industrial sector during the pandemic, despite the mean Listing Gain being lower compared to the pre-COVID period, the maximum return achieved was higher, accompanied by a standard deviation of 48.09.

This hints at relatively stable returns during the pandemic period. Moreover, the positive skewness suggests a longer right tail in the distribution, indicating the potential for higher returns. This aligns with the notion that, although the average listing gains might have decreased, the presence of an extended right tail implies the possibility of occasional substantial gains in the Industrial sector during the pandemic.

Table 2. Descriptive statistics

Market Return	Pre-covid (January10-December19)			During Covid (January 20-December 23)		
	Industrial	**Service**	**Financial**	**Industrial**	**Service**	**Financial**
No of Firms	59	73	23	28	11	8
Mean	1.08	1.04	.9604	1.05	1.01	1.07
Minimum	1.03	1.00	.92	1.01	1.00	1.00
Maximum	1.15	1.09	.99	1.09	1.03	1.17
St. Deviation	.029	.015	.018	.019	.007	.048
Skewness	-.046	-.508	-.427	.114	-1.57	.572
Kurtosis	-.414	.924	.056	-.490	3.40	2.5
Listing Gain:						
Mean	97.90	93.70	108.13	70.84	65.58	1.92
Minimum	-4.30	-17.11	32.71	2.31	4.95	1.00
Maximum	198.50	205.55	183.14	206.76	150.48	2.54
St. Deviation	45.33	48.10	39.17	48.09	41.72	.49
Skewness	-.035	.026	.088	.851	.613	-.662
Kurtosis	-.426	-.368	-.538	.870	.355	.563
Issue Price:						
Mean	3.18	3.38	3.31	3.62	3.53	3.48
Minimum	2.04	2.00	2.45	2.78	2.52	2.40
Maximum	4.25	4.12	4.22	4.49	4.24	4.09
St. Deviation	.438	.4342	.467	.437	.5396	.5260
Skewness	.191	-.758	.083	-.112	-.345	-1.3
Kurtosis	.202	.687	-.772	-.364	-.548	2.2
Issue Size:						
Mean	3.21	3.45	3.87	3.78	3.88	4.20
Minimum	2.37	2.36	2.53	2.78	3.00	3.65
Maximum	5.19	4.27	4.78	4.59	4.97	5.01
St. Deviation	.537	.4528	.574	.369	.4786	.479
Skewness	.829	-.409	-.734	-.712	.743	.526
Kurtosis	1.54	.676	.652	1.56	3.00	-.736
Over-Subscription:						
Mean	1.68	1.73	1.66	2.03	2.07	1.65
Minimum	1.05	1.00	1.07	1.02	1.32	1.20
Maximum	2.89	2.77	2.69	2.91	2.87	2.55
St. Deviation	.421	.399	.442	.537	.514	.417

continued on following page

Table 2. Continued

Market Return	Pre-covid (January10-December19)			During Covid (January 20-December 23)		
	Industrial	**Service**	**Financial**	**Industrial**	**Service**	**Financial**
Skewness	.545	.243	.364	-.102	.332	1.57
Kurtosis	-.077	-.259	-.421	-1.08	-.732	3
Nifty 50:						
Mean	3.12	3.45	3.87	2.78	3.88	4.20
Minimum	2.49	2.36	2.53	2.78	3.00	3.65
Maximum	4.19	4.27	4.78	4.59	4.97	5.01
St. Deviation	.437	.4528	.574	.369	.4786	.479
Skewness	.829	-.409	-.734	-.712	.743	.526
Kurtosis	1.54	.676	.652	1.56	3.00	-.736

*Note.*This table explains the descriptive statistics. Source: Authors computation

The kurtosis values provide insight into the distribution of data and its level of asymmetry. In the case of the Industrial Sector, the kurtosis value suggests that data was asymmetric and exhibited heavy tails, which is leptokurtic. This indicates that returns in this sector during the COVID-19 pandemic could be highly volatile. Conversely, during the pre-COVID period, the data was less volatile, with lighter tails, indicating a platykurtic distribution (Obadire and Obadire, 2023). Similarly, in the Service Sector, the average and maximum returns earned during the pandemic were lower compared to the period before the pandemic. The positive skewness and kurtosis values indicate positively skewed data with an asymmetric distribution and leptokurtic characteristics, implying volatility in returns from this sector. implying volatility in returns from this sector and influencing investor risk perception.

In the Financial Sector, both the average and maximum returns earned during the pandemic were lower compared to the pre-COVID period. Positive skewness and kurtosis values again indicate positively skewed data with an asymmetric distribution and leptokurtic characteristics, signalling higher volatility in returns which could increase investor risk..The study also examined the issue price of IPOs during the pandemic, revealing that, strangely, the capital markets did not appear to be significantly affected by the pandemic's warning effects. IPOs were issued at higher prices during the pandemic compared to the period before the pandemic, indicating that companies were willing to issue shares at higher valuations (Li et al., 2017). This is supported by data from Prime Database, which showed that IPOs raised Rs 26,770 crore in the pandemic year, a substantial increase compared to Rs 12,985 crore in 2019.Regarding the issue size, the mean issue size was higher during the pre-COVID period in the Financial Sector, with a minimum value of 2.45 and a maximum value of 4.22, along with a standard deviation of 0.467.

This suggests that the issue price of IPOs in the financial sector was influenced by the pandemic. Skewness values indicate positively skewed data with asymmetric distribution during both pre-COVID and COVID periods. Kurtosis values are positive, indicating heavy-tailed data that is leptokurtic during the COVID period and platykurtic during the pre-COVID period.

In the Industrial Sector, the average issue size during the COVID period was higher, with a minimum value of 2.78 and a maximum value of 4.59. This suggests that companies sought to take advantage of the strong rebound in the Indian indices by raising a substantial amount of capital. Regulatory changes, such as the reduction in the holding period for pre-issue capital and amendments to discretionary allotments, encouraged companies to issue more public shares during the pandemic. Skewness values were negative during the COVID period, indicating a longer left tail of distribution, while during the pre-COVID period, skewness values were positive, suggesting a longer right tail of distribution. Kurtosis values were positive in both periods, signifying heavy-tailed data that is leptokurtic.In the Service Sector and Financial Sector, the average issue size was also higher during the COVID period, indicating a similar trend. Skewness values were positive during both periods, indicating positively skewed data with asymmetric distribution. Kurtosis values were positive, indicating heavy-tailed data that is leptokurtic during the COVID period and platykurtic for the Financial Sector during this period. For risk-averse investors, the higher mean market returns and maximum returns in the Industrial and Service sectors before the pandemic might have provided a sense of security and confidence in market stability.

Furthermore, the study explored the mean values of over-subscription, revealing that the Industrial and Service Sectors experienced higher averages during the pandemic compared to the pre-COVID period. This suggests that more investors were participating in IPOs during the pandemic. However, in the Financial Sector, there was not much change, with the average remaining consistent across both periods. Skewness values were positive, indicating positively skewed data with asymmetric distribution for both periods, except for the Industrial Sector, which exhibited positively skewed data during the pre-COVID period. Kurtosis values indicated light-tailed, platykurtic distributions for all sectors during both periods, except for the Financial Sector, which exhibited heavy-tailed, leptokurtic characteristics during the COVID period.

4.1 Market Adjusted Abnormal Return Computations

Hypothesis 1:Market-Adjusted Abnormal Returns (MAAR) are zero.

The t-test results presented in Table 4 provide evidence to assess Hypothesis 1. The p-values for the Industrial, Service, and Financial sectors, both during the pre-COVID and COVID-19 periods, are all found to be less than 0.05. Therefore, the null hypothesis that MAAR is zero is rejected. This suggests that IPOs in these sectors are not priced at zero MAAR; instead, they exhibit underpricing.

This finding aligns with the prevailing notion in financial literature that IPOs often experience abnormal returns, indicating market inefficiencies or investor mispricing during the listing process (Black, 1986). The mispricing will influence the investor sentiment and the risk pattern (Chen & Zheng, 2021; Bhullar et al., 2024; Xia et al., 2024). Furthermore, the variations in the number of firms across sectors suggest a dynamic market landscape, potentially influenced by changes in IPO activity. The descriptive statistics in Table 3, including the minimum, maximum, mean, and standard deviation of MAAR, offer insights into the distribution of abnormal returns across sectors during both pre-COVID and COVID-19 periods. For instance, the lower mean in the Industrial sector during the COVID-19 period may indicate challenges or different trends for IPOs in this sector during the pandemic. The elevated standard deviation in the Financial sector suggests that IPOs in this domain might have contributed to increased market volatility, impacting investor sentiment and trading behavior. This aligns with the understanding that financial sector IPOs, due to their intrinsic connection with market dynamics, can have a more pronounced effect on market volatility.

Table 3. Market adjusted abnormal return (MAAR)

Particulars	Pre-Covid-19 (January10-december19)			During Covid-19 (January20–December23)		
	Industrial	Service	Financial	Industrial	Service	Financial
No of firms	59	73	23	28	11	8
Minimum	-.0005	-.0010	-.0031	.9951	.5249	.0000
Maximum	2.37	2.39	2.25	2.30	2.09	1.5093
Mean	1.8851	1.86	1.90	1.55	1.62	1.045
St. Deviation	.39943	.410	.549	.544	.448	0.494

Note. Descriptive Statistics of MAAR. Source: Authors Computation

Table 4. t-test results of MAAR

Particulars	Pre-Covid-19 (January10-December19)			During Covid-19 (January20–December 23)		
	Industrial	Service	Financial	Industrial	Service	Financial
No of firms	59	73	23	28	11	8
Mean	1.88	1.86	1.90	1.55	1.62	1.04
St. Deviation	.399	.410	.549	.544	.448	.494
St. Error Mean	.052	.048	.114	.102	.135	.174
t-test	36.25	38.71	16.60	15.12	12.02	5.98
p value	.000	.000	.000	.000	.000	.001

Note. Results of t-test for MAAR of Industrial, Service and Financial Sector. Source: Authors computation. Significance at 5%.

In summary, the rejection of Hypothesis 1 supports the idea that IPOs in the Industrial, Service, and Financial sectors exhibit non-zero MAAR, emphasizing the presence of underpricing. The variations in descriptive statistics further underscore the nuanced impact of IPOs on market dynamics, with potential sector-specific influences during the COVID-19 period.

4.2 Ordinary Least Square Regression

Hypotheses 2(a)-(e):Significant Impact of Market Return, Listing Gain, Issue Price, Issue Size, and Oversubscription on IPO Underpricing.

The study formulated Hypotheses 2(a)-(e) to investigate the significant impact of Market Return, Listing Gain, Issue Price, Issue Size, and Oversubscription on IPO underpricing. The results of the multiple regression analyses, presented in Table 6, Table 7, and Table 8, provide insights into the acceptance or rejection of these hypotheses.

Industrial Sector: In the Industrial sector, the results suggest that Listing Gain significantly influences IPO underpricing during both pre-COVID and COVID periods. This aligns with the expectations of Hypothesis 2(b), indicating that the immediate gains realized by investors at the time of listing have a notable impact on the subsequent underpricing of IPOs in the Industrial sector (Loughran and Ritter, 2004). On the other hand, Market Return, Issue Price, Issue Size, and Oversubscription do not show significant impacts on underpricing in this sector during either period, contrary to the hypotheses (2a, 2c, 2d, and 2e) because the sector specific risk gets average in the industry evaluation. This suggests that factors like market conditions, the size of the issue, and investor demand, as measured by oversubscription, do not play a significant role in shaping underpricing for Industrial sector IPOs and influencing overall risk assessment.This aligns with the observations of Bradley and Jordan (2002), who emphasized the importance of industry characteristics in shaping IPO outcomes. Understanding that factors influencing underpricing may differ across sectors emphasizes the need for targeted strategies and considerations when analyzing and investing in IPOs. Notably, the study explores the impact of the COVID-19 pandemic on IPO underpricing. The findings suggest potential shifts in the significance of certain variables during this period and impacting investor risk perceptions and strategies.

Service Sector: The Service sector exhibits a more nuanced picture. During the pre-COVID period, both Listing Gain and Issue Price significantly impact underpricing, aligning with Hypotheses 2(b) and 2(c). However, during the COVID period, only Listing Gain remains significant. This suggests that, while immediate gains at the time of listing consistently affect underpricing, the influence of issue pricing on underpricing may vary during different market conditions. Such temporal variations in the determinants of underpricing echo the sentiments expressed by academic researchers like Ljungqvist et al. (2006), who highlighted the influence of external economic conditions on IPO outcomes. Additionally, Market Return, Issue Size, and Oversubscription do not significantly impact underpricing in the Service sector during either period, contrasting with Hypotheses 2(a), 2(d), and 2(e) but will affect the investor sentiment and risk.

Financial Sector: In the Financial sector, Listing Gain, Issue Price, and Issue Size significantly affect underpricing during the pre-COVID period, in line with Hypotheses 2(b), 2(c), and 2(d). However, during the COVID period, only Oversubscription emerges as a significant factor. This indicates that, during periods of heightened market uncertainty, investor demand, as reflected in oversubscription levels, becomes a more crucial determinant of underpricing in the Financial sector. As liquidity risk, default risk and interest rate risk majorly influence the investor sentiment while relying on financial sector companies IPO process. At the same time, its stimuluses the equity market and ultimately Nifty 50 (Beaulieu & Mrissa, 2015). On the other hand, Market Return does not show a significant impact during either period, contrary to Hypothesis 2(a).

These findings provide nuanced insights into the factors influencing IPO underpricing in different sectors and periods. While Listing Gain consistently emerges as a significant factor, the impact of other variables varies across sectors and study periods. Loughran and Ritter (2004) have noted that initial listing gains often reflect market mispricing and are indicative of short-term investor behavior. This reaffirms the importance of immediate market reactions in shaping IPO underpricing, emphasizing the role of investor sentiment and perception. The study's nuanced results regarding the impact of Market Return, Issue Price, Issue Size, and Oversubscription diverge from some earlier studies. The study thus contributes to a better understanding of the complex dynamics that shape the underpricing of IPOs in the Industrial, Service, and Financial sectors during both pre-COVID and COVID periods.

Table 5. Regression outputs

	Pre Covid-19 (January 2010-December 2019)			During Covid-19 (January20–December23)		
	Industrial	**Service**	**Financial**	**Industrial**	**Service**	**Financial**
R	.951	.919	.906	.983	.992	.996
R square	.904	.844	.821	.967	.985	.991
Ad. R Square	.895	.832	.778	.960	.970	.970
F-stat	100.06	72.565	19.27	129.21	65.64	45.61
p value	.000	.000	.000	.000	.000	.022

Note. Result of regression analysis of Industrial, Service and Financial Sectors Source: Authors Computation Significance at 5%.

Table 6. Regression analysis for industrial sector

Industrial Sector	Pre covid (January 10-December 19)			During Covid (January 20– December 23)		
	β	**t -test**	**P-value**	**B**	**t -test**	**P- Value**
Constant	1.141	6.027	.000	.403	1.456	.160
Market return	-.032	-.740	.463	.074	1.828	.081
Listing gain	.934	21.080	.000	.954	20.040	.000
Issue price	-.073	-1.282	.205	.104	2.392	.026
Issue size	.105	1.788	.080	.001	.021	.984
Over subscription	.067	1.431	.158	.021	.396	.696
Nifty 50	-0.23	-.456	.567	-.032	.465	.081

Dependent Variable: under-pricing Source: Authors Computation Significance at 5%.

Table 7. Regression analysis for service sector

Service Sector	Pre covid (January10-December 19)			During Covid (January 20– December 23)		
	β	**t-test**	**P- Value**	**B**	**t-test**	**P- Value**
Constant	.902	3.173	.002	2.26	4.055	.010
Market return	.081	1.652	.103	-.119	-1.662	.157
Listing gain	.916	16.615	.000	1.061	13.632	.000
Issue price	-.184	-3.193	.002	.093	1.492	.196
Issue size	.039	.640	.524	.055	.750	.487
Over subscription	-.089	-1.543	.127	-.086	-1.010	.359
Nifty 50	.087	1.89	.001	-.132	-1.78	.167

Dependent Variable: under-pricing Source: Authors Computation Significance at 5%.

Table 8. Regression analysis of financial sector

Financial Sector	Pre Covid(January10-December 19)			During Covid (January20– December 23)		
	B	t -test	P – Value	B	t-test	P- Value
Constant	1.01	1.553	.135	.401	3.984	.058
Market return	.010	.094	.926	.353	4.221	.052
Listing gain	.873	8.033	.000	.445	4.212	.052
Issue price	-.222	-2.116	.046	-.117	-1.497	.273
Issue size	.263	2.216	.038	.326	3.208	.085
Over subscription	-.119	-1.026	.317	.602	4.803	.041
Nifty 50	.012	.087	.145	.389	4.678	.067

Dependent Variable: under-pricing Source: Authors Computation Significance at 5%.

The study's sector-specific variations in the impact of independent variables on underpricing contribute valuable insights. While some findings align with prior research, the sector-specific nuances offer fresh perspectives. These insights contribute to the ongoing academic discourse on IPOs, enriching our understanding of the market dynamics.In conclusion, the study's findings contribute valuable insights into the determinants of IPO underpricing, emphasizing the consistent influence of Listing Gain and highlighting sector-specific variations. While aligning with certain established trends, the study brings nuance to the discussion by uncovering sector-specific dynamics and exploring the impact of the COVID-19 pandemic. The comparisons with other authors' findings underscore the complex and multifaceted nature of IPO markets, urging researchers and practitioners to consider both general trends and sector-specific characteristics in their analyses.

5.MANAGERIAL IMPLICATIONS AND POLICY RECOMMENDATION

Managerial Implications: Underpricing is majorly influenced by underwriters pricing procedure knows as book building. The underwriter designs the prospects including all the listing details to the investors to create IPO market after the valuation. Here the underwriter plays a significant role in pricing the IPO of the company. At the same time, when the total proceeds of IPO are lower from the exchange then there is a high chance of underpricing and the marketing cost for the new IPO will be reduced. This strategy aims to create the perception that the company's stock is a good value, encouraging investors to purchase all the shares being offered. In addition to that, When the board of directors is given incentives, such as stock ownership, to monitor CEO performance, the level of underpricing witnessed on the IPO company's first day of trade can change. Firms with the lowest levels of insider ownership on the board exhibit less initial day underpricing than firms with the greatest levels of insider ownership. Thus, underwriter, CEO incentives or performance, board of directors' decision, level of insider ownership, investor risk perspective etc. are the major factors which influence the IPO underpricing.

Policy Recommendation: The company should properly evaluate the IPO pricing so that the analyst can easily recommend to retail investors and HNIs. Specifically, the company history, offer price, capital structure, risks, investment rewards and overall recommendations. In addition to this, the company should also focus on ESG compliance, cyber security safeguard, risks, and technology ecosystem to drive the IPO pricing in a productive mechanism (Earle, 2010; Baker et al., 2021; Escobar-Anel & Jiao, 2024).

6. CONCLUSION

This study delved into the evaluation of IPO performance and underpricing across diverse sectors, dissecting the research period into pre-pandemic and pandemic phases. Notably, the industrial sector emerged as a standout performer during the COVID-19 phase, showcasing robust performance compared to other sectors. The computation of Adjusted Abnormal Market Returns revealed persistent undervaluation of IPOs across all three sectors in both pandemic and pre-pandemic periods. Regression analysis underscored the pivotal role of Listing Gain in influencing underpricing across all sectors during both phases, except in the financial sector where Oversubscription demonstrated significant impact during the COVID period. This emphasizes the resilience of India's industrial IPOs amid the challenges posed by the pandemic.

Furthermore, the study highlighted the consistent underpricing of IPOs across sectors, with independent variables such as Listing Gain, Issue Price, Issue Size, and Oversubscription influencing underpricing dynamics in the Industrial, Service, and financial sectors. As a noteworthy observation, recent IPO performances should be factored into investment decisions, emphasizing the relevance of short-term returns compared to long-term prospects. This underscores the evolving nature of the IPO landscape and the need for investors to adapt their strategies based on sector-specific trends and current market conditions.

REFERENCES

Anand, R., & Singh, B. (2019). Effect of composition of board and promoter group retained ownership on underpricing of Indian IPO firms: An empirical study. *Indian Journal of Corporate Governance*, 12(1), 21–38. DOI: 10.1177/0974686219836539

Arora, N., & Singh, B. (2019). Impact of auditor and underwriter reputation on underpricing of SME IPOs in India. *Management and Labour Studies*, 44(2), 193–208. DOI: 10.1177/0258042X19829285

Baig, A. S., & Chen, M. (2022). Did the COVID-19 pandemic (really) positively impact the IPO Market? An Analysis of information uncertainty. *Finance Research Letters*, 46, 102372. DOI: 10.1016/j.frl.2021.102372 PMID: 35431676

Bajo, E., & Raimondo, C. (2017). Media sentiment and IPO underpricing. *Journal of Corporate Finance*, 46, 139–153. DOI: 10.1016/j.jcorpfin.2017.06.003

Baker, E. D., Boulton, T. J., Braga-Alves, M. V., & Morey, M. R. (2021). ESG government risk and international IPO underpricing. *Journal of Corporate Finance*, 67, 101913. DOI: 10.1016/j.jcorpfin.2021.101913

Beaulieu, M. C., & Mrissa Bouden, H. (2015). Firm-specific risk and IPO market cycles. *Applied Economics*, 47(50), 5354–5377. DOI: 10.1080/00036846.2015.1047091

Bhullar, P. S., Grover, K. L., & Tiwari, R. (2024). IPO underpricing: A comparative analysis of risk factor disclosures in the financial and non-financial sectors. *The Bottom Line (New York, N.Y.)*, 37(3), 332–350. Advance online publication. DOI: 10.1108/BL-04-2023-0123

Bhuyan, R., Çetin, C., İzgi, B., & Talukdar, B. (2021). A model of dynamic information production for initial public offerings. *Quantitative Finance*, •••, 1–18. DOI: 10.1080/14697688.2023.2273975

Black, F. (1986). Noise. *The Journal of Finance*, 41(3), 529–543. DOI: 10.2307/2328481

Bradley, D. J., & Jordan, B. D. (2002). Partial Adjustment to Public Information and IPO Underpricing. *Journal of Financial and Quantitative Analysis*, 37(4), 595–616. DOI: 10.2307/3595013

Chandler, J. A., Payne, G. T., Moore, C. B., & Brigham, K. H. (2019). Family involvement signals in initial public offerings. *Journal of Family Business Strategy*, 10(1), 8–16. DOI: 10.1016/j.jfbs.2019.01.004

Chang, H. H., Chen, A., Kao, L., & Wu, C. S. (2014). IPO price discovery efficiency under alternative regulatory constraints: Taiwan, Hong Kong and the US. *International Review of Economics & Finance*, 29, 83–96. DOI: 10.1016/j.iref.2013.05.001

Chatterjee, M., Bhattacharjee, T., & Chakraborty, B. (2023). *Studies on Indian IPO: systematic review and future research agenda.* Qualitative Research in Financial Markets., DOI: 10.1108/QRFM-10-2021-0175

Chen, H., & Zheng, M. (2021). IPO underperformance and the idiosyncratic risk puzzle. Journal of Banking &amp. *Journal of Banking & Finance*, 131, 106190. DOI: 10.1016/j.jbankfin.2021.106190

Dambra, M., Field, L. C., Gustafson, M. T., & Pisciotta, K. (2018). The consequences to analyst involvement in the IPO process: Evidence surrounding the JOBS Act. *Journal of Accounting and Economics*, 65(2–3), 302–330. DOI: 10.1016/j.jacceco.2017.12.001

Das, G., Saha, M., & Kundu, A. (2016). Analyzing long-run performance of select initial public offerings using monthly returns: Evidence from India. *Vision (Basel)*, 20(3), 237–248. DOI: 10.1177/0972262916652809

Datar, V., & Mao, D. Z. (2006). Deep underpricing of China's IPOs: Sources and implications. *International Journal of Financial Services Management*, 1(2-3), 345–362. DOI: 10.1504/IJFSM.2006.009635

Deng, Q., Dai, L., Yang, Z., Zhou, Z. G., Hussein, M., Chen, D., & Swartz, M. (2023). The impacts of regulation regime changes on ChiNext IPOs: Effects of 2013 and 2020 reforms on initial return, fair value and overreaction. *International Review of Financial Analysis*, 89, 102794. DOI: 10.1016/j.irfa.2023.102794

Dong, Y., & Huang, J. (2022). Price limits, investor sentiment, and initial public offering underpricing: A quasi-natural experiment based on ChiNext. *Emerging Markets Review*, 51, 100893. DOI: 10.1016/j.ememar.2022.100893

Earle, T. C. (2010). Trust in risk management: A model-based review of empirical research. Risk Analysis. *International Journal (Toronto, Ont.)*, 30(4), 541–574. DOI: 10.1111/j.15396924.2010.01398.x PMID: 20522197

Engelen, P. J., Heugens, P., Van Essen, M., Turturea, R., & Bailey, N. (2020). The impact of stakeholders' temporal orientaton on short-and long-term IPO outcomes: A meta-analysis. *Long Range Planning*, 53(2), 101853. DOI: 10.1016/j.lrp.2018.10.003

Escobar-Anel, M., & Jiao, Y. (2024). Robust Portfolio Optimization with Environmental, Social, and Corporate Governance Preference. *Risks*, 12(2), 33. DOI: 10.3390/risks12020033

Fama, E. F. (1970). Efficient Capital Markets: A Review of Theory and Empirical Work. *The Journal of Finance*, 25(2), 383–417. DOI: 10.2307/2325486

Fama, E. F., & French, K. R. (1993). Common Risk Factors in the Returns on Stocks and Bonds. *Journal of Financial Economics*, 33(1), 3–56. DOI: 10.1016/0304-405X(93)90023-5

Fasanya, I. O., & Akinwale, O. A. (2022). Exchange Rate Shocks and Sectoral Stock Returns in Nigeria: Do Asymmetry and Structural Breaks Matter? *Cogent Economics & Finance*, 10(1), 2045719. DOI: 10.1080/23322039.2022.2045719

Füllbrunn, S., Neugebauer, T., & Nicklisch, A. (2020). Underpricing of initial public offerings in experimental asset markets. *Experimental Economics*, 23(4), 1002–1029. DOI: 10.1007/s10683-019-09638-7

Gupta, V., Singh, S., & Yadav, S. S. (2023). Disaggregated IPO returns, economic uncertainty and the long-run performance of SME IPOs. *International Journal of Emerging Markets*, 18(10), 3847–3867. DOI: 10.1108/IJOEM-09-2020-1098

Honjo, Y. (2021). Public or perish? From founding to initial public offering. *Review of Managerial Science*, 15(6), 1573–1610. DOI: 10.1007/s11846-020-00390-4

Killins, R. N. (2019). An investigation of the short-term performance of the Canadian IPO market. *Research in International Business and Finance*, 47, 102–113. DOI: 10.1016/j.ribaf.2018.07.004

Kumar, A., & Sahoo, S. (2021). Do anchor investors affect long run performance? Evidence from Indian IPO markets. *Pacific Accounting Review*, 33(3), 322–346. DOI: 10.1108/PAR-09-2020-0149

Li, X., Wang, S. S., & Wang, X. (2017). Trust and stock price crash risk: Evidence from China. *Journal of Banking & Finance*, 76, 74–91. DOI: 10.1016/j.jbankfin.2016.12.003

Liu, L. X., Lu, R., Sherman, A. E., & Zhang, Y. (2023). IPO Underpricing and Limited Attention: Theory and Evidence. *Journal of Banking & Finance*, 106932, 106932. Advance online publication. DOI: 10.1016/j.jbankfin.2023.106932

Ljungqvist, A.. (2003). Hot Markets, Investor Sentiment, and IPO Pricing. *The Journal of Business*, 76(2), 293–318. DOI: 10.1086/503644

Ljungqvist, A., Jenkinson, T., & Wilhelm, W. J. (2006). Global Integration in Primary Equity Markets: The Role of U.S. Banks and U.S. Investors. *Review of Financial Studies*, 19(4), 1051–1082. DOI: 10.1093/rfs/16.1.0063

Loughran, T., & Ritter, J. R. (2004). Why Has IPO Underpricing Changed Over Time? *Financial Management*, 33(3), 5–37. DOI: 10.2307/3666172

Lowry, M., Michaely, R., & Volkova, E. (2017). Initial public offerings: A synthesis of the literature and directions for future research. *Foundations and Trends® in Finance, 11*(3-4), 154-320. http://dx.doi.org/DOI: 10.1561/0500000050

Luigi, A., Mohsen, B., Xihui, C., & Concetto, P. V. (2021). Knowledge spillovers and technical efficiency for cleaner production: An economic analysis from agriculture innovation. *Journal of Cleaner Production*, 320, 128830. DOI: 10.1016/j.jclepro.2021.128830

Manjunath, B. R., Raju, J. K., & Rehaman, M. (2020). Short-run performance evaluation of under-priced Indian IPOs. *Law and Financial Markets Review*, 14(3), 170–175. DOI: 10.1080/17521440.2020.1759239

Mazur, M., Dang, M., & Vega, M. (2021). COVID-19 and the march 2020 stock market crash. Evidence from S&P1500. *Finance Research Letters*, 38, 101690. DOI: 10.1016/j.frl.2020.101690 PMID: 32837377

Mohsen, B., Bruna, B., Karambir, S. D., Luca, E., & Anna, P. (2024). From manure to megawatts: Navigating the sustainable innovation solution through biogas production from livestock waste for harnessing green energy for green economy. *Heliyon*, 10(14), e34504. https://www.sciencedirect.com/science/article/pii/S240584402410535X. DOI: 10.1016/j.heliyon.2024.e34504

Obadire, A., & Obadire, K. (2023). The Impact of Bank Regulation on Bank Performance: A Novel Analysis of the Pre-Covid Era with Cross-Country Evidence. *American Journal of Industrial and Business Management*, 13(3), 118–139. DOI: 10.4236/ajibm.2023.133009

Payne, G. T., Trudell, L. T., Moore, C. B., Petrenko, O. V., & Hayes, N. T. (2023). Ambiguous signals and information asymmetry in the initial public offering process: Examining ownership concentration, process time, and underpricing. *Group & Organization Management*, 48(5), 1467–1502. DOI: 10.1177/10596011221090036

Rathnayake, D. N., Louembe, P. A., Kassi, D. F., Sun, G., & Ning, D. (2019). Are IPOs underpriced or overpriced? Evidence from an emerging market. *Research in International Business and Finance*, 50, 171–190. DOI: 10.1016/j.ribaf.2019.04.013

Shapiro, S. S., & Wilk, M. B. (1965). An analysis of variance test for normality (complete samples). *Biometrika*, 52(3/4), 591–611. DOI: 10.2307/2333709

Sundarasen, S., Goel, S., & Zulaini, F. A. (2017). Impact of investors' protection, transparency level and legal origin on initial public offering (IPO) initial returns. *Managerial Finance*, 43(7), 738–760. DOI: 10.1108/MF-08-2016-0230

Teti, E., & Montefusco, I. (2022). Corporate governance and IPO underpricing: Evidence from the italian market. *The Journal of Management and Governance*, 26(3), 851–889. DOI: 10.1007/s10997-021-09563-z

Thomadakis, S., Nounis, C., & Gounopoulos, D. (2012). Long-term performance of Greek IPOs. *European Financial Management*, 18(1), 117–141. DOI: 10.1111/j.1468-036X.2010.00546.x

Wang, Y., & Wang, G. (2021). IPO underpricing and long-term performance in China: The perspective of price limit policy. *Managerial Finance*, 47(9), 1233–1252. DOI: 10.1108/MF-08-2020-0428

Wasiuzzaman, S., Yong, F. L. K., Sundarasen, S. D. D., & Othman, N. S. (2018). Impact of disclosure of risk factors on the initial returns of initial public offerings (IPOs). *Accounting Research Journal*, 31(1), 46–62. DOI: 10.1108/ARJ-09-2016-0122

Xia, H., Weng, J., Boubaker, S., Zhang, Z., & Jasimuddin, S. M. (2024). Cross-influence ofinformation and risk effects on the IPO market: Exploring risk disclosure with a machine learning approach. *Annals of Operations Research*, 334(1), 761–797. DOI: 10.1007/s10479-022-05012-8 PMID: 36312208

Zou, G., Cheng, Q., Chen, W., & Meng, J. G. (2020). What causes the IPO underpricing? New evidence from China's SME market. *Applied Economics*, 52(23), 2493–2507. DOI: 10.1080/00036846.2019.1693017

Chapter 4
Blue Ocean Strategies and Firm Performance: Exploring the Ideas and Concepts in New Normal

Muhammad Faisal Sultan
Khadim Ali Shah Bukhari Institute of Technology, Pakistan

Erum Shaikh
https://orcid.org/0000-0002-3198-2786
Shaheed Benazir Bhutto University, Pakistan

Kashif Mehmood
Khadim Ali Shah Bukhari Institute of Technology, Pakistan

Muhammad Nawaz Tunio
https://orcid.org/0000-0003-1376-5371
University of Sufism and Modern Sciences, Bhitshah, Pakistan

ABSTRACT

This study is one of the descriptive studies written to highlight the importance and use of Blue Ocean Strategies. Previous research that indicates the use and significance of Blue Ocean Strategies is very few. Hence, there is a need for a thorough study that may make readers understand the importance and role of Blue Ocean Strategies in the performance of the firm. Hence, this study is designed to foster the understanding that may foster research and better policymaking. Therefore, the significance of this study has multiple folds and may be found to be fruitful for numerous stakeholders.

DOI: 10.4018/979-8-3693-5723-1.ch004

INTRODUCTION

A good strategy is required to make the company appropriately plotted in the competitive arena. However, there is always a need for effective execution and implementation of strategy to be in the competitive arena for the required period of time. On the other side studies also revealed that the purpose of effective strategy formulation is to create and deliver value (Alam & Islam, 2017).

However, strategies can be developed in two different forms, i.e., the Blue Ocean Strategy and Red Ocean Strategy are termed as two distinct sets of strategies that are formulated to compete in either competitive or competitionless markets (Kim & Mauborgne, 2005). However, moving from red-ocean strategies to blue-ocean strategies is a complex task and firms may face serious troubles and problems in converting towards Blue Ocean Strategies. According to the studies using the Blue Ocean Strategy may not force firms to increase production, invest heavily in marketing or R&D, etc. However, pursuing the Blue Ocean Strategy may result in customers who are not interested in the value proposition developed by the company (Yunus & Sijabat, 2021).

Differences Between Red-Ocean and Blue-Ocean Strategies

Blue Ocean Strategies are based upon the creation of new values and creation of products that are unique and address new and differentiated markets. On the other side, Red Ocean Strategies are used to outperform competitors to grab the largest slice of market share (Rawabdeh et al., 2012). Hence, on the basis of these parameters, the major differences between Red Ocean Strategies and Blue Ocean Strategies are as under:

Table 1. Table to Highlight Differences between ROS and BOS

RED OCEAN STRATEGIES (ROS)	BLUE OCEAN STRATEGIES (BOS)
Used to compete in intensive competitive markets	Used to formulate un-contested markets
Used to best competitors	Used to make competition irrelevant
Used to exploit current demands	Used to create demand for new products
Used to make customer experience tradeoffs between value and cost	Used to break tradeoff between value and cost
Used to make the entire system of the firm related with strategic choices of strategies like differentiation and low-cost.	Used to make the entire system of the firm pursue differentiation and low-cost strategies

Characteristics of Blue Ocean Strategies

According to studies, there are three major characteristics of Blue Ocean Strategies, i.e., Focus, Divergence, and Compelling Tagline. Hence, in line with these characteristics, the Blue Ocean strategies are developed to make it self-differentiated and distant from the rest of the competitors by getting focused on untapped arenas and continuing to focus on these arenas until the compelling tagline remains consistent for the company (Alam & Islam, 2017)

Developing Blue Ocean Strategy

Framework for Developing Blue Ocean Strategy

Kim and Mauborgne (2017) launched their book to address the transformation of the firm's strategy to "***Blue Ocean***" from "***Red Ocean***". Hence, the book stressed the importance of the cognitive sides of the blue ocean strategy which also required management to possess a blue mindset. To have a Blue Mindset management must need to follow some fundamental rules and values that are listed below:

Rules

Three important rules that management must govern for the effective implementation of Blue Ocean strategies are as under: (Kim & Mauborgne, 2017)

a) Need to change industrial boundaries and must not believe in any fix structure of the industry
b) Must focus on success that lies beyond the competition
c) Focus on new markets rather than conventional markets

Values

Focus toward Blue Ocean is based upon following three complementary dimensions without which effective launch of Blue Ocean strategies seems to be impossible (Kim & Mauborgne, 2017)

a) Humanness
b) Self-Confidence
c) Creative Competence

Tools, Tactics, and Techniques for Implementing Blue Ocean Strategy

Blue Ocean Strategy is developed by using Strategic Canvas which requires the strategist to ensure three prime activities. Initially, strategies are required to list all the factors that affect or may affect the working and operations in the particular industry and have the tendency to affect all the players (Rosenthal, 2017). Secondly, strategists are required to formulate the strategic profile of all the competitors operating or having the tendency to operate in the market. Lastly, strategists are required to develop a value curve by using a strategic canvas that is the practical indication of activities that the company will perform by considering the current and future competition. The value curve developed through strategic canvas is used to reflect vividly upon four questions through systematic action plans (Rosenthal, 2017).

i. What are the factors that are taken for granted in any of the specific industries? How should these factors be eliminated?
ii. What are the factors that must be reduced to well below the standards of the industry?
iii. What are those factors that must be raised well above the standards of the industry?
iv. What factors must now be created for the first time? How these initially developed factors may provide value to the customers.

Hence, the tool is used to reduce or to make management invest in the critically less important and critically important factors (Rosenthal, 2017).

Frame Work

Studies also presented a framework that must be used to implement the Blue Ocean Strategy effectively and efficiently. This framework is based action plan that is based upon four elements namely ***a)*** Eliminate ***b)*** Reduce ***c)*** Raise and ***d)*** Create. Following this framework will increase the firm's overall performance and goodwill (Kim & Mauborgne, 2017). Therefore, there is a thorough need to understand the principle and associated points in detail. Thus, the principles that are included in the action plan of Blue Ocean Strategies are as under:

i. **Eliminate:** To omit practices that are outdated or do not have value for customers in contemporary work settings (Kim & Mauborgne, 2017)

ii. **Reduce:** It is important to find out the elements that are least attractive for industry participation & also for customers. Hence, these elements must be reduced to the least possible and acceptable level of standards (Kim & Mauborgne, 2017).
iii. **Raise:** Other than eliminate and reduce companies are also required to understand which elements are essential and have high value for the industry and customers. Hence, the level of these elements must be improved to provide better value to the customers (Kim & Mauborgne, 2017)
iv. **Create:** Lastly, to follow Blue Ocean Strategies rigorously companies are also required to identify new sources that may provide desired value to the customers (Kim & Mauborgne, 2017)

STATEMENT OF PROBLEM

Studies are continuously indicating about the Blue Ocean Strategies but there is a substantial lack of studies that reflect upon the pragmatic advantages that may be obtained through applying Blue Ocean Strategies (Yunus & Sijabat, 2021).

LITERATURE REVIEW

Strategies defined by Michael Porters e.g., cost leadership, focus, and differentiation are used by traditional firms to capture market share and to become prominent in the industry. However, companies may define separate, differentiated, and uncontested markets for themselves by using a set of strategies that are termed "Blue Ocean Strategies" (Sang & Kimitei, 2021). Initial studies conducted to understand the Blue Ocean Strategies through data collection from Finnish companies reflected that the use of Blue Ocean strategies resulted in active strategic networking. These points cause value through changing and optimizing business models, networking, and industry-related goals. Hence, the firm became able to sell expertise that creates superior value to consumers (Alam & Islam, 2017).

One of the initial studies based upon applying Blue Ocean strategies by private sector firms operating in Jordan indicated that the use of Blue Ocean Strategies resulted in the creation of new products that resulted in the formation of new (Blue Ocean) markets (Rawabdeh et al., 2012). Hence, the implementation of Blue Ocean Strategies is found significant for improving the firm's strategic position. However, there is a need to implement Blue Ocean Strategies along with Red Ocean Strategies to accelerate firm performance in highly competitive markets (Kiptoon, 2014).

EMPIRICAL EVIDENCE AND SYSTEMATIC LITERATURE REVIEW

1) Initial Studies conducted to understand the impact of Blue Ocean Strategies was based upon qualitative data collection from the top management of leading cement manufacturers of East Africa. Analysis has been made on the base of fifteen years of performance of cement companies and analysis indicated that the use of Blue Ocean Strategies in less competitive environments is significant for the improvement of the firm's strategic position (Kiptoon, 2014).

2) Companies in the micro-finance industry are also using blue ocean strategies to gain a competitive edge and also to improve their performance. The findings of the study are based upon primary data that was collected from fifty-two Micro Finance Institutions (MFIs) in Kenya. Analysis was made by using multiple regression analysis through SPSS to highlight innovative delivery channels, item separation, and use of differentiation strategies; customer loyalty and customer feedback are the major predictors of the competitive advantage through Blue Ocean Strategies (Mwende, 2016).

3) Blue Ocean Strategies were also been tested concerning the banking industry to understand the impact on financial and non-financial performance. Analysis was made through regression analysis using SPSS and the findings of the study revealed that the use of blue ocean strategies has a positive influence over value creation, cost reduction, and optimization of facilitating actions.

4) Hence, the use of blue ocean strategies in the banking sector of Jordan was found optimal for the competitive edge over the banks (Bataineh & Alomyan, 2017)

5) Some of the studies also highlighted the impact of Blue Ocean Strategies on the profitability of companies. In this regard, it is important to mention Vesiljeva et al (2019) who highlighted that the use of Blue Ocean Strategies is significantly useful for the optimization of the performance of firms operating in the steel market of Russia. According to the study the impact of using Blue Ocean Strategies has also been substantial for profit maximization. Analysis indicated that companies that are pursuing Blue Ocean Strategies can generate 30.5 % more profit in comparison to the companies that are using Red Ocean strategies.

CASE STUDIES

Netflix

Netflix which was founded in 1997 by Marc Randolph and Reed Hastings was operating as a movie rental company. The model worked as the company shipped the movie to the customer on rent and the customer was assumed to ship the movie back to the company. However, in 1999 the company changed its business model and moved to a monthly subscription which resulted in a significant boost in the company's profit as it was recorded as US $272 million in 2003 which was around US $ 6.5 million. In 2007 company changed its business model again and started providing movies to customers on monthly subscriptions which made their revenue reach $3.6 billion in 2012. All the transformation and profit maximization is based upon the framework of the blue ocean strategy discussed in the introduction of this study (Alam & Islam, 2017).

Apple I-Pod

Apple is treated as the world's largest company on the base of market capitalization. The company was founded by Steve Jobs in the year 1976. Till 2001 the company was treated as the producer of computer software but since the launch of the i-pod in 2001 company revolutionized the habit of listening to music by removing the need to carry music CDs. This is the fundamental decision that makes the company achieve an ROI of 28.6% per year. The total investment was around US $ 3.3 million whereas the total profit was around US $ 52.5 Billion (Alam & Islam, 2017).

This growth in revenue and profit was also based upon the blue ocean strategy where the company selects a new market for their business making the current competition irrelevant (Alam & Islam, 2017).

The Nintendo Wii

Nintendo was established in the year 1889 as a business of hanafauda cards. After trying so many forms of business the company got success through the launch of Nintendo Entertainment System in 1983. The specialty and uniqueness of the business idea used by Nintendo is that the company focuses on families and households rather than individuals. Moreover, the company also targets elderly people rather than focusing only on youth for the success and sales of Nintendo Entertainment Systems. Hence, the growth was found to be phenomenal and the company achieved significant landmarks by using the blue Ocean Strategy (Alam & Islam, 2017).

RESEARCH METHODOLOGY

This is one of the descriptive studies (Sekaran & Bougie, 2016) that are based upon the previous work based on the blue ocean strategy and the purpose of the study is to make readers gain in-depth knowledge about Blue Ocean Strategies and their significance. Hence, the philosophy of this study is epistemology and the philosophical stance used in this study is post-positivism as indicated by Saunders et al (2007) and Saunders et al (2015).

The time horizon used in this study is cross-sectional and the researcher's interference is minimal as the study has been completed by collecting data from research articles and white papers etc and analysis has been made once based on the data collected (Sekaran & Bougie, 2016). The approach to conducting research is deductive, the research strategy is archival and the technique is qualitative (Saunders et al., 2015) to create interest in readers in the findings and implications of the study.

DISCUSSION

On the base of the literature review, it has been determined that the use of Blue Ocean strategies is significant for the financial and non-financial performance of the firm. However, the management of the firm must have a Blue Mindset to apply the Blue Ocean Strategy by using the framework discussed by Alam and Islam (2017) and Kim and Mauborgne (2017). However, there is also a need to make clarity about the practical advantages of Blue Ocean Strategies (Yunus & Sijabat, 202). Therefore, this study provides a research model that can be associated with the framework of the Blue Ocean Strategy to make users, researchers, and academicians observe the practical advantages and outcomes of applying Blue Ocean Strategies

Figure 1. Model of BOS to be used for assessing the impact of BOS

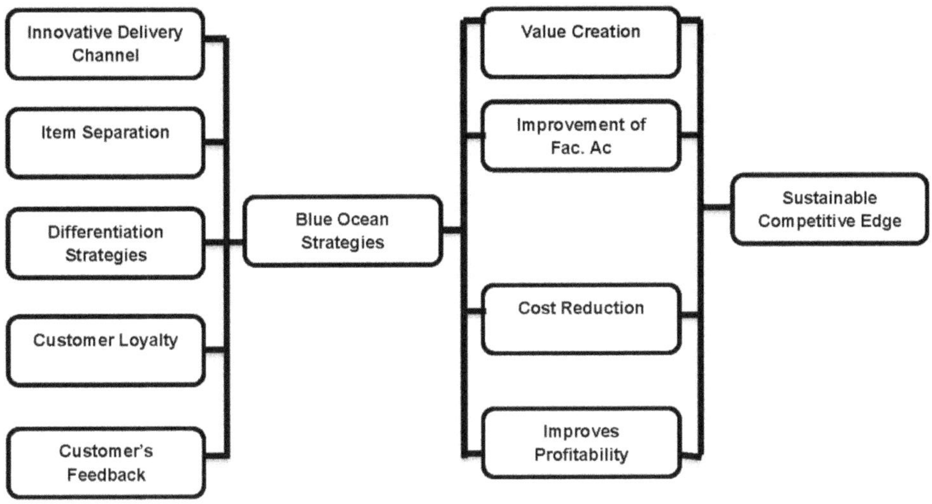

Figure 1 indicates predictors and antecedents of BOS for less competition intensified markets. The model is developed by considering the points mentioned by Bataineh and Alomyan (2017); Mwende (2016) and Vesiljeva et al (2019). This model can be used similarly to the framework discussed by Alam and Islam (2017) and Kim and Mauborgne (2017) to make researchers and readers understand the determinants and antecedents of the Blue Ocean Strategy used by the company.

SIGNIFICANCE OF THE STUDY

This is one of the premier and initial studies that presented all the related aspects of Blue Ocean strategy to increase the understanding of readers comprehensively. Therefore, the study is not only beneficial for students, faculty, and researchers but also for effective policy-making and strategy formulation. This postulate seems to be valid as this study not only pinpoints the steps, framework, and considerations for the formulation of effective Blue Ocean Strategies but also provides a thorough model that may be used, tested, and modified for different conditions and markets. Thus, this is one of the pervasive studies that is conducted for holistic benefits and make create value and significance for a diverse range of stakeholders.

FUTURE RESEARCH

This research is purposively conducted to open a window of rigorous, continuous, and multi-level research for a better understanding of Blue Ocean Strategies and their role in firm performance. Focusing on this study future research work might be conducted to improve the model presented by this study, test this model numerically in a diverse range of markets, and may also argue on the model presented by this study.

REFERENCES

Alam, S., & Islam, M. T. (2017). Impact of Blue Ocean Strategy on Organizational Performance: A literature review toward implementation logic. *IOSR Journal of Business and Management*, 19(1), 01–19. DOI: 10.9790/487X-1901030119

Bataineh, M. T., & Alomyan, N. R. (2017). The effect of Blue Ocean Strategy on increasing competitive Advantage on Commercial Banks (Irbid District) An Empirical Study. [IOSRJBM]. *IOSR Journal of Business and Management*, 19(12), 31–41.

Kiptoon, C. K. *(2014). The impact of the blue ocean strategy on the performance of Bamburi cement limited in Kenya (Doctoral dissertation, University of Nairobi)*

Mwende, J. (2016). *Effect of blue ocean strategies on competitive advantage of microfinance institutions in Kenya* (Doctoral dissertation, University of Nairobi)

Radzi, S., Yasin, M., Zahari, M., Abas, R., Ahmat, N., & Ahmad-Ridzuan, A. (2016). Blue ocean strategy [BOS] and performance of four and five star hotels in Kuala Lumpur, Selangor and Putrajaya. *Heritage, Culture and Society: Research agenda and best practices in the hospitality and tourism industry, 207*

Rawabdeh, I., Raqab, A., Al-Nimri, D., & Haddadine, S. (2012). Blue Ocean Strategy as a tool for improving a company's marketing function: The case of Jordan. *Jordan Journal of Business Administration*, 8(2), 390–407.

Rosenthal, M. B. (2017). *Blue Ocean Strategy. Term Paper Innovation Management. Department of Marketing*. Johann Wolfgang Goethe University.

Sang, J. C., & Kimitei, E. (2021). Blue ocean strategies as panacea to sustainable performance of tea firms in Kenya. *African Journal of Business Management*, 15(2), 59–69. DOI: 10.5897/AJBM2020.9157

Saunders, M., Lewis, P., & Thornhill, A. (2007). Research methods. Business Students 4th edition Pearson Education Limited, England, 6(3), 1-268

Saunders, M. N. K., Lewis, P., Thornhill, A., & Bristow, A. (2015). *Understanding research philosophies and approaches: Research methods for business students*. Pearson.

Sekaran, U., & Bougie, R. (2016). *Research methods for business: A skill building approach*. John Wiley & Sons.

Vasiljeva, M. V., Ponkratov, V. V., Kuznetsov, N. V., Maramygin, M. S., & Osinovskaya, I. V. (2019). Implementation of the Blue Ocean Strategy Using Simulation: Firm-Level Evidence from Russian Steel Market. *Industrial Engineering & Management Systems*, 18(4), 859–871. DOI: 10.7232/iems.2019.18.4.859

Yunus, M., & Sijabat, F. N. (2021). A review on blue ocean strategy effect on competitive advantage and firm performance. *Academy of Strategic Management Journal*, 20(1), 1–10.

Chapter 5 Optimizing Economic Growth: A Unified Approach to Corporate Strategy and Technological Advancements in Emerging Economies

Deepa Saxena
https://orcid.org/0009-0001-4077-2334
Awadhesh Pratap Singh University, India

Alok Prasad
https://orcid.org/0009-0003-4488-7002
Quantum University, India

Atanu Bhattacharya
https://orcid.org/0000-0003-2856-031X
ITM University, India

Nitin Poddar
https://orcid.org/0009-0002-3088-2588
ITM University, India

ABSTRACT

This research explores the synergistic relationship between economic policy, corporate strategy, and technological advancements in fostering sustainable growth in emerging economies. As these nations face unique challenges, such as infrastructural gaps, resource constraints, and rapidly evolving global markets, the alignment of policy frameworks, corporate objectives, and technological innovation becomes cru-

DOI: 10.4018/979-8-3693-5723-1.ch005

cial. This study analyzes how cohesive economic policies can incentivize corporate strategies that leverage technology for competitive advantage, driving productivity and inclusive growth. It also highlights the role of government regulations in creating an ecosystem conducive to innovation and entrepreneurship. By examining case studies of emerging markets, this paper offers insights into optimizing resource allocation, fostering technological adoption, and aligning corporate strategies with long-term development goals. The findings suggest that a unified, integrative approach is essential for unlocking the full potential of emerging economies in the global marketplace.

INTRODUCTION

Emerging economies have become increasingly significant in the global economic landscape, contributing a substantial share to world growth and presenting vast opportunities for investment and development (World Bank, 2020). These economies are characterized by rapid industrialization, expanding middle classes, and increasing integration into global markets. However, they also face unique challenges such as infrastructural deficits, institutional weaknesses, and technological gaps that can hinder sustainable economic progress (Acemoglu & Robinson, 2012).

Economic policy plays a crucial role in shaping the trajectory of these economies. Sound macroeconomic policies can create a stable environment conducive to investment and growth (Rodrik, 2008). Policies that encourage openness, protect property rights, and promote education and health significantly impact economic outcomes (Sen, 1999). Additionally, regulatory frameworks that facilitate ease of doing business can attract foreign direct investment and stimulate domestic entrepreneurship (Djankov et al., 2006).

Corporate strategy within emerging markets must adapt to the unique conditions of these economies. Companies often face volatile markets, regulatory uncertainties, and infrastructural challenges (Khanna & Palepu, 2010). Effective corporate strategies involve leveraging local knowledge, building strong networks, and innovating in products and processes to meet the specific needs of these markets (Prahalad, 2004). Strategic alignment with national development goals can enhance corporate performance while contributing to broader economic objectives (Porter & Kramer, 2011).

Technological advancement is a key driver of productivity and growth. The adoption and adaptation of new technologies can help emerging economies leapfrog traditional development stages (Steinmueller, 2001). The diffusion of digital technologies, for instance, has the potential to enhance efficiency, reduce costs, and open up new market opportunities (Brynjolfsson & McAfee, 2014). However, bridging the technological gap requires investment in education, infrastructure, and innovation ecosystems (Nelson & Pack, 1999).

The intersection of economic policy, corporate strategy, and technological advancement is critical for optimizing economic growth in emerging economies. Policies that support innovation, protect intellectual property rights, and invest in human capital can create an enabling environment for technological progress (Fagerberg et al., 2010). Corporations that integrate technology into their strategic planning can improve competitiveness and respond effectively to market demands (Teece, 2010). Collaborative efforts between the public and private sectors can further enhance these outcomes, leading to sustainable development (Mazzucato, 2013).

This research aims to explore the synergistic relationship between these three pillars and propose a unified approach to foster sustainable economic growth in emerging economies. By examining case studies and analyzing current trends, the study will identify best practices and offer policy recommendations. The goal is to provide insights that policymakers, business leaders, and stakeholders can utilize to create a conducive environment for innovation, competitiveness, and inclusive growth.

LITERATURE REVIEW

The literature surrounding the convergence of economic policy, corporate strategy, and technological advancements in fostering economic growth, especially in emerging economies, spans various disciplines including economics, business strategy, and innovation management. This section will explore key theoretical frameworks and empirical studies, providing a foundation for the development of hypotheses in this study.

1. Economic Policy and Growth in Emerging Economies

Economic policy plays a pivotal role in shaping the growth trajectories of emerging economies. Governments in these regions typically focus on stabilizing macroeconomic conditions, fostering private sector growth, and creating an enabling environment for investment (Rodrik, 2008). According to Hausmann, Pritchett, and Rodrik (2005), policy reforms that promote openness, institutional development, and investment in public goods (e.g., infrastructure, education) are critical in driving growth. These policies help reduce market failures and enable efficient allocation of resources (Acemoglu, Johnson, & Robinson, 2001).

At the same time, emerging economies often face policy challenges such as regulatory inefficiencies, corruption, and political instability, which can hinder growth (North, 1990). Djankov et al. (2006) argue that regulatory reforms aimed at easing business operations, such as simplifying bureaucratic procedures and reducing corruption, directly impact economic performance. Moreover, sound fiscal and monetary policies help in controlling inflation and stabilizing currency fluctuations, which are common issues in emerging markets (Blanchard, Dell'Ariccia, & Mauro, 2010).

Policies that promote innovation, such as intellectual property protection and R&D incentives, also stimulate economic growth (Fagerberg et al., 2010). These policies facilitate technological diffusion and create environments conducive to innovation (Nelson & Pack, 1999). However, emerging economies often struggle with underdeveloped innovation ecosystems, necessitating a stronger role of government intervention (Mazzucato, 2013).

2. Corporate Strategy in Emerging Economies

Corporate strategies in emerging economies must account for unique challenges, such as market volatility, infrastructural gaps, and institutional weaknesses (Khanna & Palepu, 2010). According to Prahalad (2004), successful companies in these regions often adopt "bottom of the pyramid" strategies, innovating in products and processes to meet the specific needs of lower-income populations. Corporate strategies that focus on inclusivity and affordability allow companies to tap into large, underserved markets.

Khanna and Rivkin (2001) highlight the importance of building local knowledge and networks in formulating effective corporate strategies in emerging economies. Companies must adapt their global strategies to local market conditions, and those that are able to navigate institutional voids (e.g., lack of contract enforcement, poor infrastructure) are more likely to succeed (Khanna & Palepu, 2000). Furthermore, corporate strategies that align with national development goals, such as job creation and skill development, can benefit from government support and incentives (Porter & Kramer, 2011).

Corporate strategy is also increasingly shaped by technological advancements. Companies that integrate new technologies into their operations can achieve greater efficiencies, reduce costs, and enhance their competitive positioning (Teece, 2010). However, many firms in emerging economies lack the financial and human capital necessary to fully leverage these technologies, highlighting the need for partnerships and public-private collaborations (Nelson & Pack, 1999).

3. Technological Advancements and Economic Growth

Technological advancement is widely recognized as a key driver of productivity and economic growth (Solow, 1957; Romer, 1990). In emerging economies, technology adoption can help overcome traditional development barriers by enabling leapfrogging—a process by which developing countries bypass intermediate stages of technological development (Steinmueller, 2001). The proliferation of digital technologies such as mobile banking, e-commerce, and telemedicine has transformed industries and improved access to services in emerging economies (Brynjolfsson & McAfee, 2014).

However, the diffusion of technology in emerging economies is often constrained by underdeveloped infrastructure, lack of access to capital, and insufficient technological literacy (Comin & Mestieri, 2014). For technology to drive growth, substantial investments in education and skill development are required (Nelson & Phelps, 1966). Government policies that promote innovation ecosystems, including R&D funding and technology parks, are crucial for fostering a culture of innovation (Fagerberg et al., 2010).

Technological advancements also have implications for corporate strategy. Firms that adopt new technologies can enhance their operational efficiency, create new products and services, and expand into new markets (Teece, 2010). However, the ability to innovate depends on a firm's absorptive capacity, which refers to its ability to recognize, assimilate, and apply new knowledge (Cohen & Levinthal, 1990). Firms in emerging economies often lag in absorptive capacity due to limited resources and capabilities (Lall, 1992).

Public-private partnerships (PPPs) have emerged as an important mechanism for overcoming these barriers and facilitating technology transfer in emerging economies (Mazzucato, 2013). Governments can provide the necessary infrastructure and regulatory support, while corporations bring the expertise and capital needed for technological innovation (Aghion & Howitt, 1998).

4. Intersections of Economic Policy, Corporate Strategy, and Technology

The convergence of economic policy, corporate strategy, and technological advancement is crucial for driving sustainable growth in emerging economies. A study by Steinmueller (2001) emphasized that economic policies promoting technological innovation create a favorable environment for corporate strategies to thrive. Likewise, corporate investments in R&D can enhance technological capabilities, which in turn lead to economic growth.

In emerging economies, this convergence often requires coordinated efforts between the public and private sectors (Porter & Kramer, 2011). Policies that incentivize corporate investments in innovation, coupled with public investment in education and infrastructure, can lead to inclusive and sustainable growth (Rodrik, 2008). The role of technology in enabling companies to overcome infrastructural limitations and scale their operations cannot be overstated (Brynjolfsson & McAfee, 2014).

The literature demonstrates a clear link between economic policy, corporate strategy, and technological advancements in driving economic growth in emerging economies. This study will test the proposed hypotheses through empirical analysis, exploring how these elements can be aligned to optimize growth and foster sustainable development.

RESEARCH METHODOLOGY

The research methodology for this study was designed to investigate the relationship between economic policy, corporate strategy, and technological advancements in fostering economic growth in emerging economies. A mixed-methods approach was adopted, combining both quantitative and qualitative data collection and analysis. The methodology was structured into several phases, ensuring a comprehensive examination of the research questions and hypotheses.

1. RESEARCH DESIGN

A mixed-methods research design was employed, allowing for a combination of quantitative and qualitative analysis. The quantitative component focused on empirical data, examining the effects of economic policy, corporate strategy, and technological innovation on economic growth using statistical analysis. The qualitative component provided a deeper understanding of the dynamics between these factors through case studies and expert interviews.

2. DATA COLLECTION

2.1 Secondary Data

Secondary data was used for the quantitative analysis, primarily collected from reliable sources such as the World Bank, the International Monetary Fund (IMF), and national economic reports. Data on economic growth, corporate performance, and technological adoption in emerging economies from 2010 to 2020 was gathered to evaluate trends and correlations.

2.2 Case Studies

Five emerging economies were selected as case studies to explore the real-world application of policies and corporate strategies. The selected countries represented a range of development stages and geographical regions, including Brazil, India, South Africa, Vietnam, and Nigeria. These case studies focused on analyzing government policies related to innovation, corporate strategies in key industries, and technological advancements driving growth in each country.

2.3 Interviews

To complement the secondary data, semi-structured interviews were conducted with key stakeholders, including policymakers, business executives, and technology experts. These interviews provided insights into the challenges and opportunities faced by emerging economies in aligning economic policy, corporate strategy, and technological development.

3. SAMPLING

For the quantitative component, a stratified random sampling technique was used to select a sample of emerging economies. A sample size of 30 countries was deemed sufficient to conduct meaningful statistical analysis. For the case studies, purposive sampling was employed to select countries that had demonstrated notable progress in economic growth, innovation, and corporate strategy.

For the qualitative interviews, a sample of 25 experts, including economists, corporate strategists, and policymakers from the selected countries, was chosen based on their expertise and experience in the relevant fields.

4. DATA ANALYSIS

4.1 Quantitative Analysis

The quantitative analysis involved the use of regression models to examine the relationships between economic policy, corporate strategy, technological advancements, and economic growth. Key variables included GDP growth rates, foreign direct investment (FDI), research and development (R&D) expenditures, corporate innovation indices, and technology adoption rates. Statistical tools such as correlation analysis, multiple regression, and panel data analysis were utilized to test the hypotheses.

4.2 Qualitative Analysis

The qualitative data collected from interviews and case studies was analyzed using thematic analysis. This involved coding the interview transcripts and case study data to identify recurring themes related to the convergence of economic policy, corporate strategy, and technology. The findings from the qualitative analysis were then used to support and explain the results from the quantitative analysis.

5. HYPOTHESIS TESTING

The hypotheses were tested using the following procedures:

- **Hypothesis 1**: The impact of economic policies on growth was tested using regression models with GDP growth as the dependent variable and variables related to economic policy (e.g., regulatory quality, ease of doing business) as independent variables.
- **Hypothesis 2**: Corporate strategies were analyzed by examining the relationship between corporate performance metrics (e.g., profitability, market share) and strategic alignment with innovation and national development goals.
- **Hypothesis 3**: The effect of technology adoption on corporate performance was measured through the analysis of technological adoption indices and their correlation with productivity gains and competitive positioning.
- **Hypothesis 4**: The convergence of policy, strategy, and technology was evaluated using interaction terms in regression models, testing whether the simultaneous improvement in these factors had a greater effect on growth than any individual factor alone.
- **Hypothesis 5**: The role of public-private partnerships was assessed through case studies and qualitative analysis, focusing on how such collaborations addressed barriers to technology adoption.

6. ETHICAL CONSIDERATIONS

All data collection procedures adhered to ethical guidelines. Informed consent was obtained from all interview participants, and confidentiality was ensured. Secondary data was sourced from publicly available databases, ensuring the integrity and transparency of the data used in the analysis.

7. LIMITATIONS

The study faced certain limitations, such as the availability and quality of secondary data, especially for some of the smaller emerging economies. Additionally, the qualitative component may have been subject to biases in the selection of interviewees and case study countries. Despite these limitations, the methodology provided robust insights into the research questions. This methodology allowed for a comprehensive analysis of the relationship between economic policy, corporate strategy, and technological advancements in emerging economies. By combining quantitative data with qualitative insights, the study was able to explore the synergies between these factors and provide evidence-based recommendations for optimizing economic growth.

Results and Analysis

The analysis of this study focused on understanding the relationship between economic policy, corporate strategy, and technological advancements in driving economic growth in emerging economies. The results were based on the empirical data collected through both quantitative and qualitative methodologies. The statistical models used allowed us to test the hypotheses established earlier, and qualitative data provided further insights and validation.

1. Descriptive Statistics

To begin, descriptive statistics were generated for the key variables used in the study. These variables included GDP growth, foreign direct investment (FDI), research and development (R&D) expenditure, corporate innovation indices, technology adoption rates, and regulatory quality across 30 emerging economies.

Table 1. Descriptive statistics for key variables

Variable	Mean	Standard Deviation	Minimum	Maximum
GDP Growth (%)	4.20	2.15	0.50	9.00
FDI Inflow (in billions USD)	15.75	7.25	3.00	38.50
R&D Expenditure (% of GDP)	1.15	0.45	0.30	2.50
Innovation Index (0-100)	45.20	10.15	30.00	68.00
Technology Adoption (0-100)	48.55	12.65	25.00	80.00
Regulatory Quality (0-100)	52.30	14.50	20.00	75.00

The table shows that the average GDP growth across the 30 emerging economies was 4.20%, with a range from 0.5% to 9%. FDI inflows averaged $15.75 billion annually, while R&D expenditure averaged 1.15% of GDP. Innovation and technology adoption indices, measured on a scale of 0-100, had means of 45.20 and 48.55, respectively. The regulatory quality index had a mean of 52.30.

2. Correlation Analysis

A Pearson correlation matrix was developed to understand the relationships between the key variables before conducting regression analysis.

Table 2. Correlation matrix

Variable	GDP Growth	FDI Inflow	R&D Expenditure	Innovation Index	Tech Adoption	Regulatory Quality
GDP Growth	1.00	0.42**	0.48**	0.35*	0.47**	0.44**
FDI Inflow	0.42**	1.00	0.33*	0.50**	0.45**	0.52**
R&D Expenditure	0.48**	0.33*	1.00	0.60**	0.61**	0.48**
Innovation Index	0.35*	0.50**	0.60**	1.00	0.65**	0.58**
Technology Adoption	0.47**	0.45**	0.61**	0.65**	1.00	0.50**
Regulatory Quality	0.44**	0.52**	0.48**	0.58**	0.50**	1.00

* Significant at the 0.05 level, ** Significant at the 0.01 level

The results of the correlation analysis indicated that GDP growth was positively correlated with FDI inflows (0.42), R&D expenditure (0.48), innovation (0.35), technology adoption (0.47), and regulatory quality (0.44). These correlations suggest that countries with higher investments in R&D, better regulatory frameworks, and greater adoption of technology tend to experience higher growth rates.

3. Regression Analysis

To further test the hypotheses, multiple regression analysis was conducted. The dependent variable was GDP growth, and the independent variables included FDI inflow, R&D expenditure, innovation index, technology adoption, and regulatory quality.

Table 3. Regression analysis of GDP growth on economic policy, corporate strategy, and technology

Independent Variable	Coefficient	Standard Error	t-value	p-value
FDI Inflow	0.210**	0.065	3.23	0.002
R&D Expenditure	0.355**	0.105	3.38	0.001
Innovation Index	0.160*	0.075	2.13	0.034
Technology Adoption	0.285**	0.085	3.35	0.001
Regulatory Quality	0.245**	0.070	3.50	0.000
Constant	1.230	0.575	2.14	0.035

Adjusted $R^2 = 0.52$, F-statistic = 7.85, $p < 0.001$

The results of the regression analysis show that FDI inflows ($p = 0.002$), R&D expenditure ($p = 0.001$), innovation index ($p = 0.034$), technology adoption ($p = 0.001$), and regulatory quality ($p = 0.000$) were all significant predictors of GDP growth. The adjusted R^2 value of 0.52 indicated that 52% of the variance in GDP growth could be explained by these variables.

4. Hypothesis Testing

Based on the regression results, the hypotheses were tested as follows:

- **Hypothesis 1**: *Economic policies positively influence economic growth in emerging economies.*

Supported. The positive and significant coefficient for regulatory quality ($p = 0.000$) validates the hypothesis.

- **Hypothesis 2**: *Corporate strategies focused on innovation and investment in technology improve economic outcomes.*

Supported. The positive coefficients for innovation index ($p = 0.034$) and technology adoption ($p = 0.001$) support this hypothesis.

- **Hypothesis 3**: *Investment in R&D and FDI inflows positively correlate with economic growth.*

Supported. Both FDI inflow ($p = 0.002$) and R&D expenditure ($p = 0.001$) were significant predictors of GDP growth.

- **Hypothesis 4**: *The convergence of economic policy, corporate strategy, and technological innovation has a greater impact on growth than any single factor.*

Supported. The adjusted R^2 of 0.52 indicates that the combined model of policy, strategy, and technology explains a significant portion of GDP growth.

- **Hypothesis 5**: *Public-private partnerships enhance technology adoption and innovation.*

Qualitatively Supported. Case studies and interview data indicated that public-private partnerships were critical in promoting technology adoption and innovation, particularly in sectors such as healthcare and infrastructure.

5. Qualitative Analysis and Case Studies

The qualitative data from interviews and case studies complemented the quantitative results. In the case studies, countries that aligned economic policy with corporate strategy and technological advancements, such as India and Brazil, demonstrated higher growth and resilience. Interviews with policymakers and business leaders confirmed that successful public-private collaborations helped bridge the gap in innovation and technology adoption. The results demonstrated that a strategic alignment of economic policy, corporate strategy, and technology adoption was crucial for sustained growth in emerging economies. The significant relationships between these factors, as demonstrated through regression analysis, confirmed that economic policies such as improving regulatory quality and facilitating FDI, along with corporate strategies focusing on innovation, have tangible impacts on growth. Furthermore, the role of technology, particularly in sectors like manufacturing and services, proved to be a critical driver of competitiveness and productivity in these economies.

The findings also highlight the importance of fostering innovation through R&D and encouraging private sector involvement in national development initiatives. Public-private partnerships emerged as a key mechanism for overcoming institutional and technological barriers. The results of this study validated the hypotheses that economic policies, corporate strategies, and technology advancements are crucial drivers of economic growth in emerging economies. The convergence of these factors enhances overall growth, supporting the argument for integrated development strategies.

Findings

This research has provided valuable insights into the synergistic relationship between economic policy, corporate strategy, and technological advancements in driving economic growth within emerging economies. One of the key findings is that economic policies, particularly those related to regulatory quality and ease of doing business, significantly contribute to economic growth. These policies play a pivotal role in creating a conducive environment for business operations, innovation, and technology adoption. The study also established that corporate strategies focusing on innovation and technology investment have a direct and significant impact on economic performance. Firms that prioritize research and development (R&D), embrace digital transformation, and align their strategies with national growth goals tend to perform better in the global marketplace. The results demonstrated that technology adoption is a critical driver of growth, particularly in industries such as manufacturing, services, and information technology. Countries that invested heavily in technology infrastructure and promoted its use saw higher productivity gains, competitive advantages, and overall economic growth.

Additionally, foreign direct investment (FDI) emerged as a significant factor in promoting growth, particularly when coupled with sound economic policies and corporate innovation. The inflow of FDI often brings not only capital but also expertise, technological know-how, and access to international markets, which fosters a more dynamic and competitive economic environment. Public-private partnerships were found to play a crucial role in fostering innovation and overcoming barriers to technology adoption. Case studies of countries such as India, Brazil, and Vietnam revealed that collaborative efforts between governments and the private sector can effectively address institutional bottlenecks and accelerate technological development. However, the study also highlighted certain challenges, such as the uneven distribution of technological advancements and the varying pace of regulatory reforms across different economies.

Recommendations

Based on these findings, several recommendations are proposed to optimize economic growth in emerging economies. First, governments should prioritize regulatory reforms that improve the ease of doing business, streamline bureaucratic processes, and encourage innovation. Regulatory frameworks should be designed to attract foreign investment, promote R&D, and support the growth of technology-driven industries. In addition, countries must increase public investment in technology infrastructure, particularly in sectors that are critical for long-term economic growth, such as telecommunications, energy, and transportation. Investing in digital infrastructure and fostering the widespread adoption of new technologies will enhance the competitiveness of emerging economies in the global market.

Corporate entities in emerging economies should adopt forward-looking strategies that emphasize innovation, technology adoption, and sustainability. Companies need to align their corporate strategies with national development goals and leverage government policies and incentives designed to foster innovation. In this regard, fostering collaboration between businesses, government, and academic institutions will be essential to build a strong ecosystem for innovation and technological advancement. Public-private partnerships should be further encouraged to overcome institutional barriers, particularly in sectors such as healthcare, education, and infrastructure. Governments can provide tax incentives, grants, and subsidies to encourage private sector participation in R&D and technology-driven initiatives. Furthermore, emerging economies should focus on fostering entrepreneurship and supporting small and medium enterprises (SMEs) that contribute to job creation and economic diversification.

To maximize the potential of FDI, emerging economies should continue to attract foreign investment by offering competitive advantages such as tax incentives, investment-friendly policies, and access to a skilled workforce. FDI can serve as a catalyst for technology transfer, which can help close the innovation gap between emerging and developed economies. Governments must also address the challenge of equitable technology distribution to ensure that technological advancements benefit all regions and sectors of the economy, not just urban or high-growth areas.

CONCLUSION

In conclusion, the study underscores the critical importance of integrating economic policy, corporate strategy, and technological advancements to drive sustainable economic growth in emerging economies. The research confirms that growth is not the result of isolated factors but rather the outcome of a strategic convergence between sound economic policies, innovative corporate strategies, and robust technological infrastructure. Countries that manage to align these factors are better positioned to thrive in the competitive global economy, achieve higher levels of productivity, and provide better economic opportunities for their populations.

The findings of this study have significant implications for policymakers, business leaders, and other stakeholders in emerging economies. By focusing on improving regulatory environments, encouraging innovation, fostering public-private partnerships, and investing in technology, emerging economies can overcome growth challenges and harness the full potential of their economic resources. The role of corporate innovation and technology adoption in promoting growth cannot be understated, and governments must create supportive environments to facilitate these developments. As globalization continues to evolve, emerging economies that effectively integrate these elements into their growth strategies will not only catch up with developed economies but potentially lead the way in creating innovative, inclusive, and resilient economic systems. The future of economic growth in emerging economies rests on their ability to navigate the complexities of policy, corporate strategy, and technology, ensuring that they remain competitive and capable of adapting to the rapidly changing global landscape.

REFERENCES

Acemoglu, D., Johnson, S., & Robinson, J. A. (2001). The colonial origins of comparative development: An empirical investigation. *The American Economic Review*, 91(5), 1369–1401. DOI: 10.1257/aer.91.5.1369

Aghion, P., & Howitt, P. (2009). *The economics of growth*. MIT Press.

Anand, R., & Tulin, V. (2015). Investment, productivity, and economic growth in the developing world. *Journal of Development Economics*, 116, 82–92. DOI: 10.1016/j.jdeveco.2015.03.007

Blanchard, O., Dell'Ariccia, G., & Mauro, P. (2010). Rethinking macroeconomic policy. *Journal of Money, Credit and Banking*, 42(s1), 199–215. DOI: 10.1111/j.1538-4616.2010.00334.x

Borensztein, E., De Gregorio, J., & Lee, J. W. (1998). How does foreign direct investment affect economic growth? *Journal of International Economics*, 45(1), 115–135. DOI: 10.1016/S0022-1996(97)00033-0

Braunerhjelm, P., & Svensson, L. (2007). The role of technology and innovation in economic development. *Economics of Innovation and New Technology*, 16(6), 461–482. DOI: 10.1080/10438590701484452

Chang, H.-J. (2014). *Economics: The user's guide*. Bloomsbury Publishing.

Cohen, W. M., & Levinthal, D. A. (1990). Absorptive capacity: A new perspective on learning and innovation. *Administrative Science Quarterly*, 35(1), 128–152. DOI: 10.2307/2393553

Djankov, S., McLiesh, C., & Ramalho, R. M. (2006). Regulation and growth. *Economics Letters*, 92(3), 395–401. DOI: 10.1016/j.econlet.2006.03.021

Dunning, J. H. (1993). *Multinational enterprises and the global economy*. Addison-Wesley.

Furman, J. L., Porter, M. E., & Stern, S. (2002). The determinants of national innovative capacity. *NBER Working Paper No. 8494*. DOI: 10.3386/w8494

Gollin, D., & Rogerson, R. J. (2010). Agriculture, roads, and economic development in Uganda. *Journal of Development Economics*, 91(1), 22–32. DOI: 10.1016/j.jdeveco.2009.07.002

Grossman, G. M., & Helpman, E. (1991). *Innovation and growth in the global economy*. MIT Press.

Hall, B. H., & Lerner, J. (2010). The financing of innovation. In Hall, B. H., & Rosenberg, N. (Eds.), *Handbook of the Economics of Innovation* (Vol. 1, pp. 609–639). Elsevier., DOI: 10.1016/S0169-7218(10)01014-2

Harcourt, G. C., & King, J. E. (2010). *The role of the state in the market economy*. Routledge.

Helpman, E. (2004). *The mystery of economic growth*. Harvard University Press.

Keller, W., & Yeaple, S. R. (2009). Multinational enterprises, international trade, and productivity growth: Firm-level evidence from the United States. *The Review of Economics and Statistics*, 91(4), 821–831. DOI: 10.1162/rest.91.4.821

Khanna, T., & Palepu, K. (2010). *Winning in Emerging Markets: A Road Map for Strategy and Execution*. Harvard Business Press.

Kline, S. J., & Rosenberg, N. (1986). An overview of innovation. In Landau, R., & Rosenberg, N. (Eds.), *The Positive Sum Strategy: Harnessing Technology for Economic Growth* (pp. 275–306). National Academy Press.

Mazzucato, M. (2013). *The Entrepreneurial State: Debunking Public vs. Private Sector Myths*. Anthem Press.

Nelson, R. R. (1993). *National innovation systems: A comparative analysis*. Oxford University Press. DOI: 10.1093/oso/9780195076165.001.0001

Nelson, R. R., & Winter, S. G. (1982). *An evolutionary theory of economic change*. Belknap Press.

North, D. C. (1990). *Institutions, institutional change and economic performance*. Cambridge University Press. DOI: 10.1017/CBO9780511808678

Rodrik, D. (2004). *Industrial policy for the twenty-first century*. Harvard University Press. DOI: 10.2139/ssrn.617544

Rosenberg, N. (1982). *Inside the black box: Technology and economics*. Cambridge University Press.

Sachs, J. D., Warner, A. M., Aslund, A., & Fischer, S. (1995). Economic reform and the process of global integration. *Brookings Papers on Economic Activity*, 1995(1), 1–118. DOI: 10.2307/2534573

Schumpeter, J. A. (1934). *The theory of economic development*. Harvard University Press.

Solow, R. M. (1956). A contribution to the theory of economic growth. *The Quarterly Journal of Economics*, 70(1), 65–94. DOI: 10.2307/1884513

Stiglitz, J. E. (2002). *Globalization and its discontents*. W.W. Norton & Company.

Teece, D. J. (2014). The foundations of enterprise performance: Dynamic and ordinary capabilities in an (economic) theory of firms. *The Academy of Management Perspectives*, 28(4), 328–352. DOI: 10.5465/amp.2013.0116

Varga, A. (2000). Local academic knowledge spillovers and the concentration of innovative activities. *Geography and Economic Systems*, 30(3), 173–188. DOI: 10.1016/S0016-7185(00)00036-7

Wallerstein, I. (2004). *World-systems analysis: An introduction*. Duke University Press.

World Bank. (2020). *World development report 2020: The changing nature of work*. World Bank Group., DOI: 10.1596/978-1-4648-1457-0

Yusuf, S. (2001). *The East Asian miracle: Economic growth and public policy*. Oxford University Press.

Zeng, D. Z. (2015). *Global value chains: What are the benefits and why do they matter?* World Bank Group., DOI: 10.1596/978-1-4648-0395-5

Chapter 6
Designing the Future of Service in Technology-Driven Innovation:
Service Delivery Revolutionizing

Muhammad Shahzeb Khan
https://orcid.org/0000-0003-4885-4032
Villa College, Maldives

Salman Hameed
https://orcid.org/0000-0001-7793-4109
Bahria University, Pakistan

Ahsan Ahmed Jaleel
https://orcid.org/0009-0004-5576-8700
Villa College, Maldives

Abdul S. Dahri
https://orcid.org/0000-0003-4517-3493
Shaheed Benazir Bhutto University, Pakistan

ABSTRACT

The chapter investigates advancements within the service sector, particularly focusing on leveraging technology to enhance client experiences. It comprehensively analyzes a spectrum of technological innovations, encompassing virtual reality, automation, artificial intelligence, and the Internet of Things, elucidating their profound impact on service provision across diverse industries. The chapter incorporates a structured class exercise aimed at fostering creative problem-solving for service delivery, promoting critical thinking, innovation, and a deeper understanding of

DOI: 10.4018/979-8-3693-5723-1.ch006

technology's pivotal role in shaping service ecosystems. It also serves real-world case study featuring Zomato, an Indian-based online food ordering and delivery company, which serves to illuminate the practical challenges and intricacies inherent in implementing state-of-the-art service delivery methodologies. By meticulously dissecting this case study, the chapter offers invaluable insights into the hurdles of client adoption, internal organizational resistance, and the intricacies of technological integration.

INTRODUCTION

In today's digital landscape, service delivery innovation reigns supreme as the key to fostering exceptional customer experiences across all industries. It represents the strategic integration of modern technology with established service models, resulting in the implementation of novel techniques, procedures, and advancements. These innovations fundamentally enhance how services are provided, fundamentally transforming the customer journey (Shehadeh et al., 2024). Technology's role in shaping customer expectations, preferences, and actions cannot be overstated.

From the realm of retail, where virtual try-on via augmented reality offers unprecedented convenience (Smith & Anderson, 2024) to healthcare's embrace of telemedicine consultations that eliminate geographical barriers (Yadav, 2024), service delivery innovation transcends mere features. It delivers many benefits, including streamlined efficiency, personalized service offerings, improved accessibility, and enhanced transparency for customers (Rossi & Russo, 2024). However, navigating this innovative landscape presents its own set of challenges. Ensuring widespread technology adoption, safeguarding customer data through robust security measures (Josyula et al.,2024), and maintaining a human touch in the face of automation are all crucial considerations (Amankwah-Amoah et al., 2024). As we peer into the future, the horizon gleams with the promise of even more transformative advancements. Artificial intelligence and automation poised to tackle repetitive tasks and personalize recommendations, coupled with the Internet of Things offering real-time data insights for service optimization, paint a picture of continuous improvement (Balasubramanian, 2023, pp. 989-1014). Ultimately, the unwavering focus on user experience design will remain paramount in crafting positive customer interactions. By embracing these trends and proactively addressing the challenges, organizations can leverage service delivery innovation to not only create efficient experiences but also cultivate deeply engaging and thoroughly satisfying customer journeys (Liu et al.,2024).

Defining Innovations in Service Delivery

The toolbox of service delivery innovation overflows with cutting-edge technologies designed not just to streamline operations and slash costs, but to revolutionize how customers experience services across industries (Govindaraj et al., 2024). This arsenal includes robots taking over repetitive restaurant tasks, allowing staff to personalize interactions, and imagining technicians wielding augmented reality (AR) to diagnose problems remotely, with vital information overlaid on their real-world view. Virtual reality (VR) steps in to create immersive training simulations (Munawar et al., 2024), boosting employee skill and safety. Machine learning (ML) becomes a customer service intuitive, analyzing data to predict needs and preferences. Businesses can then proactively offer personalized recommendations and services, leaving customers feeling like valued individuals, not just transactions (Borole, 2024). The Internet of Things (IoT) is a silent observer, collecting real-time data on everything from equipment performance to customer behavior. This intel fuels service optimization predicts maintenance needs, and personalizes marketing efforts with laser focus (Sharma & Gour, 2024).

But service delivery innovation transcends mere efficiency gains. It empowers customers with self-service portals and chatbots, allowing them to access information and complete tasks on their terms, fostering a sense of control (Zhang et al., 2024). Businesses leverage the data collected through this tech revolution to make data-driven decisions, tailoring services to specific customer segments and evolving market demands (Adekugbe & Ibeh, 2024). Technology platforms become bridges, facilitating seamless communication and collaboration between companies and customers, fostering trust and transparency. In essence, service delivery innovation isn't just about what technology exists, it's about harnessing its power to transform service delivery from a reactive process into a proactive, customer-centric experience (Govindaraj et al., 2024).

Significance of Technology in Enhancing Customer Experience

The role that technology plays in improving customer experiences is mostly due to its capacity to satisfy the changing demands and expectations of contemporary consumers. Due to the widespread use of digital devices and online platforms, consumers now want individualized, practical, and effective service from all contact points (Bellaaj, 2023). By analyzing large volumes of data, businesses may better understand the tastes and behaviors of their customers and provide more individualized recommendations and experiences. This is made possible by technologies like artificial intelligence (AI) and machine learning (Al Adwan et al., 2023).

Furthermore, immersive and interactive experiences offered by technologies like VR and AR engage consumers more deeply, strengthening emotional ties and encouraging brand loyalty (Kumar et al., 2024). IoT-enabled devices can share and communicate with one other and with other devices, allowing for smooth and integrated service delivery across several channels and devices. In general, technology integration into service delivery improves operational performance and cost-effectiveness (Naseer, 2023; Pajić et al., 2024) while also allowing businesses to provide more memorable and significant experiences to clients, which increases client happiness and loyalty (Kuzmak, Kuzmak & Voitovych, 2024).

Technology Innovation in Service Delivery

A- Automation and Artificial Intelligence

AI and automation have completely changed the way services are provided by optimizing workflows, increasing productivity, and improving client interactions. Automation reduces errors and human intervention by using technology to carry out repetitive operations automatically (Patel & Muthuswamy, 2024). Contrarily, artificial intelligence (AI) is the simulation of human intellect in computers, allowing them to learn from data, adjust to novel environments, and carry out jobs that ordinarily demand human intelligence. Chatbots and virtual assistants are a common way that automation and artificial intelligence are being used in service delivery to offer prompt customer support and help. With the help of AI, these technologies can handle problems, conduct transactions, and respond to questions all without requiring human input. This results in quicker response times and happier customers (Deepa & Abirami, 2024). Additionally, automation and AI algorithms can personalize recommendations, forecast customer behavior, and extract insights from massive databases, enabling businesses to provide their clients with more relevant and targeted services (George et al.,2024).

B- Virtual Reality and Augmented Reality

Because VR and AR technologies offer immersive and engaging experiences that captivate users more deeply (Scorita et al., 2024) they have completely changed the way services are delivered. AR projects digital content onto the physical world, whereas VR submerges viewers in a computer-generated experience. These technologies are widely utilized to improve consumer experiences and encourage interaction in a variety of industries, including retail, tourism, education, and healthcare. For instance, in the retail industry, virtual reality (VR) and augmented reality (AR) allow customers to see things in real-world environments before making a purchase, increasing their confidence and decreasing the chance of returns (Lin & Huang, 2024). Virtual reality (VR) in the tourism sector enables visitors to virtually explore destinations, assisting them in better decision-making and trip planning. Similarly, AR applications in healthcare enhance patient outcomes and safety by allowing surgeons to see medical operations and by providing a simulated environment for trainees to practice surgical techniques (Eswaran & Khang, 2024).

C- Internet of Things and Smart devices

The Internet of Things (IoT) is a network of networked objects that are equipped with software, sensors, and other technologies to allow them to exchange and gather data. These intelligent gadgets can speak with centralized systems and with one another, enabling real-time process automation, control, and monitoring (Gokhale, Bhat & Bhat, 2018). Among other applications, the Internet of Things has made it possible to construct connected cars (Jabeen & Potturu,2024, January), smart cities (Nassereddine & Khang, 2024), and smart homes (Rock, Tajudeen & Chung,2024) in terms of service delivery. For example, homeowners can enjoy increased convenience, comfort, and security by using smartphone apps to operate smart home appliances like lighting controls, security cameras, and thermostats remotely. IoT-enabled automobiles in the transportation industry can interact with traffic control systems to improve safety, ease traffic, and optimize routes. Additionally, IoT sensors integrated into industrial machinery can track performance, identify malfunctions, and send out maintenance warnings, reducing downtime and boosting productivity (Rath, Khang & Roy, 2024).

Impact on Customer Experience

A- Personalization and Customization

In service delivery, personalization and customization are important factors that contribute to improved customer experiences (Bhuiyan,2024). Organizations may now customize their products and services to meet the unique demands of each client by using AI algorithms and data analytics to obtain insights into the preferences, behaviors, and wants of their customers thanks to technological breakthroughs. In addition to raising consumer pleasure, personalized experiences also promote client retention and loyalty. Organizations can provide customers with personalized content, recommendations, and promotions based on their past interactions and preferences by utilizing data-driven customization tactics (Deepa & Abirami, 2024).

Recommendation engines, for instance, are used by e-commerce platforms to make product recommendations based on past browsing and purchase activity from users, increasing sales and conversion rates. In a similar vein, streaming services use user behavior data to make content recommendations that boost interest and pleasure (Lin & Huang, 2024).

Personalization isn't a service delivery fad, it's a game-changer. From customizing dream cars to dietary-conscious food options, it empowers customers. Music apps curate playlists, and interfaces anticipate needs, all for a frictionless, engaging experience (Chan, 2024). Travel, entertainment, finance, and retail all join the party with personalized recommendations and rewards. But wielding this power ethically is key. Balancing data privacy, avoiding filter bubbles, and maintaining a human touch is crucial (Jiang, 2024). By achieving this balance, businesses can create service delivery experiences that are not only efficient but also deeply personal, fostering trust and loyalty for a win-win on all sides (Patel,2024).

B- Seamless and Convenient Interaction

Customer encounters have been converted into more fluid, convenient, and efficient ones because of technology-enabled service delivery. Customers can interact with brands at their convenience through digital channels including websites, mobile apps, and social media platforms, which offer them 24/7 access to information, assistance, and transactions (Liu et al., 2024). Additionally, omnichannel experiences improve the consumer experience by allowing users to navigate between channels without losing context (Aripin, Saepudin & Gunawan, 2024, February). Self-service kiosks and smartphone apps, for instance, enable users to schedule appointments, place orders, and check in for services without requiring assistance from a human, cutting down on wait times and increasing productivity. Similarly to this, chatbots and virtual assistants offer clients instant help and assistance by responding to their questions, addressing their problems, and assisting them in real time through challenging procedures (Noonia et al., 2024).

Advanced technology and AI algorithms are driving automation in service delivery, minimizing errors and streamlining procedures. Digital wallets and predictive analytics exemplify this. The former ensures seamless transactions, while the latter allows businesses to anticipate customer needs, leading to proactive service and higher satisfaction. Automation benefits both sides: it enhances the customer experience and generates cost savings and efficiencies for businesses (Abutaha & Dinler, 2024).

C- Enhanced Efficiency and Effectiveness

Innovations enabled by technology have greatly increased the efficacy and efficiency of service delivery procedures, allowing businesses to provide higher-quality services faster and for less money (Casillo et al., 2024; Giannoukou, 2024). Artificial intelligence (AI) algorithms and automation can free up human resources to work on more valuable tasks by automating monotonous jobs. Robotic process automation (RPA), for instance, lowers mistakes and processing times by automating data entry, document processing, and other repetitive processes (Lo et al.,2024). Predictive analytics and machine learning algorithms additionally help firms anticipate demand, allocate resources optimally, and make better decisions. Predictive maintenance algorithms, for example, use equipment performance data to identify potential problems before they arise (Postiglione & Monteleone, 2024). This enables businesses to plan maintenance proactively and minimize expensive downtime. Similarly, dynamic pricing algorithms maximize income and profitability by instantly adjusting prices in response to market conditions, competition, and other variables (Carnehl, Stenzel & Schmidt, 2024).

Technology-enabled service delivery also makes it easier for internal teams and external partners to coordinate and collaborate, which improves productivity and speeds up response times (Gunawan, Siagian & Tarigan, 2024). Real-time remote team collaboration is made possible by cloud-based collaboration tools, and digital platforms and marketplaces facilitate the connection between businesses and outside suppliers, distributors, and service providers (Bardsen et al., 2024, March). These improvements in efficacy and efficiency allow businesses to provide better services at lower prices and with more profitability (Harahap,2024).

CLASS ACTIVITY:

Designing Innovative Delivery Solutions

A- Activity Overview

Students will work in groups to develop creative, technology-driven service delivery solutions during this class exercise. Through the application of theoretical concepts gained in the course to real-world situations, the exercise will help students develop their critical thinking, creativity, and problem-solving abilities. The following steps make up the activity:

1. Putting Teams Together and Choosing a Service Sector:

The students will be split up into teams, with three to five people on each squad. During the exercise, each team will choose a particular service industry to concentrate on. Healthcare, hospitality, retail, transportation, and any other industry with a sizable customer-facing workforce can all be considered service industries.

2. Developing an Idea for a Cutting-Edge Service Delivery Solution:
    - Teams will use technology to generate ideas for creative service delivery solutions after deciding on their relevant service industry.
    - Teams will take into account the unique requirements, complaints, and inclinations of clients in the service sector of their choice.
    - Teams will create a thorough concept for their creative solution based on the design thinking principles, taking into account aspects like usability, functionality, and feasibility.
    - Depending on the needs of the selected service industry, technologies such as blockchain, augmented reality, internet of Things (IoT), artificial intelligence, and others may be taken into consideration.
3. Conceptual Presentation:
    - Each team will create a presentation to highlight their creative approach to service delivery after designing their concepts.
    - A summary of the selected service sector, a thorough justification of the suggested remedy, and an illustration of how technology will be incorporated to improve the client experience will all be covered in the presentations.
    - Teams will also note any possible advantages of their solution, like increased customer satisfaction, cost savings, efficiency gains, and competitive advantage.
    - Teams will also talk about possible obstacles or hurdles to implementation and suggest ways to get beyond them.
    - Students will enhance their awareness of how technology is changing service delivery while also gaining practical experience in ideation, conceptualization, and presenting abilities through this assignment.
    - Students will gain the ability to use a variety of viewpoints and areas of expertise when working in groups to create creative solutions to problems that arise in the real world.

B- Learning Outcomes

1. Enhance Your Critical Thinking and Creativity:

- Students will hone their creative and critical thinking abilities by coming up with original solutions to pressing problems through the collaborative design process.
- Students will be inspired to explore unorthodox ideas and think creatively by participating in iterative design and problem-solving processes.

2. Understanding how technology is used in service delivery:
   - Students will have a greater grasp of how technology is changing the service industry by creating creative, technology-driven service delivery solutions.
   - They will look at ways to use AI, IoT, and AR/VR to improve consumer experiences, optimize workflows, and spur company expansion.
3. Acquire Knowledge of Opportunities and Challenges:
   - Students will learn about the opportunities and difficulties of applying creative ideas in practical settings through the presentation of their notions.
   - They will have the ability to foresee possible adoption roadblocks, such as legal restrictions, technological setbacks, or organizational resistance, and create plans of action to successfully overcome these obstacles.

CASE STUDY

1. Background

Collaborative business platforms are reshaping industries by enabling digital transformation and fostering innovation, especially in sectors like online food delivery (OFD). Swiggy, Fresh-Menu, Faasos, and Zomato are significant players in the Indian OFD market. Start-ups such as Zomato, an Indian-based online food ordering and delivery company, exemplify this transformation. Initially a restaurant discovery platform, Zomato strategically expanded its services to include online food ordering and delivery, tapping into new revenue streams and offering comprehensive services. Its success lies in leveraging a collaborative platform to connect a vast network of restaurants and delivery partners, while also maintaining a strong focus on understanding and meeting the needs of both businesses and customers through data analytics and customer insights. Zomato's business model innovation and customer-centric approach have enabled it to gain a competitive advantage in a fiercely competitive market. By continuously iterating its business model, Zomato has stayed ahead of rivals, captured a significant market share, and redefined the online food delivery industry. This case study underscores the significance of business model innovation in driving digital transformation and achieving competitive success, highlighting the role of collaborative platforms and customer-centricity as key factors in Zomato's journey.

Zomato`s History

Zomato initially launched in 2008 as "Foodiebay," transitioned to its current name, Zomato Media Pvt. Ltd., on January 18, 2010. The company was co-founded by Deepinder Goyal and Pankaj Chaddah, both of whom are graduates of the Indian Institute of Technology (IIT). Before founding Zomato, Deepinder worked at Bain and Company in New Delhi, where he observed long queues of people waiting to view menus in the office pantry before ordering food. This experience inspired him to create an online platform that would make menus easily accessible. In 2008, Deepinder left Bain to start Zomato from his condominium, taking charge of its strategic direction and product development. Similarly, Pankaj Chaddah, who also had a background at Bain and Company in New Delhi, joined Zomato and currently oversees strategies and operations for both local and international markets (DSIM report, 2015).

Zomato is India's leading OFD with a valuation of $3.3 billion, making it one of India's most valuable startups as of 2019. By 2020, it expanded to 24 countries and over 10,000 cities globally. In India, it lists over 250,000 restaurants and has a delivery network of over 200,000 partners across approximately 500 cities. With an active user base of over 80 million, Zomato saw significant growth in user engagement and order volume during the first half of fiscal year 2020, with monthly orders nearly quadrupling from the previous year. The company reported dining-out revenue of over $27 million and a gross merchandise value (GMV) growth of over $820 million during this period. By the fiscal year 2022, Zomato's revenue exceeded 55 billion Indian rupees, with food delivery contributing significantly to its income (Digital Food Lab, 2019, April).

Figure 1. Share of the online food delivery (platform) MARKET IN India as of Secember 2020 by company

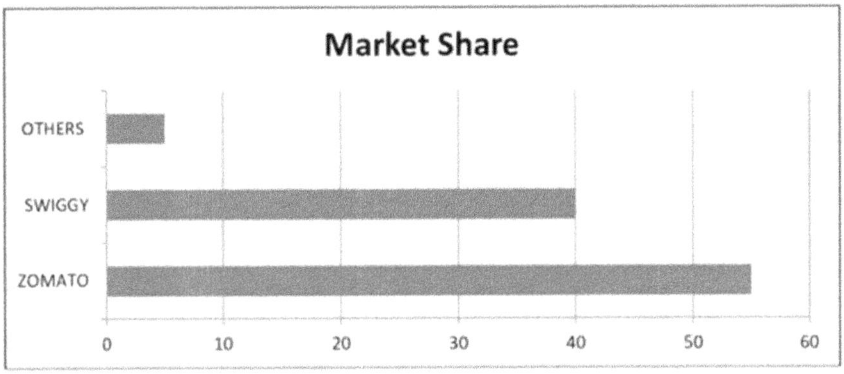

Source: Statista 2020

In 2020, Zomato reported revenues of approximately 26 billion Indian rupees, slightly surpassing its competitor Swiggy's earnings of around 25 billion Indian rupees, as indicated in Figure 2. As the leading player in online food delivery, Zomato's higher revenue underscores its superior service offerings and extensive menu selection for over 250,000 restaurants worldwide. Despite Swiggy being ranked as the second most popular food delivery app in India according to a Rakuten Insight survey from August 2021, Zomato remains the most recognized and preferred choice among consumers in India, as shown in Figure 3.

Figure 2. Revenue of online food delivery in India from the financial year 2017 to 2021 by the company (in billion Indian rupees)

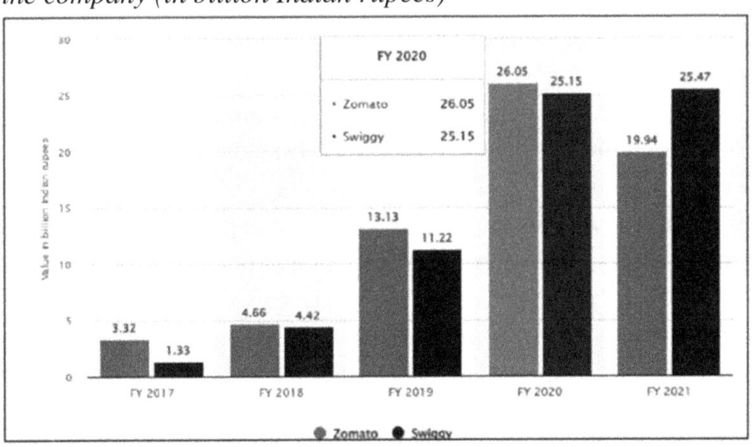

Source: Statista, 2021

Figure 3. Most popular food delivery companies across India as of August 2021

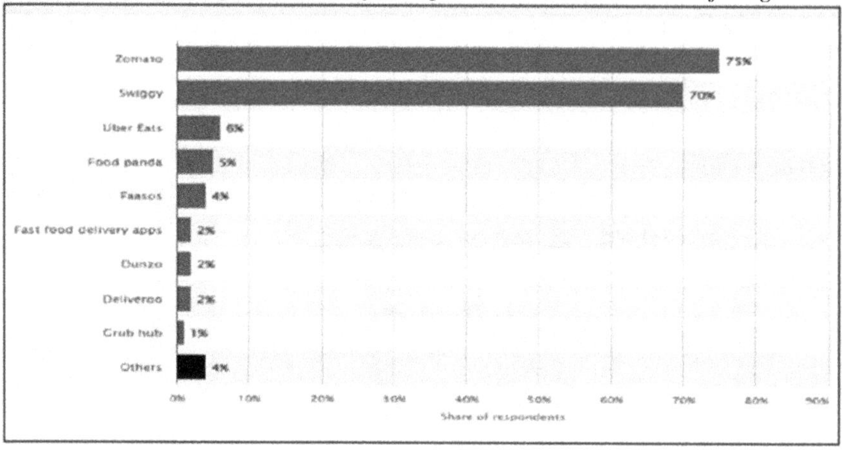

Source: Statista, 2022

2. Overview of the Company's Innovative Technology Adoption Initiative:

Recognizing the dynamic shifts in the online food delivery sector, Zomato proactively chose to harness the power of advanced technologies. To stay abreast of industry trends and enhance its service quality, Zomato initiated a comprehensive effort to infuse its operations with state-of-the-art technology. The company's leadership was keen on elevating productivity, refining service standards, and enriching the overall customer journey. A pivotal technological upgrade Zomato implemented was the creation of intuitive and user-friendly menus. Understanding the significance of an effortless and visually engaging ordering process, Zomato invested in crafting menus that are both easy to use and visually pleasing. This customer-focused menu design streamlines the ordering experience, allowing restaurants to effectively showcase their offerings and enhance the overall user experience. The Zomato platform features smart search engine filters designed to display only restaurants that match the entered keyword. When users search using keywords or phrases related to restaurants, Zomato provides them with relevant information about potential dining options.

Furthermore, Zomato emphasized the importance of real-time customer interactions as a critical technological feature. Valuing timely and personalized communication, Zomato introduced systems to ensure swift responses to customer queries, feedback, and concerns. This capability for immediate interaction empowers Zomato to promptly address customer needs, efficiently resolve issues, and cultivate stronger customer relationships. Through these technological integrations, Zomato has not just elevated its service delivery but has also reinforced its leadership position in the online food delivery market. These strategic technological investments highlight Zomato's dedication to innovation and customer satisfaction, enabling it to adapt to changing customer preferences and maintain its competitive edge.

B. Part 2: Challenges Faced

1. Technological Barriers and Integration Complexities:

Navigating the integration of new technology into its existing systems presented Zomato with substantial challenges, despite its thorough planning. The journey was complicated by issues such as system compatibility, data migration, and interoperability, which required significant resources and expertise to address effectively. As Zomato worked to align diverse systems and ensure smooth integration across various departments, it encountered delays and setbacks that tested its resolve. System compatibility emerged as a key challenge for Zomato. Ensuring that new technologies harmonized with the existing infrastructure was a complex endeavor. The tech teams had to invest considerable effort in identifying and resolving conflicts between different software and hardware elements to achieve seamless integration.

Data migration posed another significant hurdle. Transferring vast amounts of data from older systems to new platforms without compromising its integrity or security was a delicate operation. Zomato had to devise robust strategies and employ sophisticated tools to facilitate a smooth and secure data transition, essential for maintaining service continuity and customer satisfaction.

Furthermore, ensuring interoperability between various technologies across different departments was crucial but challenging. Zomato had to develop APIs and middleware solutions to enable seamless communication and data exchange between disparate systems, fostering operational coherence.

Despite these integration challenges leading to delays and setbacks, Zomato remained committed to its technological advancement objectives. Adopting a phased integration approach, Zomato prioritized key systems and processes while gradually expanding its technological capabilities across the organization. This methodical approach allowed Zomato to address immediate issues, learn from its experiences, and refine its integration strategies to minimize disruptions. In conclusion, while Zomato's technological integration journey was marked by obstacles and setbacks, it underscored the company's resilience and commitment to innovation. By navigating these challenges and leveraging its experience, Zomato strengthened its ability to harness technology effectively, enhancing its service delivery and customer experience in the long run.

2. Obstacles to customer adoption and acceptance:

Securing customer acceptance and support for its new technology presented a major challenge for Zomato. Despite the company's belief that these innovative solutions would enhance the customer experience, it faced resistance and skepticism from some of its customers. Addressing these concerns became a top priority for Zomato to successfully roll out its new service delivery methods.

To overcome this obstacle, Zomato launched targeted marketing and educational campaigns to address customer apprehensions and emphasize the benefits of its new technologies. These initiatives aimed to demonstrate how the new approaches could streamline the ordering process, improve delivery efficiency, and ultimately elevate customer satisfaction. Alongside these awareness-building efforts, Zomato executed comprehensive commercial campaigns across both print and electronic media platforms. These campaigns were designed to reach a wider audience, reinforce Zomato's dedication to innovation, and build trust with its customers. Through these initiatives, Zomato sought to establish credibility and encourage customers to embrace the new service delivery methods, as these methods tend to capture emotional value propositions coupled with consumers to evoke their positive emotions and feelings. In its latest advertisements, Zomato appeals to emotions. One ad shows a daughter visiting her father, who attempts to cook pasta despite his separation from her mother. When the pasta turns out burnt, the daughter saves the meal by revealing she ordered it through the Zomato app. In another ad, a son calls his mother through the Zomato app during his visit, sparing her from cooking.

Facing resistance within its workforce, Zomato also grappled with challenges related to its customer base, a significant portion of whom lacked tech proficiency. This added complexity to Zomato's efforts to integrate new technologies, including Artificial Intelligence (AI), to enhance its services. While Zomato was keen on innovating with AI to elevate its offerings, it was vital to make these advancements accessible to all customers. Acknowledging the varying tech comfort levels among its clientele, Zomato took the initiative to bridge this digital gap and make its AI-powered features more user-friendly. Actively seeking customer feedback, Zomato refined its approach based on their concerns and preferences. This feedback-driven approach allowed Zomato to better tailor its messaging and services to meet the diverse needs of its customer base.

To educate customers about the benefits of AI and other new technologies, Zomato organized workshops, webinars, and interactive sessions. These educational efforts aimed to offer customers practical guidance on leveraging the new service delivery methods effectively. Through these initiatives, Zomato sought to empower its customers with the knowledge and confidence to embrace AI-driven features and enhance their dining experiences. Moreover, Zomato integrated targeted marketing and comprehensive commercial campaigns into its strategy to promote the benefits of its new technologies to customers. These campaigns were crafted to resonate with a broad audience, including those who may be less tech-savvy, and to highlight the user-friendly features of the new service delivery methods. By combining customer feedback, educational initiatives, targeted marketing, and commercial campaigns, Zomato successfully navigated the challenge of gaining customer acceptance for its new technology. As customers began to experience the advantages of the new service delivery methods firsthand and saw how user-friendly they were, initial resistance gradually gave way to acceptance and appreciation.

In conclusion, while Zomato faced challenges from both its workforce and customer base during its technological transformation, its commitment to listening to customers, providing educational opportunities, and crafting targeted messaging proved instrumental in overcoming these obstacles. By prioritizing accessibility and user-friendliness in its technology adoption strategy, Zomato successfully fostered acceptance and appreciation among its diverse customer base, reinforcing its position as a customer-centric industry leader. In conclusion, while overcoming customer resistance to the new technology was a significant challenge for Zomato, its strategic approach to marketing, education, and engagement proved effective in building trust and fostering acceptance. By consistently communicating the value of its innovative solutions, Zomato strengthened its bond with its customer base and solidified its position as an industry leader in online food delivery.

3. Overcoming Organizational Resistance to Change and Cultural Shifts:

Zomato faced resistance to change within its workforce, particularly from experienced employees who were accustomed to traditional methods and hesitant to adopt new technologies. This resistance highlighted the need for more than just technical adjustments; it required a profound shift in the organization's mindset and culture. Overcoming this cultural inertia became a central challenge in Zomato's journey towards technological transformation, demanding thoughtful organizational change management strategies. The reluctance to embrace new technologies was partly due to employees' attachment to established workflows and the fear of disruptions or diminished expertise. To address these concerns and cultivate a culture that values innovation, Zomato's leadership took proactive steps to drive the transformation agenda and create a supportive environment for change.

Zomato's leadership emphasized the benefits of the new technologies and encouraged a mindset that views change as an opportunity for growth and improvement. They also ensured that employees had the necessary resources, training, and support to adapt to the new technologies effectively. This included offering comprehensive training programs and workshops to help employees understand the new systems and their advantages. Moreover, Zomato's leadership actively engaged with employees, seeking their feedback, addressing their concerns, and involving them in decision-making processes. This inclusive approach helped to build trust, alleviate fears, and foster a sense of ownership among the workforce. By implementing these strategies, Zomato's leadership successfully navigated the challenges posed by cultural inertia and resistance to change. As employees became more familiar with the new technologies and recognized their benefits, skepticism gradually transformed into acceptance, leading to a more open and adaptable organizational culture.

In summary, while overcoming resistance to change was a significant hurdle for Zomato, effective leadership, clear communication, and advanced AI-based technology strengthened their strategies driving toward organizational transformation. By fostering a culture that values innovation, providing the necessary support and resources, and actively engaging with customers and employees, Zomato's leadership laid the groundwork for successful technological adoption and a more resilient, adaptive workforce.

CONCLUSION

The chapter explores into the transformative impact of technological advancements on traditional service delivery methods across various industries. It underscores the increasing importance for businesses to integrate these technological innovations into their operations to remain competitive in today's fast-paced and ever-changing market landscape. By adopting these technologies, companies can not only meet the evolving needs and preferences of their clients but also optimize their operational processes for greater efficiency and effectiveness.

Using Zomato as a detailed case study, the chapter examines the complexities businesses face when striving to elevate their service delivery standards in the digital age. It highlights the challenges of navigating technological changes, managing resistance to new technologies, and ensuring a seamless transition for both employees and customers. Despite these challenges, the chapter also shines a light on the abundant opportunities available to businesses that successfully implement and leverage these technological advancements.

Furthermore, the chapter offers a comprehensive overview of the strategies and best practices that organizations can adopt to embrace digital transformation. It emphasizes the importance of cultivating a culture of innovation within the company and fostering a mindset that views technological change as an opportunity rather than a threat. By doing so, businesses can differentiate themselves from competitors, enhance stakeholder experiences, and create a sustainable competitive advantage in the marketplace. Additionally, the chapter serves as a valuable resource for businesses navigating the complexities of technology integration and service innovation. It provides practical insights, actionable recommendations, and a roadmap for organizations looking to adapt to technological changes effectively. As businesses continue to grapple with the challenges of digital transformation, the knowledge, and guidance offered in this chapter become increasingly important, helping companies stay ahead of the curve and unlock new avenues for growth and success in an era defined by constant change and disruption.

REFERENCES

Abutaha, F., & Dinler, C. (2024). Adopting Robotic Process Automation (RPA) in the Construction Industry. In *Complex AI Dynamics and Interactions in Management* (pp. 273-310). IGI Global.

Adekugbe, A. P., & Ibeh, C. V.Arenike Patricia AdekugbeChidera Victoria Ibeh. (2024). Innovating service delivery for underserved communities: Leveraging data analytics and program management in our context. *International Journal of Applied Research in Social Sciences*, 6(4), 472–487. DOI: 10.51594/ijarss.v6i4.986

Al Adwan, A., Kokash, H., Al Adwan, R., & Khattak, A. (2023). Data analytics in digital marketing for tracking the effectiveness of campaigns and inform strategy. *International Journal of Data and Network Science*.

Amankwah-Amoah, J., Abdalla, S., Mogaji, E., Elbanna, A., & Dwivedi, Y. K. (2024). The impending disruption of creative industries by generative AI: Opportunities, challenges, and research agenda. *International Journal of Information Management*, 79, 102759. DOI: 10.1016/j.ijinfomgt.2024.102759

Aripin, Z., Saepudin, D., & Gunawan, A. (2024, February). The impact of omni-channel integrated marketing communications (IMC) on retail product and service satisfaction in Indonesia: An analysis with an open access approach. *Journal of Jabar Economic Society Networking Forum*, 1(3), 33–48.

Balasubramanian, P. (2023). Automation in Data Science, Software, and Information Services. In *Springer Handbook of Automation* (pp. 989–1014). Springer International Publishing. DOI: 10.1007/978-3-030-96729-1_46

Bardsen, J., Nilsen, B. E. S., Froyland, T., Ramondenc, P., Segura, J., Gabdullin, A., . . . Fonseca, S. H. (2024, March). Cloud-Based Planning and Real-Time Algorithms Improve Coiled Tubing Cleanout Efficiency. In *SPE/ICoTA Well Intervention Conference and Exhibition* (p. D021S008R003). SPE. DOI: 10.2118/218290-MS

Bellaaj, M. (2023). Why and how do individual entrepreneurs use digital channels in an emerging market? Determinants of use and channel coordination. *International Journal of Emerging Markets*, 18(9), 2735–2764. DOI: 10.1108/IJOEM-08-2020-0882

Bhuiyan, M. S. (2024). The Role of AI-Enhanced Personalization in Customer Experiences. *Journal of Computer Science and Technology Studies*, 6(1), 162–169. DOI: 10.32996/jcsts.2024.6.1.17

Borole, P. J. (2024). Analysis and Implications of Adopting AI and Machine Learning in Marketing, Servicing, and Communications Technology. [IJAIML]. *International Journal of Artificial Intelligence and Machine Learning*, 13(1), 1–11. DOI: 10.4018/IJAIML.338379

Carnehl, C., Stenzel, A., & Schmidt, P. (2024). Pricing for the stars: Dynamic pricing in the presence of rating systems. *Management Science*, 70(3), 1755–1772. DOI: 10.1287/mnsc.2023.4771

Casillo, M., Cecere, L., Colace, F., Lorusso, A., & Santaniello, D. (2024). Integrating the Internet of Things (IoT) in SPA Medicine: Innovations and Challenges in Digital Wellness. *Computers*, 13(3), 67. DOI: 10.3390/computers13030067

Chan, E. Y. (2024). Consumer Behavior in the Future. In *Consumer Behavior in Practice: Strategic Insights for the Modern Marketer* (pp. 251–263). Springer Nature Switzerland. DOI: 10.1007/978-3-031-50947-6_13

Deepa, S., & Abirami, A. (2024). The Impact of AI on Customer Experience. In *Balancing Automation and Human Interaction in Modern Marketing* (pp. 263–285). IGI Global. DOI: 10.4018/979-8-3693-2276-5.ch014

Deepa, S., & Abirami, A. (2024). The Impact of AI on Customer Experience. In *Balancing Automation and Human Interaction in Modern Marketing* (pp. 263–285). IGI Global. DOI: 10.4018/979-8-3693-2276-5.ch014

Digital Food Lab. (2019, April). Foodtech in India Startup and investment activity. https://www.digitalfoodlab. com/reports/2019-india/download

DSIM report. (2015). Case Study- Zomato: An Indian Start-up acquiring the world. DSIM. https://dsim.in/ blog/2015/04/14/zomato-an-indian-startup-acquiring-the-world/Assessed

Eswaran, U., & Khang, A. (2024). 8 Augmented Reality (AR) and Virtual Reality (VR) Technologies in Surgical Operating Systems. *AI and IoT Technology and Applications for Smart Healthcare Systems*, 113.

Giannoukou, I. (2024). Revolutionizing Hospitality: Strategic Integration of Innovation Management Embracing Technological Innovation for Enhanced Customer Experiences. *Technium Business and Management*, 7, 24–39. DOI: 10.47577/business.v7i.10585

Gokhale, P., Bhat, O., & Bhat, S. (2018). Introduction to IOT. *International Advanced Research. Journal of Science, Engineering and Technology*, 5(1), 41–44.

Govindaraj, M., Gnanasekaran, C., Kandavel, R., Khan, P., & Hoang, S. D. (2024). Revolutionizing Service Productivity: A Roadmap of Innovative Technologies. In *Innovative Technologies for Increasing Service Productivity* (pp. 41-60). IGI Global. DOI: 10.4018/979-8-3693-2019-8.ch003

Gunawan, K., Siagian, H., & Tarigan, Z. (2024). The impact of supply chain integration on operational performance with supply chain capability. *Uncertain Supply Chain Management*, 12(2), 977–988. DOI: 10.5267/j.uscm.2023.12.010

Harahap, K. (2024). Harmonizing Differentiation and Cost Leadership Strategies in Culinary Businesses. *Research Horizon*, 4(2), 31–46.

Jabeen, S., & Potturu, S. R. (2024, January). Survey on security and privacy of connected vehicles and cloud platforms for communication. In *AIP Conference Proceedings* (Vol. 2512, No. 1). AIP Publishing. DOI: 10.1063/5.0159381

Jiang, S. (2024). Analysis Of the Impact of Information Filtering on People's Thinking—Take Filter Bubble as An Example. *Journal of Education. Humanities and Social Sciences*, 28, 759–763.

Josyula, H. P., Reddi, L. T., Parate, S., & Rajagopal, A. (2024). A Review on Security and Privacy Considerations in Programmable Payments. *International Journal of Intelligent Systems and Applications in Engineering*, 12(9s), 256–263.

Kumar, H., Tuli, N., Singh, R. K., Arya, V., & Srivastava, R. (2024). Exploring the role of augmented reality as a new brand advocate. *Journal of Consumer Behaviour*, 23(2), 620–638. DOI: 10.1002/cb.2227

Kuzmak, O., Kuzmak, O., & Voitovych, S. (2024). Business Development Towards the Application of Innovative Customer Relationship Management (CRM) Technologies in the Context of Global Transformational Changes. In *Data-Centric Business and Applications: Modern Trends in Financial and Innovation Data Processes 2023* (Vol. 2, pp. 47–69). Springer Nature Switzerland. DOI: 10.1007/978-3-031-53984-8_3

Lin, K. Y., & Huang, T. K. (2024). Shopping in the digital world: How augmented reality mobile applications trigger customer engagement. *Technology in Society*, 77, 102540. DOI: 10.1016/j.techsoc.2024.102540

Liu, S., Ali Vakeel, K., Smith, N., Alavipour, R. S., Wei, C., & Wirtz, J. (2024). AI concierge in the customer journey: What is it and how can it add value to the customer? *Journal of Service Management*, 35(6), 136–158. DOI: 10.1108/JOSM-12-2023-0523

Lo, W., Yang, C. M., Zhang, Q., & Li, M. (2024). Increased Productivity and Reduced Waste with Robotic Process Automation and Generative AI-Powered IoE Services. *Journal of Web Engineering*, 23(1), 53–87. DOI: 10.13052/jwe1540-9589.2313

Munawar, A., Li, Z., Nagururu, N., Trakimas, D., Kazanzides, P., Taylor, R. H., & Creighton, F. X. (2024). Fully immersive virtual reality for skull-base surgery: Surgical training and beyond. *International Journal of Computer Assisted Radiology and Surgery*, 19(1), 51–59. DOI: 10.1007/s11548-023-02956-5 PMID: 37347346

Naseer, I. (2023). AWS Cloud Computing Solutions: Optimizing Implementation for Businesses. *Statistics. Computing and Interdisciplinary Research*, 5(2), 121–132. DOI: 10.52700/scir.v5i2.138

Nassereddine, M., & Khang, A. (2024). Applications of Internet of Things (IoT) in smart cities. In *Advanced IoT Technologies and Applications in the Industry 4.0 Digital Economy* (pp. 109–136). CRC Press. DOI: 10.1201/9781003434269-6

Noonia, A., Beg, R., Patidar, A., Bawaskar, B., Sharma, S., & Rawat, H. (2024). Chatbot vs Intelligent Virtual Assistance (IVA). *Conversational Artificial Intelligence*, 655-673.

Pajić, V., Andrejić, M., Jolović, M., & Kilibarda, M. (2024). Strategic warehouse location selection in business logistics: A novel approach using imf SWARA–MARCOS—a case study of a Serbian logistics service provider. *Mathematics*, 12(5), 776. DOI: 10.3390/math12050776

Patel, D., & Muthuswamy, S. (2024). Machining Process Automation in Computer Numerical Control Turning Using Robot-Assisted Imaging and CNN-Based Machine Learning. *Journal of Manufacturing Science and Engineering*, 146(4), 041004–1. DOI: 10.1115/1.4064626

Patel, K. (2024). Ethical reflections on data-centric AI: Balancing benefits and risks. *SSRN*, 2(1), 1–17. DOI: 10.2139/ssrn.4993089

Postiglione, A., & Monteleone, M. (2024). Predictive Maintenance with Linguistic Text Mining. *Mathematics*, 12(7), 1089. DOI: 10.3390/math12071089

Rath, K. C., Khang, A., & Roy, D. (2024). The Role of Internet of Things (IoT) Technology in Industry 4.0 Economy. In *Advanced IoT Technologies and Applications in the Industry 4.0 Digital Economy* (pp. 1-28). CRC Press.

Rock, L. Y., Tajudeen, F. P., & Chung, Y. W. (2024). Usage and impact of the internet-of-things-based smart home technology: A quality-of-life perspective. *Universal Access in the Information Society*, 23(1), 345–364. DOI: 10.1007/s10209-022-00937-0 PMID: 36407566

Rossi, M., & Russo, G. (2024). Innovative Solutions: Cloud Computing and AI Synergy in Software Engineering. *MZ Journal of Artificial Intelligence*, 1(1), 1–9.

Scorita, K. B., Hendayani, N., Kusuma, M. A., & Al-Shreifeen, I. A. (2024). The integration of augmented reality in marketing: enhancing customer experience and brand engagement: literature review. *International Journal of Economic Literature*, 2(3), 713–725.

Sharma, R., & Gour, S. (2024). Internet of Things (IoT) Case Studies and Application. *AI and IoT Technology and Applications for Smart Healthcare Systems*, 333.

Shehadeh, M., Atta, A., Barrak, T., Lutfi, A., & Alrawad, M. (2024). Digital transformation: An empirical analysis of operational efficiency, customer experience, and competitive advantage in Jordanian Islamic banks. *Uncertain Supply Chain Management*, 12(2), 695–708. DOI: 10.5267/j.uscm.2024.1.015

Smith, J., & Anderson, J. (2024). *Augmented Realms, Digital Dreams: a Lengthy Expedition into the Synergies of Augmented Reality and E-Commerce, Unraveling the Threads of Innovation Woven into the Fabric of Online Shopping (No. 11965).* EasyChair.

Yadav, S. (2024). Transformative frontiers: A comprehensive review of emerging technologies in modern healthcare. *Cureus*, 16(3). Advance online publication. DOI: 10.7759/cureus.56538 PMID: 38646390

Zhang, X., Singh, S., Li, J., & Shao, X. (2024). Exploring the effects of value co-creation strategies in event services on attendees' citizenship behaviors: The roles of customer empowerment and psychological ownership. *Journal of Retailing and Consumer Services*, 76, 103619. DOI: 10.1016/j.jretconser.2023.103619

Chapter 7
Production Sector Dynamics:
Technological Advances in Manufacturing and Production

Muhammad Shahzeb Khan
https://orcid.org/0000-0003-4885-4032
Villa College, Maldives

Salman Hameed
https://orcid.org/0000-0001-7793-4109
Bahria University, Pakistan

Abdul S. Dahri
https://orcid.org/0000-0003-4517-3493
Shaheed Benazir Bhutto University, Pakistan

ABSTRACT

This chapter deeply explores the production sector's complex dynamics, emphasizing the revolutionary effects of manufacturing technology breakthroughs. This chapter explains how automation, additive manufacturing, and the Internet of Things (IoT) revolutionize production processes, increase efficiency, and improve supply chain operations. It does this by exploring these technologies in detail. The unique contributions of each technology are that automation enhances productivity and consistency while lowering costs and minimizing human error; additive manufacturing, or 3D printing, allows for mass customization, decreases waste, and speeds up prototyping; and IoT enables real-time monitoring, predictive maintenance, and supply chain optimization. These technologies are propelling the development of smart factories and Industry 4.0, leading to highly efficient, flexible, and responsive

DOI: 10.4018/979-8-3693-5723-1.ch007

production systems. A practical experience that simulates the establishment of an intelligent factory enhances students' comprehension of Industry 4.0 technology and in digitalized environment.

1. INTRODUCTION

A- Defining Production Section Dynamics

The production sector includes various operations, from raw material extraction to final product delivery, creating commodities and services (Kokotinis et al., 2024; Lee et al., 2013). According to the World Bank, the estimated global manufacturing output in 2023 reached USD 15.7 trillion World Bank (2023). In this industry, "dynamics" refers to the different forces and causes influencing how this sector operates and changes over time. Global economic situations, market demands, regulatory frameworks, and technological improvements impact these dynamics (Ololade, 2024; Schuh et al., 2017). Various forces and causes influence how the production sector operates and evolves. These factors include global economic situations, market demands, regulatory frameworks, and technological advancements, each playing a crucial role in shaping production dynamics. These forces interact complexly, driving changes and presenting manufacturers with challenges and opportunities. A study by McKinsey & Company estimated that supply chain disruptions cost businesses an average of 4% to 6% of their sales globally. This underscores the critical importance of strategically managing factors that disrupt production flow, such as dependence on single-source suppliers or geopolitical tensions (Accelerating sustainable and inclusive growth, 2023). Understanding and strategically managing these influences is crucial for companies aiming to thrive in the modern production environment.

Companies in the production industry must comprehend these dynamics to respond to changes and stay competitive in the market. Industry players must grasp the complexities of global economic trends, shifting market demands, regulatory compliance, and technological advancements to maintain competitiveness. This involves adapting operations, innovating products, ensuring regulatory adherence, and leveraging technology to enhance efficiency. A strategic and agile approach allows companies to navigate changes effectively and capitalize on emerging opportunities in the dynamic production environment.

B- Significance of Technological Advancement in Manufacturing and Production

The manufacturing and production landscape is significantly shaped by technological advancements (Alkunte et al., 2024; Lu & Ramakrishnan, 2019). The industry is undergoing a significant transition due to Industry 4.0 and the incorporation of digital technology into conventional production processes. Studies suggest that Industry 4.0 can lead to substantial productivity improvements. A PwC report estimates that manufacturers could achieve up to 30% productivity gains by leveraging digital technologies (PwC, 2016). The production of goods is revolutionized by technologies like automation, robotics, additive manufacturing, and the Internet of Things (IoT), resulting in enhanced flexibility, efficiency, and personalization (Irpan & Shaddiq, 2024; Schuh et al., 2017). Companies invest in SMART manufacturing solutions to optimize operations and reduce costs while maintaining product quality. Embracing this digital revolution empowers companies to stay competitive by leveraging real-time monitoring, predictive maintenance, and rapid adaptation to market changes. A study by BCG found that companies leveraging real-time data and analytics can achieve productivity improvements of up to 20%. This results in significant cost savings and increased output (BCG, 2023). The manufacturing sector worldwide has recently transitioned towards digital production systems and smart factories (Kolasani, 2024; Lee et al., 2013). As a result of this change, intelligent production environments have emerged, which can foresee maintenance requirements, optimize operations independently, and guarantee real-time visibility throughout the production chain. For example, GE Aviation utilizes digital tools to monitor jet engines in real-time, enabling predictive maintenance and reducing downtime; Siemens has developed a cloud-based operating system for factories that connects machines, facilitates data analysis, and improves production efficiency and Adidas leverages 3D printing technology to create customized shoes, offering greater product variety and faster production cycles.

Manufacturers can increase operational effectiveness, decrease waste, cut downtime, and become more competitive. Additionally, technical advancements in the manufacturing sector have made possible new production paradigms and business models like mass customization and dispersed manufacturing (Mourtzis et al., 2024; Schuh et al., 2017). A report by McKinsey & Company estimates that predictive maintenance techniques enabled by digital technologies can result in up to a 40% reduction in maintenance costs and a 10% improvement in equipment uptime (*Quantum Black*, 2024). These models optimize resource usage and shorten lead times, enabling businesses to fulfill the increasing demand for customized products. Technological advancements in production and manufacturing significantly impact economies, enterprises, and society; they stimulate economic growth, innovation, and sustainable development.

2. TECHNOLOGICAL INNOVATION IN MANUFACTURING

C- Automation and Robotics in Production Process

Manufacturing processes have undergone a revolution thanks to automation and robotics, which have increased output, efficiency, and flexibility (Al Bashar et al., 2024; Roser et al., 2016). A 2023 study by the International Federation of Robotics (IFR) found that the global robot stock has grown more than tenfold over the past two decades, reaching an estimated 3.5 million industrial robots worldwide. This substantial increase in robotic automation significantly boosts production output (IFR et al. of Robotics, n.d.). Human labor was traditionally indispensable in production operations, but the introduction of automation technology has led to machines taking over tasks previously performed by humans. This transition has reshaped the workforce, with some jobs being replaced by automated systems while others require new skills to operate and maintain these technologies. While automation enhances efficiency and reduces costs, it raises concerns about job displacement and the need for workforce reskilling and upskilling initiatives. Balancing the benefits of automation with the preservation of employment opportunities remains a crucial challenge for industries embracing technological advancements. Automation systems integrate several technologies to optimize production processes, such as robotic arms, conveyors, sensors, and programmable logic controllers (PLCs) (Payal et al., 2024; Ramesh et al., 2017). A 2022 report by the American Society of Safety Engineers (ASSE) found that occupational injuries and illnesses in the United States declined by 2.6% in 2021, with automation contributing to this trend (*Work-Related Fatalities up Nearly Six Percent in 2022*, n.d.).

In contemporary manufacturing facilities, robots are essential because they can precisely and reliably carry out jobs like welding, assembly, painting, and material handling (IMOH, 2024; Roser et al., 2016). Automating labour-intensive and repetitive processes can make businesses more efficient, cut expenses, and produce better products. Furthermore, robots can work continuously without becoming tired, which increases production throughput and uptime.

D- Additive Manufacturing and 3D Printing

According to Huang et al. (2013), additive manufacturing, also called 3D printing, has become a disruptive technology in the industrial sector (Zhou et al., 2024). Additive manufacturing, utilizing digital design files, constructs objects layer by layer, a departure from traditional subtractive methods that involve cutting material from a solid block to shape apart. This approach offers several advantages, including minimized material waste, rapid prototyping capabilities, and greater design flexibility. By precisely adding material only where needed, additive manufacturing reduces waste and enables the creation of intricate geometries that are challenging or impossible to achieve through subtractive techniques. The Wohlers Report 2023 estimates that the global additive manufacturing market will reach USD 37.2 billion in 2023, with a projected compound annual growth rate (CAGR) of 19.4% over the next five years. This signifies the rapid adoption of this technology across various industries (*Wohlers Report 2023- Wohlers Associates*, 2023). Additionally, the ability to swiftly produce prototypes facilitates iterative design processes and accelerates product development cycles, ultimately enhancing innovation and time-to-market. (Mallakpour, Radfar, & Hussain, 2024).

Numerous industries, including consumer products, automotive, aerospace, and healthcare, can benefit from 3D printing technologies (Gibson et al., 2014; Subramani et al., 2024). A survey by HUBS found that 73% of companies use 3D printing for prototyping (HUBS, 2021). In the aircraft industry, 3D printing technology fabricates intricate, lightweight parts characterized by sophisticated geometries, enhancing performance and fuel efficiency. This innovative approach allows for producing components with precisely engineered designs that optimize aerodynamics and structural integrity. By leveraging 3D printing, manufacturers can create lighter and stronger parts than those produced through traditional manufacturing methods. This weight reduction contributes to overall fuel efficiency, lowering operational costs and environmental impact. Moreover, the flexibility of 3D printing enables rapid prototyping and customization, facilitating the development of tailored solutions to meet specific aircraft requirements. As a result, the aircraft industry continues to embrace 3D printing as a key technology for advancing aviation capabilities and achieving sustainable performance goals. 3D printing revolutionizes healthcare by enabling personalized prosthetics and medical implants tailored to each patient's unique anatomy. This technology allows for precise customization, enhancing comfort, functionality, and overall patient satisfaction. By leveraging digital design and rapid prototyping, medical professionals can rapidly iterate and refine solutions, ultimately improving mobility and well-being for individuals requiring prosthetic limbs or implants.

E- Internet of Things in Smart Manufacturing

Smart manufacturing is being made possible in large part by the Internet of Things (IoT), which is turning conventional factories into intelligent and networked ecosystems (Rath et al., 2024; Wang et al., 2016). IoT technology empowers manufacturers to collect real-time data from machines, sensors, and production equipment, providing crucial insights into the functionality and condition of their assets. This data allows for proactive monitoring, predictive maintenance, and optimization of production processes. By harnessing IoT, manufacturers can enhance operational efficiency, reduce downtime, and improve overall equipment effectiveness. The World Economic Forum also emphasizes the importance of data-driven decision-making and connected machines in Industry 4.0 (*Mastering et al. for Successful Adoption of AI in Manufacturing*, 2024). This real-time visibility enables informed decision-making and facilitates continuous improvement initiatives, ultimately driving productivity and competitiveness in the manufacturing sector. By examining this data, businesses can reduce downtime, forecast maintenance requirements, and optimize production processes (Whig et al., 2024). Communication between IoT-enabled devices and centralized control systems makes autonomous decision-making and adaptive workflows possible in innovative manufacturing environments (Anarbayevich, 2024; Monostori et al., 2016). Sensors built into machinery can identify abnormalities or faults and initiate repairs before the equipment breaks down. Comparably, IoT platforms can optimize energy use by modifying machine settings in response to current utility rates and demand (Varone et al., 2024). Research conducted by the Department of Energy's Advanced Manufacturing Office indicates that manufacturing systems enabled by the Internet of Things (IoT) can decrease energy usage by as much as 20% (*Industries & Technologies*, n.d.).

3. IMPACT ON PRODUCTION EFFICIENCY

A- Streamlined Operations and Increased Productivity

Industrial settings have seen a considerable increase in productivity and operational efficiency due to technological advancements in manufacturing. According to Lee et al. (2015), organizations have improved overall efficiency, decreased cycle times, and optimized manufacturing processes through automation, robots, and digitalization (Sergeeva et al., 2024). Manufacturers can rapidly meet increasing demands and enhance throughput rates by automating repetitive tasks and minimizing manual intervention. Automation streamlines production processes reduces human error and accelerates task completion. According to a study published in the Harvard Business Review, automation has the potential to decrease defect rates by up to 80% in specific industries (Jesuthasan, 2018). Manufacturers can scale operations efficiently by deploying automated systems to keep pace with growing demand without compromising quality or efficiency. This enables them to respond swiftly to market fluctuations and customer requirements, ensuring timely product delivery while optimizing resource utilization. Ultimately, automation empowers manufacturers to achieve higher productivity levels, improve operational agility, and remain competitive in dynamic market environments. Research conducted by the McKinsey Global Institute suggests that automation could result in a 20% boost in productivity across various industries (McKinsey Global Institute, 2017).

Furthermore, the product development lifecycle has been entirely transformed by technologies like computer-aided design (CAD) and computer-aided manufacturing (CAM), which allow businesses to design and prototype new items quickly (Chabhadia et al., 2024, March; Rajput & Kosta, 2015). Engineers can build tool paths for machining operations, simulate manufacturing processes, and construct intricate 3D models of components using CAD/CAM software. This integrated strategy simplifies time-to-market, and producers are better equipped to react swiftly to evolving client demands (Abdulrahman & Baba, 2024).

B- Quality Control and Error Reduction

Two other significant effects of technology breakthroughs in production are the enhancement of quality control procedures and the decrease in manufacturing errors. According to Mouratzis et al. (2016), automation and robotics systems are outfitted with sensors and cameras that track production parameters in real-time, facilitating the early identification of flaws and deviations from quality standards (Al Bashar et al., 2024). The global number of connected sensors is projected to surpass 43 billion by 2025, indicating the increasing uptake of Internet of Things (IoT) technology in industrial environments (Statista, 2023, July 27). Manufacturers may save scrap and rework expenses by proactively identifying and resolving problems before they worsen (Nithia, 2024). Manufacturers can detect anomalies and potential failures in equipment or processes through real-time monitoring and data analysis provided by IoT technologies and predictive maintenance systems. By intervening early, they can prevent costly defects, minimize production downtime, and avoid the need for extensive rework. This proactive approach enhances product quality and customer satisfaction and optimizes resource utilization and operational efficiency. Ultimately, by leveraging proactive problem-solving strategies, manufacturers can realize substantial cost savings and maintain a competitive edge in the market.

In addition, predictive maintenance is made possible by sophisticated analytics and machine learning algorithms, assisting in averting equipment malfunctions and interruptions to production (Lee et al., 2016). According to a study by the Aberdeen Group, organizations implementing predictive maintenance practices can extend their equipment's lifespan by as much as 30% (Aberdeen, 2017). Manufacturers can maximize equipment uptime and productivity by scheduling maintenance during off-peak hours and anticipating maintenance needs by analyzing historical data and performance metrics (Sharma & Gurung, 2024). Manufacturers can mimic and optimize manufacturing processes risk-free to improve quality and efficiency using digital twins or virtual copies of actual assets (Tao et al., 2018; Yazdi, 2024). As per a study conducted by Gartner, it is forecasted that by 2021, 50% of manufacturers will incorporate digital twins into their operations, resulting in a projected 10% rise in productivity (Gartner, 2017). This predictive capability reduces maintenance costs and enhances reliability, ensuring uninterrupted production and meeting customer demands more effectively.

C- Supply Chain Optimization

Innovations in technology have also changed the way supply chain management is done, making global industrial networks more resilient and efficient. Blockchain, artificial intelligence, and the Internet of Things (IoT) have enabled greater visibility, traceability, and collaboration across supply chains (Odimarha et al., 2024; Chen et al., 2018). Blockchain, IoT sensors, and advanced analytics have made real-time insight into supply chain operations possible. Walmart utilizes blockchain technology to trace the origin and movement of food products throughout its supply chain. This enables swift identification and resolution of potential contamination issues, enhancing food safety standards and bolstering consumer confidence (*Blockchain in the Food Supply Chain - What Does the Future Look Like?* n.d.). This has allowed producers to track shipments, monitor inventory levels, and spot possible bottlenecks (Ivanov et al., 2019). This improved visibility allows businesses to cut lead times, optimize inventory levels, and react quickly to supply fluctuations and interruptions (Mubarik & Khan, 2024). Real-time data analytics and predictive modelling tools enhance decision-making, enabling proactive risk management and demand forecasting. According to a study conducted by Accenture, companies that effectively utilize data analytics experience a notable increase in profitability, ranging from 10% to 15% (*Companies Are Satisfied With Business Outcomes From Big Data and Recognize Big Data as Very Important to Their Digital Transformation, Accenture Study Shows*, n.d.). Additionally, automation and robotics streamline warehouse operations and transportation, reducing lead times and improving overall efficiency. These technological innovations empower businesses to adapt quickly to disruptions, optimize inventory levels, and enhance customer satisfaction. As a result, supply chains have become more agile, responsive, and resilient in the face of evolving market dynamics and unforeseen challenges (Nair et al., (2024).

Additionally, 3D printing and additive manufacturing make localized production and on-demand manufacturing possible, lessening the need for conventional supply chains and lowering the hazards involved in long-distance transportation (Roozkhosh et al., 2024; Weller et al., 2015). By utilizing digital manufacturing technologies, businesses may create flexible and responsive supply chains that can better adjust to changing market conditions and consumer preferences.

4. CLASS ACTIVITY: SIMULATION OF SMART FACTORY IMPLEMENTATION

A- Activity Overview

By simulating smart factory deployment, students can gain practical experience in comprehending the advantages and challenges of incorporating Internet of Things-enabled technology into manufacturing processes. The activity aims to give participants a real-world understanding of how intelligent manufacturing solutions are implemented and the difficulties that come with them. Through this activity, participants will engage in practical exercises simulating scenarios encountered in deploying technologies like automation and IoT. Data integration issues and organizational resistance are addressed, fostering critical thinking and problem-solving skills. Ultimately, the activity bridges theory and practice, equipping participants with the knowledge and skills to drive innovation in manufacturing operations.

Roles are assigned: Students are split into teams, and each team represents a distinct department in the intelligent factory, such as management, production, quality assurance, logistics, and maintenance. This division promotes cooperation and teamwork by allowing members to perform defined roles and duties. This approach promotes a deeper understanding of how various departments interact and rely on each other to achieve common goals in a dynamic manufacturing environment. Through active participation and role-playing, students develop essential teamwork skills while learning about the complexities of intelligent factory operations.

Development of Scenarios: Using IoT-enabled solutions, teams must solve a predetermined scenario or a series of manufacturing difficulties presented by the simulation. Teams might be entrusted, for instance, with boosting output while upholding standards for product quality or maximizing equipment use to reduce downtime.

Data Analysis and Decision-Making: During the simulation, teams examine data produced in real-time by Internet of Things (IoT) sensors mounted on industrial machinery, inventory management systems, and other linked devices. This data contains indicators related to product quality, inventory levels, energy consumption, and machine performance. Teams use this data to inform strategic decisions on allocating resources, streamlining production processes, and dealing with new problems.

Application of IoT Solutions: To solve the problems found during the simulation, teams suggest and implement IoT-enabled solutions. These might include implementing RFID-based inventory tracking systems to improve supply chain visibility, deploying predictive maintenance algorithms to prevent equipment failures, or integrating intelligent sensors to monitor environmental conditions and guarantee product quality.

Performance Evaluation: At the end of the simulation, teams assess the efficacy of their IoT solutions based on predetermined performance criteria, including production output, resource utilization, defect rates, and overall equipment effectiveness (OEE). They evaluate how their decisions affect key performance indicators to determine areas for optimization or improvement.

By participating in this simulation, students get critical insights into the challenges of integrating IoT-enabled technologies in manufacturing environments. They gain analytical, decision-making, and critical thinking abilities as they work through the difficulties of streamlining production procedures and utilizing technology to promote operational excellence.

5. CASE STUDY: ADOPTION OF 4.0 TECHNOLOGY BY XYZ MANUFACTURING COMPANY.

A- Background of the Study

XYZ Manufacturing Company Overview: A major force in the industrial sector, XYZ Industrial Company specializes in creating automotive components. With decades of experience using traditional manufacturing techniques, the business has built a solid reputation for providing clients with high-quality products.

Proposal to Combine Industry 4.0 Technologies: XYZ Manufacturing Company launched an initiative to incorporate Industry 4.0 technology into its manufacturing processes after realizing the necessity to maintain competitiveness in a world that is becoming more digitally connected. The objective was to optimize processes, boost productivity, and improve product quality by utilizing cutting-edge digital technologies, including automation, data analytics, and the Internet of Things.

B- Challenges Faced

Resistance to Change: One of the main issues XYZ Manufacturing Company had to deal with was opposition to change among staff members who were used to conventional manufacturing techniques. At first, many workers were dubious about adopting new technologies because they thought digitization and automation would cause them to lose their jobs or force them to learn new skills. Overcoming this opposition and cultivating an innovative and continuous improvement culture proved a significant challenge for the company.

Integration Difficulties: The deployment of Industry 4.0 technology has presented integration complexity and interoperability problems between new digital solutions and legacy systems. The combination of legacy gear and equipment used by XYZ Manufacturing Company made it challenging to integrate IoT sensors, automation systems, and data analytics platforms with ease. It requires careful planning and investments in technical infrastructure to ensure compatibility and interoperability amongst these platforms.

Security Concerns: Security became significant when XYZ Manufacturing Company used IoT devices and linked systems to collect real-time data from its manufacturing environment. Implementing IoT devices posed certain cybersecurity risks that the organization had to handle. These risks included potential disruptions to manufacturing operations, unauthorized access, and data breaches. Ensuring data privacy and protecting sensitive information by implementing strong security measures and protocols became the company's primary concern.

XYZ Manufacturing Company overcame these obstacles and maintained its competitive advantage in the market by transforming its operations and implementing a thorough plan for implementing Industry 4.0 technology.

CONCLUSION

Investigating production sector dynamics and technological advances in manufacturing and production has gained deep insights into the revolutionary potential of Industry 4.0 technologies. As we wrap up this chapter, we must consider the most important lessons learned and how they affect the industrial sector.

We explored many facets of technological advancements in manufacturing throughout this chapter, beginning with automation and robotics. These productivity, accuracy, and efficiency innovations have entirely changed the manufacturing sector. The relevance of real-time data-driven approaches in production planning and scheduling is highlighted by research by Lu et al. (2017), emphasizing its transformative impact on conventional manufacturing practices (Takeda-Berger& Frazzon, 2024). Furthermore, 3D printing and additive manufacturing have become disruptive technologies, allowing on-demand production and quick prototyping. Additive manufacturing lowers lead times and costs by layering materials to build complicated geometries (Schuh, Anderl, & Gausemeier, 2017). Because of this technology, businesses can respond to shifting market demands with more flexibility and agility. The Internet of Things (IoT) has completely transformed smart manufacturing by integrating machines, gadgets, and sensors to collect real-time data and enhance production procedures. As a result of the integration of IoT technologies, supply chain visibility, quality control, and manufacturing efficiency have all significantly improved (Kandarkar & Ravi, 2024; Lee et al., 2015).

Technological advancements have improved manufacturing quality control, boosted productivity, and streamlined processes. They provide clients with products of the highest caliber while cutting down on waste and downtime (Kamta & Sharma, 2024, pp. 261-279; Thoben et al., 2017). The intelligent factory implementation simulation gave students a practical learning experience that helped them understand contemporary manufacturing systems. Through cooperative teamwork and data analysis, students gained a deeper grasp of IoT-enabled solutions and their role in streamlining industrial processes (Singh, 2024).

Furthermore, the real-world case study of XYZ Manufacturing Company's use of Industry 4.0 technology provided insight into the prospects and difficulties related to manufacturing's digital transformation. The company's experience demonstrated how crucial it is to deal with employee resistance, overcome integration challenges, and prioritize cybersecurity. Technological advancements will continue to change the manufacturing sector. Businesses that embrace digital transformation and use cutting-edge technologies will obtain a competitive edge. However, success in the digital age involves more than technical aptitude; it also calls for an innovative culture, strategic vision, and a dedication to lifelong learning (Singha & Singha, 2024; Taherdoost, H. (2024)).

In conclusion, the manufacturing sector has great potential due to technological improvements and changes in the dynamics of the production sector. Manufacturers can achieve unprecedented productivity, efficiency, and competitiveness levels by adopting Industry 4.0 technologies such as automation, additive manufacturing, and the Internet of Things. We must develop the next generation of leaders and provide them with the tools they need to succeed in an increasingly digital environment as stakeholders in the industrial ecosystem (Schiuma et al., 2024).

REFERENCES

Abdulrahman, K. O., & Baba, R. A. (2024). Additive Manufacturing Technologies for On-Demand Production of Customised Goods in the Era of the 4th Industrial Revolution. In *Advances in Industrial Engineering in the Industry 4.0 Era* (pp. 127-146). CRC Press.

Aberdeen (2017). Asset Performance Management https://resources.altium.com/sites/default/files/uberflip_docs/file_964.pdf

Accelerating sustainable and inclusive growth. (2023, September 18). McKinsey & Company. https://www.mckinsey.com/about-us/overview/sustainable-and-inclusive-growth

Al Bashar, M., Taher, M. A., Islam, M. K., & Ahmed, H. (2024). The Impact Of Advanced Robotics And Automation On Supply Chain Efficiency In Industrial Manufacturing: A Comparative Analysis Between The Us And Bangladesh. *Global Mainstream Journal of Business, Economics. Development & Project Management*, 3(03), 28–41.

Alkunte, S., Fidan, I., Naikwadi, V., Gudavasov, S., Ali, M. A., Mahmudov, M., Hasanov, S., & Cheepu, M. (2024). Advancements and Challenges in Additively Manufactured Functionally Graded Materials: A Comprehensive Review. *Journal of Manufacturing and Materials Processing*, 8(1), 23. DOI: 10.3390/jmmp8010023

Anarbayevich, A. R. (2024). EXPLORING THE PRACTICAL APPLICATIONS OF IoT TECHNOLOGIES. *International Journal of Advances in Scientific Research*, 4(02), 88–100. DOI: 10.37547/ijasr-04-02-15

BCG. (2023).Reaching New Heights in Uncertain Times (2023). Reaching New Heights in Uncertain Times. https://media-publications.bcg.com/BCG_Most-Innovative-Companies-2023_Reaching-New-Heights-in-Uncertain-Times_May-2023.pdf

Blockchain in the food supply chain - What does the future look like? (n.d.). Blockchain in the Food Supply Chain - What Does the Future Look Like? https://tech.walmart.com/content/walmart-global-tech/en_us/blog/post/blockchain-in-the-food-supply-chain.html

Chabhadia, N., Jain, P., & Doshi, S. (2024, March). A review on digital manufacturing systems. In *AIP Conference Proceedings* (Vol. 3013, No. 1). AIP Publishing. DOI: 10.1063/5.0202021

Chen, M., Mao, S., & Liu, Y. (2018). Big data: A survey. *Mobile Networks and Applications*, 19(2), 171–209. DOI: 10.1007/s11036-013-0489-0

Companies Are Satisfied with Business Outcomes from Big Data and Recognize Big Data as Very Important to Their Digital Transformation, Accenture Study Shows. (n.d.). https://newsroom.accenture.com/news/2014/companies-are-satisfied-with-business-outcomes-from-big-data-and-recognize-big-data-as-very-important-to-their-digital-transformation-accenture-study-shows

Gartner (2017). Prepare for the impact of digital twins. https://www.gartner.com/smarterwithgartner/prepare-for-the-impact-of-digital-twins

Gibson, I., Rosen, D., & Stucker, B. (2014). Additive Manufacturing Technologies: 3D Printing, Rapid Prototyping, and Direct Digital Manufacturing. Springer. https://www.mckinsey.com/~/media/BAB489A30B724BECB5DEDC41E9BB9FAC.ashx

Huang, Y., Leu, M. C., & Mazumder, J. (2013). A review of 3D printing technologies for soft polymer materials. *Virtual and Physical Prototyping*, 8(3), 187–200.

HUBS. (2021). Additive manufacturing trend report 2021. https://f.hubspotusercontent10.net/hubfs/4075618/Additive%20manufacturing%20trend%20report%202021.pdf

IFR International Federation of Robotics. (n.d.). *World Robotics 2023 Report: Asia ahead of Europe and the Americas.* https://ifr.org/ifr-press-releases/news/world-robotics-2023-report-asia-ahead-of-europe-and-the-americas

IMOH, I. (2024). A Technical Survey on The Role of Robotics in Conventional Manufacturing Process: An Element of Industry 4.0. *FUPRE Journal of Scientific and Industrial Research (FJSIR), 8*(2), 172-192.

Industries & Technologies. (n.d.). Energy.gov. https://www.energy.gov/eere/iedo/industries-technologies

Irpan, M., & Shaddiq, S. (2024). Industry 4.0 and Industry 5.0—Inception, Conception, Perception, and Rethinking Loyalty Employment. *INTERNATIONAL JOURNAL OF ECONOMICS, MANAGEMENT* [IJEMBIS]. *BUSINESS, AND SOCIAL SCIENCE*, 4(1), 95–114.

Ivanov, D., Dolgui, A., & Sokolov, B. (2019). The Ripple Effect in supply chains: Trade-off 'efficiency-flexibility-resilience' in disruption management. *International Journal of Production Research*, 57(3), 829–846. DOI: 10.1080/00207543.2018.1488086

Jesuthasan, R. (2018, October 11). *What we often get wrong about automation.* Harvard Business Review. https://hbr.org/2018/10/what-we-often-get-wrong-about-automation

Kamta, H., & Sharma, S. K. (2024). Multiagent-Based Manufacturing: Foundations, Applications, and Future Directions. In *The Convergence of Self-Sustaining Systems With AI and IoT* (pp. 261-279). IGI Global.

Kandarkar, P. C., & Ravi, V. (2024). Investigating the impact of smart manufacturing and interconnected emerging technologies in building smarter supply chains. *Journal of Manufacturing Technology Management*, 35(5), 984–1009. DOI: 10.1108/JMTM-11-2023-0498

Kokotinis, G., Michalos, G., Arkouli, Z., & Makris, S. (2024). A Behavior Trees-based architecture towards operation planning in hybrid manufacturing. *International Journal of Computer Integrated Manufacturing*, 37(3), 324–349. DOI: 10.1080/0951192X.2023.2228254

Kolasani, S. (2024). Revolutionizing manufacturing, making it more efficient, flexible, and intelligent with Industry 4.0 innovations. *International Journal of Sustainable Development Through AI. ML and IoT*, 3(1), 1–17.

Lee, J., Bagheri, B., & Kao, H. A. (2015). A cyber-physical systems architecture for industry 4.0-based manufacturing systems. *Manufacturing Letters*, 3, 18–23. DOI: 10.1016/j.mfglet.2014.12.001

Lee, J., Kao, H. A., & Yang, S. (2014). Service innovation and smart analytics for industry 4.0 and big data environment. *Procedia CIRP*, 16, 3–8. DOI: 10.1016/j.procir.2014.02.001

Lee, J., Lapira, E., Bagheri, B., & Kao, H. A. (2013). Recent advances and trends in predictive manufacturing systems in big data environment. *Manufacturing Letters*, 1(1), 38–41. DOI: 10.1016/j.mfglet.2013.09.005

Lu, Y., & Ramakrishnan, R. (2019). Convergence of IoT and big data in healthcare. *Healthcare Informatics Research*, 25(3), 139–141. PMID: 31406605

Lu, Y., Xu, X., Huang, Y., & Duan, H. (2017). Real-time data-driven production planning and scheduling in cyber-physical manufacturing systems. *Robotics and Computer-integrated Manufacturing*, 44, 226–238.

Mallakpour, S., Radfar, Z., & Hussain, C. M. (2024). Advanced application of additive manufacturing in the footwear industry: from customized insoles to fully 3D-printed shoes. In *Medical Additive Manufacturing* (pp. 153–178). Elsevier. DOI: 10.1016/B978-0-323-95383-2.00015-9

Mastering AI quality for successful adoption of AI in manufacturing. (2024, January 16). World Economic Forum. https://www.weforum.org/agenda/2024/01/mastering-ai-quality-successful-adoption-ai-manufacturing/

McKinsey Global Institute. (2017). JOBS LOST, JOBS GAINED: WORKFORCE TRANSITIONS IN A TIME OF AUTOMATION. https://www.mckinsey.com/~/media/BAB489A30B724BECB5DEDC41E9BB9FAC.ashx

Monostori, L., Kádár, B., Bauernhansl, T., Kondoh, S., Kumara, S., Reinhart, G., Sauer, O., Schuh, G., Sihn, W., & Ueda, K. (2016). Cyber-physical systems in manufacturing. *CIRP Annals*, 65(2), 621–641. DOI: 10.1016/j.cirp.2016.06.005

Mourtzis, D., Panopoulos, N., Stavropoulos, P., & Papakostas, N. (2024). Artificial Intelligence for Production Management and Control Towards Mass Personalization of Global Networks. In *CIRP Novel Topics in Production Engineering* (Vol. 1, pp. 267–312). Springer Nature Switzerland. DOI: 10.1007/978-3-031-54034-9_8

Mourtzis, D., Vlachou, E., Milas, N., & Xanthakis, E. (2016). Big data analytics challenges and application in manufacturing. *Procedia CIRP*, 55, 126–131.

Mubarik, M. S., & Khan, S. A. (2024). Digital Supply Chain and Industry 4.0 Technologies. In *The Theory, Methods and Application of Managing Digital Supply Chains* (pp. 121-132). Emerald Publishing Limited.

Nair, J. (2024). Reconfiguration and transformation for resilience: Building service organizations towards sustainability. *Journal of Services Marketing*, 38(4), 404–425. DOI: 10.1108/JSM-04-2023-0144

Nithia, A. (2024). *SUCCESSFUL MANUFACTURING TRANSFORMATION: RAPIDLY GET OUT OF MANUFACTURING CRISIS AND ACHIEVE GLOBAL MANUFACTURING COMPETITIVENESS*. Partridge Publishing Singapore.

Odimarha, A. C., Ayodeji, S. A., & Abaku, E. A.Agnes Clare OdimarhaSodrudeen Abolore AyodejiEmmanuel Adeyemi Abaku. (2024). The role of technology in supply chain risk management: Innovations and challenges in logistics. *Magna Scientia Advanced Research and Reviews*, 10(2), 138–145. DOI: 10.30574/msarr.2024.10.2.0052

Ololade, Y. J.Yinka James Ololade. (2024). SME financing through fintech: An analytical study of trends in Nigeria and the USA. *International Journal of Management & Entrepreneurship Research*, 6(4), 1078–1102. DOI: 10.51594/ijmer.v6i4.1001

Payal, A., Nimbkar, S., Bharathi, R. M., Moses, J. A., & Anandharamakrishnan, C. (2024). Robotics and automation in the food industry. In *Emerging Technologies for the Food Industry* (pp. 31–62). Apple Academic Press. DOI: 10.1201/9781003413660-2

PwC. (2016). Industry 4.0: Building the digital enterprise.https://www.pwc.com/gx/en/industries/industries-4.0/landing-page/industry-4.0-building-your-digital-enterprise-april-2016.pdf

QuantumBlack. (2024, March 13). McKinsey & Company. https://www.mckinsey.com/capabilities/quantumblack/how-we-help-clients?cid=aob-pse-gaw-mog-mog-oth-

Rajput, S., & Kosta, Y. P. (2015). The adoption of CAD/CAM technologies in small manufacturing industry. *International Journal of Advanced Engineering Research and Applications*, 3(3), 1–8.

Ramesh, R., Jayakrishna, K., Karunamoorthy, L., & Kumaran, S. T. (2017). Review on CNC machining parameters optimization. *Materials Today: Proceedings*, 4(2), 1970–1979.

Rath, K. C., Khang, A., & Roy, D. (2024). The Role of Internet of Things (IoT) Technology in Industry 4.0 Economy. In *Advanced IoT Technologies and Applications in the Industry 4.0 Digital Economy* (pp. 1-28). CRC Press.

Roozkhosh, P., Pooya, A., Soleimani Fard, O., & Bagheri, R. (2024). Revolutionizing supply chain sustainability: An additive manufacturing-enabled optimization model for minimizing waste and costs. *Process Integration and Optimization for Sustainability*, 8(1), 285–300. DOI: 10.1007/s41660-023-00368-1

Roser, C., Akbulut, A., & Westkämper, E. (2016). Towards cyber-physical production systems. *Procedia CIRP*, 41, 173–178.

Schiuma, G., Santarsiero, F., Carlucci, D., & Jarrar, Y. (2024). Transformative leadership competencies for organizational digital transformation. *Business Horizons*, 67(4), 425–437. DOI: 10.1016/j.bushor.2024.04.004

Schuh, G., Anderl, R., & Gausemeier, J. (2017). Enabling the digital transformation of manufacturing with Industry 4.0. *CIRP Annals*, 66(2), 839–862.

Sergeeva, S., Belova, N., Shichiyakh, R., Bobrova, A., Vaslavskaya, I., Bankova, N., Vetrova, E., & Hajiyev, H. (2024). Implementation of Lean Manufacturing Principles and Fast Structured Logic Methods in the Organizational Culture: Addressing Challenges and Maximizing Efficiency. *International Journal of Sustainable Development and Planning*, 19(3), 1195–1201. DOI: 10.18280/ijsdp.190337

Sharma, R., & Gurung, S. (2024). Implementing Big Data Analytics and Machine Learning for Predictive Maintenance in Manufacturing Facilities in South Korea. *AI. IoT and the Fourth Industrial Revolution Review*, 14(2), 1–17.

Singh, N., Panigrahi, P. K., Zhang, Z., & Jasimuddin, S. M. (2024). Cyber-physical systems: A bibliometric analysis of literature. *Journal of Intelligent Manufacturing*, •••, 1–37. DOI: 10.1007/s10845-024-02380-9

Singha, R., & Singha, S. (2024). Educational Innovation Transforming Higher Education for Workforce Readiness. In *Advancing Student Employability Through Higher Education* (pp. 37–55). IGI Global. DOI: 10.4018/979-8-3693-0517-1.ch003

Statista. (2023, July 27). *IoT connected devices worldwide 2019-2030* | Statista. https://www.statista.com/statistics/1183457/iot-connected-devices-worldwide/

Subramani, R., Mustafa, M. A., Ghadir, G. K., Al-Tmimi, H. M., Alani, Z. K., Haridas, D., ... & Kumar, A. P. (2024). Advancements in 3D printing materials: A comparative analysis of performance and applications. *Applied Chemical Engineering*, 3867-3867.

Taherdoost, H. (2024). *Digital Transformation Roadmap: From Vision to Execution*. CRC Press. DOI: 10.1201/9781003471226

Takeda-Berger, S. L., & Frazzon, E. M. (2024). An inventory data-driven model for predictive-reactive production scheduling. *International Journal of Production Research*, 62(9), 3059–3083. DOI: 10.1080/00207543.2023.2217297

Tao, F., Cheng, J., Qi, Q., Zhang, M., Zhang, H., & Sui, F. (2018). Digital twin-driven product design, manufacturing and service with big data. *International Journal of Advanced Manufacturing Technology*, 94(9-12), 3563–3576. DOI: 10.1007/s00170-017-0233-1

Thoben, K. D., Wiesner, S., & Wuest, T. (2017). State of the art and challenges for digitalization in the manufacturing industry. *IFAC-PapersOnLine*, 50(1), 9995–10000.

Varone, A., Heilmann, Z., Porruvecchio, G., & Romanino, A. (2024). Solar parking lot management: An IoT platform for smart charging EV fleets, using real-time data and production forecasts. *Renewable & Sustainable Energy Reviews*, 189, 113845. DOI: 10.1016/j.rser.2023.113845

Wang, S., Wan, J., Zhang, D., Li, D., & Zhang, C. (2016). Towards smart factory for Industry 4.0: A self-organized multi-agent system with big data based feedback and coordination. *Computer Networks*, 101, 158–168. DOI: 10.1016/j.comnet.2015.12.017

Weller, C., Kleer, R., & Piller, F. T. (2015). Economic implications of 3D printing: Market structure models in light of additive manufacturing revisited. *International Journal of Production Economics*, 164, 43–56. DOI: 10.1016/j.ijpe.2015.02.020

Whig, P., Kouser, I. S., Bhatia, A. B., Nadikattu, I. R. R., & Alkali, Y. J. (2024). 6 IoT Industrial. *Wireless Communication Technologies: Roles, Responsibilities, and Impact of IoT, 6G, and Blockchain Practices*, 101.

Wohlers Associates. (2023, May 31). *Wohlers Report (2023)*. Wohlers Associates. https://wohlersassociates.com/product/wr2023/

Work-Related fatalities up nearly six percent in 2022. (n.d.). American Society of Safety Professionals. https://www.assp.org/news-and-articles/work-related-fatalities-up-nearly-six-percent-in-2022

World Bank. (2023). Food-Security-Update 2023 https://thedocs.worldbank.org/en/doc/40ebbf38f5a6b68bfc11e5273e1405d4-0090012022/related/Food-Security-Update-XCVI-November-30-23.pdf. Retrieved on 29th May 2024.

Yazdi, M. (2024). Digital Twins and Virtual Prototyping for Industrial Systems. In *Advances in Computational Mathematics for Industrial System Reliability and Maintainability* (pp. 155–168). Springer Nature Switzerland. DOI: 10.1007/978-3-031-53514-7_9

Zhou, L., Miller, J., Vezza, J., Mayster, M., Raffay, M., Justice, Q., Al Tamimi, Z., Hansotte, G., Sunkara, L. D., & Bernat, J. (2024). Additive Manufacturing: A Comprehensive Review. *Sensors (Basel)*, 24(9), 2668. DOI: 10.3390/s24092668 PMID: 38732776

Chapter 8
OpenStreetMap Empowering Digital Infrastructure for Emerging Markets

Munir Ahmad
https://orcid.org/0000-0003-4836-6151
Survey of Pakistan, Pakistan

Trupti Dandekar Humnekar
https://orcid.org/0000-0002-5676-0100
Jain University, India

Maida Maqsood
Government College Women University, Sialkot, Pakistan

Houssem Chemingui
https://orcid.org/0000-0002-3351-250X
Brest Business School, France

ABSTRACT

OpenStreetMap offers significant advantages for emerging markets, including cost-effectiveness, local knowledge utilization, scalability, adaptability, and integration with digital services. These benefits empower communities to map their environments, fostering economic growth, mobility, and access to services. OSM's democratized mapping data enables local entrepreneurs to innovate without high financial burdens. Leveraging local knowledge ensures maps are accurate and up-to-date, reflecting dynamic infrastructure landscapes and fostering community resilience. However, limited internet connectivity, low digital literacy, inadequate mapping resources,

DOI: 10.4018/979-8-3693-5723-1.ch008

and political and social barriers can hinder OSM's effective use. Ensuring data accuracy and sustaining community engagement are crucial. Solutions like offline editing tools, lightweight mapping applications, community-driven network initiatives, and training and continuous support are essential.

INTRODUCTION

The digital revolution has fundamentally reshaped our interactions with the world, revolutionizing how we navigate and engage with our surroundings (Fischer et al., 2020; Lazzeretti, 2022). Central to this transformation is the availability of precise and current spatial data, which forms the bedrock of modern digital landscapes. Yet, in numerous emerging markets, the dearth of dependable geospatial information continues to impede progress, stalling developmental initiatives and limiting the expansive capabilities of digital technologies. The absence of comprehensive and freely accessible geospatial data in emerging markets presents a formidable obstacle. Conventional approaches to map generation are frequently prohibitively expensive and labor-intensive, resulting in extensive regions being left unmapped.

This deficiency in data severely impedes the advancement of essential digital services such as ride-hailing applications, navigation systems, and disaster response platforms. These services are reliant upon up-to-date geographical data to operate with efficacy and reliability (R. Liu et al., 2022; Sarker et al., 2020; Topete et al., 2024; Tzavella et al., 2022; Wang, Zhang, et al., 2024; Yan, 2024; Yang et al., 2024). Without access to updated maps, urban planning initiatives are stymied, transportation networks struggle to optimize efficiency, and emergency responders face heightened challenges in reaching those in need swiftly. The unmet demand for geospatial information perpetuates a cycle of underdevelopment, hindering economic growth and societal resilience in regions where reliable infrastructure is most crucial. Addressing this disparity is paramount to unlocking the full potential of digital innovation in emerging markets, fostering inclusive development, and improving the quality of life across diverse communities.

OpenStreetMap (OSM) presents a compelling remedy to this pressing challenge. Functioning as a collaborative platform, OSM enables and empowers local communities to actively participate in mapping their immediate environments (Gjura Godec & Nikšič, 2023; Herfort et al., 2021; Muhamad et al., 2023; Schröder-Bergen, 2024). This inclusive approach not only cultivates a sense of ownership among community members but also guarantees that the mapped data accurately portrays the dynamic realities of rapidly evolving regions. By harnessing local knowledge and insights, OSM fills critical gaps in geospatial information that traditional mapping methods often overlook or struggle to update promptly. Moreover, OSM's collaborative model facilitates the continuous improvement and validation of data over time. This iterative process ensures that the maps remain current and relevant, reflecting ongoing developments and changes in infrastructure and geography. As a result, digital services and innovations that rely on accurate spatial data, such as urban planning tools, logistics optimization systems, and disaster preparedness applications, can operate more effectively and adaptably in these diverse and often challenging environments.

By empowering communities to contribute their local expertise, OpenStreetMap not only enhances the accessibility and reliability of geographical data but also strengthens resilience and fosters sustainable development in emerging markets (Ahmad, 2023, 2024; Ahmad & Ali, 2023; Borkowska & Pokonieczny, 2022; Van Den Hoek et al., 2021). This grassroots approach to mapping not only bridges existing data gaps but also lays a foundation for inclusive growth and equitable access to digital resources across diverse communities worldwide. Therefore, this chapter aims to demonstrate how OpenStreetMap empowers digital infrastructure for emerging markets. We explore the functionalities of OSM, its advantages for developing regions, and the challenges encountered in implementing this approach. The chapter also discusses the future potential of OSM in bridging the digital divide and fostering sustainable development in emerging markets.

FUNCTIONALITIES OF OPENSTREETMAP

OpenStreetMap can provide a robust platform for communities in emerging markets, offering a suite of features designed to facilitate the creation, access, and utilization of high-quality geospatial data.

Collaborative Mapping

OSM thrives on inclusivity, inviting anyone with a smartphone or internet access to contribute their local knowledge. This participatory approach can empower users to enrich the map with diverse data points, including:

- Users can map various linear elements such as roads (whether paved, unpaved, or tracks), rivers, streams, canals, power lines, and other infrastructure crucial for connectivity and development planning.
- OSM allows mapping of essential area features like buildings, parks, forests, agricultural lands, cemeteries, and other land uses that define the local landscape and community infrastructure.

- Users can mark and detail points of interest vital for community life, such as hospitals, schools, shops, bus stops, ATMs, historical landmarks, and recreational facilities, enhancing the map's utility for navigation and resource planning.
- Beyond basic mapping, contributors can add nuanced attributes to enhance data accuracy and usefulness. This includes information like street names, building heights, details about one-way streets, accessibility features for persons with disabilities, and other specific characteristics that enhance the map's functionality for diverse user needs.

By facilitating collaborative mapping, OSM not only democratizes access to spatial data but also ensures that the map reflects local realities accurately (Herfort et al., 2021). This grassroots effort not only bridges information gaps but also empowers communities to make informed decisions about urban planning (Atwal et al., 2022; Cohen & Dalyot, 2021), disaster preparedness (San Martin & Painho, 2019), economic development (B. Liu et al., 2020; Wang, Zheng, et al., 2024), and public services (Truden et al., 2022). As a result, OSM serves as a catalyst for inclusive growth and sustainable development in emerging markets, fostering resilience and community empowerment through accessible and accurate geospatial information.

Open Data Licensing

Open Data Licensing is a cornerstone of OSM's appeal, offering substantial advantages over proprietary mapping solutions. OSM adopts an open data approach, licensing its data under the Open Data Commons Open Database License (ODbL). This licensing framework grants unrestricted access to OSM's map data, empowering users worldwide to freely access, download, modify, and distribute geographic information for any purpose, including commercial ventures (Le Guilcher et al., 2022; Sarretta et al., 2023). The ODbL enables a dynamic ecosystem of innovation by removing barriers that traditionally restrict access to proprietary data. This openness encourages collaboration among developers, researchers, and community contributors, fostering the creation of diverse and innovative location-based services. Furthermore, the flexibility of the ODbL promotes transparency and accountability in how geographic data is used and shared. It ensures that improvements and updates made to the map by contributors remain accessible to the global community, continually enriching the quality and accuracy of the data. This collaborative model not only democratizes access to geospatial information but also empowers local stakeholders to actively participate in the digital economy, driving economic growth and social development in their regions.

Data Quality Tools

Maintaining high data accuracy is paramount for OpenStreetMap, and the platform employs several robust mechanisms to achieve this goal as elaborated below.

- OSM utilizes version control to track every edit made to the map. This feature allows users to view the history of changes and revert to previous versions if needed, ensuring transparency and accountability in the editing process (Sarkar & Anderson, 2022).
- OSM implements a user reputation system to recognize and reward active contributors who consistently make accurate edits (D. Zhang et al., 2021). Contributors earn reputation scores based on the quality and reliability of their contributions over time. Higher reputation scores increase the trustworthiness of their edits, helping to maintain overall data integrity.
- OSM provides validation tools that enable users to compare map data with satellite imagery and other authoritative sources. This functionality helps identify discrepancies, such as missing roads or misplaced landmarks, allowing contributors to propose corrections promptly. By integrating these tools into the editing workflow, OSM enhances the accuracy and completeness of its map data (Kashian et al., 2019).
- Local communities play a crucial role in verifying and validating data contributed to OSM (Minghini et al., 2022). Local mappers, who possess intimate knowledge of their surroundings, review and confirm the accuracy of data entries. This grassroots verification process ensures that the map reflects current on-the-ground conditions and local nuances accurately.

Offline Maps

Recognizing the variability of internet access in emerging markets, OpenStreetMap offers robust support for offline maps, providing users with the ability to download map data for specific regions. This functionality is particularly valuable where reliable internet connectivity is scarce or unavailable altogether.

- OSM's offline map feature allows users to download detailed map data onto their devices, including smartphones, tablets, and GPS devices. Once downloaded, users can access these maps without requiring a continuous internet connection. This capability ensures that individuals and organizations can navigate urban and rural areas, plan routes, and utilize location-based services even in remote or poorly connected regions.

- OSM enables users to customize their offline map downloads by selecting specific regions or areas of interest. This flexibility allows users to tailor their offline maps based on their navigation needs, whether for local commuting, tourism, fieldwork, or emergency response.
- OSM provides mechanisms for offline map users to periodically update their downloaded map data. This ensures that users have access to the most current information available, including recent edits and additions contributed by the OSM community. Users can sync their offline maps when they have access to the internet, keeping their maps relevant and up-to-date.
- The availability of offline maps through OSM supports various community needs, such as improved transportation logistics, emergency preparedness, and access to healthcare services. Local businesses, tourism operators, and humanitarian organizations can leverage offline maps to enhance their operations and serve local populations more effectively.

ADVANTAGES OF OSM FOR EMERGING MARKETS

OpenStreetMap offers a compelling set of advantages that make it particularly valuable for emerging markets.

Cost-Effectiveness

Traditional methods of map creation often involve substantial expenses, including the procurement of expensive surveying equipment and licensing fees for proprietary software. OSM revolutionizes this paradigm by harnessing the collective efforts of local communities. Through crowdsourcing, individuals contribute their local knowledge and map their surroundings at minimal cost, significantly reducing the financial barriers to creating and updating accurate maps. This democratization of mapping data empowers local entrepreneurs and organizations to innovate and develop location-based services without the upfront investment typically required by proprietary mapping solutions. For instance, a startup in a developing country can utilize OSM data to launch a ride-hailing application, providing essential transportation services to communities without the financial burden of high licensing fees. By leveraging OSM's open data model, entrepreneurs can focus resources on enhancing service quality and expanding market reach, thereby fostering economic growth and improving mobility options for local residents.

Local Knowledge

OpenStreetMap stands out in emerging markets by harnessing the power of local knowledge to capture the dynamic and rapidly evolving infrastructure landscapes (Fonte et al., 2019; Klonner et al., 2021). In many emerging markets, infrastructure development is rapid and often informal. OSM enables local residents—who possess intimate knowledge of their neighborhoods—to actively contribute to mapping efforts. This grassroots approach allows for the timely inclusion of newly built roads, paths through informal settlements, and other local features that may not be captured by traditional top-down mapping methods. As a result, OSM maps evolve continuously to reflect the current state of infrastructure development, providing a comprehensive and up-to-date resource for planners, developers, and service providers.

OSM's inclusive platform encourages residents from all walks of life to participate in mapping their surroundings. Whether through mobile devices or community mapping events, individuals can contribute details about their communities that are crucial for various applications. For instance, local knowledge can pinpoint hidden footpaths used by residents daily but overlooked by official maps, improving accessibility and connectivity within neighborhoods. The local knowledge integrated into OSM has profound implications for practical applications. For instance, accurate maps aid emergency responders in navigating remote villages during crises, ensuring timely assistance reaches those in need (Minghini et al., 2022; Tzavella et al., 2022). Similarly, logistics companies can use detailed maps to optimize delivery routes and expand services to previously unmapped areas, enhancing economic opportunities and access to goods and services.

By empowering communities to map their own environments, OSM fosters a sense of ownership and resilience. Local residents become active participants in shaping the digital infrastructure that supports their daily lives, fostering community pride and a shared responsibility for maintaining accurate geographic data.

Scalability and Adaptability

OpenStreetMap demonstrates exceptional scalability and adaptability in dynamic emerging markets, where rapid urbanization and infrastructure development are prevalent. OSM thrives on its collaborative model, allowing local contributors to continuously update map data to reflect real-time changes in their communities. This dynamic approach ensures that the map remains current amidst rapid urban growth, where new neighborhoods, roads, and facilities emerge frequently. Unlike static, pre-made maps that quickly become outdated, OSM evolves organically with local input, capturing the evolving landscape accurately. Local residents play a pivotal role in expanding and refining OSM's coverage. They contribute firsthand knowledge about newly constructed streets, buildings, and landmarks, ensuring that navigation apps, delivery services, and emergency responders have access to reliable and detailed information. This community involvement not only enhances the accuracy of the map data but also fosters a sense of ownership and pride among residents, who see their contributions making a tangible impact on their surroundings.

The scalability of OSM supports a wide range of practical applications in emerging markets. For example, as cities expand and new suburbs develop, OSM's updated maps facilitate efficient urban planning, transportation management, and service delivery. Navigation apps can seamlessly integrate new areas into their routing algorithms, improving accessibility for residents and businesses alike. Moreover, humanitarian organizations and disaster response teams rely on OSM's real-time updates to navigate and coordinate relief efforts in rapidly changing environments. OSM's adaptability extends beyond infrastructure updates to include cultural and local context. Contributors can add details about local amenities, cultural landmarks, and community services that are crucial for enhancing the map's utility and relevance to residents. This localized approach ensures that OSM not only keeps pace with physical changes but also reflects the unique characteristics and needs of diverse communities.

Integration with Digital Services

OpenStreetMap facilitates seamless integration with various digital services, unlocking a multitude of opportunities that are particularly crucial for development in emerging markets. Accurate and up-to-date maps are indispensable for ride-hailing services. OSM's detailed and freely accessible map data enables these platforms to operate effectively in emerging markets. By leveraging OSM, ride-hailing apps can expand their coverage to previously unmapped or underserved areas without the high costs associated with proprietary mapping solutions. This expansion enhances transportation accessibility, connects drivers with passengers more efficiently, and supports economic opportunities in local communities.

Delivery services can rely on location data to optimize delivery routes, reach new customers, and provide timely service. OSM's comprehensive map data allows these platforms to accurately navigate diverse urban and rural landscapes in emerging markets. Integration with OSM enables delivery platforms to expand their service areas, improve delivery efficiency, and enhance customer satisfaction by ensuring accurate delivery estimates and reliable service coverage. During emergencies, detailed and reliable maps are essential for effective disaster response and humanitarian aid efforts. OSM's open data can be integrated into disaster response platforms to identify affected areas, coordinate rescue operations, and allocate resources efficiently. The real-time updates and community-contributed data on OSM provide critical information to aid organizations and government agencies, facilitating swift and targeted responses to natural disasters, humanitarian crises, and public health emergencies in emerging markets.

CHALLENGES OF IMPLEMENTING OSM IN EMERGING MARKETS

While OSM offers significant advantages for emerging markets, several challenges can hinder its full potential.

Limited Internet Connectivity

Access to reliable internet connectivity is crucial for both contributing data and accessing OSM resources. However, many emerging markets face significant challenges with limited or unreliable internet infrastructure, particularly in rural areas (Hambly & Rajabiun, 2021; Morris et al., 2022; Y. Zhang et al., 2021). This limitation poses several barriers to the effective use and contribution of OSM.

Firstly, individuals in remote villages often lack access to internet-enabled devices or mobile data plans. The high-cost data services can be prohibitive (Reddick et al., 2020), leaving many potential contributors unable to participate in mapping activities. Even where devices are available, the connectivity may be intermittent or slow (Graves et al., 2021), further complicating efforts to upload data or interact with the OSM platform in real-time. Secondly, the infrastructure to support robust internet connectivity is often underdeveloped in these regions (Graves et al., 2021). Rural areas may have limited access to cell towers, fiber-optic networks, or broadband services, resulting in unreliable or slow internet speeds. This infrastructural gap means that even when communities are motivated to contribute to OSM, they face practical hurdles in doing so.

Moreover, limited internet bandwidth can make it difficult to download large map datasets for offline use, which is often necessary in areas with unstable connectivity. This constraint hinders the ability of local communities and organizations to utilize OSM data for planning and development projects. For instance, downloading detailed maps for use in field surveys, disaster response, or infrastructure development becomes a cumbersome process, potentially delaying critical activities. Additionally, the challenge of limited connectivity is compounded by the lack of local internet service providers (ISPs) capable of offering affordable and reliable services. In many emerging markets, the ISP market is either monopolized or underdeveloped, leading to high costs and poor service quality. This situation not only restricts access but also limits the potential for competitive improvements in infrastructure and service delivery.

To mitigate these challenges, innovative solutions such as offline editing tools, lightweight mapping applications, and community-driven network initiatives are essential. Offline editing tools allow users to collect and store data locally, which can then be uploaded when a stable internet connection becomes available. Lightweight mapping applications designed to function with minimal bandwidth can help users interact with the OSM platform more efficiently. Community-driven initiatives, such as the establishment of local Wi-Fi networks or the use of satellite internet services, can also play a crucial role in bridging the connectivity gap. By empowering communities to develop their own solutions, these initiatives can enhance both access and participation in OSM, fostering a more inclusive and comprehensive mapping effort.

Lack of Digital Literacy

In many emerging markets, a significant portion of the population may not be digitally literate (Jamil, 2021). This lack of familiarity with digital tools and platforms can prevent people from effectively using and contributing to OpenStreetMap, posing a substantial barrier to the platform's widespread adoption and utility. Firstly, digital literacy encompasses more than just the ability to use a smartphone or computer (Pangrazio et al., 2020). It includes understanding how to navigate online platforms, recognize and avoid misinformation, and utilize digital tools for specific tasks such as mapping and data entry (Radovanović et al., 2020). In regions where educational opportunities are limited, many individuals may lack these essential skills, making it difficult for them to engage with OSM. Training and educational programs are often necessary to build the requisite digital literacy. These programs need to cover a range of skills, from basic computer and internet use to more advanced topics like GPS data collection, map editing, and the principles of geospatial information systems (GIS). However, implementing these programs can be resource-intensive. It requires not only financial investment but also access to skilled trainers and appropriate training materials, which may be scarce in emerging markets.

Additionally, there is often a cultural component to digital literacy (Martínez-Bravo et al., 2022; Pangrazio et al., 2020). In some communities, especially those with limited exposure to technology, there may be resistance to adopting new tools and methods. Overcoming this resistance requires culturally sensitive approaches that involve local leaders and influencers who can advocate for the benefits of digital literacy and mapping. Sustained engagement is another critical factor. Initial training sessions, while important, are not sufficient on their own. Continuous support, follow-up training, and opportunities for practical application are necessary to ensure that newly acquired skills are retained and utilized. This ongoing support can be facilitated through online forums, local user groups, and partnerships with educational institutions or non-governmental organizations (NGOs).

Inadequate Mapping Resources

High-quality mapping requires various resources, including GPS devices, high-resolution satellite imagery, and up-to-date geographical data. In emerging markets, these resources may be scarce or too expensive for local communities and organizations to obtain. Without access to these tools, creating accurate and detailed maps becomes challenging. Firstly, GPS devices are essential for data collection in mapping projects (Nowak et al., 2020). These devices, which provide precise location data, are often costly and may not be readily available in emerging markets. Even when available, the cost can be prohibitive for individuals or small organizations. As a result, local mappers might rely on less accurate methods, which can lead to errors and inconsistencies in the maps.

Secondly, high-resolution satellite imagery is crucial for creating detailed maps (Corbane et al., 2021; Morell-Monzó et al., 2020). This imagery allows mappers to see and trace features such as roads, buildings, and natural landmarks. However, access to high-resolution satellite imagery often comes with a high price tag, putting it out of reach for many in emerging markets. Free alternatives, while helpful, may not offer the necessary resolution or frequency of updates needed for high-quality mapping. Up-to-date geographical data is another critical resource for mapping. This data includes information on boundaries, place names, infrastructure, and natural features. In many emerging markets, such data may either be outdated, incomplete, or entirely unavailable. The lack of current and comprehensive geographical data makes it difficult to create maps that accurately reflect the current state of an area, leading to potential issues in planning and development efforts.

Moreover, the availability of skilled personnel to collect, process, and analyze mapping data is often limited in emerging markets. Training individuals to use mapping tools and technologies effectively requires investment in education and capacity-building initiatives. Without a pool of trained mappers, even when tools and data are available, the quality of the maps produced may suffer. Additionally, the infrastructure needed to support mapping activities, such as reliable electricity and internet connectivity, is often inadequate in these regions. Mapping projects that rely on electronic devices and online platforms can be hampered by frequent power outages or slow, unreliable internet connections, further complicating efforts to produce high-quality maps.

Political and Social Barriers

In some regions, political instability or social tensions can significantly hinder mapping efforts. These barriers can manifest in various ways, impacting the accessibility, accuracy, and inclusiveness of OpenStreetMap initiatives.

Political Barriers

Firstly, governments may restrict access to certain geographical data or impose regulations that limit the use of mapping technologies. These restrictions can stem from national security concerns, where governments fear that detailed maps could be used for military or terrorist activities. In other cases, political regimes may wish to control or censor geographical information to maintain power or suppress dissent. Such restrictions can lead to incomplete or outdated maps, limiting their usefulness for development and humanitarian efforts. Moreover, political instability itself can disrupt mapping activities. In regions experiencing conflict, civil unrest, or frequent changes in government, the continuity and safety of mapping projects can be jeopardized. Mappers may face risks to their personal safety, and the logistical challenges of operating in unstable environments can be formidable. These conditions can lead to a lack of reliable data from affected areas, further complicating efforts to provide accurate and comprehensive maps.

Social Barriers

Social barriers, such as language differences and cultural practices, can also affect the participation of local communities in OSM initiatives. In many emerging markets, multiple languages and dialects are spoken, and the primary language used on OSM platforms may not be widely understood. This language barrier can prevent potential contributors from effectively engaging with the platform, reducing the diversity and richness of the data collected. Cultural practices and social norms can also impact participation. In some cultures, there may be gender norms or other social hierarchies that discourage certain groups, such as women or lower social classes, from participating in public or technological activities. This exclusion can lead to a lack of representation and a narrow perspective in the mapping data, which may not fully reflect the needs and realities of all community members.

Data Accuracy and Validation

Ensuring the accuracy and reliability of contributed data is crucial for the success of OpenStreetMap. In emerging markets, where formal geographic data may be sparse, validating the information provided by contributors can be particularly challenging. There may also be fewer local experts available to review and correct inaccuracies, leading to potential errors in the maps.

In many emerging markets, official geographic data may be limited, outdated, or incomplete. This lack of baseline data makes it difficult to validate new contributions against authoritative sources. Without reliable reference points, ensuring the accuracy of user-contributed data becomes a significant challenge. **Moreover, c**ontributors to OSM come from diverse backgrounds and varying levels of expertise. While some may be highly skilled in mapping, others may be novices. This variation in skill levels can result in inconsistent data quality. Errors in data entry, misinterpretation of satellite imagery, and incorrect use of mapping tools can all contribute to inaccuracies.

Accurate mapping often requires local knowledge to correctly identify and label geographic features. In emerging markets, there may be a shortage of local experts who can review and validate contributed data. This lack of expertise can lead to persistent errors and reduce the overall reliability of the maps. Furthermore, many emerging markets are experiencing rapid development and urbanization. Roads, buildings, and other infrastructure can change quickly, making it challenging to keep maps up-to-date. Contributors may provide accurate data at the time of collection, but this data can quickly become outdated if not regularly updated and validated.

Sustainability of Community Engagement

Building and maintaining a vibrant community of contributors is essential for the ongoing success of OpenStreetMap. In emerging markets, sustaining community engagement can be particularly challenging due to economic constraints, limited access to technology, and competing priorities. Continuous support and motivation are needed to keep contributors active and involved in the mapping process. Many individuals in emerging markets face economic challenges that limit their ability to participate in voluntary activities like mapping. The need to prioritize work and family responsibilities over unpaid mapping contributions can lead to lower levels of engagement. Moreover, access to necessary technology, such as smartphones, computers, and reliable internet connectivity, is often limited in emerging markets. Without these tools, potential contributors may find it difficult to participate in OSM activities.

CONCLUSION

OpenStreetMap presents a transformative opportunity for emerging markets, providing significant advantages in cost-effectiveness, utilization of local knowledge, scalability, adaptability, and integration with digital services. These benefits enable communities to actively participate in mapping their environments, fostering economic growth, enhancing mobility, and improving access to essential services. The democratization of mapping data through OSM allows local entrepreneurs and organizations to innovate without the financial burdens associated with proprietary mapping solutions. By leveraging the power of local knowledge, OSM ensures that maps are accurate, up-to-date, and reflective of the dynamic infrastructure landscapes in emerging markets. This continuous community involvement not only enhances the quality of the map data but also instills a sense of ownership and resilience among residents.

However, the implementation of OSM in emerging markets is not without challenges. Limited internet connectivity, a lack of digital literacy, inadequate mapping resources, and political and social barriers can hinder the effective use and contribution to OSM. Additionally, ensuring the accuracy and validation of contributed data, as well as sustaining community engagement, are critical factors that need to be addressed to maximize the platform's potential. To overcome these obstacles, innovative solutions such as offline editing tools, lightweight mapping applications, and community-driven network initiatives are essential. Training and educational programs, culturally sensitive approaches, and continuous support are also vital for building digital literacy and maintaining active participation.

REFERENCES

Ahmad, M. (2023). Exploring the Role of OpenStreetMap in Mapping Religious Tourism in Pakistan for Sustainable Development. In J. P. D. M. Vítor, A. G. da R. N. João, L. de J. P. Maria, & A. de M. C. Liliana (Eds.), *Experiences, Advantages, and Economic Dimensions of Pilgrimage Routes* (pp. 23–40). IGI Global. DOI: 10.4018/978-1-6684-9923-8.ch002

Ahmad, M. (2024). Unleashing Business Potential: Harnessing OpenStreetMap for Intelligent Growth and Sustainability. In Singh, S., Rajest, S. S., Hadoussa, S., Obaid, A. J., & Regin, R. (Eds.), *Data-Driven Intelligent Business Sustainability* (pp. 177–198). IGI Global., DOI: 10.4018/979-8-3693-0049-7.ch013

Ahmad, M., & Ali, A. (2023). Mapping the future of sustainable development through cloud-based solutions: A case study of openstreetmap. In *Promoting Sustainable Management Through Technological Innovation* (pp. 153–176). IGI Global., DOI: 10.4018/978-1-6684-9979-5.ch011

Atwal, K. S., Anderson, T., Pfoser, D., & Züfle, A. (2022). Predicting building types using OpenStreetMap. *Scientific Reports*, 12(1), 19976. Advance online publication. DOI: 10.1038/s41598-022-24263-w PMID: 36404337

Borkowska, S., & Pokonieczny, K. (2022). Analysis of OpenStreetMap Data Quality for Selected Counties in Poland in Terms of Sustainable Development. *Sustainability (Basel)*, 14(7), 3728. Advance online publication. DOI: 10.3390/su14073728

Cohen, A., & Dalyot, S. (2021). Route planning for blind pedestrians using OpenStreetMap. *Environment and Planning. B, Urban Analytics and City Science*, 48(6), 1511–1526. Advance online publication. DOI: 10.1177/2399808320933907

Corbane, C., Syrris, V., Sabo, F., Politis, P., Melchiorri, M., Pesaresi, M., Soille, P., & Kemper, T. (2021). Convolutional neural networks for global human settlements mapping from Sentinel-2 satellite imagery. *Neural Computing & Applications*, 33(12), 6697–6720. Advance online publication. DOI: 10.1007/s00521-020-05449-7

Fischer, G., Lundin, J., & Lindberg, J. O. (2020). Rethinking and reinventing learning, education and collaboration in the digital age—From creating technologies to transforming cultures. *International Journal of Information and Learning Technology*, 37(5), 241–252. Advance online publication. DOI: 10.1108/IJILT-04-2020-0051

Fonte, C. C., Lopes, P., See, L., & Bechtel, B. (2019). Using OpenStreetMap (OSM) to enhance the classification of local climate zones in the framework of WUDAPT. *Urban Climate*, 28, 100456. Advance online publication. DOI: 10.1016/j.uclim.2019.100456

Gjura Godec, M., & Nikšič, M. (2023). Empowering Public Engagement in Spatial Planning: A Collaborative Mapping Approach. *Igra Ustvarjalnosti - Creativy Game, 2023*(11). DOI: 10.15292/IU-CG.2023.11.066-071

Graves, J. M., Abshire, D. A., Amiri, S., & Mackelprang, J. L. (2021). Disparities in Technology and Broadband Internet Access across Rurality: Implications for Health and Education. *Family & Community Health*, 44(4), 257–265. Advance online publication. DOI: 10.1097/FCH.0000000000000306 PMID: 34269696

Hambly, H., & Rajabiun, R. (2021). Rural broadband: Gaps, maps and challenges. *Telematics and Informatics*, 60, 101565. Advance online publication. DOI: 10.1016/j.tele.2021.101565

Herfort, B., Lautenbach, S., Porto de Albuquerque, J., Anderson, J., & Zipf, A. (2021). The evolution of humanitarian mapping within the OpenStreetMap community. *Scientific Reports*, 11(1), 3037. Advance online publication. DOI: 10.1038/s41598-021-82404-z PMID: 33542423

Jamil, S. (2021). From digital divide to digital inclusion: Challenges for wide-ranging digitalization in Pakistan. *Telecommunications Policy*, 45(8), 102206. Advance online publication. DOI: 10.1016/j.telpol.2021.102206

Kashian, A., Rajabifard, A., Richter, K. F., & Chen, Y. (2019). Automatic analysis of positional plausibility for points of interest in OpenStreetMap using coexistence patterns. *International Journal of Geographical Information Science*, 33(7), 1420–1443. Advance online publication. DOI: 10.1080/13658816.2019.1584803

Klonner, C., Usón, T. J., Aeschbach, N., & Höfle, B. (2021). Participatory Mapping and Visualization of Local Knowledge: An Example from Eberbach, Germany. *International Journal of Disaster Risk Science*, 12(1), 56–71. Advance online publication. DOI: 10.1007/s13753-020-00312-8

Lazzeretti, L. (2022). What is the role of culture facing the digital revolution challenge? Some reflections for a research agenda. *European Planning Studies*, 30(9), 1617–1637. Advance online publication. DOI: 10.1080/09654313.2020.1836133

Le Guilcher, A., Olteanu-Raimond, A. M., & Balde, M. B. (2022). Analysis of massive imports of open data in openstreetmap database: A study case for france. *ISPRS Annals of the Photogrammetry, Remote Sensing and Spatial Information Sciences*, 5(4), 99–106. Advance online publication. DOI: 10.5194/isprs-annals-V-4-2022-99-2022

Liu, B., Shi, Y., Li, D. J., Wang, Y. D., Fernandez, G., & Tsou, M. H. (2020). An economic development evaluation based on the openstreetmap road network density: The case study of 85 cities in china. *ISPRS International Journal of Geo-Information*, 9(9), 517. Advance online publication. DOI: 10.3390/ijgi9090517 PMID: 33511044

Liu, R., Yu, H., Ren, Y., & Liu, S. (2022). The Analysis of Classification and Spatiotemporal Distribution Characteristics of Ride-Hailing Driver's Driving Style: A Case Study in China. *International Journal of Environmental Research and Public Health*, 19(15), 9734. Advance online publication. DOI: 10.3390/ijerph19159734 PMID: 35955090

Martínez-Bravo, M. C., Chalezquer, C. S., & Serrano-Puche, J. (2022). Dimensions of Digital Literacy in the 21st Century Competency Frameworks. *Sustainability (Basel)*, 14(3), 1867. Advance online publication. DOI: 10.3390/su14031867

Minghini, M., Sarretta, A., & Napolitano, M. (2022). OpenStreetMap Contribution to Local Data Ecosystems in COVID-19 Times: Experiences and Reflections from the Italian Case. *Data*, 7(4), 39. Advance online publication. DOI: 10.3390/data7040039

Morell-Monzó, S., Estornell, J., & Sebastiá-Frasquet, M. T. (2020). Article Comparison of Sentinel-2 and high-resolution imagery for mapping land abandonment in fragmented areas. *Remote Sensing (Basel)*, 12(12), 2062. Advance online publication. DOI: 10.3390/rs12122062

Morris, J., Morris, W., & Bowen, R. (2022). Implications of the digital divide on rural SME resilience. *Journal of Rural Studies*, 89, 369–377. Advance online publication. DOI: 10.1016/j.jrurstud.2022.01.005

Muhamad, N., Muhamad Hakimi, F. H., & Mahadzir, M. D. A. (2023). Community Activation for Disaster Risk Reduction Through OpenStreetMap: A Scoping Review. *Journal of Advanced Geospatial Science & Technology*, 3(2), 25–50. Advance online publication. DOI: 10.11113/jagst.v3n2.68

Nowak, M. M., Dzióbb, K., Ludwisiak, Ł., & Chmiel, J. (2020). Mobile GIS applications for environmental field surveys: A state of the art. In *Global Ecology and Conservation* (Vol. 23). DOI: 10.1016/j.gecco.2020.e01089

Pangrazio, L., Godhe, A. L., & Ledesma, A. G. L. (2020). What is digital literacy? A comparative review of publications across three language contexts. *E-Learning and Digital Media*, 17(6), 442–459. Advance online publication. DOI: 10.1177/2042753020946291

Radovanović, D., Holst, C., Banerjee Belur, S., Srivastava, R., Vivien Houngbonon, G., Le Quentrec, E., Miliza, J., Winkler, A. S., & Noll, J. (2020). Digital literacy key performance indicators for sustainable development. *Social Inclusion (Lisboa)*, 8(2), 151–167. Advance online publication. DOI: 10.17645/si.v8i2.2587

Reddick, C. G., Enriquez, R., Harris, R. J., & Sharma, B. (2020). Determinants of broadband access and affordability: An analysis of a community survey on the digital divide. *Cities (London, England)*, 106, 102904. Advance online publication. DOI: 10.1016/j.cities.2020.102904 PMID: 32921864

San Martin, R., & Painho, M. (2019). Geospatial preparedness: Empirical study of the joint effort to provide geospatial support to disaster response. *Transactions in GIS*, 23(3), 481–494. Advance online publication. DOI: 10.1111/tgis.12537

Sarkar, D., & Anderson, J. T. (2022). Corporate editors in OpenStreetMap: Investigating co-editing patterns. *Transactions in GIS*, 26(4), 1879–1897. Advance online publication. DOI: 10.1111/tgis.12910

Sarker, M. N. I., Peng, Y., Yiran, C., & Shouse, R. C. (2020). Disaster resilience through big data: Way to environmental sustainability. In *International Journal of Disaster Risk Reduction* (Vol. 51). DOI: 10.1016/j.ijdrr.2020.101769

Sarretta, A., Napolitano, M., & Minghini, M. (2023). OPENSTREETMAP AS AN INPUT SOURCE FOR PRODUCING GOVERNMENTAL DATASETS: THE CASE OF THE ITALIAN MILITARY GEOGRAPHIC INSTITUTE. *The International Archives of the Photogrammetry, Remote Sensing and Spatial Information Sciences, XLVIII-4/W7-2023*, 193–200. DOI: 10.5194/isprs-archives-XLVIII-4-W7-2023-193-2023

Schröder-Bergen, S. (2024). Crowd-Based Geodata Production and Platform Capitalism: The Case of OpenStreetMap. In *Geographies of the Platform Economy: Critical Perspectives* (pp. 49–59). Springer.

Topete, A., He, C., Protzko, J., Schooler, J., & Hegarty, M. (2024). How is GPS used? Understanding navigation system use and its relation to spatial ability. *Cognitive Research: Principles and Implications*, 9(1), 16. Advance online publication. DOI: 10.1186/s41235-024-00545-x PMID: 38504081

Truden, C., Kollingbaum, M. J., Reiter, C., & Schasché, S. E. (2022). A GIS-based analysis of reachability aspects in rural public transportation. *Case Studies on Transport Policy*, 10(3), 1827–1840. Advance online publication. DOI: 10.1016/j.cstp.2022.07.012

Tzavella, K., Skopeliti, A., & Fekete, A. (2022). Volunteered geographic information use in crisis, emergency and disaster management: A scoping review and a web atlas. *Geo-Spatial Information Science*. Advance online publication. DOI: 10.1080/10095020.2022.2139642

Van Den Hoek, J., Friedrich, H. K., Ballasiotes, A., Peters, L. E. R., & Wrathall, D. (2021). Development after displacement: Evaluating the utility of openstreetmap data for monitoring sustainable development goal progress in refugee settlements. *ISPRS International Journal of Geo-Information*, 10(3), 153. Advance online publication. DOI: 10.3390/ijgi10030153

Wang, Z., Zhang, Y., Jia, B., & Gao, Z. (2024). Comparative Analysis of Usage Patterns and Underlying Determinants for Ride-hailing and Traditional Taxi Services: A Chicago Case Study. *Transportation Research Part A, Policy and Practice*, 179, 103912. Advance online publication. DOI: 10.1016/j.tra.2023.103912

Wang, Z., Zheng, J., Han, C., Lu, B., Yu, D., Yang, J., & Han, L. (2024). Exploring the Potential of OpenStreetMap Data in Regional Economic Development Evaluation Modeling. *Remote Sensing (Basel)*, 16(2), 239. Advance online publication. DOI: 10.3390/rs16020239

Yan, Y. (2024). Research on optimal path planning technology for vehicle positioning and navigation system. *Applied Mathematics and Nonlinear Sciences*, 9(1), 20230397. Advance online publication. DOI: 10.2478/amns.2023.1.00397

Yang, X., Zhang, Y., Chen, X., Huang, L., & Qiu, X. (2024). Limitations and Management of Dynamic Navigation System for Locating Calcified Canals Failure. *Journal of Endodontics*, 50(1), 96–105. Advance online publication. DOI: 10.1016/j.joen.2023.10.010 PMID: 37890613

Zhang, D., Ge, Y., Stein, A., & Zhang, W. (2021). Ranking of VGI contributor reputation using an evaluation-based weighted pagerank. *Transactions in GIS*, 25(3), 1439–1459. Advance online publication. DOI: 10.1111/tgis.12735

Zhang, Y., Love, D. J., Krogmeier, J. V., Anderson, C. R., Heath, R. W., & Buckmaster, D. R. (2021). Challenges and Opportunities of Future Rural Wireless Communications. *IEEE Communications Magazine*, 59(12), 16–22. Advance online publication. DOI: 10.1109/MCOM.001.2100280

KEY TERMS AND DEFINITIONS

Collaborative mapping: refers to the process of creating and maintaining maps through the collective efforts of a community or group of contributors. This approach leverages the knowledge, skills, and resources of multiple individuals to produce detailed, accurate, and up-to-date maps. Collaborative mapping is often used in projects like OpenStreetMap, where volunteers contribute geographic data, or in crisis mapping, where crowdsourced information helps respond to emergencies.

Digital literacy: refers to the ability to effectively use digital technologies, tools, and platforms to find, evaluate, create, and communicate information. It encompasses a range of skills, including using computers, smartphones, the internet, and software applications, as well as understanding digital security, privacy, and the ethical use of technology. Digital literacy is crucial in today's information-driven society.

Digital services: are online services delivered through digital platforms, typically via the Internet. These services can include anything from e-commerce, online banking, and streaming media, to government services, cloud computing, and social media. Digital services are designed to be accessible, efficient, and user-friendly, often providing a digital alternative to traditional, physical services.

OpenStreetMap (OSM): is a collaborative, open-source mapping platform that allows users to create and edit a global map. It is freely accessible and maintained by a community of volunteers who contribute geographic data, such as roads, buildings, and landmarks. OSM is widely used for various purposes, including navigation, research, and urban planning, due to its comprehensive and regularly updated map data.

Spatial data: refers to information about the physical location and shape of objects on Earth, typically represented in coordinates and geometries such as points, lines, and polygons. This data is used in geographic information systems (GIS) to map, analyze, and interpret various phenomena on the Earth's surface. Examples include maps, satellite images, and GPS data.

Chapter 9
Catalyzing Growth: Charting a Path to 50 Lakh New Job Openings in India's IT and Software Sector

Natasha Saqib
https://orcid.org/0000-0003-1676-557X
University of Kashmir, India

Manasha Saqib
Islamic University of Science and Technology, India

ABSTRACT

The Indian Information Technology/Software industry has emerged as a prominent global force, exerting an unparalleled influence on the nation of India. This paper aims to explore the transformative potential of India's Information Technology (IT) and Software sector, with a focus on generating 50 lakh new job opportunities within the next two years. Through an analysis of key drivers such as digital transformation, emerging technologies, and government initiatives, the study identifies strategies for job creation. Findings suggest that by adopting a strategic approach towards skill development, innovation, and regulatory reforms, India can leverage its strengths in the sector to achieve this ambitious goal. The implications of achieving this target extend beyond economic growth, encompassing fostering innovation, enhancing technological advancement, and addressing unemployment challenges.

DOI: 10.4018/979-8-3693-5723-1.ch009

INTRODUCTION

The origins of India's IT industry can be traced back to the 1960s and 1970s when a few select organizations began developing software for export. However, it was in the early 1990s that the sector experienced a significant transformation with the liberalization of the Indian economy. This policy shift allowed foreign investments, technology imports, and the establishment of software technology parks. The liberalization era, coupled with India's strong education system, provided the impetus for the growth of IT services companies. Companies like Infosys, Wipro, and Tata Consultancy Services (TCS) emerged as pioneers, offering a range of services such as software development, maintenance, and business process outsourcing (BPO). They not only catered to the domestic market but also expanded their footprint on the global stage. The USA, the largest software and service market in the world, diversified business opportunities by using India's skilled labor. American MNCs played a role in showing that India has great IT software and services work talent. Both American, as well as Indian entrepreneurs, availed this opportunity by leveraging their business operations. India has become one of the largest IT capitals of the modern world, with all the top IT firms in the world present in the country. Bangalore city is known as Silicon Valley of India due to its dominance in exports, accounting for 77% of total revenue from the Indian IT industry (Malik & Anandarao, 2023). The Indian Information Technology/ Software industry is a global powerhouse today, and its impact on India has been incomparable. It has contributed immensely in positioning the country as a preferred investment destination amongst global investors and creating hug job opportunities in India (MEIT report, 2023). According to National Association of Software and Service Companies (NASSCOM), the Indian IT industry's revenue touched US$ 227 billion in FY22, a 15.5% growth and is estimated to have touched US$ 245 billion in FY23(Figure 1).

Figure 1. Domestic revenue of the information technology industry in India from financial year 2019 to 2022, with estimate of 2023 (in billion U.S. dollars) (Statista, 2023)

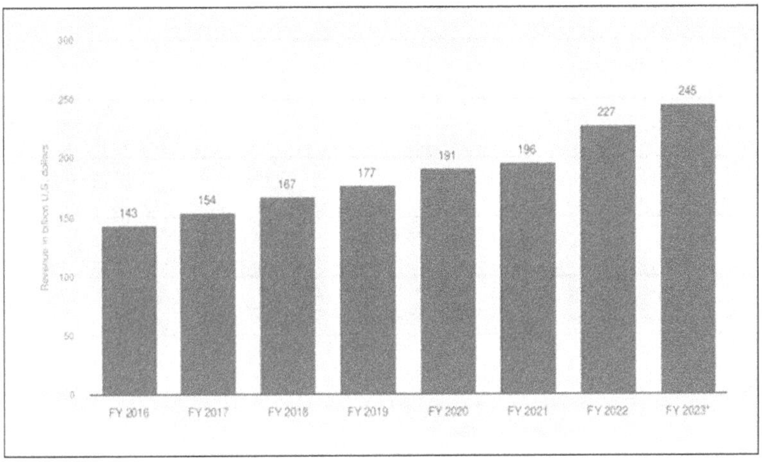

Based on estimates provided by Gartner, it is projected that the expenditure on information technology (IT) in India will witness a rise to US$ 101.8 billion in the year 2022, compared to an estimated amount of US$ 81.89 billion in the preceding year of 2021. In the fiscal year 2020, the data annotation market in India was valued at US$ 250 million, with the United States market accounting for 62% of the total value. The software industry in India witnessed a revenue of 7.3 billion U.S. dollars in the year 2022, with enterprise software contributing the highest revenue of 1.5 billion dollars. Subsequently, the application development software segment reached a valuation of $1.8 billion. The software industry's revenue during the 1990s ranged from approximately 30 to 40 million dollars (Figure 2).

Figure 2. Revenue of the software market worldwide from 2016 to 2027, by segment (in billion U.S. dollars) (Statista, 2023)

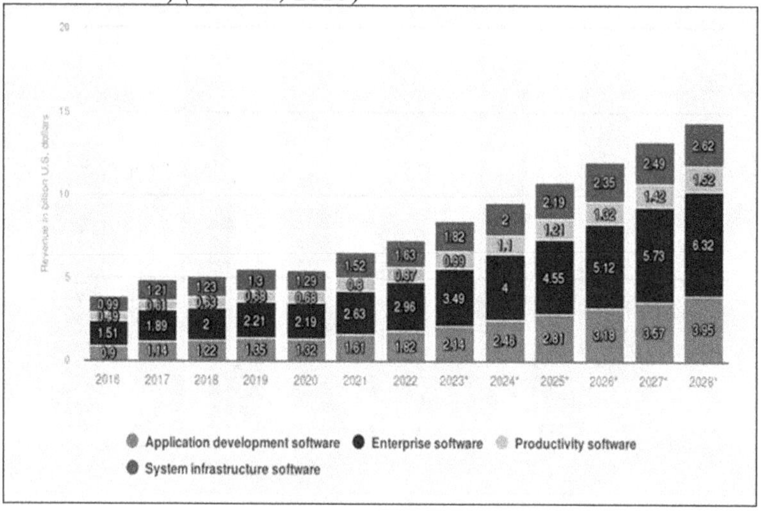

The Indian information technology (IT) industry holds a prominent position on the global stage and has been steadily making significant contributions to the generation of employment opportunities. In the fiscal year 2023, the Information Technology (IT) industry experienced a notable increase in employment, with the addition of 290,000 new jobs. As a result, the total workforce within the industry reached a significant figure of 5.4 million individuals. The IT sector in India is recognized as the largest source of employment and has given rise to a wide range of opportunities for leading IT companies. These firms have demonstrated their competence in providing services to clients worldwide, both within the country and abroad. Furthermore, the emergence of new technologies has opened up a whole new spectrum of possibilities for these companies. The Indian IT/Software industry is known for its cost-effectiveness, high quality, strong reliability, efficient delivery, and utilization of cutting-edge technologies on a global scale.

Table 1. Employment in Indian IT/software industry

Description	2018-19	2019-20	2020-21	2021-22	2022-23 (E)
Employment (In Millions)	4.1	4.36	4.47	5.1	5.4
Net Addition	200000	205000	138000	445000	290000

Expected Potential for Employment Creation in the Sector

The expected potential for employment creation in India's IT and software sector is substantial, and it can play a pivotal role in driving economic growth and job generation. The factors that contribute to this potential and provide an estimate of the employment opportunities that can be created in the sector over the next few years are as follows

- ***Digital Transformation***: The potential of the digital transformation of industrial entities has garnered significant attention in recent years. According to Vial (2019), the organization commits to generating novel market prospects, fostering innovative product development, enhancing adaptability in production procedures, and augmenting overall operational effectiveness. The current and continuous process of digital transformation across various industries is resulting in a growing need for information technology (IT) and software solutions. Organizations are increasingly inclined towards the integration of digital technologies in order to sustain their competitiveness, thereby generating a rising demand for IT professionals and software developers.
- ***Emerging Technologies***: The concept of Industry 4.0 is a transformative phenomenon that holds significant implications for a wide range of industries across the globe. Industry 4.0 serves as a technological catalyst that facilitates rapid growth by enabling systematic adaptation and the utilization of state-of-the-art engineering tools. The successful realization of Industry 4.0 relies on the integration and collaboration of various key technologies, including Internet of Things (IoT), Blockchain, Artificial Intelligence (AI), Augmented Reality (AR), 3D printing, Big-data analytics, and cloud computing. According to the study conducted by Shrivastava et al. (2023), Organizations are allocating resources towards these domains in order to maintain a competitive edge in terms of technological advancements, resulting in a notable increase in the need for professionals with expertise in these particular disciplines.
- ***Global Demand***: India has gained recognition for its exports of IT services, and there is a persistent increase in the worldwide demand for outsourcing and offshoring services. Based on the findings of Malik and Anandarao (2023), it can be observed that India possessed a notable comparative advantage in the field of computer and information services (CIS) in comparison to China, the Philippines, Malaysia, and Brazil. This suggests that India's relative export performance in this sector was superior to that of China, Malaysia, the Philippines, and Brazil. According to the cross-service index, India exhibited a higher degree of relative specialization in the Commonwealth of

Independent States (CIS) compared to the average level of specialization observed globally. The fiscal year 2022 witnessed India's IT sector exports reaching approximately 178 billion U.S. dollars. The export market was largely controlled by IT services, which accounted for a significant share of 104 billion dollars. The information technology exports have emerged as the dominant force within the industry, accounting for a significant portion of the overall revenue. Nevertheless, the domestic market has exhibited promising patterns as well. This situation provides a favorable circumstance for Indian IT companies to augment their labor force in order to cater to the demands of global clientele. In fiscal year 2023, India's IT export revenue experienced a growth of 11.4% in constant currency terms, reaching a total of US$ 194 billion. The fiscal year 2022 witnessed exports from the Indian IT industry amounting to a total of US$ 178 billion. The exportation of information technology (IT) services has emerged as the primary driver, constituting over 51% of the overall export of IT goods and services, encompassing hardware as well. During the fiscal year 2021, Business Process Management (BPM), Engineering and Research & Development (ER&D), and software products export each contributed 20.78% to the overall exports in the field of Information Technology (IT). According to projections, the market for Engineering Research and Development (ER&D) is anticipated to expand significantly, reaching a value of US$ 42 billion by the year 2022. (Figure 3) .

Figure 3. Value of export revenue of the IT sector across India from financial year 2016 to 2022, with an estimate for 2023 (in billion U.S. dollars) (Statista, 2023)

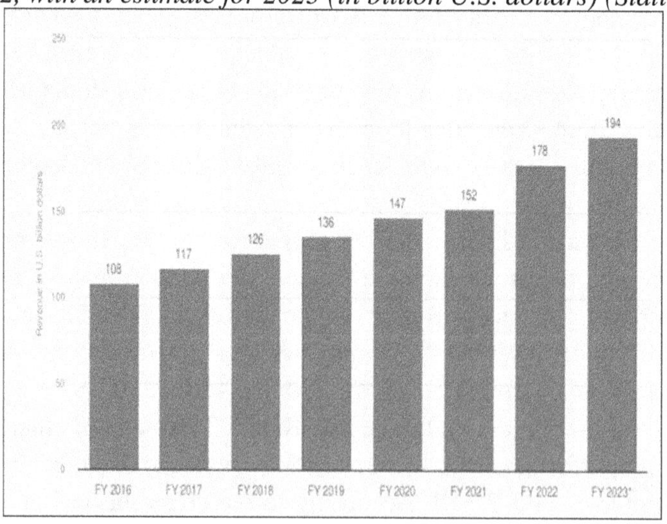

In financial year 2022, the United States was estimated to remain the biggest importer of India's IT and BPM industry, with an export revenue share of 62 percent. With a much smaller share of 17 percent, the United Kingdom maintained its second position (Figure-4).

Figure 4. Share of information technology and business process management industry export revenue in India in financial year 2022, by region (Statista, 2023)

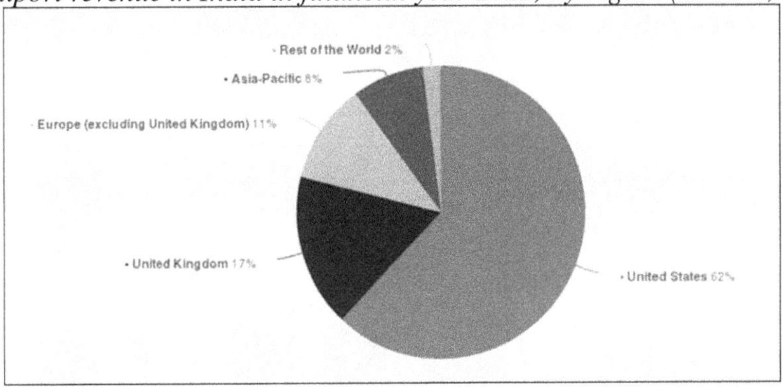

- ***Startups and Innovation***: India's burgeoning entrepreneurial performance has led certain analysts to regard it as the prospective Asian miracle (Huang, 2008). India's startup ecosystem is notable for being the third largest in the world, according to projections from Startup India (2019). It is anticipated that this ecosystem will experience a year-on-year growth rate of 12-15%. Furthermore, there is a particular emphasis on technology and software within this ecosystem. In the year 2022, the Indian startup ecosystem garnered a cumulative funding amounting to approximately 25 billion U.S. dollars. Among the cumulative funding of 25 billion U.S. dollars acquired by Indian startups, fintech startups secured a funding amount exceeding four billion U.S. dollars, while Ecommerce startups received a funding of four billion dollars. In the year 2022, the Indian market witnessed the emergence of more than 303 enterprisetech startups, which collectively secured funding through various deals amounting to approximately four billion U.S. dollars. Moreover, during that specific time frame, a significant portion of the funding allocated to enterprise technology, specifically 79 percent, was directed towards the Software as a Service (SaaS) industry. These startup companies necessitate the employment of proficient individuals, thereby fostering job generation as they progress and broaden their activities. In the year 2022, the total count of employment opportunities documented by established startups participating in the Startup India initiative, administered by the central government of the country, exceeded 238,767. There was a notable rise in comparison to the preceding year. According to official government data, there has been an increase in employment opportunities by approximately 860,000 positions since the implementation of the Startup India initiative (Figure -5).

Figure 5. Number of reported jobs within Startup India initiative from 2016 to 2022 (Statista, 2023)

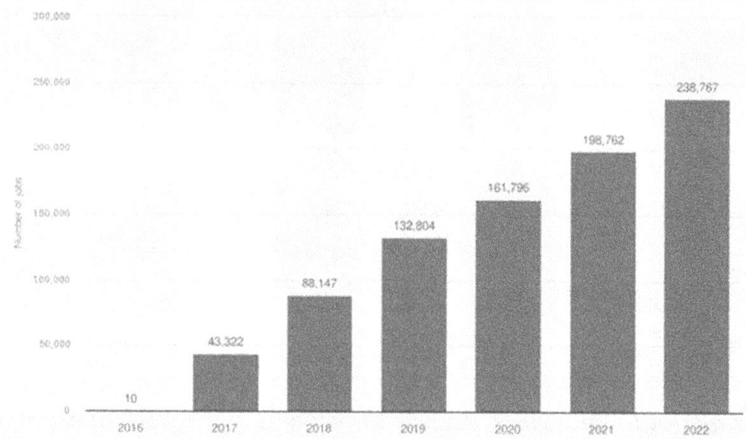

- ***Government Initiatives:*** Recent investments made by the Indian government have significantly strengthened India's standing as a flourishing center for startups, cultivating a culture of innovation and entrepreneurship among its populace. Several initiatives and schemes, such as Startup India, Atal Innovation Mission, and Meity Startup Hubs, have been introduced with the aim of offering aspiring entrepreneurs the essential assistance and facilitating their access to capital. To foster the growth of startups, various measures have been implemented, including the implementation of streamlined regulations, provision of tax exemptions, and the establishment of intellectual property rights protection. These initiatives aim to create an environment that is conducive to the development and success of startups. In addition, a range of ministries and state governments administer funding, incubation, and mentorship initiatives aimed at providing support to small startups. Examples of such programs include those offered by the Department of Biotechnology (DBT), the Department of Science and Technology (DST), and the Defense

Research and Development Organization (DRDO). The Make in India initiative, which was initiated in 2014, has been instrumental in promoting the establishment of startups through its ability to attract endorsement from global business leaders and potential investors. The objective of the campaign is to establish India as a prominent player in the global manufacturing and design industries, leading to substantial investments, particularly in foreign direct investment (FDI), across various sectors including railways, defense, and space. The aforementioned statement underscores the significance of implementing efficient regulatory frameworks that promote investment and improve the business climate in India (Wasnik & Jain, 2023). These programs establish a favorable ecosystem for IT enterprises to flourish, thereby resulting in an increase in employment prospects.

The expected potential for employment creation in India's IT and software sector is significant. It is plausible to envision that the sector could create several million new job openings over the next two years, especially if the right strategies and initiatives are implemented to foster growth and competitiveness. These job openings will not only benefit the workforce but also contribute to India's economic development and technological advancement.

Methods

The generation of employment opportunities within India's IT and software sector necessitates the implementation of a comprehensive strategy that encompasses diverse dimensions of workforce enhancement, industry expansion, and economic policy considerations. Implementing these strategies will create a conducive environment for employment generation in India's IT and software sector. The various strategies for efficiently creating employment prospects within the sector are as follows

Skill Development and Education:

- *Upskilling and Reskilling*: The implementation of comprehensive upskilling and reskilling initiatives on a national scale is being pursued in order to augment the skill sets of the current workforce. The emphasis of these programs should be directed towards burgeoning technologies such as Artificial Intelligence, Machine Learning, Data Science, and Cybersecurity.
- *Promote STEM Education*: Advocating for the provision of specialized STEM (Science, Technology, Engineering, and Mathematics) programs by educational institutions that are in line with the demands and requirements of

the industry. One potential approach to encourage students to pursue STEM fields is the implementation of scholarships and incentives.

- *Online Learning Platforms*: Advocate for and provide backing to online learning platforms that facilitate the independent acquisition of IT skills by individuals. Engage in partnerships with these platforms to provide cost-effective and readily available educational courses.

Encouraging Entrepreneurship and Innovation:

- *Incubators and Innovation Hubs:* The implementation of innovation hubs and incubators nationwide is being pursued in order to cultivate entrepreneurial activities and provide assistance to technology-based startups. These hubs have the capacity to offer mentorship, infrastructure, and funding prospects.
- *Startup Ecosystem:* Developing an ecosystem that fosters the proliferation of technology startups. Providing tax incentives, grants, and facilitating access to venture capital in order to stimulate innovation and foster the creation of employment opportunities.
- *Research and Development Grants*: One potential strategy to stimulate and support research and development endeavors, particularly in emerging technology domains, involves the provision of monetary incentives and grants. Promoting collaboration between research institutions and the private sector.

Regulatory Reforms:

- *Streamlined Processes:* The aim is to streamline and accelerate the regulatory procedures for IT enterprises, encompassing the processes of authorization, licensing, and adherence to regulatory standards. Streamlining administrative processes to minimize bureaucratic obstacles, thereby facilitating the establishment and operation of startups.
- *Taxation Reforms*: The implementation of tax reforms aimed at alleviating the tax burden on information technology (IT) companies, with a particular focus on startups. Offering incentives to encourage investments in research and development (R&D)
- *Ease of Doing Business*: Enhancing the ease of conducting business rankings can be achieved through the implementation of measures such as streamlining bureaucratic procedures, digitizing administrative processes, and providing online platforms for the facilitation of approvals and permits across different sectors.

Infrastructure Development:

- Digital Infrastructure: Investment in high-speed internet connectivity, encompassing both urban and rural regions, is imperative to ensure comprehensive access to dependable digital infrastructure across the entire nation.
- *IT Parks and Clusters*: The implementation of IT parks and technology clusters equipped with cutting-edge infrastructure, collaborative workspaces, and contemporary facilities is aimed at attracting both enterprises and skilled professionals.
- *Power* Supply: One crucial aspect for IT companies is the guarantee of a consistent and dependable power supply, as their operations heavily depend on electricity.

Export Promotion:

- *Global Market Access*: The objective is to assist IT companies in their global expansion endeavors through the provision of market access assistance, trade missions, and diplomatic initiatives aimed at facilitating entry into untapped markets.
- *Trade Agreements:* One potential strategy to enhance IT exports and facilitate opportunities for Indian companies overseas is through the negotiation of advantageous trade agreements with partner countries.
- *Marketing Campaigns*: One potential strategy for attracting international clients involves the development of marketing campaigns that highlight India's IT capabilities, talent pool, and success stories.

Diversity and Inclusion:

- *Promote Diversity*: Promoting diversity within the IT workforce through the implementation of diversity hiring initiatives. Propose measures to provide incentives for companies to increase their recruitment and employment of women, minorities, and individuals with disabilities.
- *STEM Education for All*: The objective is to create initiatives that address the disparity in STEM education between genders, spanning from early childhood to higher education. Promoting the engagement of girls and underrepresented groups in Science, Technology, Engineering, and Mathematics (STEM) professions.
- *Inclusive Workplace* Culture: The cultivation of an inclusive culture within IT workplaces can be facilitated through the implementation of various

strategies such as awareness campaigns, training initiatives, and mentorship programs.

Government-Industry Collaboration:

- *Industry Advisory Boards*: One proposed strategy involves the establishment of industry advisory boards that include representatives from both the public and private sectors. These boards would serve as platforms for fostering ongoing dialogue, collaboration, and policy alignment.
- *R&D Partnerships*: Promoting collaborative endeavors between public and private entities in the realm of research and development. It is recommended to allocate financial grants and incentives to facilitate collaborative initiatives aimed at fostering innovation.
- *Skill Councils*: The establishment of skill development councils in collaboration with industry associations is proposed as a means to delineate skill standards, curricula, and certification programs.

Rural and Semi-Urban Expansion:

- *IT Skill Centers:* The proposal involves the establishment of information technology (IT) skill development centers in rural and semi-urban regions with the aim of harnessing the potential of underutilized talent reservoirs. Offering incentives to information technology (IT) companies to establish satellite offices in these regions can be a viable strategy.
- *Incentives for Rural Entrepreneurs*: Proposing incentives and assistance to rural entrepreneurs seeking to establish IT-oriented enterprises or deliver IT services within their local communities.
- *Digital Literacy Programs*: Promoting digital literacy programs in rural schools and communities with the aim of equipping individuals with the necessary skills and knowledge required for employment in the field of information technology.

Action Plan for Implementation

The implementation of an action plan aimed at creating employment opportunities in India's IT and software sector is of utmost importance in order to accomplish the objective of generating 50 lakh new job openings within the sector over the course of the next two years. Figure 6 illustrates a comprehensive action plan that delineates the sequential steps and strategic approaches necessary for the successful execution of a particular initiative.

Step 1- ***Implementing the strategies***: By addressing skill development and education entrepreneurship and innovation, regulatory reforms, infrastructure development, export promotion, diversity and inclusion, government-industry collaboration and rural and semi-urban expansion India can capitalize on its strengths in the IT and Software Services sector to create 50 lakh jobs over the next two years, driving economic growth, innovation, and technological advancement

Step 2- ***Monitoring and Evaluation***: To ensure the successful implementation of strategies aimed at creating 50 lakh new job openings in India's IT and software sector over the next two years, robust monitoring and evaluation processes are essential.

- *Establish a Dedicated Committee*: Establish a dedicated committee tasked with the responsibility of overseeing the monitoring and evaluation endeavors' is imperative to ensure the participation of individuals representing government agencies, industry associations, educational institutions, and independent experts. It is imperative to ascertain that the committee possesses the requisite jurisdiction and allocation of resources to effectively execute its designated tasks.
- *Define Key Performance Indicators (KPIs):* The first step is to identify and establish Key Performance Indicators (KPIs) that are closely aligned with the objectives outlined in the action plan. Key performance indicators (KPIs) that are commonly utilized may encompass metrics such as the quantity of job opportunities generated, the level of investments garnered, the rate of export expansion, the outcomes of skill development initiatives, and advancements in diversity and inclusion. It is imperative to ensure that Key Performance Indicators (KPIs) possess the qualities of being quantifiable, measurable, and time-bound.
- *Regular Data Collection and Reporting*: To ensure real-time progress tracking, it is imperative to establish and execute a methodical data collection process. It is imperative to mandate that all pertinent stakeholders provide regular reports and data pertaining to their individual initiatives. The data should be compiled and analyzed in order to produce performance reports that can be presented to both the committee and the general public.
- *Feedback Mechanism*: Implement a feedback mechanism to collect input from various industry stakeholders, educational institutions, and civil society organizations. Promote the establishment of transparent communication channels to facilitate the reporting of both obstacles and achievements pertaining to the implementation of the action plan by relevant stakeholders. Utilize this feedback to implement data-driven modifications to the strategies.

- *Data Transparency*: To promote transparency, it is essential to provide public access to pertinent data and reports. Develop an accessible web-based platform that facilitates the monitoring of the implementation progress of the action plan by both individuals and enterprises. It is advisable to promote the implementation of independent audits and evaluations in order to enhance the credibility of the subject matter.
- *Regular Reviews and Adjustments*: It is recommended to establish regular evaluations, occurring no less than once every quarter, in order to evaluate the efficacy and efficiency of the implemented action plan. It is advisable to take into account external evaluations in order to obtain an impartial assessment of the progress being made. In light of the research outcomes, it is imperative to implement requisite modifications and enhancements to the proposed strategy in order to effectively tackle emerging patterns or obstacles.
- *Reporting to Stakeholders*: Regular updates should be provided to various stakeholders, including the public, government bodies, and industry associations. The individual is requested to provide an account of both accomplishments and obstacles encountered, and to elucidate the manner in which feedback has been incorporated into the strategic framework. Adopting a transparent and accountable approach is crucial in order to foster trust and garner support.

Step 3- Public Awareness and Engagement: In order to effectively execute the strategies designed to generate 5 million job opportunities in India's IT and software industry, it is imperative to actively involve the public and cultivate awareness regarding the available prospects and governmental initiatives.

- *Launch a Public Awareness Campaign:* Design and implement an all-encompassing public awareness initiative aimed at disseminating information to the general populace regarding employment prospects within the Information Technology (IT) industry. Employ a diverse range of communication channels, encompassing television, radio, social media, print media, and community events. Emphasize the government's dedication to fostering employment opportunities and the prospects for professional advancement within the information technology and software sector.
- *Engage with Industry Associations:* Engage in strategic partnerships with industry associations and organizations to secure their endorsement and facilitate the dissemination of the action plan. Utilize their professional networks as a means to engage with prospective job applicants and provide them with comprehensive information regarding the industry's prospects. Promote the

active engagement of industry leaders in public events, seminars, and workshops as a means to disseminate their valuable insights and experiences.

- *Academic Institutions and Schools:* Establish collaborative partnerships with educational institutions to integrate IT and software sector awareness and education within their academic curriculum. Organize career counselling sessions, seminars, and workshops within educational institutions, such as schools and colleges, with the aim of providing students with an opportunity to gain exposure to various information technology (IT) career pathways. It is imperative to advocate for the implementation of internship programs that offer students genuine opportunities to gain practical experience within their respective fields.
- *Civil Society Organizations:* Engage in partnerships with non-governmental organizations that prioritize education and employment. These organizations have the capacity to serve as intermediaries between the government and individuals seeking employment opportunities. Collaborate with non-governmental organizations (NGOs) to implement outreach programs and initiatives aimed at fostering skill development.
- *Feedback and Collaboration:* Establish communication channels to facilitate public engagement, encompassing various stakeholders such as individuals seeking employment, parents, and community members, in order to solicit input on the proposed action plan. Facilitate town-hall meetings or webinars to foster direct engagement between government representatives and the public, enabling the latter to voice their concerns and receive responses. Promote and foster public engagement in the IT sector's expansion, encouraging individuals to become active stakeholders in the process.
- *Showcasing Success Stories:* Share success stories of individuals who have achieved employment or entrepreneurial success in the IT and software sector. Enhance the accessibility of opportunities by incorporating relatable narratives and exemplary figures. Utilize these narratives as a means of eliciting inspiration and fostering motivation among individuals seeking employment opportunities.
- *Leverage Online Platforms:* Establishing a specialized online platform or website that offers a comprehensive array of resources, employment opportunities, and informational content pertaining to the field of information technology. Interact with individuals seeking employment by utilizing social media platforms, conducting webinars, and organizing online question and answer sessions. Utilize digital platforms as a means to effectively engage a broad spectrum of individuals, with particular emphasis on the younger demographic.

Step 5- Budget Allocation: In order to accomplish the objective of creating 50 lakh fresh employment opportunities within India's IT and software industry over the forthcoming biennium, it is imperative to allocate sufficient financial resources to bolster the implementation strategy. The following is a systematic methodology for the allocation of budgetary resources:

- *Determine Specific Budgets:* It is recommended to allocate dedicated financial resources to each of the action points delineated in the implementation plan. These action points encompass skill development, regulatory reforms, infrastructure development, export promotion, diversity and inclusion, government-industry collaboration, and rural expansion.
- It is imperative to ensure that the allocated budgets are both realistic and adequate in order to effectively achieve the objectives associated with each strategy.
- *Prioritize Key Initiatives:* Identify the initiatives that are deemed most critical and have a high impact within each strategy. In order to optimize the effectiveness of these high-priority projects, it is recommended to allocate a substantial portion of the budget towards them.
- *Seek Funding Sources:* One should consider exploring a variety of funding sources in order to provide financial support for the budget. Possible sources of information may include: Government budgetary allocations should be directed towards the implementation of employment creation initiatives within the IT and software sector. The promotion of domestic investments entails fostering private sector engagement and venture capital funding in the realm of IT-related startups and projects. International support can be sought by securing financial resources from multilateral organizations, foreign governments, and international institutions that prioritize the promotion of job creation. Public-Private Partnerships (PPPs) entail the establishment of collaborative alliances with private sector entities for the purpose of jointly financing and executing designated projects. Tax incentives can be provided to businesses and individuals who contribute to the creation of jobs in the IT sector, thereby offering them tax benefits or advantages.
- *Allocation Transparency:* It is imperative to establish and maintain a high level of transparency in the process of allocating the budget. Disseminate information regarding the allocation and utilization of financial resources. Develop an intelligible and inclusive financial reporting framework that enables stakeholders to effectively oversee and track expenditures.
- *Resource Management:* Effectively oversee allocated resources through the reduction of waste and the optimization of expenditures. Develop and estab-

lish a comprehensive framework to ensure the responsible management of resources and conduct periodic financial audits.

- *Emergency Contingency*: It is recommended to designate a specific portion of the budget as an emergency contingency fund in order to effectively address unanticipated challenges or potential opportunities. The utilization of this fund enables prompt responses to dynamic circumstances or fluctuations in the economy.
- *Regular Review and Adjustments*: It is advisable to conduct regular evaluations of the budget allocation in order to determine the efficiency of fund utilization. It is advisable to be adequately prepared to make necessary adaptations in response to evolving requirements, emerging trends, and feedback obtained from the monitoring and evaluation process.

Step 6- Periodic Reviews and Adjustments

Periodic Reviews and Adjustments: Establish a prearranged timetable for conducting comprehensive evaluations of the action plan. It is recommended that these reviews be conducted on a quarterly or semi-annual basis. The evaluation process should encompass the participation of various important actors, such as government officials, industry representatives, educational institutions, and civil society organizations.

- *Performance Assessment:* During each evaluation, it is imperative to appraise the effectiveness of the action plan in relation to the predetermined key performance indicators (KPIs). This analysis aims to assess the accomplishments and obstacles encountered by each strategy employed, as well as the overall advancement made towards the objective of creating 50 lakh job openings.
- *Stakeholder Input:* Seek input from various stakeholders, such as industry leaders, educators, job seekers, and the general public. Promote the solicitation of transparent and honest feedback pertaining to the efficacy and influence of the implemented strategies.
- *Data-Driven Decision-Making*: It is imperative to base adjustments on reliable data and compelling evidence. When faced with strategies that are underperforming or surpassing expectations, it is crucial to make well-informed decisions regarding potential adjustments. It is advisable to maintain a flexible approach towards revising timelines, reallocating budgets, and introducing new initiatives as necessary.
- Scenario Planning: Formulate contingency plans for various scenarios. This can facilitate the action plan's ability to effectively address unforeseen challenges or capitalize on unexpected opportunities. It is imperative to maintain

the plan's agility and adaptability in response to evolving economic and technological trends.

- *Budget Adjustments:* If deemed necessary, it may be prudent to make modifications to the budget in order to redistribute resources towards strategies or initiatives that demonstrate the greatest potential and effectiveness. It is imperative to reassess the financial requirements of each strategy and ascertain that they continue to be in accordance with the objectives outlined in the action plan.
- *Communication and Transparency:* It is imperative to effectively disseminate the outcomes of the regular evaluations and modifications to the general public, stakeholders, and the media. Ensure transparency and exhibit the government's dedication to promoting openness and accountability.
- *External Evaluation:* It is advisable to consider the inclusion of independent evaluators or experts in order to obtain impartial assessments of the action plan. External evaluations provide valuable insights and recommendations for enhancing performance.
- Benchmarking: Examine the progress and outcomes of the action plan in the IT and software sector by comparing them to international benchmarks and best practices. The practice of benchmarking can yield valuable insights that can be utilized to refine and optimize strategies.
- Continuous Learning: Promote a culture that fosters ongoing learning and enhancement among all individuals involved. Utilize the knowledge acquired from the evaluations to modify and enhance the tactics in order to achieve a more significant influence.

Furthermore, implementing this comprehensive action plan will require close coordination between government agencies, industry stakeholders, educational institutions, and civil society. Regular communication, transparency, and a commitment to the vision of creating 50 lakh new job openings in India's IT and software sector will be essential for success.

Figure 6. Action plan for creating 50 Lakh jobs over the next two years in Indian information technology/ software industry(Authors own compilation)

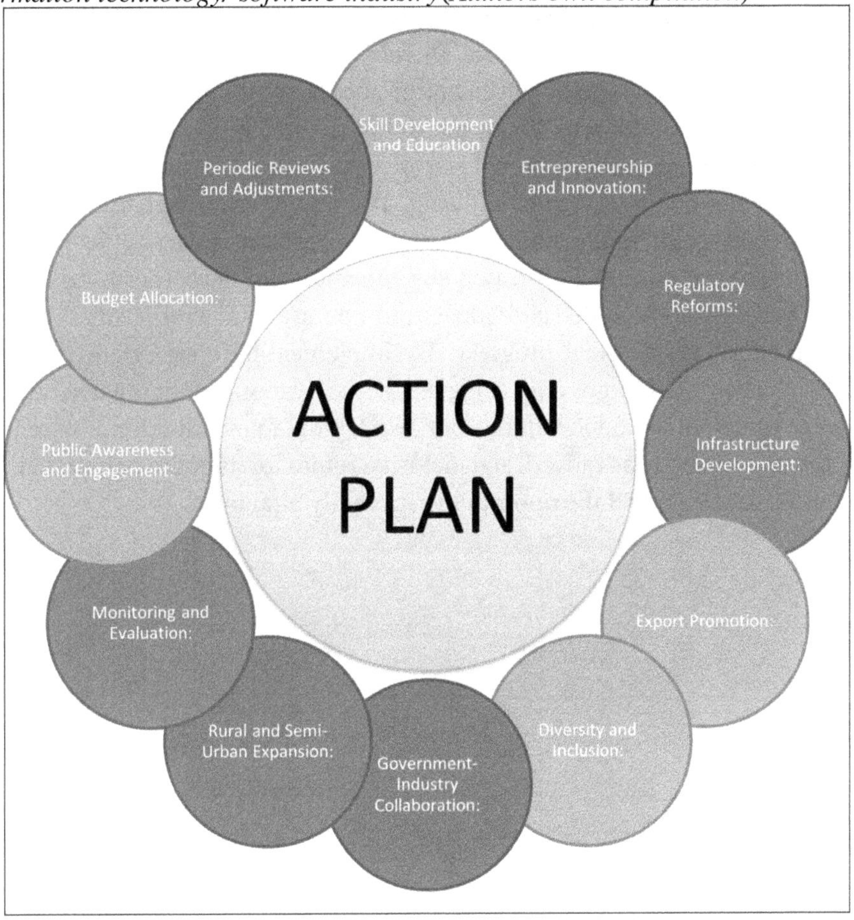

4. CONCLUSION

The objective of generating 5 million new employment opportunities in India's IT and software industry within the next two years is an ambitious yet feasible goal. The IT industry in India has exhibited notable resilience, innovation, and expansion throughout its history, establishing itself as a prominent global leader. India has the potential to enhance its position in the global IT landscape and address crucial employment needs by executing a comprehensive action plan encompassing skill development, innovation, regulatory reforms, infrastructure enhancement, export promotion, diversity, and government-industry collaboration. This endeavor encompasses more than just the creation of job opportunities; it encompasses the promotion of economic growth, the cultivation of innovation, and the guarantee of inclusivity. The information technology (IT) sector has the potential to act as a catalyst for comprehensive economic development, thereby yielding advantages for both urban and rural communities. The achievement of success will be contingent upon the dedication and cooperation of various stakeholders, encompassing governmental bodies, industry pioneers, educational establishments, and the broader civil society. The implementation of regular monitoring, evaluation, and adaptability will play a crucial role in attaining the intended results. As India progresses in its pursuit of becoming a prominent global IT leader, it is imperative for the nation to maintain its dedication to cultivating skilled individuals, promoting a conducive business climate, and embracing technological progress. By implementing appropriate strategies, India has the potential to not only achieve its objective of generating a substantial number of employment opportunities but also lay the foundation for a more prosperous, technologically advanced, and inclusive future for its entire population. The potential is extensive, and the opportunity is readily attainable.

REFERENCES

Huang, Y. (2008). The next Asian miracle. *Foreign Policy*, (167), 32–40.

Malik, M. H., Anandarao, S., & Dar, A. A. (2023). An appraisal of India's comparative advantage in information technology exports. *Journal of Chinese Economic and Foreign Trade Studies*, 16(2), 136–152. DOI: 10.1108/JCEFTS-08-2022-0051

Shrivastava, A., Krishna, K. M., Rinawa, M. L., Soni, M., Ramkumar, G., & Jaiswal, S. (2023). Inclusion of IoT, ML, and blockchain technologies in next generation industry 4.0 environment. *Materials Today: Proceedings*, 80, 3471–3475.

Startup India. (2019)., Retrieved from https://www.startupindia.gov.in/content/dam/invest india/Templates/public/5_years_Achievement_report%20_%20final%20(1).pdf Accessed on 10th October, 2023

Statista 2023, Indian IT industry report, Retrieved from https://www-statista-com.mdilibrary.remotexs.in/statistics/1247634/startup-india-number-of-reported-jobs/ Accessed on 10th October, 2023

Vial, G. (2009). Understanding digital transformation: A review and a research agenda. *The Journal of Strategic Information Systems*, 28(2), 118–144. DOI: 10.1016/j.jsis.2019.01.003

Wasnik, A. P., & Jain, A. (2023). Government Support for Startups: A Comprehensive Analysis of Funding Initiatives and the Role of the Indian Government in Nurturing the Startup Ecosystem. *Economics and Business Quarterly Reviews*, 6(3), 98–107. DOI: 10.31014/aior.1992.06.03.523

Chapter 10
Discrimination, Gender, and Immigration:
European Social Survey Investigation

Annamaria Nese
https://orcid.org/0000-0001-9356-4320
University of Salerno, Italy

Mohsen Brahmi
https://orcid.org/0000-0002-0995-0761
University of Sfax, Tunisia

Luigi Aldieri
https://orcid.org/0000-0001-9300-6804
University of Salerno, Italy

ABSTRACT

This work examines any ethnic gaps between self-identified ethnic minorities and the majority of the population across Western European regions, taking into consideration the variations within native population and ethnic minorities due to family background (i.e., parents' education and occupation). The analysis shows that self-identified ethnic minorities and national majorities have significantly different socioeconomic levels; the observed ethnic gaps cannot be fully explained by individual educational attainment, family history, or challenges related to migration. Micro data from the European Social Survey are used in this investigation. The findings show that overestimating any ethnic gaps may result from ignoring social origins: parents with high socioeconomic status may better target their children in their decision-making, which may imply further disadvantages for ethnic minorities,

DOI: 10.4018/979-8-3693-5723-1.ch010

particularly for the offspring of migrants who typically have low social origins. The findings also highlight how little intergenerational mobility there is in Europe.

INTRODUCTION

The ethnic mix of many European countries[1] has rapidly increased due to the migration of people from less developed to more developed countries over the past few decades. As a result, more research is now required to determine whether and to what extent members of ethnic minorities are integrated into the labor market and host society (Alba et al. 2011). In addition to wasting money and creating inefficiencies, discrimination of any kind regarding employment and educational opportunities is a serious public health risk since it weakens social cohesiveness and can lead to social instability.

The majority of recent empirical findings show that people of ethnic minorities face considerable, occasionally severe barriers to obtaining higher education and employment opportunities (Hehewisch and Liepmann, 2013; Kim, 3013; Kahanec et al., 2010 summarize the results for European countries). The severity of these drawbacks differs by nation and ethnic group, as is to be expected. The primary characteristic, though, is the variation in the data and approaches employed by the various research to gauge any ethnic prejudice.

Some studies focus solely on comparing the average employment outcomes or socio-economic conditions of immigrants, ethnic minorities, and natives, while others take into account additional factors such as age and education levels (Borjas, 1990, 1995, Adsera and Chiswick, 2007; Cheung and Heath, 2007; Kahanec and Zaiceva, 2009; Kahanec et al., 2010; Kahanec and Zimmerman, 2010). Lefranc (2010) also considers family background in the French labor market to illustrate the various social and economic factors that can contribute to ethnic disadvantages.

In this context, the primary challenge for researchers is defining and measuring "ethnicity." The term "ethnic minority" can include immigrants and their offspring, as well as indigenous minority groups who have not been absorbed into the larger population. Max Weber (1978, p. 389)defines ethnic groups as those "human groups that entertain a subjective belief in their common descent because of similarities of physical type or of customs or both, or because of memories of colonization and migration" (see also, Heath and Cheung, 2007).

Considering this definition, there are challenges in accurately measuring ethnicity. For instance, using individuals' and parents' birthplaces can be misleading, as children of ex-colonists may be mistaken for indigenous populations (Lefranc, 2010). Additionally, many migrant-sending countries have diverse ethnicities, such as India with its numerous linguistic and ethnic groups. Relying on nationality alone does not distinguish naturalized citizens' ethnic origins. Self-reporting ancestry may also be biased, as some ancestries may be stigmatized and individuals may choose to conceal them (Heath and Cheung, 2007).

The further limitation for researchers in this context is the scarcity of adequate data, particularly in Europe (Kahanec et al., 2010; OECD, 2018).

In contrast to the United States, where diverse ethnic populations have led to the creation of large datasets, European studies often rely on national surveys and various methods to determine minority status. The identification of ethnic minorities poses challenges within individual countries and across Europe due to the varying characteristics of these populations (see also Bauer et al., 2001). Some countries have significant ethnic minorities due to post-colonial migration or labor recruitment policies, while others have indigenous minorities or are experiencing increasing migration flows of asylum seekers and refugees.

This study aims to examine inequalities experienced by ethnic minorities in the labor market across European countries using data from the 8th wave of the European Social Survey. The ESS provides valuable information on individual characteristics, labor market outcomes, family background, and a key variable for this study - whether respondents identify as ethnic minority members. This variable helps distinguish between individuals with immigrant backgrounds and those from indigenous minority groups, with self-identification being the preferred method for identifying an individual's ethnic group (United Nations, 2017; ILO, 1989).

The research examines disparities between self-identified ethnic minorities and the majority population, as well as differences within ethnic minority groups based on their individual characteristics and family backgrounds. By overlooking social origins, there is a risk of exaggerating ethnic gaps, as parents with high socioeconomic status are more likely to guide their children towards successful educational and career paths. This could potentially create further challenges for ethnic minorities, especially the offspring of migrants with lower social origins.

Multilevel models have been estimated where the dependent variable is the individual outcome in society and the labor market in terms of education, income and occupational status. The intercept and coefficient for ethnicity are allowed to vary across regions (random-intercept, random coefficient models): multilevel models allow to explain any variations in the individual outcomes in the labor market with the individual characteristics (age, education, family background and ethnicity) and region-level variables (i.e., unemployment rate and endowment of social capital) simultaneously, while also allowing for the impact of individual characteristics – i.e. minority membership – on the individual outcome to vary across regions.

The paper is set out as follows. Section 2 reviews current literature, section 3 describes the methodology and data used in the analysis, section 4 displays the results; concluding remarks are reported in section 5.

LITERATURE REVIEW

According to the basic theory of labor economics, firms that prioritize profits rationally pay employees based on their marginal productivity. This means that in a competitive labor market that functions well, workers with equal skills have an equal chance of finding employment and earning the same salary. The issue of labor market discrimination based on race, gender, or ethnicity has received a great deal of attention from empirical studies (Altoniji and Blank, 1999). These studies have highlighted the existence of ethnic penalties; among them are Cheung and Heath (2007), Hegewisch and Liepman (2013), and Kim (2013); Kananec et al. (2010) and Kahanec and Zimmerman (2010) provide a summary of the findings across European countries.

Neoclassical authors (e.g., Abowd and Killingsworth, 1984; Heckman, 1998; Trejo, 1997) assert that racial and ethnic variations in earnings, jobs, and income are determined by the lower levels of education, work experience, and training among ethnic minorities. Neoclassical theory critics point out, however, that even when skill levels are taken into consideration, racial and ethnic minorities still earn less money than equivalent white workers (Cheung and Heath, 2007; Kim, 2007; Smith, 2012). Minority job seekers are also less likely to be invited for an interview, according to field tests (see Bertrand and Mullainathan, 2004; OECD, 2013; Neumark, 2016; Zschirnt and Ruedin, 2016). Immigrants with ethnic backgrounds are likely to fare worse than natives in the labor market for a variety of reasons.

First of all, immigrants may not speak the language of the host nation well, which could reduce their productivity in a variety of roles. Second, because their native countries have relatively underdeveloped educational institutions, migrants from less developed nations frequently have low competency levels. Additionally, employers in the host nation could not have appreciated the migrants' skills since they were unable to appropriately identify their international qualifications (OECD, 2013). Furthermore, social networks are seen to be crucial sources of knowledge about job opportunities, but immigrants are less likely to be part of them (see Mortensen, 1986; Granovetter, 1973).

When endogenous ethnic minorities or the descendants of immigrants are taken into account, these arguments, however, do not justify barriers to employment or income because the descendants of immigrants were born in the host community and received their education in the same educational system. In other words, ethnic minorities may be impacted by prejudice and discrimination (Burstein, 1994). Research on employment practices also indicates that businesses choose white employees over black Americans who are comparable to them but not "visible ethnic minorities" (Kirschenman and Neckerman, 1991). Another argument might be that employers frequently fall back on outdated prejudices as a result of issues with asymmetric information regarding employees' productivity (for more on this, see Pager and Karafin, 2009).

As was previously indicated, the numerous measures of ethnic disadvantage that are frequently employed in empirical works may capture a variety of reasons that contribute to the poorer socioeconomic (Arabiun et al. 2023). accomplishment of ethnic minorities, but they do not always imply racial discrimination (Brahmi & Zouari, 2014). For example, Cheung and Heath (2007) and Phalet and Heath (2007) distinguish between two empirical measures of the ethnic gap: on the one hand, differences between the members of the ethnic minority and the majority population evaluated age and education (net disadvantage); on the other hand, differences in the mean outcome between the ethnic minority and the population majority (gross ethnic disadvantage), which may be biased by unobserved differences in the individual characteristics.

DATA AND METHODOLOGY

Individual data were drawn from the tenth edition of the European Social Survey (ESS8, 2016-2018), carried out in the European regions. The ESS dataset was used for this study due to its wide range of data on household and individual characteristics, as well as a critical variable pertaining to the respondents' self-definition as members of an ethnic minority. This characteristic makes it possible to distinguish between people who are members of autochthonous minority and people with an immigrant background. The most accurate way to determine a person's ethnic group is thought to be by self-identification (see United Nations, 2017; ILO, 1989).

One major limitation of the ESS survey is that, unlike studies that analyze migration issues, ethnic minorities are not oversampled. As a result, the number of observations for working-age members of ethnic minorities is relatively low, making it difficult to make extensive comparisons among different ethnic groups or at the national level. Conversely, studies focusing on certain minority typically don't have a representative sample of the majority population that has the data needed to achieve this goal (OECD, 2019). Considering the constraints of the data, consideration was given to any distinctions that may exist between the majority population and ethnic minorities, as well as whether and to what degree these distinctions are influenced by observable personal and familiar traits.

Multiple linear regression and logit models were estimated, where the dependent variables represent individual performance in the society and labor market; the individual outcome is measured through various indicators. First, individual education is measured in full-time years of schooling. Second, the labor market position is measured distinguishing between employed/self-employed and unemployed people in search of job. In addition, "insecurity in the labor market" is represented by using two distinct questions, defining i) whether the respondents have been unemployed for more than 3 months in the past 5 years and ii) whether they are afraid of losing their job in the following 12 months. Two indicators identify the individual positions in the society, respectively i) individual occupations, coded according to the ISCO classification and ii) a question defining whether respondents live comfortably on their family income.

We take explicitly into account how regional characteristics – in addition to individual factors – may influence individual performances, and that attitudes toward immigrants and immigration policies may vary across regions (Crawley 2005; Crawley et al., 2013) as a consequence of different cultural and economic characteristics and/or different place-specific immigrant integration policies. Hence, the intercept and coefficient for ethnicity are allowed to vary across regions (random-intercept, random coefficient multilevel models). The design weights provided in the ESS data, which correct for country differences in sampling are also applied. The correlates comprise the following individual characteristics: sex, age, and education, place of birth, familial background, and ethnic background. The primary justification for controlling age is that life-cycle factors partially influence individual outcomes; comparing people at different phases of life would yield biased findings. The dummies for sex and the place of birth should highlight any gender gap as well as the effects on individual performances of mobility across countries.

The unemployment rate in each of the European regions included in NUTS-2 and the degree of social capital endowment serve as indicators of the socioeconomic conditions at the regional level. Social capital is widely acknowledged for promoting human contacts and reciprocal action, which facilitates many facets of economic activity. (Colemann, 1988; Putnam, 1993; &Knack and Keefer, 1995). Fukuyama (1995) identifies social trust as social capital and underlines its function: "trust acts like a lubricant that makes any group or organization run more efficiently"; some recent works highlight a positive correlation between social trust, social distance, and local economic development (Guangyi, 2017). Thus, the indicators of social trust and social distance available in the ESS survey are included. Social trust is measured through the opinions expressed on the following subjects: "most people can be trusted, or you can't be too careful; most people try to take advantage of you, or try to be fair; most of the time people are helpful or they are mostly looking out for themselves". Social distance toward ethnic minorities is proxies by two variables: a first question asked respondents if they would mind having a boss who an immigrant is and belongs to a racial/ethnic minority group; respondents were also asked if they would mind if a close relative married an immigrant who is also member of a racial/ethnic minority. Focusing on social distance is particularly interesting for the aim of this work since it allows observing whether and to what extent anti-immigrant sentiments vary across European regions. Hence, two exogenous regional indicators of social capital have been drawn from a previous wave of the survey (ESS7).

DESCRIPTIVE STATISTICS

The focus of the paper is on individual outcomes in the labor market, the sample retains individuals aged between 15 to 64 years old. Ethnic minorities' members born in the country of the interview (see Table 1a-b, columns III and VI) should have performances similar to those observed for national majorities' members (Table 1a, columns I and IV) since they grew up and socialized in the same country, whereas first-generation migrants should bear the cost of migration decisions. The descriptive statistics in Table 1b suggest that overall majority population members have better performances in the labor market than ethnic minorities since they are more likely to be employed, are engaged in jobs that require a plenty of communication (and a lower physical burden), and live more comfortably on their present household income. The observed ethnic disadvantages seem not due to education since ethnic minorities' members born in the host country also have a higher education level than majority members; as expected, the ethnic disadvantages are higher when first generation migrants are included in the sample.

Table 1a. Summary statistics- Our elaborations on ESS data

Variables	Females – mean (std dev.)			Males – mean (std dev.)		
	I National majorities	II Ethnic minorities	III born minorities	IV National majorities	V Ethnic minorities	VI born minorities
Age	44.502(0.162)	44.156(0.633)	38.383(1.024)	43.977(0.166)	39.285(0.769)	40.375(1.211)
Own education	13.771(0.048)	13.734(0.256)	13.821(0.395)	13.633(0.049)	13.693(0.279)	13.747(0.382)
Mother's education	2.297 (0.024)	2.355 (0.127)	2.336(0.197)	2.282 (0.025)	2.034(0.119)	1.989 (0.151)
Father's education	2.398 (0.028)	2.416 (0.142)	2.177 (0.201)	2.506 (0.029)	2.338 (0.150)	2.178 (0.197)
Mother's occup.	7.274(0.040)	7.348(0.186)	7.247 (0.280)	7.325 (0.041)	8.057 (0.180)	7.625(0.285)
Father's occup.	6.072 (0.034)	6.018 (0.173)	6.292 (0.263)	6.021 (0.036)	6.347 (0.180)	6.537 (0.219)
ISCOlevel	3.982(0.035)	4.651(0.198)	4.085 (0.237)	4.562 (0.039)	5.243 (0.185)	4.768 (0.283)
Household income	1.908 (0.010)	2.113 (0.047)	2.140 (0.075)	1.845 (0.010)	2.074(0.056)	2.079(0.079)
Binary Variables	%			%		
Employment	78.63	72.23	71.88	89.53	85.47	87.30
Unemploym. last 5 yrs	34.77	46.27	43.94	34.44	46.55	41.97
Unemployment risk	33.32	44.09	44.08	28.83	41.82	42.53
n. observations	13.785	743	348	12835	739	351

Legend:

Ethnic minorities: respondents who identified themselves as members of ethnic minorities. born minorities: respondents born in the country of the interview who identified themselves as members of ethnic minorities. Education: years of full time schooling.

Mother's/father's occupation when respondent was aged 14: 10=not employed; 9: elementary occupation; 8: plant and machine operators and assemblers; 7: craft and related workers; 6: skilled agricultural and fishery workers; 5: service workers and shop and market sales workers; 4: clerks; 3: technicians and associate professionals; 2: professionals; 1=legislators, senior officials and managers. Mother's/father's education is measured according to ISCED classification.

Occupational prestige: 9: elementary occupation; 8: plant and machine operators and assemblers; 7: craft and related workers; 6: skilled agricultural and fishery workers; 5: service workers and shop and market sales workers; 4: clerks; 3: technicians and associate professionals; 2: professionals; 1=legislators, senior officials and managers. Household income: respondent'sfeeling about household's income on a scale 0-3 (0 if living comfortably/coping on present income, 3 if very difficult).

Employment: dummy equal to if employed, 0 otherwise.

Unemploym. last 5 yrs: dummy equal to 1 if the respondent experienced at least 3 months of unemployment and work seeking in the 5 years preceding the interview, 0 otherwise.

Unemployment risk: dummy equal to 1 if the respondent considers very likely unemployment and work seeking in the next 12 months, 0 otherwise.

Table 1b. Years of schooling– Linear regression model with random intercepts and random slopes

Variables	Coefficients (std errors)			
	No family origins	**Full model**	**Full model**	**Full model with region-level variables**
ethnic minorities	-0.580**(0.221)	-0.255(0.208)	-0.192 (0.221)	-0.190(0.220)
female	0.153***(0.069)	0.152***(0.064)	0.168**(0.073)	0.167**(0.073)
foreign born	-0.595***(0.197)	-	-0.474**(0.190)	-0.476**(0.189)
mother's education		0.513***(0.171)	0.254***(0.024)	0.254***(0.023)
father's education		0.267***(0.024)	0.269***(0.023)	0.268***(0.023)
mother's occupation		0.282***(0.023)	-	-0.099***(0.012)
father's occupation		-	0.099***(0.012)	-0.199***(0.023)
regional indicators	no	0.099***(0.012)	-	yes
		-	0.120***(0.027)	
		0.204***(0.020)	no	
		no		
N. observations	26380	26380	24097	24097
n. parameters	27	36	36	39
n. countries	21	21	19	19
LL random		-68750.405		-59843.09
intercepts	-70843.006	-68678.873	-59777.542	-59773.671
LL random				
coefficients	1.367(0.174)	1.279(0.181)	1.294 (0.181)	1.283(0.179)
RE parameters	0.559(0.072)	0.442(0.061)	0.452(0.065)	0.427(0.066)
sd (ethnic)	3.498(0.088)	3.224(0.080)	3.197(0.088)	3.197(0.089)
sd (constant)				
sd (residuals)				

Legend: the dependents variable is full-time years of schooling;LL random intercepts: log-likelihood reported for the model including only random intercepts; LL random coefficients: log-likelihood reported for the model including both random intercepts and random slopes. See also legend in Table 3.1. Notes: robust standard errors; sample weights included.

Note: Our Elaborations on ESS data

RESULTS AND DISCUSSION

1. Education Variable

Since education is a strong predictor of socio-economic status, guaranteeing equal access to education, is necessary to pursue equal opportunities in the labor market. It has therefore been analyzed whether and to what extent ethnic origins, other than parents' socioeconomic status, affects educational attainment (Brahmi et al. 2022). The dependent variables are individual education in full-time years of schooling. The results obtained on the whole sample are shown in Table 2.

Table 2. Employment probabilities/versus unemployment – Logit estimates with random intercepts

Variables	Coefficients (std errors) [Odds ratios]					
	No own education	**No family origins**	**No education, no family origins**	**Full model**	**Full model**	**Full with region – level variables**
Education	-	0.225***(0.011)	-0.407***(0.078)	0.172	0.166 ***(0.013)	0.166*** (0.013)
	0.329***(0.079)	[1.253]	[0.665]	***(0.012)	[1.181]	[1.182]
ethnic minority	[0.719]	-0.364***(0,079)	-0.901***(0.039)	[1.187]	-0.375***(0.093)	-0.358***(0.082)
	-	[0.695]	[0.405]	-	[0.699]	[0.699]
female	0.921***(0.039)	-0.965***(0.039)	-0.305***(0.058)	0.328***(0.079)	-0.940***(0.042)	-0.939***(0.042)
	[0.398]	[0.381]	[0.738]	[0.720]	[0.391]	[0.391]
foreign born	-	-0.318***(0.059)		-	-0.302***(0.063)	-0.302***(0.063)
	0.311***(0.059)	[0.728]		0.963***(0.039)	[0.739]	[0.741]
mother's educ.	[0.732]			[0.382]	0.043***(0.015)	0.042**(0.015)
	0.066***(0.015)			-	[1.044]	[1.043]
father's	[1.068]			0.318***(0.059)	0.040***(0.013)	0.040**(0.013)
education	0.618***(0.013)			[0.728]	[1.041]	[1.041]
	[1.064]			-	-0.036***(0.008)	-0.036***(0.008)
mother'soccup.	-			0.034***(0.008)	[0.964]	[0.964]
	0.042***(0.007)		no	[1.041]	-0.017*(0.009)	-0.017**(0.009)
father'soccup.	[0.958]			-0.021**(0.009)	[0.983]	[0.982]
	-	no		[1.038]	no	yes
Regional	0.038***(0.009)			0.040**(0.015)		
indicators	[1.064]			[0.966]		
	no			0.040**(0.013)		
				[0.978]		
				no		
N. Obs.	23755	23755	23755	23755	21540	22540
n. countries	21	21	21	21	19	19
n. parameters	35	28	27	36	36	38
LL random				-9451.503		-8458.790
coeffic.	-9559.905	-9505.9564	-9720.776	-9451.682	-8458.752	-8458.895
LL random						
intercepts	0.302 (0.037)	0.306 (0.037)	0.316 (0.037)	0.299(0.037)	0.189(0.042)	0.193 (0.042)
RE parameter						
Sd (constant)						

Legend: the dependent variable is a dummy equal to if employed, 0 otherwise. See also Legend in Table 3.1
Note: Our Elaborations on ESS data

A potential problem is that unobserved heterogeneity across the countries could have influenced the results; for this reason country fixed effects have been included in all the specifications of the model and, in the last column, a control for region-level variables (i.e., unemployment rates, social distance and social trust). Dummy variables for foreign born and females also capture any penalties due to recent transition from other countries (emigrants that come back or first-generation immigrants) or to gender discrimination.

Our results can be summarized as follows. When we control for family background, ethnic disadvantages are no longer significant. Parents' education matters on their children's scholastic career, thus highlighting that parents' cultural beliefs and attitudes to education foster children motivation to make effort in school. As expected, there is a statistically significant difference between natives and recent movers to the country of the interview.

A Likelihood Ratio (LRT) test also suggests that the random coefficient model is appropriate (the log-likelihood functions evaluated for the random coefficient model and for the random intercept are reported only for the full model specification). The main conclusions remain substantially stable when controlling for region level variables in the last column; once again, a Likelihood Ratio (LRT) test suggests that the random coefficient model is appropriate.

2. Employment Status

This section focuses on individual unemployment probabilities and interprets the differentials in these probabilities between self-identified ethnic minorities and majority population members as measures of integration in the EU-countries. The selected sample includes working-age population, aged 15 to 64, excluding anyone who is disabled, member of the military, a student or retired. The unemployment rate is the proportion of people who are employed (vs unemployed) in the labor force.

Table 2 reports the estimates of employment probabilities; a multilevel logit model with intercept random to account for heterogeneity at region level is the final specification of the model. The results in the third column show that minorities experience probabilities of employment lower than national majorities, particularly if female and foreign born; the coefficient on "ethnic minority" is shared by all the European regions, but regions vary in their intercept.

Both individual education and family background explain part of the observed ethnic penalties (in the fourth column), but the probabilities of being employed are still lower than those observed for the national majority members. Finally, the inclusion among the correlates of region-level variables in the last column does not improve significantly the explicative power of the model.

The observed unemployment probabilities may reflect both a high risk of being unemployed and a low probability of exiting unemployment; even if a micro-econometric analysis of unemployment dynamics is beyond the aim of this study, the probability of having been unemployed for long periods (at last three months) in the previous five years and the probabilities of exiting employment in the following year were also focused on. Both of the last indicators are useful in order to highlight insecurity at work.

When considering the unemployment probabilities in the previous five years in Table 3, the results highlight that the gross ethnic disadvantage shown in the fourth column cannot be entirely explained by differences in individual characteristics even if controlling for own education and family background reduces the ethnic differentials. As expected, first generation migrants/movers from other countries experience higher difficulties of being employed in the previous 5 years (in the host country as well as in another country). The results remain substantially the same when including the region-level (i.e., the regional indicators of social trust and social distance) variables in the last column. A likelihood ratio test suggests that the random intercept model is appropriate.

Table 3. Employment status in the last 5 years – Logit estimates with random intercepts

Variables	**Coefficients (std errors) [Odds ratios]**					
	No own education	**No family origins**	**No family origins, no own education**	**Full model**	**Full model**	**Full model with region-level variables**
Education	0.379***(0.059)	-0.103***	0.414***	-	-	-0.070***(0.008)
	[1.461]	(0.008)	(0.058)	0.069***(0.008)	0.071***(0.008)	[0.932]
ethnic minority	0.018(0.026)	[0.902]	[1.512]	[0.933]	[0.932]	0.417***(0.061)
	[1.018]	0.415***	0.017	0.364***(0.075)	0.414***(0.061)	[1.518]
female	0.338***(0.045)	(0.059)	(0.026)	[1.439]	[1.513]	0.044(0.027)
	[1.401]	[1.514]	[1.016]	0.032(0.026)	0.044*(0.028)	[1.045]
foreign born	-0.032***(0.010)	0.039	0.339***	[1.032]	[1.045]	0.325***(0.047)
	[0.969]	(0.026)	(0.044)	0.351***(0.045)	0.320***(0.046)	[1.384]
mother's educ.	-0.049***(0.009)	[1.040]	[1.404]	[1.419]	[1.377]	-0.022**(0.010)
	[0.952]	0.355***		-0.021**(0.010)	-0.022**(0.010)	[0.978]
father's education	0.013**(0.005)	(0.045)		[0.978]	[0.978]	-0.042* (0.009)
	[1.013]	[1.425]		-	-	[0.959]
mother'soccup.	0.020***(0.006)			0.040***(0.009)	0.042***(0.009)	0.011**(0.006)
	[1.020]			[0.960]	[0.959]	[1.011]
father'soccup.	no		no	0.010*(0.005)	0.011*(0.006)	0.011*(0.007)
				[1.010]	[1.011]	[1.011]
Regional indicators		no		0.013**(0.006)	0.011*(0.007)	yes
				[1.013]	[1.011]	
				no	no	
N. Obs.	27105	27105	27105	27105	24717	24717
n. parameters	35	28	27	36	36	38
n. countries	21	21	21	21	19	19
L.L. random interc.	-16385.292	-16839.805	-16947.347	-16781.717	-15315.91	-15311.589
LL. random coeff.				-16780.961		-15311.145
RE parameter Sd (constant)	0.241(0.028)	0.238 (0.028)	0.247(0.028)	0.236(0.027)	0.208 (0.028)	0.184(0.027)

Legend: the dependent variable is a dummy equal to 1 if the respondent experienced at least 3 months of unemployment and work seeking in the 5 years preceding the interview, 0 otherwise. See also legend in Table 3.1

Note: Our Elaborations on ESS data

The probability of becoming unemployed in the following year (as declared by the respondents) is analyzed in Table 4. Familiar background significantly improves respondents' labor perspectives(the full specification model is reported in the fourth column), but once again there are still unexplained ethnic penalties. First generation migrants experience even higher rates of precariousness whereas lower differences emerge between native males and females. The inclusion of region level variables (social trust and social distance) does not improve the explicative power of the model in the last column; the final estimates rely on a random coefficient model.

Table 4. Fear losing job - logit estimates with random intercepts and random slopes

Variables	Coefficients (std errors) [Odds ratios]					
	No own education	**No family origins**	**No family origins, no own education**	**Full model**	**Full model**	**Full model with region-level variables**
Education ethnic minority female foreign born mother's educ. father's education mother'soccup. father'soccup.	0.325***(0.088) [1.384] 0.229***(0.027) [1.253] 0.464***(0.046) [1.594] - 0.046***(0.010) [0.955] - 0.040***(0.009) [0.960] 0.015**(0.006) [1.015] 0.040***(0.007) [1.041] no	- 0.185***(0.008) [0.831] 0.377***(0.087) [1.458] 0.266***(0.027) [1.305] 0.480***(0.046) [1.618] no	0.391***(0.087) [1.384] 0.225***(0.027) [1.256] 0.461***(0.046) [1.588] no	-0.151***(0.009) [0.859] 0.344***(0.088) [1.411] 0.259***(0.027) [1.296] 0.481***(0.046) [1.618] -0.025**(0.010) [0.975] -0.021**(0.009) [1.027] 0.009(0.006) [1.009] 0.027***(0.007) [1.027] no	-0.145***(0.009) [0.865] 0.377***(0.091) [1.458] 0.245*** (0.028) [1.278] 0.434***(0.049) [1.548] -0.025**(0.011) [0.976] -0.022**(0.009) [0.978] 0.011*(0.006) [1.011] 0.027***(0.007) [1.028] no	- 0.145***(0.009) [0.865] 0.378***(0.091) [1.460] 0.245***(0.029) [1.278] 0.436***(0.049) [1.549] -0.025**(0.011) [0.976] -0.022**(0.009) [0.978] 0.011*(0.006) [1.011] 0.027***(0.007) [1.028] yes
N. Obs.	28873	28873	28873	28873	26304	26304
n. countries	21	21	21	21	19	19
n. parameters	35	28	27	36	36	38
L.L. random coeff.	-16353.027	-16234.135	-16505.216	-16188.714	-14774.339	-14773.851
L.L. random interc.				-16204.407		-14789.477
RE parameters						
Sd (constant)	0.216(0.026)	0.214 (0.026)	0.23 (0.027)	0.209(0.025)	0.180(0.027)	0.177(0.027)
Sd (ethnic)	0.404(0.085)	0.392 (0.085)	0.403(0.087)	0.398(0.085)	0.401(0.088)	0.400(0.088)

Legend: the dependent variable is a dummy equal to 1 if the respondent considers very likely unemployment and work seeking in the next 12 months, 0 otherwise. See also legend in Table 3.1

Note: Our Elaborations on ESS data

3. Socioeconomic Conditions

The analysis of the labor market status provides incomplete information to evaluate the welfare consequences of ethnic differences in the society. Any differences may arise in relation to the type of job (e.g., migrants are more likely to accept jobs that do not correspond to their educational qualification Dhayal et al. 2023) or because minorities experience lower earnings than majority members. This section focuses on two additional indicators, economic conditions and the ISCO classification of a given job. Likelihood ratio tests suggested to retain both random intercept and random slope in the final specification of the model (as above, the log-likelihood values reported, respectively, for the random intercept model and for the random coefficients model are shown only for the full model specification).

Table 5 focuses on economic conditions: the respondents' during the interview revealed their feelings about the household income on a scale from 1 (living comfortably on present income) to 4 (very difficult). The estimates are based on a linear random intercept model; binary and ordered logitestimates have also been considered in previous estimates. According to the results in the third column, the ethnic gap is lower when controlling for individual education and family background. Family origins explain most of the observed gap between ethnic minorities and national majorities. For immigrants, as expected, the economic conditions are even lower. The estimates remain substantially the same when including the region-level variables.

Table 5. Economic conditions - linear multilevel model with random intercepts and random slopes

Variable	Coefficients (std errors) [odds ratios]					
	No owneducation	**No family origins**	**No family origins, no own education**	**Full model**	**Full model**	**Full model with region-level variables**
Education	0.239***(0.040)	-	0.265***(0.042)	-0.025(0.005)	-	-
ethnic	0.056***(0.013)	0.035***(0.007)	0.059***(0.014)	0.232***(0.040)	0.023***(0.006)	0.023***(0.006)
minority	0.222***(0.029)	0.276***(0.041)	0.238***(0.032)	0.057***(0.013)	0.235***(0.042)	0.234***(0.042)
female	-0.030***(0.005)	0.060***(0.014)		0.222***(0.029)	0.062***(0.014)	0.062***(0.014)
born abroad	-0.034***(0.005)	0.239***(0.031)		-0.027***(0.004)	0.199***(0.029)	0.199***(0.029)
mother's	0.009***(0.003)			-0.032***(0.004)	-	-
educ.	0.031***(0.003)			0.009***(0.003)	0.024***(0.004)	0.024***(0.004)
father's	no		no	0.029***(0.004)	-	-
education				no	0.031***(0.004)	0.030***(0.004)
mother'soccup.		no			0.007**(0.003)	0.007**(0.003)
father'soccup.					0.028***(0.004)	-
regional					no	0.030***(0.004)
indicators						yes
N. Obs.	29436	29436	29436	29436	26801	26801
n. countries	21	21	21	21	19	19
n. parameters	35	28	27	36	36	38
LL random	-32820.593	-33379.804	-33709.692	-32655.585	-28069.378	-28054.946
coeff.				-32721		-28123.237
LL random						
interc.	0.113(0.013)	0.117(0.012)	0.121(0.013)	0.112(0.013)	0.095(0.012)	0.074 (0.010)
RE	0.304(0.038)	0.301(0.035)	0.316(0.036)	0.292(0.037)	0.299(0.038)	0.299(0.038)
parameters	0.719(0.011)	0.732(0.012)	0.740(0.012)	0.715(0.011)	0.706(0.011)	0.706(0.011)
Sd(constant)						
Sd(ethnic)						
Sd (residual)						

Legend: dependent variable is respondent'sfeeling about household's income on a scale 0-3 (0 if living comfortably/coping on present income, 3 if very difficult). See also legend in Table 3.1. Notes: robust standard errors; sample weights included.

Note: Our Elaborations on ESS data

Finally, Table 6focuses on occupational status; relying on the ISCO classification, the considered levels are the following: 9: elementary occupation; 8:plant and machine operators and assemblers; 7:craft and related workers; 6:skilled agricultural and fishery workers; 5:service workers and shop and market sales workers; 4:clerks;3:technicians and associate professionals; 2:professionals; 1=legislators, senior officials and managers. The results are based on the estimation of a liner random coefficient model, with the slope varying across regions.

Table 6. Occupation-ISCO level - Linear multilevel model random intercepts and random slopes

Variable	Coefficients (std errors)					
	No owneducation	**No family origins**	**No family origins, no own education**	**Full model**	**full model**	**Full model with region-level vars**
Education	-	-	0.324**(0.137)	-	-0.162***(0.049)	-0.161***(0.050)
Ethnic minority	0.163(0.145)	0.209***(0.054)	0.962***(0.122)	0163***(0.045)	0.306**(0.155)	0.309**(0.155)
female	-0.546***(0.057)	0.418**(0.153)	0.575***(0.062)	0.262*(0.151)	-0.503***(0.062)	-0.503***(0.062)
born abroad	0.924***(0.0111)	-		-	0.846***(0.107)	0.852***(0.108)
mother's	-0.129***(0.020)	0.536***(0.063)		0.523***(0.058)	-0.104***(0.021)	-0.104***(0.021)
education	-0.149***(0.019)	0.970***(0.118)		0.934***(0.108)	-0.134***(0.020)	-0.134***(0.020)
father's education	0.051***(0.009)			-	0.044***(0.010)	0.045***(0.010)
mother's	0.136***(0.013)		no	0.523***(0.058)	0.109***(0.013)	0.108***(0.013)
occupation	no			-	no	yes
father'soccupation				0.134***(0.020)		
Regionalindicators		no		0.045***(0.009)		
				0.114***(0.013)		
				no		
N. Obs.	19543	19543	19543	19543	17864	17864
n. countries	21	21	21	21	19	19
n. parameters	35	28	27	36	36	38
LL random coeff.	-42544.386	-42916.976	-43660.537	-42056.406	-36904.634	-36898.400
LL random intercept				-42100		-36937.971
RE parameters						
Sd (constant)	0.233(0.036)	0.463(0.039)	0.319(0.045)	0.218(0.034)	0.229(0.035)	0.199(0.030)
Sd (ethnic)	0.843(0.209)	0.957(0.150)	0.742(0.140)	0.920(0.191)	0.910(0.195)	0.894(0.197)
Sd(residuals)	2.189(0.023)	2.226(0.036)	2.318(0.027)	2.134(0.029)	2.137(0.032)	2.127(0.032)

Legend: dependent variable Occupation (ISCO level): 9 farm worker; 8=unskilled worker;...2= higher administrator occupation; 1=professional and technical occupation (ISCOclassification). See also legend in Table 3.1. Notes: robust standard errors; sample weights included.

Note: Our Elaborations on ESS data

Ethnic minorities are more likely to be engaged in job characterized by a higher physical burden. Family background explains much of this gap since its omission in the second column increases the ethnic gap. Not surprisingly, the coefficient for individuals born abroad is very high; as mentioned above, migrants may lack fluency in the language of the host country, and this may explain why they are allocated in positions that do not require a plenty of communication. Secondly, migrants coming from less developed countries have often low competencies since the educational systems in their home country is usually quite limited, or more simply, employers in the new country may be unable to properly evaluate their scholastic qualifications (OECD, 2013); however, when immigrants can rely on family support, their disadvantage goes down.

CONCLUSION

The analysis in the previous sections reveals the presence of sizeable differences in the socio-economic achievement comparing self-identified ethnic minorities and national majorities across European countries. The observed ethnic penalties cannot be entirely attributed to migration difficulties since even native ethnic minorities experience disadvantages in the labor market. One possibility is that the observed "ethnic penalties" may reflect differences in human capital and family socioeconomic conditions. In the reported estimates, own education improves individual probabilities of employment; with respect to education, no significant differences are observed between minority groups and national majorities when family origins are taken into account; with respect to employment probabilities, the observed ethnic disadvantage is slightly lower when controlling for family background. This draws further attention on the low intergenerational mobility in Europe.

Overall, when controlling for own education, family background and place of birth, sizeable ethnic penalties remain. It is possible to admit the presence of discriminatory behavior in the labor market, varying across the different European regions; much of the heterogeneity across regions explained by social capital indicators – i.e., social trust and social distance –other than by local unemployment rates. Nonetheless, we are unable to conclusively link prejudice to the noted ethnic disadvantages. One potential problem is that the observed variables were not a good indicator of the individual's and the family's background. For instance, an individual's education did not fully explain their productivity at work, and parents from similar socioeconomic backgrounds might have different access to social networks. Reports of ethnic gaps may be biased if the unexplained heterogeneity among people was associated with their ethnic origins (and the direction of the bias would not be contested). Secondly, self-identified minorities, such as native ethnic minorities who have not fully assimilated, could make their disadvantage worse. However, it is important noting that the observed ethnic disparities are sizeable, too large to be fully explained only by measurement issues.

REFERENCES

Abowd, J. M., & Killingsworth, M. R. (1984). Do minority/white unemployment differences really exist? *Journal of Business & Economic Statistics*, 2(1), 64–72. DOI: 10.1080/07350015.1984.10509370

Adsera, A., & Chiswick, B. R. (2007). Are gender and country of origin differences in immigrant labor market outcomes across European destinations? *Journal of Population Economics*, 20(3), 495–526. DOI: 10.1007/s00148-006-0082-y

Alba, R. D., Kasinitz, P. M. C., & Waters, M. C. (2011). The kids are (mostly) alright: Second generation assimilation. *Social Forces*, 89, 763–774.

Altonji, J. G., & Blank, R. M. (1999). Race and gender in the labor market. Chapter 48 in *Handbook of Labor Economics,* Vol. 3, O. Ashenfeher and D. Card eds.

Arabiun, A., Hosseini, E., Mahmoodi, K., & Mohsen, B. (2023). An Investigation of the Socio-Cultural Impacts of the Digital Transformation in Developed, Developing, and Middle: Africa and Asia Pacific. In Joshi, M., Brahmi, M., Aldieri, L., & Vinci, C. (Eds.), *Exploring Business Ecosystems and Innovation Capacity Building in Global Economics* (pp. 112–130). IGI Global., DOI: 10.4018/978-1-6684-6766-4.ch006

Atkinson, A. (1983). The measurement of economic mobility. In Atkinson, A. (Ed.), *Social Justice and Public Policy*. MIT Press.

Bertrand, M., & Mullainathan, S. (2004). Are Emily and Greg More Employable than Lakisha and Jamal? A Field Experiment on Labor Market Discrimination. *The American Economic Review*, 94(4), 991–1013. DOI: 10.1257/0002828042002561

Borjas, G. J. (1990). *Friends or Strangers: The impact of immigrants on the US economy*. Basic Books.

Borjas, G. J. (1994). Assimilation and changes in cohort quality revisited: What happened to immigrant earnings during the 1980s? *Journal of Labor Economics*, 13(2), 201–245. DOI: 10.1086/298373 PMID: 12291239

Brahmi, M., Aldieri, L., Dhayal, K. S., & Agrawal, S. (2022). Education 4.0: Can It Be a Component of the Sustainable Well-Being of Students? In Shaikh, E., & Tunio, M. (Eds.), *Sustainable Development of Human Resources in a Globalization Period* (pp. 215–230). IGI Global., DOI: 10.4018/978-1-6684-4981-3.ch014

Brahmi, M., & Zouari, S. (2014). The Employment Policy in the Mining Industry: A Critical Study on Gender Discrimination. *Journal of Asian Business Strategy*, 4(8), 98–107. https://archive.aessweb.com/index.php/5006/article/view/4130/6390

Coleman, J. S. (1988). Social Capital in the Creation of Human Capital. *American Journal of Sociology*, 94, 95–S120. DOI: 10.1086/228943

Crawley, H. (2005). Evidence on Attitudes to Asylum and Immigration: What We Know, Don't Know and Need to Know, Centre on Migration, Policy and Society *Working Paper* No. 23, University of Oxford, 2005

Crawley H., Drinkwater S., Kause S., (2013). Regional Variations in Attitudes Towards Refugees: Evidence from Great Britain. *IZA DP N*. 7647

Dardanoni, V. (1993). On measuring social mobility. *Journal of Economic Theory*, 61(2), 372–394. DOI: 10.1006/jeth.1993.1073

Dhayal, K. S., Brahmi, M., Agrawal, S., Aldieri, L., & Vinci, C. P. (2023). A Paradigm Shift in Education Systems Due to COVID-19: Its Social and Demographic Consequences. In Tunio, M., & Memon, A. (Eds.), *Frugal Innovation and Social Transitions in the Digital Era* (pp. 157–166). IGI Global., DOI: 10.4018/978-1-6684-5417-6.ch015

ESS Round 7: European Social Survey (2018): ESS-7 2014 Documentation Report. Edition 3.2. Bergen, European Social Survey Data Archive, NSD - Norwegian Centre for Research Data for ESS ERIC. DOI: 10.21338/NSD-ESS7-2014

ESS Round 7: European Social Survey Round 7 Data (2014). Data file edition 2.2. NSD - Norwegian Centre for Research Data, Norway – *Data Archive and distributor of ESS data for ESS ERIC*. DOI: 10.21338/NSD-ESS7-2014

ESS Round 8: European Social Survey (2020): ESS-8 2016 Documentation Report. Edition 2.2. Bergen, European Social Survey Data Archive, NSD - *Norwegian Centre for Research Data for ESS ERIC*. DOI: 10.21338/NSD-ESS8-2016

ESS Round 8: European Social Survey Round 8 Data (2016). Data file edition 2.2. NSD - Norwegian Centre for Research Data, *Norway Data Archive and distributor of ESS data for ESS ERIC*. DOI: 10.21338/NSD-ESS8-2016

Fukuyama, F. (1995). *Trust: The social virtues and the creation of prosperity*. The Free Press.

Granovetter, M. (1973, May). The Strength of Weak Ties. *American Journal of Sociology*, 78(6), 1360–1380. DOI: 10.1086/225469

Guangyi, S. (2017). *Essays on Social Capital and Economic Activity, PhD dissetation, Univ*. Of Leicester.

Heath, A., & Cheung, S. Y. (2007). The comparative study of ethnic minority disadvantage. *Chapter in Proccedings of the British Academy*,2007

Heckman, J. J. (1998). Detecting Discrimination. *The Journal of Economic Perspectives*, 12(2), 101–116. DOI: 10.1257/jep.12.2.101

Hegewisch, A., & Liepmann, H. (2013). Occupational Segregation and the Gender Wage Gap in the US. In Figart, D., & Warnecke, T. (Eds.), *Handbook of Research on Gender and Economic Life* (pp. 200–217). Edward Elgar. DOI: 10.4337/9780857930958.00024

Kahanec, M., & Zaiceva, A. (2009). Labour market outcomes of immigrants and non-citizens in the EU: An East-West comparison. *International Journal of Manpower*, 30(1/2), 97–115. DOI: 10.1108/01437720910948429

Kahanec M., Zaiceva A. and Zimmerman K.F. (2010). Ethnic minorities in the European Union: An overview. *IZA DP*, 5397

Kahanec, M., & Zimmerman, K. F. (Eds.). (2010). *EU Labor markets after post-enlargement migration*. Springer Verlag. DOI: 10.1007/978-3-642-02242-5

Kin, M. (2013). Race and ethnicity in the workplace. In Figart, D., & Warnecke, T. (Eds.), *Handbook of Research on Gender and Economic Life* (pp. 200–217). Edward Elgar.

Kirschenman J., Neckerman K.M., J.Kirschenman(1991)., Social Problems, 38 (4), Special Issue on the Underclass in the United States (Nov., 1991), 433-447.

Knack, S., & Keefer, P. (1995). Institutions And Economic Performance: Cross-Country Tests Using Alternative Institutional Measures. *Economics and Politics*, 7(3), 207–227. DOI: 10.1111/j.1468-0343.1995.tb00111.x

Lefranc, A. (2010). Unequal opportunities and ethnic origin: The labor market outcomes of second generationmigrants in France. *The American Behavioral Scientist*, 53(12), 1851–1882. DOI: 10.1177/0002764210368100

Mortensen, D. (1986). Job search and labor market analysis. Chapter 15 in Handbook of Labor Economics, vol. 2

Neumark, D. (2016).Experimental Research on Labor Market Discrimination, *NBER Working Paper* No. 22022

OECD. *International migration outlook*, (2019), https://www.oecd-ilibrary.org/

Pager D., Karafin D. (2009). Bayesian Bigot? Statistical Discrimination, Stereotypes, and Employer Decision Making, ANNALS, *AAPSS*, 621.

Phalet, K., & Heath, A. (2007). *From ethnic boundaries to ethnic penalties: urban economies and the Turkish second generation, technical report*. University of Utrecht.

Putnam, R. (1993). *Making Democracy Work.* Civic Traditions in Modern Italy.

Solon, G. (1999). Intergenerational Mobility in the Labor Market. In Ashenfelter, O. C., & Card, D. (Eds.), *Handbook of Labor Economics* (Vol. 3, pp. 1761–1800). North-Holland.

Trejo, S. J. (1997). Why Do Mexican Americans Earn Low Wages? *Journal of Political Economy*, 105(6), 1235–1268. DOI: 10.1086/516391

Weber, M. (1978). Ethnic groups. In Roth, G., & Wittich, C. (Eds.), *Economy and Society: an outline of interpretative sociology, 1, (II), Berkele: Univ. Of California press, 385-398*. DOI: 10.1007/978-1-349-26403-2_2

Zschirnt, E., Ruedin D., (2016) Ethnic Discrimination in Hiring Decisions: A Meta-Analysis of Correspondence Tests 1990–2015. *Journal of Ethnic and Migration Studites*, 1–19.

ENDNOTE

1 A preliminary version of this work is Ethnicminorities'disadvantages in Europe (2021) https://papers.ssrn.com/sol3/papers.cfm?abstract_id=3995458.

Chapter 11
Artificial Intelligence and Its Implications for Cattle and Buffalo Farming

Muhammad Faisal Sultan
KASB Institute of Technology, Pakistan

Muhammad Nawaz Tunio
https://orcid.org/0000-0003-1376-5371
University of Sufism and Modern Sciences, Pakistan

Muhammad Asim
Karachi University Business School, Pakistan

Erum Shaikh
https://orcid.org/0000-0002-3198-2786
Shaheed Benazir Bhutto University, Pakistan

ABSTRACT

The purpose of writing this chapter is to make readers understand the role of AI in cattle farming. Previously studies on this topic were scarce and did not contain all the possible benefits of smart-cattle farming. Therefore, this study is developed through consulting multiple studies to reflect vividly on benefits that AI may provide to cattle farmers. Hence, this study is highly significant for researchers, scholars, and academicians who as this study is not only beneficial for improvement of knowledge and conduction of further studies but may also aid better business practices and policy making associated with the use of AI in cattle farming. However, this is a generic form of study which is developed for better understanding and improvement of research activities rather than to reflect outcomes inferentially. Hence, further

DOI: 10.4018/979-8-3693-5723-1.ch011

work that may add to one's understanding must be conducted through focusing on the gist of this study.

BACKGROUND

Animal farming is an important topic all over the world and it has been practiced not only for economic benefits but also for reducing carbon footprints, rendering welfare for animals and to yield sustainable farming. However, there is one socially controversial view that is termed as animal husbandry that is related to cattle farming in a controversial manner (Hanjal et al., 2022).

In South-Asian countries farming is one of the most reliable sources for earning (Singh et al., 2022). Similar points are valid for the livestock sector in developing countries. In fact, the sector is perceived as the backbone of the economy. Similar is the case of Pakistan where the livestock sector surpasses the crop sector (Rana et al., 2021). Hence, there is a need to utilize efficient and effective methods to reduce issues associated with animal farming (Singh et al., 2022). Pakistan livestock sector comprises cows, goats, sheep; buffalos and horses etc. Hence, the sector is offering a large amount of milk, meat, skins and wool etc. In fact, the contribution of the livestock sector to the agriculture sector of Pakistan is more than 61% and around 12% in overall GDP of the country. On the other hand, the livestock sector is responsible for running around 40% of rural farmers (Rana et al., 2021).

However, besides these numerous advantages there are several challenges that are threatening the livestock sector in Pakistan. Breeding is perceived as the most important challenge associated with the business of livestock and creating havoc for the farmers. The challenge became critical day after day as most of the farmers capitalized on natural methods of insemination that not only causes genetic degradation but also several threats to animals. However, with the advent of technology a smaller slice of farmers are trying to capitalize on artificial intelligence (AI) for breeding and insemination (Rana et al., 2021). Studies highlighted that AI is the system through which we take advantage of computers to perform required activities with least efforts from human beings. In short AI-Based systems are sophistically trained for performing complex and customized tasks through utilizing advanced level knowledge embedded in the device (Singh et al., 2022).

INTRODUCTION

Cattle Farming is one of the prime branches of agriculture (Micle et al., 2021). Cattle Farming is divided into two major categories i.e., meat cattle that fulfills the need of meat as well as leather related products and dairy cattle that is required to fulfill dairy needs of the country. However, with the addition of technology in the farming industry the scope of the industry has been magnified and managing business also becomes efficient, manageable that can also be transformed to larger scales (de Oliveira Nascimento & de Oliveira Penheiro,2022).

Therefore, since longtime researchers are highlighting the role that combination of internet of things (IoT) and sensors can do for the betterment of agriculture business (Tedeschi et al., 2021). However, in the livestock or animal sector conduction of technologically integrated businesses is known as precision livestock farming, smart animal agriculture and smart livestock farming. These terminologies are based upon the holistic impact of technology that not only resulted in better production but will also result in welfare of the animal and less degradation of the environment. Studies further highlighted that smart cattle farming is one of the easiest way of doing small-scale business through applying sensor-based animal centric approach (Tedeschi et al., 2021). Therefore, the use of artificial methods for cattle farming are benefiting the sector in all the related fields like breeding and Insemination etc. However, in developing countries like Pakistan the facility is available to a very small slice of farmers where cattle and buffalo farming is the most dominant area of livestock farming (Rana et al., 2021). Hence multiple studies e.g., Anzar et al (2003); Chaudhry and Miranda (2015) and Rana et al (2022) etc. tried to increase focus towards use of AI for cattle and buffalo farming.

STATEMENT OF PROBLEM AND GRAY AREA

There are very few studies that may provide solutions to farmers to deal effectively with cattle farming and related issues (Rana et al., 2021). However, use of machine learning, applying algorithms and relating work to Artificial Intelligence has been beneficial for several industries. Thus, there is significant need to understand the role of artificial intelligence in the field of cattle farming (de Oliveira Nascimento & de Oliveira Penheiro, 2022)

LITERATURE REVIEW

According to studies, use of sensors is one of the mandatory elements for dairy cattle farming. However, with the advancement of time expectations of farmers are also getting increased. Recent studies mentioned that the devices must be durable and also able to provide behavioral and psychological support to farmers for effective decision making (Hanjal et al., 2022). Hence, use of AI is highly significant for the agriculture sector. In fact, use of AI will not only be used for decreasing of cost and increase of quality but also for assessing animals' health, emotions, moods, and walking behavior etc. Therefore, these measures will not only make farmers take better decisions about the business but also about the animal' health and wellbeing (Patel et al., 2022).

Use of AI for Automated Milking:

Use of AI for automated milking is one of the prime uses of technology in animal's husbandry. In fact, use of AI also helps in assessing the product quality as well as anomalies through utilizing smart sensors (Costa et al., 2012; Patel et al., 2022). Use of AI in the process of milking will not only reduce need of manpower, hurdles in issues but will also assure milk consistency, animal health and welfare. Hence the use of an automated milking system in husbandry of cattle is highly beneficial (Micle et al., 2021).

Use of AI for Artificial Data Collection:

Through using advanced technology farmers have the tendency to make more precise and effective decisions. These decisions now can be made on an individual basis for each of the animals which provides detailed understanding of animal health, behavior, movement, rumination, diet intake, sleep cycles and sickness etc. In fact, at the advent of AI quality of air can also be assessed at shelters of animals. Hence enable farmers to take the best possible decision for managing cattle, farm as well as quality of food (Patel et al., 2022).

Use of AI for Harvesting:

Use of AI for harvesting not only reduces the time of harvesting but also will assess the total consumption as well as quality of the cereal (Patel et al., 2022).

Adding to this point Kasera et al (2024) indicated that use of AI is also beneficial for pre-harvest, harvest and post-harvest activities. Hence, use of AI is beneficial for developing cereals, assessing quality and its effect and predicting development of cereals and meals for future.

Use of AI for Assessing Body Temperature:

Use of AI may also assess the body temperature of cows on a daily basis. In fact, this can also be done through radio frequency identification (RFID) biosensors on the lower part of an animal's ear. Other way to analyze temperature of animal's body is through using remote sensing cameras and computer vision analysis (Micle et al., 2021)

Use of Block chain Technology for improving Food Supply Chain:

Use of block chain in the food supply chain will not only improve traceability but will also optimize the level of food safety. Thus, has the potential to provide highly competitive advantage to those farmers who are lure with this form of technologies (Patel et al., 2022).

Effective & Early Determination of Lameness:

Lameness is considered as the top-ranked factor that may affect the productivity level of cattle. However, severe lameness may be easy to detect but by this time the damage has been done to animals. Therefore, treatment will not fully recover the animal. However, using precision livestock farming it is efficient to monitor every animal and detect mild or minor lameness in animals (Tedeschi et al., 2021).

Effective & Early Detection of Diseases:

Use of AI and machine learning is also effective in early detection of diseases like ketosis and meteorites. According to literature the purpose of using AI and machine learning for disease detection is beneficial especially when they become able to detect the disease earlier than humans. According to a literature survey more than 100 studies were published on the topic of use of AI and dairy sector that highlight various types of diseases e.g., health, mastitis, heat stress, body condition and physiology (De Vries et al., 2023).

Use of AI Robots for Vaccination:

This method is quite popular in poultry farming and with lowest chances of error AI-based robots perform vaccination in a minimal amount of time. Through using AI-based robots for vaccination farmers may also have idea about the level of immunity for each of the elements. Hence the use is not only beneficial for cost and time reduction but may also provide better results of vaccination than the conventional forms of vaccination (Patel et al., 2022)

METHODOLOGY

The purpose of this chapter is to develop detailed understanding about the role of AI for cattle farming. In fact the purpose of research is descriptive (Sekaran & Bougie, 2016) as the study is conducted to understand the significance and implications of AI in the field of cattle farming. Therefore, this chapter has been developed through combining literature and evidence from multiple studies which makes this study associated with epistemology that is the philosophy of knowledge (Saunders et al., 2007). The philosophical stance that is used to connect philosophy of research with research approach and methodological choices is post-positivism that is applicable to quantitative as well as qualitative studies. The research approach is deductive, methodological choices in mono-method qualitative and research strategy is archival (Saunders et al., 2007 & Saunders et al., 2015).

DISCUSSION

On the basis of literature review the following model has been proposed to be further assessed by academicians, researchers and scholars. The model developed is not a perception of researchers and has been supplemented with creative ideas, throughs and claims made by previous studies. The purpose of model development is to foster research in the vein through quantitative surveys rather than theoretical discussion and conceptualization of work.

Figure 1. Proposed model for assessing benefits of AI for cattle farming

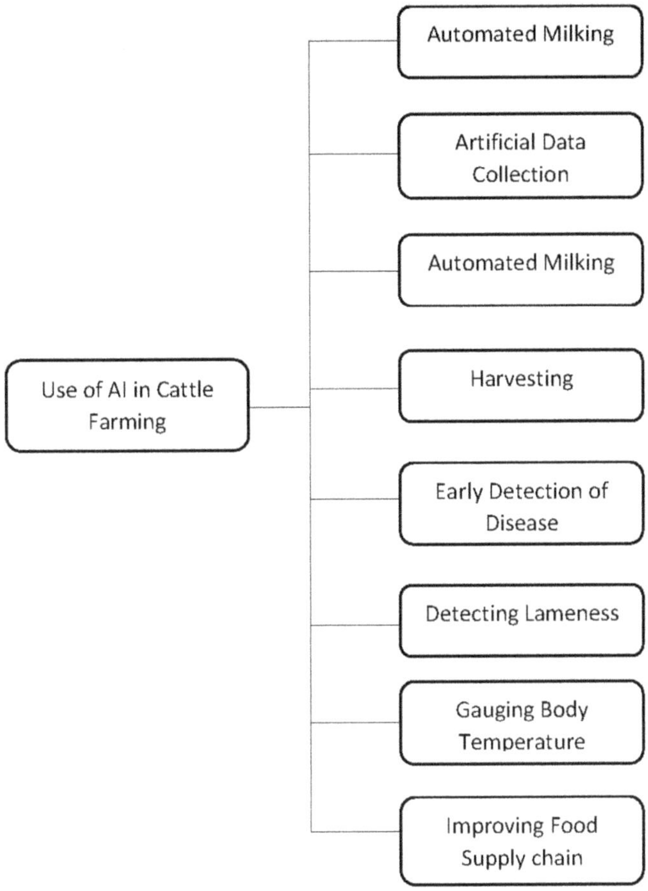

CONCLUSION

Study highlighted that cattle farming is one of the premier profession of inhabitants from developing and South Asian countries. However, there is a lack of understanding of the use of AI for agriculture sector. Thus, this chapter has been written purposively to reflect the benefits that famers may attain through using AI in cattle-farming. Hence, this study is a blend of literature from developing as well as developed sides of the world in order to make readers fully aware of the scope of the AI in the field of cattle farming.

Therefore, regardless of the nature of this study it is one of the most impactful studies conducted for understanding the significance of AI in livestock and cattle farming and can be capitalized by faculty, researchers, academicians, entrepreneurs, and policy makers for realizing academic and pragmatic benefits of this study.

REFERENCES

Anzar, M., Farooq, U., Mirza, M. A., Shahab, M., & Ahmad, N. (2003). Factors affecting the efficiency of artificial insemination in cattle and buffalo in Punjab, Pakistan. *Pakistan Veterinary Journal*, 23(3), 106–113.

Chaudhry, M. I., & Miranda, M. J. (2015). Structural Determinants of Adoption of Artificial Insemination among Livestock Farmers in Pakistan. In *2015 AAEA & WAEA Joint Annual Meeting, July 26-28, San Francisco, California* (No. 205285). Agricultural and Applied Economics Association

Costa, L. S., Pereira, D. F., Bueno, L. G. F., & Pandorfi, H. (2012). Some aspects of chicken behavior and welfare. *Revista Brasileira de Ciência Avícola*, 14(3), 159–164. DOI: 10.1590/S1516-635X2012000300001

de Oliveira Nascimento, V. S., & de Oliveira Pinheiro, G. (2022). Application of Artificial Intelligence in Cattle Farming: A Scope Review. *Revista Electrónica de Veterinaria*, •••, 30–40.

Hajnal, É., Kovács, L., & Vakulya, G. (2022). Dairy cattle rumen bolus developments with special regard to the applicable artificial intelligence (AI) methods. *Sensors (Basel)*, 22(18), 6812. DOI: 10.3390/s22186812 PMID: 36146158

Kasera, R. K., Gour, S., & Acharjee, T. (2024). A comprehensive survey on IoT and AI based applications in different pre-harvest, during-harvest and post-harvest activities of smart agriculture. *Computers and Electronics in Agriculture*, 216, 108522. DOI: 10.1016/j.compag.2023.108522

Micle, D. E., Deiac, F., Olar, A., Dren a, R. F., Florean, C., Coman, I. G., & Arion, F. H. (2021). Research on innovative business plan. Smart cattle farming using artificial intelligent robotic process automation. *Agriculture*, 11(5), 430. DOI: 10.3390/agriculture11050430

. Patel, H., Samad, A., Hamza, M., Muazzam, A., & Harahap, M. K. (2022). Role of Artificial Intelligence in Livestock and Poultry Farming. *Sinkron: jurnal dan penelitian teknik informatika, 7*(4), 2425-2429

Rana, H. A., Iftikhar, M., Wattoo, M. A., & Bilal, M. Q. (2021). Farmers' perceptions regarding artificial insemination services in Punjab, Pakistan. *International Journal of Agricultural Extension*, 9(2), 163–170.

Saunders, M., & Lewis, P. & Thornhill, A. (2007). Research methods. *Business (Atlanta, Ga.)*.

. Saunders, M. N., Lewis, P., Thornhill, A., & Bristow, A. (2015). Understand-ingnresearch philosophy and approaches to theory development, Pearson education

. Sekaran, U., & Bougie, R. (2016). Research methods for business: A skill building approach. john Wiley & Son

Singh, D., Singh, R., Gehlot, A., Akram, S. V., Priyadarshi, N., & Twala, B. (2022). An imperative role of digitalization in monitoring cattle health for sustainability. *Electronics, 11*(17), 2702 Students 4th edition Pearson Education Limited, England, 6(3), 1-268

Syed, M., & McLean, K. C. (2021). Disentangling paradigm and method can help bring qualitative research to post-positivist psychology and address the generalizability crisis. *Behavioral and Brain Sciences*, 45, 58–60. PMID: 35139943

Tedeschi, L. O., Greenwood, P. L., & Halachmi, I. (2021). Advancements in sensor technology and decision support intelligent tools to assist smart livestock farming. *Journal of Animal Science*, 99(2), skab038. DOI: 10.1093/jas/skab038 PMID: 33550395

Conclusion

As the curtains draw on this scholarly exploration, *Converging Economic Policy, Corporate Strategy, and Technology for Emerging Economies* underscores the intricate interplay of economic frameworks, strategic initiatives, and technological innovations in shaping the trajectory of emerging markets. The insights gleaned from the preceding chapters reinforce a central theme: sustainable growth in these economies necessitates a synergistic approach that aligns policy, strategy, and technology with local contexts and global aspirations.

Emerging economies occupy a unique position in the global economic order, characterized by vast potential, rapid transformations, and significant challenges. Throughout the book, authors have delved into diverse facets of this dynamic landscape, from examining investor behavior and capital structure decisions to understanding IPO underpricing and exploring the transformative power of blue ocean strategies. Each contribution offers critical perspectives, enabling policymakers, business leaders, and researchers to grasp the complexity of the issues at hand and devise innovative solutions.

A key insight from these chapters is the indispensable role of technology as a transformative force. Whether revolutionizing service delivery systems or reconfiguring manufacturing processes, technological advancements provide unparalleled opportunities for economic growth and development. However, these opportunities come with responsibilities. The integration of technologies like IoT, automation, and virtual reality requires careful navigation of challenges such as digital divides, organizational resistance, and skill gaps.

The thematic diversity of the chapters also highlights the importance of context-specific approaches. For instance, the bibliometric analysis of herding behavior in financial markets and the examination of IPO underpricing in India illustrate how local nuances shape global phenomena. Similarly, OpenStreetMap's application in emerging markets and the adoption of blue ocean strategies emphasize the need for tailored solutions that resonate with regional realities.

As editors, we recognize that the future of emerging economies hinges on fostering environments that support innovation, inclusivity, and resilience. To this end, policymakers must enact regulatory frameworks that encourage investment and entrepreneurship while ensuring equitable access to resources and opportunities. Corporate leaders, on the other hand, must align their strategies with sustainable development goals, leveraging technological advancements to drive efficiency and competitiveness.

At the heart of this book lies a call to action: a unified approach is essential to bridge the gaps between policy, strategy, and technology. Governments, corporations, and communities must collaborate to create ecosystems that nurture creativity, address systemic barriers, and unlock the latent potential of these economies. The chapters collectively serve as a blueprint for this transformative journey, offering actionable insights, thought-provoking analyses, and practical examples.

In closing, we hope that this volume serves as a catalyst for further research, dialogue, and innovation. Emerging economies are poised to be the engines of global growth, but their success will depend on the collective efforts of stakeholders to navigate complexities and seize opportunities. The road ahead is undoubtedly challenging, but with concerted effort and visionary leadership, it is possible to chart a path toward inclusive, sustainable, and technology-driven growth.

Compilation of References

Abdulrahman, K. O., & Baba, R. A. (2024). Additive Manufacturing Technologies for On-Demand Production of Customised Goods in the Era of the 4th Industrial Revolution. In *Advances in Industrial Engineering in the Industry 4.0 Era* (pp. 127-146). CRC Press.

Aberdeen (2017). Asset Performance Management https://resources.altium.com/sites/default/files/uberflip_docs/file_964.pdf

Abeywardhana, D. K. Y. (2017). 'Capital Structure Theory: An Overview', *Accounting and Finance Research*, 6.

Abowd, J. M., & Killingsworth, M. R. (1984). Do minority/white unemployment differences really exist? *Journal of Business & Economic Statistics*, 2(1), 64–72. DOI: 10.1080/07350015.1984.10509370

Abutaha, F., & Dinler, C. (2024). Adopting Robotic Process Automation (RPA) in the Construction Industry. In *Complex AI Dynamics and Interactions in Management* (pp. 273-310). IGI Global.

Accelerating sustainable and inclusive growth. (2023, September 18). McKinsey & Company. https://www.mckinsey.com/about-us/overview/sustainable-and-inclusive-growth

Acemoglu, D., Johnson, S., & Robinson, J. A. (2001). The colonial origins of comparative development: An empirical investigation. *The American Economic Review*, 91(5), 1369–1401. DOI: 10.1257/aer.91.5.1369

Adedeji, A. (1998). Does the Pecking Order Hypothesis Explain the Dividend Payout Ratios of Firms in the UK? *Journal of Business Finance & Accounting*, 25(9-10), 9–10. DOI: 10.1111/1468-5957.00230

Adekugbe, A. P., & Ibeh, C. V.Arenike Patricia AdekugbeChidera Victoria Ibeh. (2024). Innovating service delivery for underserved communities: Leveraging data analytics and program management in our context. *International Journal of Applied Research in Social Sciences*, 6(4), 472–487. DOI: 10.51594/ijarss.v6i4.986

Adsera, A., & Chiswick, B. R. (2007). Are gender and country of origin differences in immigrant labor market outcomes across European destinations? *Journal of Population Economics*, 20(3), 495–526. DOI: 10.1007/s00148-006-0082-y

Aggarwal, D., & Padhan, P. C. (2017). Impact of Capital Structure on Firm Value: Evidence from Indian Hospitality Industry. *Theoretical Economics Letters*, 07(4), 982–1000. DOI: 10.4236/tel.2017.74067

Aghion, P., & Howitt, P. (2009). *The economics of growth*. MIT Press.

Ah Mand, A., Janor, H., Abdul Rahim, R., & Sarmidi, T. (2023). Herding behavior and stock market conditions. *PSU Research Review*, 7(2), 105–116. DOI: 10.1108/PRR-10-2020-0033

Ahmad, M. (2023). Exploring the Role of OpenStreetMap in Mapping Religious Tourism in Pakistan for Sustainable Development. In J. P. D. M. Vítor, A. G. da R. N. João, L. de J. P. Maria, & A. de M. C. Liliana (Eds.), *Experiences, Advantages, and Economic Dimensions of Pilgrimage Routes* (pp. 23–40). IGI Global. DOI: 10.4018/978-1-6684-9923-8.ch002

Ahmad, M. (2024). Unleashing Business Potential: Harnessing OpenStreetMap for Intelligent Growth and Sustainability. In Singh, S., Rajest, S. S., Hadoussa, S., Obaid, A. J., & Regin, R. (Eds.), *Data-Driven Intelligent Business Sustainability* (pp. 177–198). IGI Global., DOI: 10.4018/979-8-3693-0049-7.ch013

Ahmad, M., & Ali, A. (2023). Mapping the future of sustainable development through cloud-based solutions: A case study of openstreetmap. In *Promoting Sustainable Management Through Technological Innovation* (pp. 153–176). IGI Global., DOI: 10.4018/978-1-6684-9979-5.ch011

Ahmad, M., & Wu, Q. (2022). Does herding behavior matter in investment management and perceived market efficiency? Evidence from an emerging market. *Management Decision*, 60(8), 2148–2173. DOI: 10.1108/MD-07-2020-0867

Ahmed, F., & Karira, D. (2019). Empirical analysis of Herd Behavior in Pakistan Stock exchange. *Estudios de Economía Aplicada*, 37(1), 147–169. DOI: 10.25115/eea.v37i1.2582

Ahn, K., Cong, L., Jang, H., & Kim, D. S. (2024). Business cycle and herding behavior in stock returns: Theory and evidence. *Financial Innovation*, 10(1), 6. DOI: 10.1186/s40854-023-00540-z

Akbar, U. S., Oad Rajput, S. K., & Bhutto, N. A. (2019). Do investors herd with industries or markets? Evidence from Pakistan stock exchange. *Cogent Economics & Finance*, 7(1), 1698089. DOI: 10.1080/23322039.2019.1698089

Al Adwan, A., Kokash, H., Al Adwan, R., & Khattak, A. (2023). Data analytics in digital marketing for tracking the effectiveness of campaigns and inform strategy. *International Journal of Data and Network Science*.

Al Bashar, M., Taher, M. A., Islam, M. K., & Ahmed, H. (2024). The Impact Of Advanced Robotics And Automation On Supply Chain Efficiency In Industrial Manufacturing: A Comparative Analysis Between The Us And Bangladesh. *Global Mainstream Journal of Business, Economics. Development & Project Management*, 3(03), 28–41.

Alam, S., & Islam, M. T. (2017). Impact of Blue Ocean Strategy on Organizational Performance: A literature review toward implementation logic. *IOSR Journal of Business and Management*, 19(1), 01–19. DOI: 10.9790/487X-1901030119

Alba, R. D., Kasinitz, P. M. C., & Waters, M. C. (2011). The kids are (mostly) alright: Second generation assimilation. *Social Forces*, 89, 763–774.

Alhaj-Yaseen, Y. S., & Ladd, D. (2019). Which sentiments do US investors follow when trading ADRs? *Journal of Economics and Finance*, 43(3), 506–527. DOI: 10.1007/s12197-018-9452-z

Alhaj-Yaseen, Y. S., & Yau, S. K. (2018). Herding tendency among investors with heterogeneous information: Evidence from China's equity markets. *Journal of Multinational Financial Management*, 47, 60–75. DOI: 10.1016/j.mulfin.2018.11.001

Alkunte, S., Fidan, I., Naikwadi, V., Gudavasov, S., Ali, M. A., Mahmudov, M., Hasanov, S., & Cheepu, M. (2024). Advancements and Challenges in Additively Manufactured Functionally Graded Materials: A Comprehensive Review. *Journal of Manufacturing and Materials Processing*, 8(1), 23. DOI: 10.3390/jmmp8010023

Altonji, J. G., & Blank, R. M. (1999). Race and gender in the labor market. Chapter 48 in *Handbook of Labor Economics,* Vol. 3, O. Ashenfeher and D. Card eds.

Amankwah-Amoah, J., Abdalla, S., Mogaji, E., Elbanna, A., & Dwivedi, Y. K. (2024). The impending disruption of creative industries by generative AI: Opportunities, challenges, and research agenda. *International Journal of Information Management*, 79, 102759. DOI: 10.1016/j.ijinfomgt.2024.102759

Anand, R., & Singh, B. (2019). Effect of composition of board and promoter group retained ownership on underpricing of Indian IPO firms: An empirical study. *Indian Journal of Corporate Governance*, 12(1), 21–38. DOI: 10.1177/0974686219836539

Anand, R., & Tulin, V. (2015). Investment, productivity, and economic growth in the developing world. *Journal of Development Economics*, 116, 82–92. DOI: 10.1016/j.jdeveco.2015.03.007

Anarbayevich, A. R. (2024). EXPLORING THE PRACTICAL APPLICATIONS OF IoT TECHNOLOGIES. *International Journal of Advances in Scientific Research*, 4(02), 88–100. DOI: 10.37547/ijasr-04-02-15

Ansari, A., & Ansari, V. A. (2021). Do investors herd in emerging economies? Evidence from the Indian equity market. *Managerial Finance. Vol. 47 No. 7, pp.* 951-974. https://doi.org/DOI: 10.1108/MF-06-2020-0331

Anzar, M., Farooq, U., Mirza, M. A., Shahab, M., & Ahmad, N. (2003). Factors affecting the efficiency of artificial insemination in cattle and buffalo in Punjab, Pakistan. *Pakistan Veterinary Journal*, 23(3), 106–113.

Aparisi T, S., & Ribes Giner, G. (2022). Entrepreneurial leadership factors: a bibliometric analysis for the 2000-2020 period.https://doi.org/DOI: 10.5295/cdg.211456sa

Arabiun, A., Hosseini, E., Mahmoodi, K., & Mohsen, B. (2023). An Investigation of the Socio-Cultural Impacts of the Digital Transformation in Developed, Developing, and Middle: Africa and Asia Pacific. In Joshi, M., Brahmi, M., Aldieri, L., & Vinci, C. (Eds.), *Exploring Business Ecosystems and Innovation Capacity Building in Global Economics* (pp. 112–130). IGI Global., DOI: 10.4018/978-1-6684-6766-4.ch006

Aripin, Z., Saepudin, D., & Gunawan, A. (2024, February). The impact of omni-channel integrated marketing communications (IMC) on retail product and service satisfaction in Indonesia: An analysis with an open access approach. *Journal of Jabar Economic Society Networking Forum*, 1(3), 33–48.

Arjoon, V., & Bhatnagar, C. S. (2017). Dynamic herding analysis in a frontier market. *Research in International Business and Finance*, 42, 496–508. DOI: 10.1016/j.ribaf.2017.01.006

Arora, N., & Singh, B. (2019). Impact of auditor and underwriter reputation on underpricing of SME IPOs in India. *Management and Labour Studies*, 44(2), 193–208. DOI: 10.1177/0258042X19829285

Asante Antwi, H. (2022). Mitigating the destructive outcome of negative environmental stock market behaviours on environmental health security in China. *Journal of Sustainable Finance & Investment*, 12(3), 870–885. DOI: 10.1080/20430795.2020.1809291

Atkinson, A. (1983). The measurement of economic mobility. In Atkinson, A. (Ed.), *Social Justice and Public Policy*. MIT Press.

Atwal, K. S., Anderson, T., Pfoser, D., & Züfle, A. (2022). Predicting building types using OpenStreetMap. *Scientific Reports*, 12(1), 19976. Advance online publication. DOI: 10.1038/s41598-022-24263-w PMID: 36404337

Baig, A. S., & Chen, M. (2022). Did the COVID-19 pandemic (really) positively impact the IPO Market? An Analysis of information uncertainty. *Finance Research Letters*, 46, 102372. DOI: 10.1016/j.frl.2021.102372 PMID: 35431676

Bajo, E., & Raimondo, C. (2017). Media sentiment and IPO underpricing. *Journal of Corporate Finance*, 46, 139–153. DOI: 10.1016/j.jcorpfin.2017.06.003

Baker, E. D., Boulton, T. J., Braga-Alves, M. V., & Morey, M. R. (2021). ESG government risk and international IPO underpricing. *Journal of Corporate Finance*, 67, 101913. DOI: 10.1016/j.jcorpfin.2021.101913

Baker, M., & Wurgler, J. (2002). Market Timing and Capital Structure. *The Journal of Finance*, 57(1), 1–32. DOI: 10.1111/1540-6261.00414

Balasubramanian, P. (2023). Automation in Data Science, Software, and Information Services. In *Springer Handbook of Automation* (pp. 989–1014). Springer International Publishing. DOI: 10.1007/978-3-030-96729-1_46

Balcilar, M., Demirer, R., & Hammoudeh, S. (2013). Investor herds and regime-switching: Evidence from Gulf Arab stock markets. *Journal of International Financial Markets, Institutions and Money*, 23, 295–321. DOI: 10.1016/j.intfin.2012.09.007

Balcılar, M., Demirer, R., & Ulussever, T. (2017). Does speculation in the oil market drive investor herding in emerging stock markets? *Energy Economics*, 65, 50–63. DOI: 10.1016/j.eneco.2017.04.031

Bardsen, J., Nilsen, B. E. S., Froyland, T., Ramondenc, P., Segura, J., Gabdullin, A., . . . Fonseca, S. H. (2024, March). Cloud-Based Planning and Real-Time Algorithms Improve Coiled Tubing Cleanout Efficiency. In *SPE/ICoTA Well Intervention Conference and Exhibition* (p. D021S008R003). SPE. DOI: 10.2118/218290-MS

Baskin, J. (1989). An Empirical Investigation of the Pecking Order Hypothesis. *Financial Management*, 18(1), 18. DOI: 10.2307/3665695

Bataineh, M. T., & Alomyan, N. R. (2017). The effect of Blue Ocean Strategy on increasing competitive Advantage on Commercial Banks (Irbid District) An Empirical Study. [IOSRJBM]. *IOSR Journal of Business and Management*, 19(12), 31–41.

Batten, J. A., & Vo, X. V. (2015). Foreign ownership in emerging stock markets. *Journal of Multinational Financial Management*, 32-33, 15–24. DOI: 10.1016/j.mulfin.2015.05.001

BCG. (2023).Reaching New Heights in Uncertain Times (2023). Reaching New Heights in Uncertain Times. https://media-publications.bcg.com/BCG_Most-Innovative-Companies-2023_Reaching-New-Heights-in-Uncertain-Times_May-2023.pdf

Beaulieu, M. C., & Mrissa Bouden, H. (2015). Firm-specific risk and IPO market cycles. *Applied Economics*, 47(50), 5354–5377. DOI: 10.1080/00036846.2015.1047091

Beer, F., Hamdi, B., & Zouaoui, M. (2018). Investors' sentiment and accruals anomaly: European evidence. *Journal of Applied Accounting Research*, 19(4), 500–517. DOI: 10.1108/JAAR-03-2017-0043

Belgacem, A., & Lahiani, A. (2013). Herding behavior around US macroeconomic announcements. [JABR]. *Journal of Applied Business Research*, 29(5), 1401–1410. DOI: 10.19030/jabr.v29i5.8022

Bellaaj, M. (2023). Why and how do individual entrepreneurs use digital channels in an emerging market? Determinants of use and channel coordination. *International Journal of Emerging Markets*, 18(9), 2735–2764. DOI: 10.1108/IJOEM-08-2020-0882

Benito, A. (2003). 'The capital structure decisions of firms: is there a pecking order?', *Working Papers 0310, Banco de España.*

Benz, L., Jacob, A., Paulus, S., & Wilkens, M. (2020). Herds on green meadows: The decarbonization of institutional portfolios. *Journal of Asset Management*, 21(1), 13–31. DOI: 10.1057/s41260-019-00147-z

Berger, A. N., & Bonaccorsi di Patti, E. (2006). Capital structure and firm performance: A new approach to testing agency theory and an application to the banking industry. *Journal of Banking & Finance*, 30(4), 1065–1102. DOI: 10.1016/j.jbankfin.2005.05.015

Bertrand, M., & Mullainathan, S. (2004). Are Emily and Greg More Employable than Lakisha and Jamal? A Field Experiment on Labor Market Discrimination. *The American Economic Review*, 94(4), 991–1013. DOI: 10.1257/0002828042002561

Bharti, B., & Kumar, A. (2020). Herding in fast moving consumer group sector: Equity market asymmetry and crisis. *The Journal of Asian Finance. Economics and Business*, 7(9), 39–49. DOI: 10.13106/jafeb.2020.vol7.no9.039

Bhattacharya, A. K. (2001). The Asian financial crisis and Malaysian capital controls. *Asia Pacific Business Review*, 7(3), 181–193. DOI: 10.1080/713999106

Bhuiyan, M. S. (2024). The Role of AI-Enhanced Personalization in Customer Experiences. *Journal of Computer Science and Technology Studies*, 6(1), 162–169. DOI: 10.32996/jcsts.2024.6.1.17

Bhullar, P. S., Grover, K. L., & Tiwari, R. (2024). IPO underpricing: A comparative analysis of risk factor disclosures in the financial and non-financial sectors. *The Bottom Line (New York, N.Y.)*, 37(3), 332–350. Advance online publication. DOI: 10.1108/BL-04-2023-0123

Bhuyan, R., Çetin, C., İzgi, B., & Talukdar, B. (2021). A model of dynamic information production for initial public offerings. *Quantitative Finance*, •••, 1–18. DOI: 10.1080/14697688.2023.2273975

Bikhchandani, S., Hirshleifer, D., & Welch, I. (1992). A theory of fads, fashion, custom, and cultural change as informational cascades. *Journal of Political Economy*, 100(5), 992–1026. DOI: 10.1086/261849

Bistrova, J., Lace, N., & Peleckienė, V. (2011). The Influence of Capital Structure on Baltic Corporate Performance / Kapitalo StruktŪra Baltijos ĮmonĖse. *Journal of Business Economics and Management*, 12(4), 655–669. DOI: 10.3846/16111699.2011.599414

Black, F. (1986). Noise. *The Journal of Finance*, 41(3), 529–543. DOI: 10.2307/2328481

Blanchard, O., Dell'Ariccia, G., & Mauro, P. (2010). Rethinking macroeconomic policy. *Journal of Money, Credit and Banking*, 42(s1), 199–215. DOI: 10.1111/j.1538-4616.2010.00334.x

Blockchain in the food supply chain - What does the future look like? (n.d.). Blockchain in the Food Supply Chain - What Does the Future Look Like? https://tech.walmart.com/content/walmart-global-tech/en_us/blog/post/blockchain-in-the-food-supply-chain.html

Boako, G., Tiwari, A. K., Ibrahim, M., & Ji, Q. (2019). Analysing dynamic dependence between gold and stock returns: Evidence using stochastic and full-range tail dependence copula models. *Finance Research Letters*, 31. Advance online publication. DOI: 10.1016/j.frl.2018.12.008

Bohl, M. T., Klein, A. C., & Siklos, P. L. (2014). Short-selling bans and institutional investors' herding behaviour: Evidence from the global financial crisis. *International Review of Financial Analysis*, 33, 262–269. DOI: 10.1016/j.irfa.2014.03.004

Borensztein, E., De Gregorio, J., & Lee, J. W. (1998). How does foreign direct investment affect economic growth? *Journal of International Economics*, 45(1), 115–135. DOI: 10.1016/S0022-1996(97)00033-0

Borjas, G. J. (1990). *Friends or Strangers: The impact of immigrants on the US economy*. Basic Books.

Borjas, G. J. (1994). Assimilation and changes in cohort quality revisited: What happened to immigrant earnings during the 1980s? *Journal of Labor Economics*, 13(2), 201–245. DOI: 10.1086/298373 PMID: 12291239

Borkowska, S., & Pokonieczny, K. (2022). Analysis of OpenStreetMap Data Quality for Selected Counties in Poland in Terms of Sustainable Development. *Sustainability (Basel)*, 14(7), 3728. Advance online publication. DOI: 10.3390/su14073728

Borole, P. J. (2024). Analysis and Implications of Adopting AI and Machine Learning in Marketing, Servicing, and Communications Technology. [IJAIML]. *International Journal of Artificial Intelligence and Machine Learning*, 13(1), 1–11. DOI: 10.4018/IJAIML.338379

Bowe, M., & Domuta, D. (2004). Investor herding during financial crisis: A clinical study of the Jakarta Stock Exchange. *Pacific-Basin Finance Journal*, 12(4), 387–418. DOI: 10.1016/j.pacfin.2003.09.003

Bradley, D. J., & Jordan, B. D. (2002). Partial Adjustment to Public Information and IPO Underpricing. *Journal of Financial and Quantitative Analysis*, 37(4), 595–616. DOI: 10.2307/3595013

Brahmi, M., Aldieri, L., Dhayal, K. S., & Agrawal, S. (2022). Education 4.0: Can It Be a Component of the Sustainable Well-Being of Students? In Shaikh, E., & Tunio, M. (Eds.), *Sustainable Development of Human Resources in a Globalization Period* (pp. 215–230). IGI Global., DOI: 10.4018/978-1-6684-4981-3.ch014

Brahmi, M., & Zouari, S. (2014). The Employment Policy in the Mining Industry: A Critical Study on Gender Discrimination. *Journal of Asian Business Strategy*, 4(8), 98–107. https://archive.aessweb.com/index.php/5006/article/view/4130/6390

Braunerhjelm, P., & Svensson, L. (2007). The role of technology and innovation in economic development. *Economics of Innovation and New Technology*, 16(6), 461–482. DOI: 10.1080/10438590701484452

Brealey, R. A., & Myers, S. C. (1991). *Principles of Corporate Finance* (4th ed.). McGraw-Hill.

Bui, Thi Ngoc, Xuan Hung Nguyen, and Kieu Trang Pham. (2023). 'The Effect of Capital Structure on Firm Value: A Study of Companies Listed on the Vietnamese Stock Market', *International Journal of Financial Studies*, 11.

Cakan, E., Demirer, R., Gupta, R., & Marfatia, H. A. (2019). Oil speculation and herding behavior in emerging stock markets. *Journal of Economics and Finance*, 43(1), 44–56. DOI: 10.1007/s12197-018-9427-0

Carnehl, C., Stenzel, A., & Schmidt, P. (2024). Pricing for the stars: Dynamic pricing in the presence of rating systems. *Management Science*, 70(3), 1755–1772. DOI: 10.1287/mnsc.2023.4771

Casillo, M., Cecere, L., Colace, F., Lorusso, A., & Santaniello, D. (2024). Integrating the Internet of Things (IoT) in SPA Medicine: Innovations and Challenges in Digital Wellness. *Computers*, 13(3), 67. DOI: 10.3390/computers13030067

Chabhadia, N., Jain, P., & Doshi, S. (2024, March). A review on digital manufacturing systems. In *AIP Conference Proceedings* (Vol. 3013, No. 1). AIP Publishing. DOI: 10.1063/5.0202021

Chandler, J. A., Payne, G. T., Moore, C. B., & Brigham, K. H. (2019). Family involvement signals in initial public offerings. *Journal of Family Business Strategy*, 10(1), 8–16. DOI: 10.1016/j.jfbs.2019.01.004

Chan, E. Y. (2024). Consumer Behavior in the Future. In *Consumer Behavior in Practice: Strategic Insights for the Modern Marketer* (pp. 251–263). Springer Nature Switzerland. DOI: 10.1007/978-3-031-50947-6_13

Chang, C. Y., Chen, H. L., & Jiang, Z. R. (2012). Portfolio performance in relation to herding behavior in the Taiwan stock market. *Emerging Markets Finance and Trade, 48*(sup2), 82-104.https://doi.org/DOI: 10.2753/REE1540-496X48S205

Chang, C. L., McAleer, M., & Wang, Y. A. (2020). Herding behaviour in energy stock markets during the Global Financial Crisis, SARS, and ongoing COVID-19. *Renewable & Sustainable Energy Reviews*, 134, 110349. DOI: 10.1016/j.rser.2020.110349 PMID: 34234619

Chang, E. C., & Dong, S. (2006). Idiosyncratic volatility, fundamentals, and institutional herding: Evidence from the Japanese stock market. *Pacific-Basin Finance Journal*, 14(2), 135–154. DOI: 10.1016/j.pacfin.2005.09.001

Chang, H. H., Chen, A., Kao, L., & Wu, C. S. (2014). IPO price discovery efficiency under alternative regulatory constraints: Taiwan, Hong Kong and the US. *International Review of Economics & Finance*, 29, 83–96. DOI: 10.1016/j.iref.2013.05.001

Chang, H.-J. (2014). *Economics: The user's guide*. Bloomsbury Publishing.

Chatterjee, M., Bhattacharjee, T., & Chakraborty, B. (2023). *Studies on Indian IPO: systematic review and future research agenda*. Qualitative Research in Financial Markets., DOI: 10.1108/QRFM-10-2021-0175

Chaudhry, M. I., & Miranda, M. J. (2015). Structural Determinants of Adoption of Artificial Insemination among Livestock Farmers in Pakistan. In *2015 AAEA & WAEA Joint Annual Meeting, July 26-28, San Francisco, California* (No. 205285). Agricultural and Applied Economics Association

Chen, H., & Zheng, M. (2021). IPO underperformance and the idiosyncratic risk puzzle. Journal of Banking &amp. *Journal of Banking & Finance*, 131, 106190. DOI: 10.1016/j.jbankfin.2021.106190

Chen, M., Mao, S., & Liu, Y. (2018). Big data: A survey. *Mobile Networks and Applications*, 19(2), 171–209. DOI: 10.1007/s11036-013-0489-0

Chen, T. (2013). Do investors herd in global stock markets? *Journal of Behavioral Finance*, 14(3), 230–239. DOI: 10.1080/15427560.2013.819804

Chin, A. L. L., & Shahzad, A. (2018). Are the Effects of Age Still Relevant in Predicting Malaysian Investors' Risk-Taking Behavior in Stock Market?. *International Journal of Engineering & Technology, 7*(3.21), 238-242.

Choijil, E., Méndez, C. E., Wong, W. K., Vieito, J. P., & Batmunkh, M. U. (2022). Thirty years of herd behavior in financial markets: A bibliometric analysis. *Research in International Business and Finance*, 59, 101506. DOI: 10.1016/j.ribaf.2021.101506

Choi, K. H., & Yoon, S. M. (2020). Investor sentiment and herding behavior in the Korean stock market. *International Journal of Financial Studies*, 8(2), 34. DOI: 10.3390/ijfs8020034

Choi, N., & Skiba, H. (2015). Institutional herding in international markets. *Journal of Banking & Finance*, 55, 246–259. DOI: 10.1016/j.jbankfin.2015.02.002

Chong, T. T. L., Liu, X., & Zhu, C. (2017). What explains herd behavior in the Chinese stock market? *Journal of Behavioral Finance*, 18(4), 448–456. DOI: 10.1080/15427560.2017.1365365

Christie, W. G., & Huang, R. D. (1995). Following the pied piper: Do individual returns herd around the market? *Financial Analysts Journal*, 51(4), 31–37. DOI: 10.2469/faj.v51.n4.1918

Chung, C. Y., & Wang, K. (2016). Short-term trading by individual investors in the Korean stock market. *Journal of the Asia Pacific Economy*, 21(4), 599–611. DOI: 10.1080/13547860.2016.1187798

Cohen, A., & Dalyot, S. (2021). Route planning for blind pedestrians using OpenStreetMap. *Environment and Planning. B, Urban Analytics and City Science*, 48(6), 1511–1526. Advance online publication. DOI: 10.1177/2399808320933907

Cohen, W. M., & Levinthal, D. A. (1990). Absorptive capacity: A new perspective on learning and innovation. *Administrative Science Quarterly*, 35(1), 128–152. DOI: 10.2307/2393553

Coleman, J. S. (1988). Social Capital in the Creation of Human Capital. *American Journal of Sociology*, 94, 95–S120. DOI: 10.1086/228943

Companies Are Satisfied with Business Outcomes from Big Data and Recognize Big Data as Very Important to Their Digital Transformation, Accenture Study Shows. (n.d.). https://newsroom.accenture.com/news/2014/companies-are-satisfied-with-business-outcomes-from-big-data-and-recognize-big-data-as-very-important-to-their-digital-transformation-accenture-study-shows

Corbane, C., Syrris, V., Sabo, F., Politis, P., Melchiorri, M., Pesaresi, M., Soille, P., & Kemper, T. (2021). Convolutional neural networks for global human settlements mapping from Sentinel-2 satellite imagery. *Neural Computing & Applications*, 33(12), 6697–6720. Advance online publication. DOI: 10.1007/s00521-020-05449-7

Costa, L. S., Pereira, D. F., Bueno, L. G. F., & Pandorfi, H. (2012). Some aspects of chicken behavior and welfare. *Revista Brasileira de Ciência Avícola*, 14(3), 159–164. DOI: 10.1590/S1516-635X2012000300001

Crawley H., Drinkwater S., Kause S., (2013). Regional Variations in Attitudes Towards Refugees: Evidence from Great Britain. *IZA DP N.* 7647

Crawley, H. (2005). Evidence on Attitudes to Asylum and Immigration: What We Know, Don't Know and Need to Know, Centre on Migration, Policy and Society *Working Paper* No. 23, University of Oxford, 2005

Črnigoj, M., & Mramor, D. (2014). Determinants of Capital Structure in Emerging European Economies: Evidence from Slovenian Firms. *Emerging Markets Finance & Trade*, 45(1), 72–89. DOI: 10.2753/REE1540-496X450105

Dalgıç, N., Ekinci, C., & Ersan, O. (2021). Daily and intraday herding within different types of investors in Borsa Istanbul. *Emerging Markets Finance & Trade*, 57(6), 1793–1810. DOI: 10.1080/1540496X.2019.1641082

Dambra, M., Field, L. C., Gustafson, M. T., & Pisciotta, K. (2018). The consequences to analyst involvement in the IPO process: Evidence surrounding the JOBS Act. *Journal of Accounting and Economics*, 65(2–3), 302–330. DOI: 10.1016/j.jacceco.2017.12.001

Dang, H. V., & Lin, M. (2016). Herd mentality in the stock market: On the role of idiosyncratic participants with heterogeneous information. *International Review of Financial Analysis*, 48, 247–260. DOI: 10.1016/j.irfa.2016.10.005

Danrimi, M. L., Abdullah, M., & Alfan, E. (2018). Investors' herding practice: Do IFRS and national economic culture matter? *Managerial Finance*, 44(9), 1117–1133. DOI: 10.1108/MF-08-2017-0311

Dardanoni, V. (1993). On measuring social mobility. *Journal of Economic Theory*, 61(2), 372–394. DOI: 10.1006/jeth.1993.1073

Das, G., Saha, M., & Kundu, A. (2016). Analyzing long-run performance of select initial public offerings using monthly returns: Evidence from India. *Vision (Basel)*, 20(3), 237–248. DOI: 10.1177/0972262916652809

Datar, V., & Mao, D. Z. (2006). Deep underpricing of China's IPOs: Sources and implications. *International Journal of Financial Services Management*, 1(2-3), 345–362. DOI: 10.1504/IJFSM.2006.009635

de Jong, A., Kabir, R., & Nguyen, T. (2008). 'Capital structure around the world: The roles of firm- and country-specific determinants', *Journal of Banking &amp. Finance*, 32, 1954–1969.

de Oliveira Nascimento, V. S., & de Oliveira Pinheiro, G. (2022). Application of Artificial Intelligence in Cattle Farming: A Scope Review. *Revista Electrónica de Veterinaria*, •••, 30–40.

DeAngelo, H., & Masulis, R. W. (1980). ' Optimal Capital Structure under Corporate and Personal Taxation. '. *Journal of Financial Economics*, 8(1), 3–29. DOI: 10.1016/0304-405X(80)90019-7

Deepa, S., & Abirami, A. (2024). The Impact of AI on Customer Experience. In *Balancing Automation and Human Interaction in Modern Marketing* (pp. 263–285). IGI Global. DOI: 10.4018/979-8-3693-2276-5.ch014

Demirer, R., Kutan, A. M., & Chen, C. D. (2010). Do investors herd in emerging stock markets?: Evidence from the Taiwanese market. *Journal of Economic Behavior & Organization*, 76(2), 283–295. DOI: 10.1016/j.jebo.2010.06.013

Deng, Q., Dai, L., Yang, Z., Zhou, Z. G., Hussein, M., Chen, D., & Swartz, M. (2023). The impacts of regulation regime changes on ChiNext IPOs: Effects of 2013 and 2020 reforms on initial return, fair value and overreaction. *International Review of Financial Analysis*, 89, 102794. DOI: 10.1016/j.irfa.2023.102794

Devenow, A., & Welch, I. (1996). Rational herding in financial economics. *European Economic Review*, 40(3-5), 603–615. DOI: 10.1016/0014-2921(95)00073-9

Dhayal, K. S., Brahmi, M., Agrawal, S., Aldieri, L., & Vinci, C. P. (2023). A Paradigm Shift in Education Systems Due to COVID-19: Its Social and Demographic Consequences. In Tunio, M., & Memon, A. (Eds.), *Frugal Innovation and Social Transitions in the Digital Era* (pp. 157–166). IGI Global., DOI: 10.4018/978-1-6684-5417-6.ch015

Digital Food Lab. (2019, April). Foodtech in India Startup and investment activity. https://www.digitalfoodlab. com/reports/2019-india/download

Ding, Y., & Cronin, B. (2011). Popular and/or prestigious? Measures of scholarly esteem. *Information Processing & Management*, 47(1), 80–96. DOI: 10.1016/j.ipm.2010.01.002

Djankov, S., McLiesh, C., & Ramalho, R. M. (2006). Regulation and growth. *Economics Letters*, 92(3), 395–401. DOI: 10.1016/j.econlet.2006.03.021

Donaldson, G. (1961). ' Corporate Debt Capacity: A Study of Corporate Debt Policy and the Determination of Corporate Debt Capacity. ', *Division of Research, Graduate School of Business Administration, Harvard University. Boston.*

Dong, Y., & Huang, J. (2022). Price limits, investor sentiment, and initial public offering underpricing: A quasi-natural experiment based on ChiNext. *Emerging Markets Review*, 51, 100893. DOI: 10.1016/j.ememar.2022.100893

Donthu, N., Kumar, S., Mukherjee, D., Pandey, N., & Lim, W. M. (2021). How to conduct a bibliometric analysis: An overview and guidelines. *Journal of Business Research*, 133, 285–296. DOI: 10.1016/j.jbusres.2021.04.070

DSIM report. (2015). Case Study- Zomato: An Indian Start-up acquiring the world. DSIM. https://dsim.in/ blog/2015/04/14/zomato-an-indian-startup-acquiring-the-world/Assessed

Dunning, J. H. (1993). *Multinational enterprises and the global economy*. Addison-Wesley.

Dzikowski, P. (2018). A bibliometric analysis of born global firms. *Journal of Business Research*, 85, 281–294. DOI: 10.1016/j.jbusres.2017.12.054

Earle, T. C. (2010). Trust in risk management: A model-based review of empirical research. Risk Analysis. *International Journal (Toronto, Ont.)*, 30(4), 541–574. DOI: 10.1111/j.15396924.2010.01398.x PMID: 20522197

Economou, F., Hassapis, C., & Philippas, N. (2018). Investors' fear and herding in the stock market. *Applied Economics*, 50(34-35), 3654–3663. DOI: 10.1080/00036846.2018.1436145

Eduardus Tandelilin, S., Hartono, J., & Hanafi, M. M. (2013). Detecting the existence of herding behavior in intraday data: Evidence from the Indonesia stock exchange. *Gadjah Mada International Journal of Business*, 15(1), 27–44. DOI: 10.22146/gamaijb.5399

Engelen, P. J., Heugens, P., Van Essen, M., Turturea, R., & Bailey, N. (2020). The impact of stakeholders' temporal orientaton on short-and long-term IPO outcomes: A meta-analysis. *Long Range Planning*, 53(2), 101853. DOI: 10.1016/j.lrp.2018.10.003

Escobar-Anel, M., & Jiao, Y. (2024). Robust Portfolio Optimization with Environmental, Social, and Corporate Governance Preference. *Risks*, 12(2), 33. DOI: 10.3390/risks12020033

ESS Round 7: European Social Survey (2018): ESS-7 2014 Documentation Report. Edition 3.2. Bergen, European Social Survey Data Archive, NSD - Norwegian Centre for Research Data for ESS ERIC. DOI: 10.21338/NSD-ESS7-2014

ESS Round 8: European Social Survey (2020): ESS-8 2016 Documentation Report. Edition 2.2. Bergen, European Social Survey Data Archive, NSD - *Norwegian Centre for Research Data for ESS ERIC.* DOI: 10.21338/NSD-ESS8-2016

Eswaran, U., & Khang, A. (2024). 8 Augmented Reality (AR) and Virtual Reality (VR) Technologies in Surgical Operating Systems. *AI and IoT Technology and Applications for Smart Healthcare Systems*, 113.

Ezeoha, E. (2008). Firm size and corporate financial-leverage choice in a developing economy. *The Journal of Risk Finance*, 9(4), 351–364. DOI: 10.1108/15265940810895016

Fama, E. F. (1970). Efficient Capital Markets: A Review of Theory and Empirical Work. *The Journal of Finance*, 25(2), 383–417. DOI: 10.2307/2325486

Fama, E. F., & French, K. R. (1993). Common Risk Factors in the Returns on Stocks and Bonds. *Journal of Financial Economics*, 33(1), 3–56. DOI: 10.1016/0304-405X(93)90023-5

Fama, E. F., & French, K. R. (2002). Testing Trade-Off and Pecking Order Predictions about Dividends and Debt. *Review of Financial Studies*, 15(1), 1–33. DOI: 10.1093/rfs/15.1.1

Fama, E. F., & French, K. R. (2005). Financing decisions: Who issues stock? *Journal of Financial Economics*, 76(3), 549–582. DOI: 10.1016/j.jfineco.2004.10.003

Fang, H., Lu, Y. C., & Yang, T. Y. (2013). The decomposition and causes of securities dealers' cascades in the Taiwan stock market. *Investment management and financial innovations*, (10, Iss. 3), 30-39.

Fang, H., Lu, Y. C., Yau, H. Y., & Lee, Y. H. (2013). Stock Characteristics Herded by Foreign Investors with Higher Abnormal Returns in the Taiwan Stock Market. *Romanian Journal of Economic Forecasting*, 16(4), 232–245.

Fasanya, I. O., & Akinwale, O. A. (2022). Exchange Rate Shocks and Sectoral Stock Returns in Nigeria: Do Asymmetry and Structural Breaks Matter? *Cogent Economics & Finance*, 10(1), 2045719. DOI: 10.1080/23322039.2022.2045719

Fazzari, S., Hubbard, R. G., Petersen, B., Blinder, A. S., & Poterba, J. M. (1988). Financing Constraints and Corporate Investment. *Brookings Papers on Economic Activity*, 19(1), 141–206. DOI: 10.2307/2534426

Filip, A. M., & Pochea, M. M. (2023). Intentional and spurious herding behavior: A sentiment driven analysis. *Journal of Behavioral and Experimental Finance*, 38, 100810. DOI: 10.1016/j.jbef.2023.100810

Fischer, G., Lundin, J., & Lindberg, J. O. (2020). Rethinking and reinventing learning, education and collaboration in the digital age—From creating technologies to transforming cultures. *International Journal of Information and Learning Technology*, 37(5), 241–252. Advance online publication. DOI: 10.1108/IJILT-04-2020-0051

Fonte, C. C., Lopes, P., See, L., & Bechtel, B. (2019). Using OpenStreetMap (OSM) to enhance the classification of local climate zones in the framework of WUDAPT. *Urban Climate*, 28, 100456. Advance online publication. DOI: 10.1016/j.uclim.2019.100456

Frank, Murray Z., and Vidhan K. Goyal. (2007). ' Trade-Off and Pecking Order Theories of Debt '.

Fukuyama, F. (1995). *Trust: The social virtues and the creation of prosperity*. The Free Press.

Füllbrunn, S., Neugebauer, T., & Nicklisch, A. (2020). Underpricing of initial public offerings in experimental asset markets. *Experimental Economics*, 23(4), 1002–1029. DOI: 10.1007/s10683-019-09638-7

Furman, J. L., Porter, M. E., & Stern, S. (2002). The determinants of national innovative capacity. *NBER Working Paper No. 8494*. DOI: 10.3386/w8494

Galariotis, E. C., Rong, W., & Spyrou, S. I. (2015). Herding on fundamental information: A comparative study. *Journal of Banking & Finance*, 50, 589–598. DOI: 10.1016/j.jbankfin.2014.03.014

Garfield, E., Sher, I. H., & Torpie, R. J. (1964). *The use of citation data in writing the history of science*. Institute for Scientific Information Inc Philadelphia PA. DOI: 10.21236/AD0466578

Gartner (2017). Prepare for the impact of digital twins. https://www.gartner.com/smarterwithgartner/prepare-for-the-impact-of-digital-twins

Gaviria-Marin, M., Merigo, J. M., & Popa, S. (2018). Twenty years of the Journal of Knowledge Management: A bibliometric analysis. *Journal of Knowledge Management*, 22(8), 1655–1687. DOI: 10.1108/JKM-10-2017-0497

Gavrilakis, N., & Floros, C. (2023). ESG performance, herding behavior and stock market returns: Evidence from Europe. *Operations Research*, 23(1), 3. DOI: 10.1007/s12351-023-00745-1

Ghorbel, A., Snene, Y., & Frikha, W. (2023). Does herding behavior explain the contagion of the COVID-19 crisis? *Review of Behavioral Finance*, 15(6), 889–915. DOI: 10.1108/RBF-12-2021-0263

Giannoukou, I. (2024). Revolutionizing Hospitality: Strategic Integration of Innovation Management Embracing Technological Innovation for Enhanced Customer Experiences. *Technium Business and Management*, 7, 24–39. DOI: 10.47577/business.v7i.10585

Gibson, I., Rosen, D., & Stucker, B. (2014). Additive Manufacturing Technologies: 3D Printing, Rapid Prototyping, and Direct Digital Manufacturing. Springer. https://www.mckinsey.com/~/media/BAB489A30B724BECB5DEDC41E9BB9FAC.ashx

Gjura Godec, M., & Nikšič, M. (2023). Empowering Public Engagement in Spatial Planning: A Collaborative Mapping Approach. *Igra Ustvarjalnosti - Creativy Game, 2023*(11). DOI: 10.15292/IU-CG.2023.11.066-071

Gleason, K. C., Mathur, I., & Peterson, M. A. (2004). Analysis of intraday herding behavior among the sector ETFs. *Journal of Empirical Finance*, 11(5), 681–694. DOI: 10.1016/j.jempfin.2003.06.003

Gokhale, P., Bhat, O., & Bhat, S. (2018). Introduction to IOT. *International Advanced Research. Journal of Science, Engineering and Technology*, 5(1), 41–44.

Gollin, D., & Rogerson, R. J. (2010). Agriculture, roads, and economic development in Uganda. *Journal of Development Economics*, 91(1), 22–32. DOI: 10.1016/j.jdeveco.2009.07.002

Goodfellow, C., Bohl, M. T., & Gebka, B. (2009). Together we invest? Individual and institutional investors' trading behaviour in Poland. *International Review of Financial Analysis*, 18(4), 212–221. DOI: 10.1016/j.irfa.2009.03.002

Govindaraj, M., Gnanasekaran, C., Kandavel, R., Khan, P., & Hoang, S. D. (2024). Revolutionizing Service Productivity: A Roadmap of Innovative Technologies. In *Innovative Technologies for Increasing Service Productivity* (pp. 41-60). IGI Global. DOI: 10.4018/979-8-3693-2019-8.ch003

Granovetter, M. (1973, May). The Strength of Weak Ties. *American Journal of Sociology*, 78(6), 1360–1380. DOI: 10.1086/225469

Graves, J. M., Abshire, D. A., Amiri, S., & Mackelprang, J. L. (2021). Disparities in Technology and Broadband Internet Access across Rurality: Implications for Health and Education. *Family & Community Health*, 44(4), 257–265. Advance online publication. DOI: 10.1097/FCH.0000000000000306 PMID: 34269696

Grossman, G. M., & Helpman, E. (1991). *Innovation and growth in the global economy*. MIT Press.

Guangyi, S. (2017). *Essays on Social Capital and Economic Activity, PhD dissetation, Univ*. Of Leicester.

Gunawan, K., Siagian, H., & Tarigan, Z. (2024). The impact of supply chain integration on operational performance with supply chain capability. *Uncertain Supply Chain Management*, 12(2), 977–988. DOI: 10.5267/j.uscm.2023.12.010

Gupta, S., & Shrivastava, M. (2021). Herding and loss aversion in stock markets: Mediating role of fear of missing out (FOMO) in retail investors. *International Journal of Emerging Markets*, 17(7), 1720–1737. DOI: 10.1108/IJOEM-08-2020-0933

Gupta, V., Singh, S., & Yadav, S. S. (2023). Disaggregated IPO returns, economic uncertainty and the long-run performance of SME IPOs. *International Journal of Emerging Markets*, 18(10), 3847–3867. DOI: 10.1108/IJOEM-09-2020-1098

Haghani, M., Cristiani, E., Bode, N. W., Boltes, M., & Corbetta, A. (2019). Panic, irrationality, and herding: Three ambiguous terms in crowd dynamics research. *Journal of Advanced Transportation*, 2019, 1–58. Advance online publication. DOI: 10.1155/2019/9267643

Hajnal, É., Kovács, L., & Vakulya, G. (2022). Dairy cattle rumen bolus developments with special regard to the applicable artificial intelligence (AI) methods. *Sensors (Basel)*, 22(18), 6812. DOI: 10.3390/s22186812 PMID: 36146158

Hall, B. H., & Lerner, J. (2010). The financing of innovation. In Hall, B. H., & Rosenberg, N. (Eds.), *Handbook of the Economics of Innovation* (Vol. 1, pp. 609–639). Elsevier., DOI: 10.1016/S0169-7218(10)01014-2

Halov, N., & Heider, F. (2011). 'Capital Structure, Risk and Asymmetric Information'. *The Quarterly Journal of Finance*, 1(4), 767–809. DOI: 10.1142/S2010139211000171

Hambly, H., & Rajabiun, R. (2021). Rural broadband: Gaps, maps and challenges. *Telematics and Informatics*, 60, 101565. Advance online publication. DOI: 10.1016/j.tele.2021.101565

Harahap, K. (2024). Harmonizing Differentiation and Cost Leadership Strategies in Culinary Businesses. *Research Horizon*, 4(2), 31–46.

Harcourt, G. C., & King, J. E. (2010). *The role of the state in the market economy*. Routledge.

Haritha, P. H., & Uchil, R. (2019). Impact of investor sentiment on decision-making in Indian stock market: An empirical analysis. *Journal of Advances in Management Research*, 17(1), 66–83. DOI: 10.1108/JAMR-03-2019-0041

Harris, M., & Raviv, A. (1991). ' The Theory of Capital Structure'. *The Journal of Finance*, 46(1), 297–355. DOI: 10.1111/j.1540-6261.1991.tb03753.x

Hasana, M. F., & Al-Dahanb, N. S. (2019). The herding effect of domestic investors on foreign investors: Evidence from the Iraq stock exchange. *International Journal of Innovation. Creativity and Change*, 10(6), 234–245.

Hasan, I., Tunaru, R., & Vioto, D. (2023). Herding behavior and systemic risk in global stock markets. *Journal of Empirical Finance*, 73, 107–133. DOI: 10.1016/j.jempfin.2023.05.004

Heath, A., & Cheung, S. Y. (2007). The comparative study of ethnic minority disadvantage. *Chapter in Proccedings of the British Academy*,2007

Heckman, J. J. (1998). Detecting Discrimination. *The Journal of Economic Perspectives*, 12(2), 101–116. DOI: 10.1257/jep.12.2.101

Hegewisch, A., & Liepmann, H. (2013). Occupational Segregation and the Gender Wage Gap in the US. In Figart, D., & Warnecke, T. (Eds.), *Handbook of Research on Gender and Economic Life* (pp. 200–217). Edward Elgar. DOI: 10.4337/9780857930958.00024

Helpman, E. (2004). *The mystery of economic growth.* Harvard University Press.

Herfort, B., Lautenbach, S., Porto de Albuquerque, J., Anderson, J., & Zipf, A. (2021). The evolution of humanitarian mapping within the OpenStreetMap community. *Scientific Reports*, 11(1), 3037. Advance online publication. DOI: 10.1038/s41598-021-82404-z PMID: 33542423

Hirshleifer, D., & Hong Teoh, S. (2003). Herd behaviour and cascading in capital markets: A review and synthesis. *European Financial Management*, 9(1), 25–66. DOI: 10.1111/1468-036X.00207

Honjo, Y. (2021). Public or perish? From founding to initial public offering. *Review of Managerial Science*, 15(6), 1573–1610. DOI: 10.1007/s11846-020-00390-4

Hsieh, S. F. (2013). Individual and institutional herding and the impact on stock returns: Evidence from Taiwan stock market. *International Review of Financial Analysis, 29*, 175-188. https://doi.org/DOI: 10.1016/j.irfa.2013.01.003

Huang, Y. (2008). The next Asian miracle. *Foreign Policy*, (167), 32–40.

Huang, Y., Leu, M. C., & Mazumder, J. (2013). A review of 3D printing technologies for soft polymer materials. *Virtual and Physical Prototyping*, 8(3), 187–200.

HUBS. (2021). Additive manufacturing trend report 2021. https://f.hubspotusercontent10.net/hubfs/4075618/Additive%20manufacturing%20trend%20report%202021.pdf

Hulland, J., & Houston, M. B. (2020). Why systematic review papers and meta-analyses matter: An introduction to the special issue on generalizations in marketing. *Journal of the Academy of Marketing Science*, 48(3), 351–359. DOI: 10.1007/s11747-020-00721-7

IFR International Federation of Robotics. (n.d.). *World Robotics 2023 Report: Asia ahead of Europe and the Americas.* https://ifr.org/ifr-press-releases/news/world-robotics-2023-report-asia-ahead-of-europe-and-the-americas

IMOH, I. (2024). A Technical Survey on The Role of Robotics in Conventional Manufacturing Process: An Element of Industry 4.0. *FUPRE Journal of Scientific and Industrial Research (FJSIR), 8*(2), 172-192.

Indārs, E. R., Savin, A., & Lublóy, Á. (2019). Herding behaviour in an emerging market: Evidence from the Moscow Exchange. *Emerging Markets Review*, 38, 468–487. DOI: 10.1016/j.ememar.2018.12.002

Industries & Technologies. (n.d.). Energy.gov. https://www.energy.gov/eere/iedo/industries-technologies

Irpan, M., & Shaddiq, S. (2024). Industry 4.0 and Industry 5.0—Inception, Conception, Perception, and Rethinking Loyalty Employment. *INTERNATIONAL JOURNAL OF ECONOMICS, MANAGEMENT* [IJEMBIS]. *BUSINESS, AND SOCIAL SCIENCE*, 4(1), 95–114.

Ivanov, D., Dolgui, A., & Sokolov, B. (2019). The Ripple Effect in supply chains: Trade-off 'efficiency-flexibility-resilience' in disruption management. *International Journal of Production Research*, 57(3), 829–846. DOI: 10.1080/00207543.2018.1488086

Jabeen, S., & Potturu, S. R. (2024, January). Survey on security and privacy of connected vehicles and cloud platforms for communication. In *AIP Conference Proceedings* (Vol. 2512, No. 1). AIP Publishing. DOI: 10.1063/5.0159381

Jaiyeoba, H. B., & Haron, R. (2016). A qualitative inquiry into the investment decision behaviour of the Malaysian stock market investors. *Qualitative Research in Financial Markets*, 8(3), 246–267. DOI: 10.1108/QRFM-07-2015-0027

Jalal, R. N. U. D., Sargiacomo, M., Sahar, N. U., & Fayyaz, U. E. (2020). Herding behavior and cryptocurrency: Market asymmetries, inter-dependency and intra-dependency. *The Journal of Asian Finance. Economics and Business*, 7(7), 27–34. DOI: 10.13106/jafeb.2020.vol7.no7.027

Jamil, S. (2021). From digital divide to digital inclusion: Challenges for wide-ranging digitalization in Pakistan. *Telecommunications Policy*, 45(8), 102206. Advance online publication. DOI: 10.1016/j.telpol.2021.102206

Jensen, M. C., & Meckling, W. H. (1976). Theory of the Firm: Managerial Behavior, Agency Costs and Ownership Structure. *Journal of Financial Economics*, 3(4), 3. DOI: 10.1016/0304-405X(76)90026-X

Jesuthasan, R. (2018, October 11). *What we often get wrong about automation*. Harvard Business Review. https://hbr.org/2018/10/what-we-often-get-wrong-about-automation

Jiang, R., Wen, C., Zhang, R., & Cui, Y. (2022). Investor's herding behavior in Asian equity markets during COVID-19 period. *Pacific-Basin Finance Journal*, 73, 101771. DOI: 10.1016/j.pacfin.2022.101771

Jiang, S. (2024). Analysis Of the Impact of Information Filtering on People's Thinking—Take Filter Bubble as An Example. *Journal of Education. Humanities and Social Sciences*, 28, 759–763.

Josyula, H. P., Reddi, L. T., Parate, S., & Rajagopal, A. (2024). A Review on Security and Privacy Considerations in Programmable Payments. *International Journal of Intelligent Systems and Applications in Engineering*, 12(9s), 256–263.

Kabir, M. H., & Shakur, S. (2018). Regime-dependent herding behavior in Asian and Latin American stock markets. *Pacific-Basin Finance Journal*, 47, 60–78. DOI: 10.1016/j.pacfin.2017.12.002

Kahanec M., Zaiceva A. and Zimmerman K.F. (2010). Ethnic minorities in the European Union: An overview. *IZA DP*, 5397

Kahanec, M., & Zaiceva, A. (2009). Labour market outcomes of immigrants and non-citizens in the EU: An East-West comparison. *International Journal of Manpower*, 30(1/2), 97–115. DOI: 10.1108/01437720910948429

Kahanec, M., & Zimmerman, K. F. (Eds.). (2010). *EU Labor markets after post-enlargement migration*. Springer Verlag. DOI: 10.1007/978-3-642-02242-5

Kajikawa, Y., Ohno, J., Takeda, Y., Matsushima, K., & Komiyama, H. (2007). Creating an academic landscape of sustainability science: An analysis of the citation network. *Sustainability Science*, 2(2), 221–231. DOI: 10.1007/s11625-007-0027-8

Kamil, K. H., & Abidin, S. N. Z. (2017). Does herd behavior exist among investors of Shariah-compliant equities in Malaysia? *Advanced Science Letters*, 23(5), 4968–4972. DOI: 10.1166/asl.2017.8978

Kaminsky, G. L., & Schmukler, S. L. (1999). What triggers market jitters?: A chronicle of the Asian crisis. *Journal of International Money and Finance*, 18(4), 537–560. DOI: 10.1016/S0261-5606(99)00015-7

Kamta, H., & Sharma, S. K. (2024). Multiagent-Based Manufacturing: Foundations, Applications, and Future Directions. In *The Convergence of Self-Sustaining Systems With AI and IoT* (pp. 261-279). IGI Global.

Kandarkar, P. C., & Ravi, V. (2024). Investigating the impact of smart manufacturing and interconnected emerging technologies in building smarter supply chains. *Journal of Manufacturing Technology Management*, 35(5), 984–1009. DOI: 10.1108/JMTM-11-2023-0498

Kanojia, S., Singh, D., & Goswami, A. (2020). Impact of herding on the returns in the Indian stock market: An empirical study. *Review of Behavioral Finance*, 14(1), 115–129. DOI: 10.1108/RBF-01-2020-0017

Kasera, R. K., Gour, S., & Acharjee, T. (2024). A comprehensive survey on IoT and AI based applications in different pre-harvest, during-harvest and post-harvest activities of smart agriculture. *Computers and Electronics in Agriculture*, 216, 108522. DOI: 10.1016/j.compag.2023.108522

Kashian, A., Rajabifard, A., Richter, K. F., & Chen, Y. (2019). Automatic analysis of positional plausibility for points of interest in OpenStreetMap using coexistence patterns. *International Journal of Geographical Information Science*, 33(7), 1420–1443. Advance online publication. DOI: 10.1080/13658816.2019.1584803

Kashif, M., Palwishah, R., Ahmed, R. R., Vveinhardt, J., & Streimikiene, D. (2021). Do investors herd? An examination of Pakistan stock exchange. *International Journal of Finance & Economics*, 26(2), 2090–2105. DOI: 10.1002/ijfe.1895

Kayhan, A., & Titman, S. (2004). ' Firms' Histories and Their Capital Structures ', *NBER Working Paper No. w10526, Available atSSRN:*https://ssrn.com/abstract=552889 DOI: 10.2139/ssrn.552144

Kayhan, A., & Titman, S. (2007). Firms' histories and their capital structures. *Journal of Financial Economics*, 83(1), 1–32. DOI: 10.1016/j.jfineco.2005.10.007

Keller, W., & Yeaple, S. R. (2009). Multinational enterprises, international trade, and productivity growth: Firm-level evidence from the United States. *The Review of Economics and Statistics*, 91(4), 821–831. DOI: 10.1162/rest.91.4.821

Kessler, M. M. (1963). Bibliographic coupling between scientific papers. *American Documentation*, 14(1), 10–25. DOI: 10.1002/asi.5090140103

Khanna, T., & Palepu, K. (2010). *Winning in Emerging Markets: A Road Map for Strategy and Execution*. Harvard Business Press.

Khanthavit, A. (2020). Foreign investors' abnormal trading behavior in the time of COVID-19. *The Journal of Asian Finance. Economics and Business*, 7(9), 63–74. DOI: 10.13106/jafeb.2020.vol7.no9.063

Killins, R. N. (2019). An investigation of the short-term performance of the Canadian IPO market. *Research in International Business and Finance*, 47, 102–113. DOI: 10.1016/j.ribaf.2018.07.004

Kiptoon, C. K. *(2014). The impact of the blue ocean strategy on the performance of Bamburi cement limited in Kenya (Doctoral dissertation, University of Nairobi)*

Kiran, F., & Khan, N. U. (2016, August). The Herding Behavior on Pakistan Stock Exchange. In *4th International Conference on Advances in Management, Economics and Social Science-MES* (pp. 18-19). DOI: 10.15224/978-1-63248-103-0-81

Kirschenman J., Neckerman K.M., J.Kirschenman(1991)., Social Problems, 38 (4), Special Issue on the Underclass in the United States (Nov., 1991), 433-447.

Klein, A. C. (2013). Time-variations in herding behavior: Evidence from a Markov switching SUR model. *Journal of International Financial Markets, Institutions and Money*, 26, 291–304. DOI: 10.1016/j.intfin.2013.06.006

Kline, S. J., & Rosenberg, N. (1986). An overview of innovation. In Landau, R., & Rosenberg, N. (Eds.), *The Positive Sum Strategy: Harnessing Technology for Economic Growth* (pp. 275–306). National Academy Press.

Klonner, C., Usón, T. J., Aeschbach, N., & Höfle, B. (2021). Participatory Mapping and Visualization of Local Knowledge: An Example from Eberbach, Germany. *International Journal of Disaster Risk Science*, 12(1), 56–71. Advance online publication. DOI: 10.1007/s13753-020-00312-8

Knack, S., & Keefer, P. (1995). Institutions And Economic Performance: Cross-Country Tests Using Alternative Institutional Measures. *Economics and Politics*, 7(3), 207–227. DOI: 10.1111/j.1468-0343.1995.tb00111.x

Kokotinis, G., Michalos, G., Arkouli, Z., & Makris, S. (2024). A Behavior Trees-based architecture towards operation planning in hybrid manufacturing. *International Journal of Computer Integrated Manufacturing*, 37(3), 324–349. DOI: 10.1080/0951192X.2023.2228254

Kolasani, S. (2024). Revolutionizing manufacturing, making it more efficient, flexible, and intelligent with Industry 4.0 innovations. *International Journal of Sustainable Development Through AI. ML and IoT*, 3(1), 1–17.

Komalasari, P. T., Asri, M., Purwanto, B. M., &Setiyono, B. (2021). Herding behaviour in the capital market: What do we know and what is next?. *Management Review Quarterly*, 1-43.https://doi.org/DOI: 10.1007/s11301-021-00212-1

Ko, Y. C., & Fujita, H. (2018). Evidential probability of signals on a price herd prediction: Case study on solar energy companies. *International Journal of Approximate Reasoning*, 92, 255–269. DOI: 10.1016/j.ijar.2017.10.015

Kremer, S., & Nautz, D. (2013). Causes and consequences of short-term institutional herding. *Journal of Banking & Finance*, 37(5), 1676–1686. DOI: 10.1016/j.jbankfin.2012.12.006

Krichene, H., & El-Aroui, M. A. (2018). Agent-based simulation and microstructure modeling of immature stock markets. *Computational Economics*, 51(3), 493–511. DOI: 10.1007/s10614-016-9615-y

Kudryavtsev, A., Cohen, G., & Hon-Snir, S. (2013). 'Rational'or'Intuitive': Are behavioral biases correlated across stock market investors?. *Contemporary economics, 7*(2), 31-53.

Kumar, A., Paul, J., & Unnithan, A. B. (2020). 'Masstige'marketing: A review, synthesis and research agenda. *Journal of Business Research*, 113, 384–398. DOI: 10.1016/j.jbusres.2019.09.030

Kumar, A., & Sahoo, S. (2021). Do anchor investors affect long run performance? Evidence from Indian IPO markets. *Pacific Accounting Review*, 33(3), 322–346. DOI: 10.1108/PAR-09-2020-0149

Kumar, H., Tuli, N., Singh, R. K., Arya, V., & Srivastava, R. (2024). Exploring the role of augmented reality as a new brand advocate. *Journal of Consumer Behaviour*, 23(2), 620–638. DOI: 10.1002/cb.2227

Kumar, N. K., & Yadav, A. S. (2022). A Systematic Literature Review and Bibliometric Analysis on Mobile Payments. *Vision (Basel)*, 09722629221104190. Advance online publication. DOI: 10.1177/09722629221104

Kuzmak, O., Kuzmak, O., & Voitovych, S. (2024). Business Development Towards the Application of Innovative Customer Relationship Management (CRM) Technologies in the Context of Global Transformational Changes. In *Data-Centric Business and Applications: Modern Trends in Financial and Innovation Data Processes 2023* (Vol. 2, pp. 47–69). Springer Nature Switzerland. DOI: 10.1007/978-3-031-53984-8_3

Lai, R. N., & Zhang, Y. (2020). Spillover and profitability of intraday herding on cross-listed stocks. *Chinese Economy*, 53(1), 25–61. DOI: 10.1080/10971475.2019.1625244

Lavin, J. F., & Magner, N. S. (2014). Herding in the mutual fund industry: Evidence from Chile. *Academia (Caracas)*, 27(1), 10–29. DOI: 10.1108/ARLA-09-2013-0137

Lazzeretti, L. (2022). What is the role of culture facing the digital revolution challenge? Some reflections for a research agenda. *European Planning Studies*, 30(9), 1617–1637. Advance online publication. DOI: 10.1080/09654313.2020.1836133

Le Guilcher, A., Olteanu-Raimond, A. M., & Balde, M. B. (2022). Analysis of massive imports of open data in openstreetmap database: A study case for france. *ISPRS Annals of the Photogrammetry, Remote Sensing and Spatial Information Sciences*, 5(4), 99–106. Advance online publication. DOI: 10.5194/isprs-annals-V-4-2022-99-2022

Lee, J., Bagheri, B., & Kao, H. A. (2015). A cyber-physical systems architecture for industry 4.0-based manufacturing systems. *Manufacturing Letters*, 3, 18–23. DOI: 10.1016/j.mfglet.2014.12.001

Lee, J., Kao, H. A., & Yang, S. (2014). Service innovation and smart analytics for industry 4.0 and big data environment. *Procedia CIRP*, 16, 3–8. DOI: 10.1016/j.procir.2014.02.001

Lee, J., Lapira, E., Bagheri, B., & Kao, H. A. (2013). Recent advances and trends in predictive manufacturing systems in big data environment. *Manufacturing Letters*, 1(1), 38–41. DOI: 10.1016/j.mfglet.2013.09.005

Lefranc, A. (2010). Unequal opportunities and ethnic origin: The labor market outcomes of second generationmigrants in France. *The American Behavioral Scientist*, 53(12), 1851–1882. DOI: 10.1177/0002764210368100

Lemmon, M. L., & Zender, J. F. (2010). Debt Capacity and Tests of Capital Structure Theories. *Journal of Financial and Quantitative Analysis*, 45(5), 1161–1187. DOI: 10.1017/S0022109010000499

Levi, Y., & Welch, I. (2017). Best Practice for Cost-of-Capital Estimates. *Journal of Financial and Quantitative Analysis*, 52(2), 427–463. DOI: 10.1017/S0022109017000114

Lin, K. Y., & Huang, T. K. (2024). Shopping in the digital world: How augmented reality mobile applications trigger customer engagement. *Technology in Society*, 77, 102540. DOI: 10.1016/j.techsoc.2024.102540

Li, T., Chen, H., Liu, W., Yu, G., & Yu, Y. (2023). Understanding the role of social media sentiment in identifying irrational herding behavior in the stock market. *International Review of Economics & Finance*, 87, 163–179. DOI: 10.1016/j.iref.2023.04.016

Litimi, H. (2017). Herd behavior in the French stock market. *Review of Accounting and Finance*, 16(4), 497–515. DOI: 10.1108/RAF-11-2016-0188

Liu, B., Shi, Y., Li, D. J., Wang, Y. D., Fernandez, G., & Tsou, M. H. (2020). An economic development evaluation based on the openstreetmap road network density: The case study of 85 cities in china. *ISPRS International Journal of Geo-Information*, 9(9), 517. Advance online publication. DOI: 10.3390/ijgi9090517 PMID: 33511044

Liu, L. X., Lu, R., Sherman, A. E., & Zhang, Y. (2023). IPO Underpricing and Limited Attention: Theory and Evidence. *Journal of Banking & Finance*, 106932, 106932. Advance online publication. DOI: 10.1016/j.jbankfin.2023.106932

Liu, R., Yu, H., Ren, Y., & Liu, S. (2022). The Analysis of Classification and Spatiotemporal Distribution Characteristics of Ride-Hailing Driver's Driving Style: A Case Study in China. *International Journal of Environmental Research and Public Health*, 19(15), 9734. Advance online publication. DOI: 10.3390/ijerph19159734 PMID: 35955090

Liu, S., Ali Vakeel, K., Smith, N., Alavipour, R. S., Wei, C., & Wirtz, J. (2024). AI concierge in the customer journey: What is it and how can it add value to the customer? *Journal of Service Management*, 35(6), 136–158. DOI: 10.1108/JOSM-12-2023-0523

Li, X., Wang, S. S., & Wang, X. (2017). Trust and stock price crash risk: Evidence from China. *Journal of Banking & Finance*, 76, 74–91. DOI: 10.1016/j.jbankfin.2016.12.003

Ljungqvist, A.. (2003). Hot Markets, Investor Sentiment, and IPO Pricing. *The Journal of Business*, 76(2), 293–318. DOI: 10.1086/503644

Ljungqvist, A., Jenkinson, T., & Wilhelm, W. J. (2006). Global Integration in Primary Equity Markets: The Role of U.S. Banks and U.S. Investors. *Review of Financial Studies*, 19(4), 1051–1082. DOI: 10.1093/rfs/16.1.0063

Loughran, T., & Ritter, J. R. (2004). Why Has IPO Underpricing Changed Over Time? *Financial Management*, 33(3), 5–37. DOI: 10.2307/3666172

Lo, W., Yang, C. M., Zhang, Q., & Li, M. (2024). Increased Productivity and Reduced Waste with Robotic Process Automation and Generative AI-Powered IoE Services. *Journal of Web Engineering*, 23(1), 53–87. DOI: 10.13052/jwe1540-9589.2313

Lowry, M., Michaely, R., & Volkova, E. (2017). Initial public offerings: A synthesis of the literature and directions for future research. *Foundations and Trends® in Finance, 11*(3-4), 154-320. http://dx.doi.org/DOI: 10.1561/0500000050

Luigi, A., Mohsen, B., Xihui, C., & Concetto, P. V. (2021). Knowledge spillovers and technical efficiency for cleaner production: An economic analysis from agriculture innovation. *Journal of Cleaner Production*, 320, 128830. DOI: 10.1016/j.jclepro.2021.128830

Lulin, Z., Antwi, H. A., Wang, W., Yiranbon, E., Marfo, E. O., & Acheampong, P. (2016). The effect of herd formation among healthcare investors on health sector growth in China. *International Journal for Equity in Health*, 15(1), 1–15. DOI: 10.1186/s12939-016-0393-x PMID: 27436298

Luo, B., & Lin, Z. (2013). A decision tree model for herd behavior and empirical evidence from the online P2P lending market. *Information Systems and e-Business Management*, 11(1), 141–160. DOI: 10.1007/s10257-011-0182-4

Luu, Q. T., & Luong, H. T. T.LUU. (2020). Herding behavior in emerging and frontier stock markets during pandemic influenza panics. *The Journal of Asian Finance. Economics and Business*, 7(9), 147–158. DOI: 10.13106/jafeb.2020.vol7.no9.147

Lu, Y., & Ramakrishnan, R. (2019). Convergence of IoT and big data in healthcare. *Healthcare Informatics Research*, 25(3), 139–141. PMID: 31406605

Lu, Y., Xu, X., Huang, Y., & Duan, H. (2017). Real-time data-driven production planning and scheduling in cyber-physical manufacturing systems. *Robotics and Computer-integrated Manufacturing*, 44, 226–238.

Madaan, V., & Shrivastava, M. (2020). FIIs herding in energy sector of Indian stock market. *South Asian Journal of Business Studies*, 11(2), 174–194. DOI: 10.1108/SAJBS-02-2020-0033

Mahajan, A., & Tartaroglu, S. (2008). Equity market timing and capital structure: International evidence. *Journal of Banking & Finance*, 32(5), 754–766. DOI: 10.1016/j.jbankfin.2007.05.007

Mahmud, S. F., & Tiniç, M. (2018). Herding in Chinese stock markets: A nonparametric approach. *Empirical Economics*, 55(2), 679–711. DOI: 10.1007/s00181-017-1281-y

Malik, M. H., Anandarao, S., & Dar, A. A. (2023). An appraisal of India's comparative advantage in information technology exports. *Journal of Chinese Economic and Foreign Trade Studies*, 16(2), 136–152. DOI: 10.1108/JCEFTS-08-2022-0051

Mallakpour, S., Radfar, Z., & Hussain, C. M. (2024). Advanced application of additive manufacturing in the footwear industry: from customized insoles to fully 3D-printed shoes. In *Medical Additive Manufacturing* (pp. 153–178). Elsevier. DOI: 10.1016/B978-0-323-95383-2.00015-9

Manjunath, B. R., Raju, J. K., & Rehaman, M. (2020). Short-run performance evaluation of under-priced Indian IPOs. *Law and Financial Markets Review*, 14(3), 170–175. DOI: 10.1080/17521440.2020.1759239

Marabelli, M., & Newell, S. (2014). Knowing, power and materiality: A critical review and reconceptualization of absorptive capacity. *International Journal of Management Reviews*, 16(4), 479–499. DOI: 10.1111/ijmr.12031

Marietza, F., Nurazi, R., & Santi, F. (2021). Bibliometric Analysis Of Herding Behavior In Times Of Crisis. *arXiv preprint arXiv:2106.13598*.https://doi.org//arXiv.2106.13598DOI: 10.48550

Marshakova, I. V. (1973). System of document connections based on references. *Nauchno-TekhnicheskayaInformatsiya Seriya 2-Informatsionnye Protsessy I Sistemy*, (6), 3-8.

Martínez-Bravo, M. C., Chalezquer, C. S., & Serrano-Puche, J. (2022). Dimensions of Digital Literacy in the 21st Century Competency Frameworks. *Sustainability (Basel)*, 14(3), 1867. Advance online publication. DOI: 10.3390/su14031867

Mastering AI quality for successful adoption of AI in manufacturing. (2024, January 16). World Economic Forum. https://www.weforum.org/agenda/2024/01/mastering-ai-quality-successful-adoption-ai-manufacturing/

Mavruk, T. (2022). Analysis of herding behavior in individual investor portfolios using machine learning algorithms. *Research in International Business and Finance*, 62, 101740. DOI: 10.1016/j.ribaf.2022.101740

Mazur, M., Dang, M., & Vega, M. (2021). COVID-19 and the march 2020 stock market crash. Evidence from S&P1500. *Finance Research Letters*, 38, 101690. DOI: 10.1016/j.frl.2020.101690 PMID: 32837377

Mazzucato, M. (2013). *The Entrepreneurial State: Debunking Public vs. Private Sector Myths*. Anthem Press.

McKinsey Global Institute. (2017). JOBS LOST, JOBS GAINED: WORKFORCE TRANSITIONS IN A TIME OF AUTOMATION. https://www.mckinsey.com/~/media/BAB489A30B724BECB5DEDC41E9BB9FAC.ashx

Mefteh-Wali, Salma, and Marie-Josèphe Rigobert. (2013). 'Les facteurs déterminants de l'endettement en devises des entreprises françaises', *Revue Finance ContrÃ´le StratÃ©gie*, 16: 31-47.

Mengist, W., Soromessa, T., & Legese, G. (2020). Method for conducting Systematic Literature Reviewand meta-analysis for environmental science research. *MethodsX*, 7, 100777. DOI: 10.1016/j.mex.2019.100777 PMID: 31993339

Metawa, N., Hassan, M. K., Metawa, S., & Safa, M. F. (2018). Impact of behavioral factors on investors' financial decisions: Case of the Egyptian stock market. *International Journal of Islamic and Middle Eastern Finance and Management*, 12(1), 30–55. DOI: 10.1108/IMEFM-12-2017-0333

Micle, D. E., Deiac, F., Olar, A., Dren a, R. F., Florean, C., Coman, I. G., & Arion, F. H. (2021). Research on innovative business plan. Smart cattle farming using artificial intelligent robotic process automation. *Agriculture*, 11(5), 430. DOI: 10.3390/agriculture11050430

Miller, M. H. (1977). Debt and Taxes. *The Journal of Finance*, •••, 261–275.

Minghini, M., Sarretta, A., & Napolitano, M. (2022). OpenStreetMap Contribution to Local Data Ecosystems in COVID-19 Times: Experiences and Reflections from the Italian Case. *Data*, 7(4), 39. Advance online publication. DOI: 10.3390/data7040039

Missaoui, I., Brahmi, M., & Rajeb, J. B. (2022). Ownership structure management and its effect on dividend policy in the Tunisian stock exchange enterprises: An empirical study. *International Journal of Technology Transfer and Commercialisation*, 1(1), 83–96. http://www.inderscience.com/storage/f171021139684125.pdf. DOI: 10.1504/IJTTC.2022.123084

Modigliani, F., & Miller, M. (1958). ' The Cost of Capital, Corporation Finance and the Theory of Investment. '. *The American Economic Review*, 48, 261–297.

Modigliani, F., & Miller, M. H. (1963). Corporate income taxes and the cost of capital: A correction. *The American Economic Review*, 53(3), 433–443.

Mohsen B., Espisoto L., Anna A., Karabir S D., Shruti A, Arun K G., & Loan N. (2023). The Role of Greener Innovations in Promoting Financial Inclusion to Achieve Carbon Neutrality: An Integrative Review, *Economies*, Vol. 11(7), 1-18. RePEc:gam:jecomi:v:11:y:2023:i:7:p:194-:d:1196091

Mohsen, B., & Sonia, Z. (2013). Efficiency of monetary policy approach and activist rules, *Journal of Economics and Management,* Vol. (3), 7-17, Published by University of Defense in Brno. https://www.anakan.cz/soubory/kisdis/riv-anakan-2013-14.pdf#page=21

Mohsen, B., Bruna, B., Karambir, S. D., Luca, E., & Anna, P. (2024). From manure to megawatts: Navigating the sustainable innovation solution through biogas production from livestock waste for harnessing green energy for green economy. *Heliyon*, 10(14), e34504. https://www.sciencedirect.com/science/article/pii/S240584402410535X. DOI: 10.1016/j.heliyon.2024.e34504

Mohsen, B., Ibtissem, M., & Jaleleddine Ben, R. (2018). Quantitative relationship between corruption ad development of the Tunisian stock market. *Public and Municipal Finance*, 7(2), 39–47. DOI: 10.21511/pmf.07(2).2018.04

Monostori, L., Kádár, B., Bauernhansl, T., Kondoh, S., Kumara, S., Reinhart, G., Sauer, O., Schuh, G., Sihn, W., & Ueda, K. (2016). Cyber-physical systems in manufacturing. *CIRP Annals*, 65(2), 621–641. DOI: 10.1016/j.cirp.2016.06.005

Morell-Monzó, S., Estornell, J., & Sebastiá-Frasquet, M. T. (2020). Article Comparison of Sentinel-2 and high-resolution imagery for mapping land abandonment in fragmented areas. *Remote Sensing (Basel)*, 12(12), 2062. Advance online publication. DOI: 10.3390/rs12122062

Morris, J., Morris, W., & Bowen, R. (2022). Implications of the digital divide on rural SME resilience. *Journal of Rural Studies*, 89, 369–377. Advance online publication. DOI: 10.1016/j.jrurstud.2022.01.005

Mortensen, D. (1986). Job search and labor market analysis. Chapter 15 in Handbook of Labor Economics, vol. 2

Mourtzis, D., Panopoulos, N., Stavropoulos, P., & Papakostas, N. (2024). Artificial Intelligence for Production Management and Control Towards Mass Personalization of Global Networks. In *CIRP Novel Topics in Production Engineering* (Vol. 1, pp. 267–312). Springer Nature Switzerland. DOI: 10.1007/978-3-031-54034-9_8

Mourtzis, D., Vlachou, E., Milas, N., & Xanthakis, E. (2016). Big data analytics challenges and application in manufacturing. *Procedia CIRP*, 55, 126–131.

Mubarik, M. S., & Khan, S. A. (2024). Digital Supply Chain and Industry 4.0 Technologies. In *The Theory, Methods and Application of Managing Digital Supply Chains* (pp. 121-132). Emerald Publishing Limited.

Muhamad, N., Muhamad Hakimi, F. H., & Mahadzir, M. D. A. (2023). Community Activation for Disaster Risk Reduction Through OpenStreetMap: A Scoping Review. *Journal of Advanced Geospatial Science & Technology*, 3(2), 25–50. Advance online publication. DOI: 10.11113/jagst.v3n2.68

Munawar, A., Li, Z., Nagururu, N., Trakimas, D., Kazanzides, P., Taylor, R. H., & Creighton, F. X. (2024). Fully immersive virtual reality for skull-base surgery: Surgical training and beyond. *International Journal of Computer Assisted Radiology and Surgery*, 19(1), 51–59. DOI: 10.1007/s11548-023-02956-5 PMID: 37347346

Mwende, J. (2016). *Effect of blue ocean strategies on competitive advantage of microfinance institutions in Kenya* (Doctoral dissertation, University of Nairobi)

Myers, S. C. (1984). The Capital Structure Puzzle. *The Journal of Finance*, 39(3), 574–592. DOI: 10.1111/j.1540-6261.1984.tb03646.x

Myers, S. C., & Majluf, N. S. (1984). Corporate financing and investment decisions when firms have information that investors do not have. *Journal of Financial Economics*, 13(2), 187–221. DOI: 10.1016/0304-405X(84)90023-0

Nair, J. (2024). Reconfiguration and transformation for resilience: Building service organizations towards sustainability. *Journal of Services Marketing*, 38(4), 404–425. DOI: 10.1108/JSM-04-2023-0144

Naseer, I. (2023). AWS Cloud Computing Solutions: Optimizing Implementation for Businesses. *Statistics. Computing and Interdisciplinary Research*, 5(2), 121–132. DOI: 10.52700/scir.v5i2.138

Nassereddine, M., & Khang, A. (2024). Applications of Internet of Things (IoT) in smart cities. In *Advanced IoT Technologies and Applications in the Industry 4.0 Digital Economy* (pp. 109–136). CRC Press. DOI: 10.1201/9781003434269-6

Nelson, R. R. (1993). *National innovation systems: A comparative analysis*. Oxford University Press. DOI: 10.1093/oso/9780195076165.001.0001

Nelson, R. R., & Winter, S. G. (1982). *An evolutionary theory of economic change*. Belknap Press.

Neumark, D. (2016).Experimental Research on Labor Market Discrimination, *NBER Working Paper* No. 22022

Ng, S. H., Zhuang, Z., Toh, M. Y., Ong, T. S., & Teh, B. H. (2022). Exploring herding behavior in an innovative-oriented stock market: Evidence from ChiNext. *Journal of Applied Econometrics*, 25(1), 523–542. DOI: 10.1080/15140326.2022.2050992

Nicodano, G., & Regis, L. (2019). A trade-off theory of ownership and capital structure. *Journal of Financial Economics*, 131(3), 715–735. DOI: 10.1016/j.jfineco.2018.09.001

Nithia, A. (2024). *SUCCESSFUL MANUFACTURING TRANSFORMATION: RAPIDLY GET OUT OF MANUFACTURING CRISIS AND ACHIEVE GLOBAL MANUFACTURING COMPETITIVENESS*. Partridge Publishing Singapore.

Niyitegeka, O., & Tewari, D. D. (2015). Short and long-term dynamics of herd behaviour at the Johannesburg stock exchange. *African Finance Journal*, 17(2), 84–103.

Noonia, A., Beg, R., Patidar, A., Bawaskar, B., Sharma, S., & Rawat, H. (2024). Chatbot vs Intelligent Virtual Assistance (IVA). *Conversational Artificial Intelligence*, 655-673.

North, D. C. (1990). *Institutions, institutional change and economic performance*. Cambridge University Press. DOI: 10.1017/CBO9780511808678

Nowak, M. M., Dzióbb, K., Ludwisiak, Ł., & Chmiel, J. (2020). Mobile GIS applications for environmental field surveys: A state of the art. In *Global Ecology and Conservation* (Vol. 23). DOI: 10.1016/j.gecco.2020.e01089

Obadire, A., & Obadire, K. (2023). The Impact of Bank Regulation on Bank Performance: A Novel Analysis of the Pre-Covid Era with Cross-Country Evidence. *American Journal of Industrial and Business Management*, 13(3), 118–139. DOI: 10.4236/ajibm.2023.133009

Odimarha, A. C., Ayodeji, S. A., & Abaku, E. A.Agnes Clare OdimarhaSodrudeen Abolore AyodejiEmmanuel Adeyemi Abaku. (2024). The role of technology in supply chain risk management: Innovations and challenges in logistics. *Magna Scientia Advanced Research and Reviews*, 10(2), 138–145. DOI: 10.30574/msarr.2024.10.2.0052

OECD. *International migration outlook*, (2019), https://www.oecd-ilibrary.org/

Ololade, Y. J.Yinka James Ololade. (2024). SME financing through fintech: An analytical study of trends in Nigeria and the USA. *International Journal of Management & Entrepreneurship Research*, 6(4), 1078–1102. DOI: 10.51594/ijmer.v6i4.1001

Pager D., Karafin D. (2009). Bayesian Bigot? Statistical Discrimination, Stereotypes, and Employer Decision Making, ANNALS, *AAPSS*, 621.

Pajić, V., Andrejić, M., Jolović, M., & Kilibarda, M. (2024). Strategic warehouse location selection in business logistics: A novel approach using imf SWARA–MARCOS—a case study of a Serbian logistics service provider. *Mathematics*, 12(5), 776. DOI: 10.3390/math12050776

Palmatier, R. W., Houston, M. B., & Hulland, J. (2018). Review articles: Purpose, process, and structure. *Journal of the Academy of Marketing Science*, 46(1), 1–5. DOI: 10.1007/s11747-017-0563-4

Pangrazio, L., Godhe, A. L., & Ledesma, A. G. L. (2020). What is digital literacy? A comparative review of publications across three language contexts. *E-Learning and Digital Media*, 17(6), 442–459. Advance online publication. DOI: 10.1177/2042753020946291

Parsons, Christopher A., and Sheridan Titman. (2007). 'Capital Structure and Corporate Strategy '.

Patel, D., & Muthuswamy, S. (2024). Machining Process Automation in Computer Numerical Control Turning Using Robot-Assisted Imaging and CNN-Based Machine Learning. *Journal of Manufacturing Science and Engineering*, 146(4), 041004–1. DOI: 10.1115/1.4064626

Patel, K. (2024). Ethical reflections on data-centric AI: Balancing benefits and risks. *SSRN*, 2(1), 1–17. DOI: 10.2139/ssrn.4993089

Payal, A., Nimbkar, S., Bharathi, R. M., Moses, J. A., & Anandharamakrishnan, C. (2024). Robotics and automation in the food industry. In *Emerging Technologies for the Food Industry* (pp. 31–62). Apple Academic Press. DOI: 10.1201/9781003413660-2

Payne, G. T., Trudell, L. T., Moore, C. B., Petrenko, O. V., & Hayes, N. T. (2023). Ambiguous signals and information asymmetry in the initial public offering process: Examining ownership concentration, process time, and underpricing. *Group & Organization Management*, 48(5), 1467–1502. DOI: 10.1177/10596011221090036

Phalet, K., & Heath, A. (2007). *From ethnic boundaries to ethnic penalties: urban economies and the Turkish second generation, technical report*. University of Utrecht.

Pilkington, A., & Liston-Heyes, C. (1999). Is production and operations management a discipline? A citation/co-citation study. *International Journal of Operations & Production Management*, 19(1), 7–20. DOI: 10.1108/01443579910244188

Postiglione, A., & Monteleone, M. (2024). Predictive Maintenance with Linguistic Text Mining. *Mathematics*, 12(7), 1089. DOI: 10.3390/math12071089

Putnam, R. (1993). *Making Democracy Work*. Civic Traditions in Modern Italy.

PwC. (2016). Industry 4.0: Building the digital enterprise.https://www.pwc.com/gx/en/industries/industries-4.0/landing-page/industry-4.0-building-your-digital-enterprise-april-2016.pdf

QuantumBlack. (2024, March 13). McKinsey & Company. https://www.mckinsey.com/capabilities/quantumblack/how-we-help-clients?cid=aob-pse-gaw-mog-mog-oth-

Radovanović, D., Holst, C., Banerjee Belur, S., Srivastava, R., Vivien Houngbonon, G., Le Quentrec, E., Miliza, J., Winkler, A. S., & Noll, J. (2020). Digital literacy key performance indicators for sustainable development. *Social Inclusion (Lisboa)*, 8(2), 151–167. Advance online publication. DOI: 10.17645/si.v8i2.2587

Radzi, S., Yasin, M., Zahari, M., Abas, R., Ahmat, N., & Ahmad-Ridzuan, A. (2016). Blue ocean strategy [BOS] and performance of four and five star hotels in Kuala Lumpur, Selangor and Putrajaya. *Heritage, Culture and Society: Research agenda and best practices in the hospitality and tourism industry, 207*

Rajan, R. G., & Zingales, L. (1995). ' What Do We Know about Capital Structure? Some Evidence from International Data', *Journal of Finance. American Finance Association*, 50, 1421–1460.

Rajput, S., & Kosta, Y. P. (2015). The adoption of CAD/CAM technologies in small manufacturing industry. *International Journal of Advanced Engineering Research and Applications*, 3(3), 1–8.

Ramesh, R., Jayakrishna, K., Karunamoorthy, L., & Kumaran, S. T. (2017). Review on CNC machining parameters optimization. *Materials Today: Proceedings*, 4(2), 1970–1979.

Rana, H. A., Iftikhar, M., Wattoo, M. A., & Bilal, M. Q. (2021). Farmers' perceptions regarding artificial insemination services in Punjab, Pakistan. *International Journal of Agricultural Extension*, 9(2), 163–170.

Rath, K. C., Khang, A., & Roy, D. (2024). The Role of Internet of Things (IoT) Technology in Industry 4.0 Economy. In *Advanced IoT Technologies and Applications in the Industry 4.0 Digital Economy* (pp. 1-28). CRC Press.

Rathnayake, D. N., Louembe, P. A., Kassi, D. F., Sun, G., & Ning, D. (2019). Are IPOs underpriced or overpriced? Evidence from an emerging market. *Research in International Business and Finance*, 50, 171–190. DOI: 10.1016/j.ribaf.2019.04.013

Rawabdeh, I., Raqab, A., Al-Nimri, D., & Haddadine, S. (2012). Blue Ocean Strategy as a tool for improving a company's marketing function: The case of Jordan. *Jordan Journal of Business Administration*, 8(2), 390–407.

Reddick, C. G., Enriquez, R., Harris, R. J., & Sharma, B. (2020). Determinants of broadband access and affordability: An analysis of a community survey on the digital divide. *Cities (London, England)*, 106, 102904. Advance online publication. DOI: 10.1016/j.cities.2020.102904 PMID: 32921864

Ren, R., & Wu, D. (2018). An innovative sentiment analysis to measure herd behavior. *IEEE Transactions on Systems, Man, and Cybernetics. Systems*, 50(10), 3841–3851. DOI: 10.1109/TSMC.2018.2864942

Robert, A. (1988). Bankruptcy and Agency Costs: Their Significance to the Theory of Optimal Capital Structure. *Journal of Financial and Quantitative Analysis*, 23(1), 27–38. DOI: 10.2307/2331022

Rock, L. Y., Tajudeen, F. P., & Chung, Y. W. (2024). Usage and impact of the internet-of-things-based smart home technology: A quality-of-life perspective. *Universal Access in the Information Society*, 23(1), 345–364. DOI: 10.1007/s10209-022-00937-0 PMID: 36407566

Rodrik, D. (2004). *Industrial policy for the twenty-first century*. Harvard University Press. DOI: 10.2139/ssrn.617544

Roozkhosh, P., Pooya, A., Soleimani Fard, O., & Bagheri, R. (2024). Revolutionizing supply chain sustainability: An additive manufacturing-enabled optimization model for minimizing waste and costs. *Process Integration and Optimization for Sustainability*, 8(1), 285–300. DOI: 10.1007/s41660-023-00368-1

Rosenberg, N. (1982). *Inside the black box: Technology and economics*. Cambridge University Press.

Rosenthal, M. B. (2017). *Blue Ocean Strategy. Term Paper Innovation Management. Department of Marketing*. Johann Wolfgang Goethe University.

Roser, C., Akbulut, A., & Westkämper, E. (2016). Towards cyber-physical production systems. *Procedia CIRP*, 41, 173–178.

Rossi, M., & Russo, G. (2024). Innovative Solutions: Cloud Computing and AI Synergy in Software Engineering. *MZ Journal of Artificial Intelligence*, 1(1), 1–9.

Ross, S. A. (1977). The Determination of Financial Structure: The Incentive-Signalling Approach. *The Bell Journal of Economics*, 8(1), 8. DOI: 10.2307/3003485

Sachs, J. D., Warner, A. M., Aslund, A., & Fischer, S. (1995). Economic reform and the process of global integration. *Brookings Papers on Economic Activity*, 1995(1), 1–118. DOI: 10.2307/2534573

San Martin, R., & Painho, M. (2019). Geospatial preparedness: Empirical study of the joint effort to provide geospatial support to disaster response. *Transactions in GIS*, 23(3), 481–494. Advance online publication. DOI: 10.1111/tgis.12537

Sang, J. C., & Kimitei, E. (2021). Blue ocean strategies as panacea to sustainable performance of tea firms in Kenya. *African Journal of Business Management*, 15(2), 59–69. DOI: 10.5897/AJBM2020.9157

Sarkar, D., & Anderson, J. T. (2022). Corporate editors in OpenStreetMap: Investigating co-editing patterns. *Transactions in GIS*, 26(4), 1879–1897. Advance online publication. DOI: 10.1111/tgis.12910

Sarker, M. N. I., Peng, Y., Yiran, C., & Shouse, R. C. (2020). Disaster resilience through big data: Way to environmental sustainability. In *International Journal of Disaster Risk Reduction* (Vol. 51). DOI: 10.1016/j.ijdrr.2020.101769

Sarretta, A., Napolitano, M., & Minghini, M. (2023). OPENSTREETMAP AS AN INPUT SOURCE FOR PRODUCING GOVERNMENTAL DATASETS: THE CASE OF THE ITALIAN MILITARY GEOGRAPHIC INSTITUTE. *The International Archives of the Photogrammetry, Remote Sensing and Spatial Information Sciences, XLVIII-4/W7-2023*, 193–200. DOI: 10.5194/isprs-archives-XLVIII-4-W7-2023-193-2023

Saunders, M., Lewis, P., & Thornhill, A. (2007). Research methods. Business Students 4th edition Pearson Education Limited, England, 6(3), 1-268

Saunders, M. N. K., Lewis, P., Thornhill, A., & Bristow, A. (2015). *Understanding research philosophies and approaches: Research methods for business students.* Pearson.

Saunders, M., & Lewis, P. & Thornhill, A. (2007). Research methods. *Business (Atlanta, Ga.).*

Scharfstein, D. S., & Stein, J. C. (1990). Herd behavior and investment. *The American Economic Review*, •••, 465–479.

Schiuma, G., Santarsiero, F., Carlucci, D., & Jarrar, Y. (2024). Transformative leadership competencies for organizational digital transformation. *Business Horizons*, 67(4), 425–437. DOI: 10.1016/j.bushor.2024.04.004

Schröder-Bergen, S. (2024). Crowd-Based Geodata Production and Platform Capitalism: The Case of OpenStreetMap. In *Geographies of the Platform Economy: Critical Perspectives* (pp. 49–59). Springer.

Schuh, G., Anderl, R., & Gausemeier, J. (2017). Enabling the digital transformation of manufacturing with Industry 4.0. *CIRP Annals*, 66(2), 839–862.

Schumpeter, J. A. (1934). *The theory of economic development.* Harvard University Press.

Scorita, K. B., Hendayani, N., Kusuma, M. A., & Al-Shreifeen, I. A. (2024). The integration of augmented reality in marketing: enhancing customer experience and brand engagement: literature review. *International Journal of Economic Literature*, 2(3), 713–725.

Sekaran, U., & Bougie, R. (2016). *Research methods for business: A skill building approach.* John Wiley & Sons.

Sergeeva, S., Belova, N., Shichiyakh, R., Bobrova, A., Vaslavskaya, I., Bankova, N., Vetrova, E., & Hajiyev, H. (2024). Implementation of Lean Manufacturing Principles and Fast Structured Logic Methods in the Organizational Culture: Addressing Challenges and Maximizing Efficiency. *International Journal of Sustainable Development and Planning*, 19(3), 1195–1201. DOI: 10.18280/ijsdp.190337

Shantha, K. V. A. (2019). Individual investors' learning behavior and its impact on their herd bias: An integrated analysis in the context of stock trading. *Sustainability (Basel)*, 11(5), 1448. DOI: 10.3390/su11051448

Shapira, Y., Berman, Y., & Ben-Jacob, E. (2014). Modelling the short-term herding behaviour of stock markets. *New Journal of Physics*, 16(5), 053040. DOI: 10.1088/1367-2630/16/5/053040

Shapiro, S. S., & Wilk, M. B. (1965). An analysis of variance test for normality (complete samples). *Biometrika*, 52(3/4), 591–611. DOI: 10.2307/2333709

Sharma, R., & Gour, S. (2024). Internet of Things (IoT) Case Studies and Application. *AI and IoT Technology and Applications for Smart Healthcare Systems*, 333.

Sharma, R., & Gurung, S. (2024). Implementing Big Data Analytics and Machine Learning for Predictive Maintenance in Manufacturing Facilities in South Korea. *AI. IoT and the Fourth Industrial Revolution Review*, 14(2), 1–17.

Shehadeh, M., Atta, A., Barrak, T., Lutfi, A., & Alrawad, M. (2024). Digital transformation: An empirical analysis of operational efficiency, customer experience, and competitive advantage in Jordanian Islamic banks. *Uncertain Supply Chain Management*, 12(2), 695–708. DOI: 10.5267/j.uscm.2024.1.015

Shi, Y., Zheng, Y., Guo, K., & Ren, X. (2022). Relationship between herd behavior and Chinese stock market fluctuations during a bullish period based on complex networks. *International Journal of Information Technology & Decision Making*, 21(01), 405–421. DOI: 10.1142/S0219622021400010

Shrivastava, A., Krishna, K. M., Rinawa, M. L., Soni, M., Ramkumar, G., & Jaiswal, S. (2023). Inclusion of IoT, ML, and blockchain technologies in next generation industry 4.0 environment. *Materials Today: Proceedings*, 80, 3471–3475.

Shrotryia, V. K., & Kalra, H. (2020). Herding and BRICS markets: A study of distribution tails. *Review of Behavioral Finance*, 14(1), 91–114. DOI: 10.1108/RBF-04-2020-0086

Signorelli, P. F. C. L., Camilo-da-Silva, E., & Barbedo, C. H. D. S. (2021). An Examination of Herding Behavior in the Brazilian Equity Market. *BBR.Brazilian Business Review*, 18(3), 236–254. DOI: 10.15728/bbr.2021.18.3.1

Simerly, R. L., & Li, M. (2000). Environmental dynamism, capital structure and performance: A theoretical integration and an empirical test. *Strategic Management Journal*, 21(1), 31–49. DOI: 10.1002/(SICI)1097-0266(200001)21:1<31::AID-SMJ76>3.0.CO;2-T

Singh, D., Singh, R., Gehlot, A., Akram, S. V., Priyadarshi, N., & Twala, B. (2022). An imperative role of digitalization in monitoring cattle health for sustainability. *Electronics, 11*(17), 2702 Students 4th edition Pearson Education Limited, England, 6(3), 1-268

Singha, R., & Singha, S. (2024). Educational Innovation Transforming Higher Education for Workforce Readiness. In *Advancing Student Employability Through Higher Education* (pp. 37–55). IGI Global. DOI: 10.4018/979-8-3693-0517-1.ch003

Singh, N., Panigrahi, P. K., Zhang, Z., & Jasimuddin, S. M. (2024). Cyber-physical systems: A bibliometric analysis of literature. *Journal of Intelligent Manufacturing*, •••, 1–37. DOI: 10.1007/s10845-024-02380-9

Singh, V. (2013). Did institutions herd during the internet bubble? *Review of Quantitative Finance and Accounting*, 41(3), 513–534. DOI: 10.1007/s11156-012-0320-1

Small, H. (1973). Co-citation in the scientific literature: A new measure of the relationship between two documents. *Journal of the American Society for Information Science*, 24(4), 265–269. DOI: 10.1002/asi.4630240406

Smith, J., & Anderson, J. (2024). *Augmented Realms, Digital Dreams: a Lengthy Expedition into the Synergies of Augmented Reality and E-Commerce, Unraveling the Threads of Innovation Woven into the Fabric of Online Shopping (No. 11965).* EasyChair.

Snyder, H. (2019). Literature review as a research methodology: An overview and guidelines. *Journal of Business Research*, 104, 333–339. DOI: 10.1016/j.jbusres.2019.07.039

Solon, G. (1999). Intergenerational Mobility in the Labor Market. In Ashenfelter, O. C., & Card, D. (Eds.), *Handbook of Labor Economics* (Vol. 3, pp. 1761–1800). North-Holland.

Solow, R. M. (1956). A contribution to the theory of economic growth. *The Quarterly Journal of Economics*, 70(1), 65–94. DOI: 10.2307/1884513

Spyrou, S. (2013). Herding in financial markets: A review of the literature. *Review of Behavioral Finance*, 5(2), 175–194. DOI: 10.1108/RBF-02-2013-0009

Startup India. (2019)., Retrieved from https://www.startupindia.gov.in/content/dam/invest india/Templates/public/5_years_Achievement_report%20_%20final%20(1).pdf Accessed on 10th October, 2023

Statista 2023, Indian IT industry report, Retrieved from https://www-statista-com.mdilibrary.remotexs.in/statistics/1247634/startup-india-number-of-reported-jobs/ Accessed on 10th October, 2023

Statista. (2023, July 27). *IoT connected devices worldwide 2019-2030* | Statista. https://www.statista.com/statistics/1183457/iot-connected-devices-worldwide/

Stiglitz, J. E. (2002). *Globalization and its discontents*. W.W. Norton & Company.

Subramani, R., Mustafa, M. A., Ghadir, G. K., Al-Tmimi, H. M., Alani, Z. K., Haridas, D., ... & Kumar, A. P. (2024). Advancements in 3D printing materials: A comparative analysis of performance and applications. *Applied Chemical Engineering*, 3867-3867.

Su, H. N., & Lee, P. C. (2010). Mapping knowledge structure by keyword co-occurrence: A first look at journal papers in Technology Foresight. *Scientometrics*, 85(1), 65–79. DOI: 10.1007/s11192-010-0259-8

Sundarasen, S., Goel, S., & Zulaini, F. A. (2017). Impact of investors' protection, transparency level and legal origin on initial public offering (IPO) initial returns. *Managerial Finance*, 43(7), 738–760. DOI: 10.1108/MF-08-2016-0230

Syed, M., & McLean, K. C. (2021). Disentangling paradigm and method can help bring qualitative research to post-positivist psychology and address the generalizability crisis. *Behavioral and Brain Sciences*, 45, 58–60. PMID: 35139943

Taherdoost, H. (2024). *Digital Transformation Roadmap: From Vision to Execution*. CRC Press. DOI: 10.1201/9781003471226

Tailab, Mohamed. (2014). ' The Effect of Capital Structure on Profitability of Energy American Firms ', *International Journal of Business and Management Invention* 3.

Takeda-Berger, S. L., & Frazzon, E. M. (2024). An inventory data-driven model for predictive-reactive production scheduling. *International Journal of Production Research*, 62(9), 3059–3083. DOI: 10.1080/00207543.2023.2217297

Tao, F., Cheng, J., Qi, Q., Zhang, M., Zhang, H., & Sui, F. (2018). Digital twin-driven product design, manufacturing and service with big data. *International Journal of Advanced Manufacturing Technology*, 94(9-12), 3563–3576. DOI: 10.1007/s00170-017-0233-1

Tedeschi, L. O., Greenwood, P. L., & Halachmi, I. (2021). Advancements in sensor technology and decision support intelligent tools to assist smart livestock farming. *Journal of Animal Science*, 99(2), skab038. DOI: 10.1093/jas/skab038 PMID: 33550395

Teece, D. J. (2014). The foundations of enterprise performance: Dynamic and ordinary capabilities in an (economic) theory of firms. *The Academy of Management Perspectives*, 28(4), 328–352. DOI: 10.5465/amp.2013.0116

Teti, E., & Montefusco, I. (2022). Corporate governance and IPO underpricing: Evidence from the italian market. *The Journal of Management and Governance*, 26(3), 851–889. DOI: 10.1007/s10997-021-09563-z

Theriou, N. G., Mlekanis, G., & Maditinos, D. (2011). Herding by mutual fund managers in the Athens Stock Exchange. *European Research Studies*, 14(4), 131–154. DOI: 10.35808/ersj/339

Thoben, K. D., Wiesner, S., & Wuest, T. (2017). State of the art and challenges for digitalization in the manufacturing industry. *IFAC-PapersOnLine*, 50(1), 9995–10000.

Thomadakis, S., Nounis, C., & Gounopoulos, D. (2012). Long-term performance of Greek IPOs. *European Financial Management*, 18(1), 117–141. DOI: 10.1111/j.1468-036X.2010.00546.x

Topete, A., He, C., Protzko, J., Schooler, J., & Hegarty, M. (2024). How is GPS used? Understanding navigation system use and its relation to spatial ability. *Cognitive Research: Principles and Implications*, 9(1), 16. Advance online publication. DOI: 10.1186/s41235-024-00545-x PMID: 38504081

Trejo, S. J. (1997). Why Do Mexican Americans Earn Low Wages? *Journal of Political Economy*, 105(6), 1235–1268. DOI: 10.1086/516391

Truden, C., Kollingbaum, M. J., Reiter, C., & Schasché, S. E. (2022). A GIS-based analysis of reachability aspects in rural public transportation. *Case Studies on Transport Policy*, 10(3), 1827–1840. Advance online publication. DOI: 10.1016/j.cstp.2022.07.012

Tzavella, K., Skopeliti, A., & Fekete, A. (2022). Volunteered geographic information use in crisis, emergency and disaster management: A scoping review and a web atlas. *Geo-Spatial Information Science*. Advance online publication. DOI: 10.1080/10095020.2022.2139642

Van Campenhout, G., & Verhestraeten, J. F. (2010). Herding behavior among financial analysts: A literature review.Hub Research Paper 2010/39 November 2010.

Van Den Hoek, J., Friedrich, H. K., Ballasiotes, A., Peters, L. E. R., & Wrathall, D. (2021). Development after displacement: Evaluating the utility of openstreetmap data for monitoring sustainable development goal progress in refugee settlements. *ISPRS International Journal of Geo-Information*, 10(3), 153. Advance online publication. DOI: 10.3390/ijgi10030153

Van Raan, A. (2003). The use of bibliometric analysis in research performance assessment and monitoring of interdisciplinary scientific developments. *TATuP-Zeitschrift für Technikfolgenabschätzung in Theorie und Praxis*, 12(1), 20–29. DOI: 10.14512/tatup.12.1.20

Varga, A. (2000). Local academic knowledge spillovers and the concentration of innovative activities. *Geography and Economic Systems*, 30(3), 173–188. DOI: 10.1016/S0016-7185(00)00036-7

Varone, A., Heilmann, Z., Porruvecchio, G., & Romanino, A. (2024). Solar parking lot management: An IoT platform for smart charging EV fleets, using real-time data and production forecasts. *Renewable & Sustainable Energy Reviews*, 189, 113845. DOI: 10.1016/j.rser.2023.113845

Vasiljeva, M. V., Ponkratov, V. V., Kuznetsov, N. V., Maramygin, M. S., & Osinovskaya, I. V. (2019). Implementation of the Blue Ocean Strategy Using Simulation: Firm-Level Evidence from Russian Steel Market. *Industrial Engineering & Management Systems*, 18(4), 859–871. DOI: 10.7232/iems.2019.18.4.859

Venezia, I., Nashikkar, A., & Shapira, Z. (2011). Firm specific and macro herding by professional and amateur investors and their effects on market volatility. *Journal of Banking & Finance*, 35(7), 1599–1609. DOI: 10.1016/j.jbankfin.2010.11.015

Vial, G. (2009). Understanding digital transformation: A review and a research agenda. *The Journal of Strategic Information Systems*, 28(2), 118–144. DOI: 10.1016/j.jsis.2019.01.003

Vieira, E. F. S., & Pereira, M. S. V. (2015). Herding behaviour and sentiment: Evidence in a small European market. *Revista de Contabilidad*, 18(1), 78–86. DOI: 10.1016/j.rcsar.2014.06.003

Vieito, J. P., Espinosa, C., Wong, W. K., Batmunkh, M. U., Choijil, E., & Hussien, M. (2023). Herding behavior in integrated financial markets: the case of MILA. *International Journal of Emerging Markets*. https://doi.org/DOI: 10.1108/IJOEM-08-2021-1202

Vo, X. V., & Phan, D. B. A. (2019). Herd behavior and idiosyncratic volatility in a frontier market. *Pacific-Basin Finance Journal*, 53, 321–330. DOI: 10.1016/j.pacfin.2018.10.005

Wallerstein, I. (2004). *World-systems analysis: An introduction*. Duke University Press.

Wang, C. S., Tang, H. W., & Chen, R. C. (2017). Does IPO subscription demand affect investor herd behavior in Taiwan? *International Review of Economics & Finance*, 51, 258–272. DOI: 10.1016/j.iref.2017.06.004

Wang, S., Wan, J., Zhang, D., Li, D., & Zhang, C. (2016). Towards smart factory for Industry 4.0: A self-organized multi-agent system with big data based feedback and coordination. *Computer Networks*, 101, 158–168. DOI: 10.1016/j.comnet.2015.12.017

Wang, Y., & Wang, G. (2021). IPO underpricing and long-term performance in China: The perspective of price limit policy. *Managerial Finance*, 47(9), 1233–1252. DOI: 10.1108/MF-08-2020-0428

Wang, Z., Zhang, Y., Jia, B., & Gao, Z. (2024). Comparative Analysis of Usage Patterns and Underlying Determinants for Ride-hailing and Traditional Taxi Services: A Chicago Case Study. *Transportation Research Part A, Policy and Practice*, 179, 103912. Advance online publication. DOI: 10.1016/j.tra.2023.103912

Wang, Z., Zheng, J., Han, C., Lu, B., Yu, D., Yang, J., & Han, L. (2024). Exploring the Potential of OpenStreetMap Data in Regional Economic Development Evaluation Modeling. *Remote Sensing (Basel)*, 16(2), 239. Advance online publication. DOI: 10.3390/rs16020239

Wasiuzzaman, S., Yong, F. L. K., Sundarasen, S. D. D., & Othman, N. S. (2018). Impact of disclosure of risk factors on the initial returns of initial public offerings (IPOs). *Accounting Research Journal*, 31(1), 46–62. DOI: 10.1108/ARJ-09-2016-0122

Wasnik, A. P., & Jain, A. (2023). Government Support for Startups: A Comprehensive Analysis of Funding Initiatives and the Role of the Indian Government in Nurturing the Startup Ecosystem. *Economics and Business Quarterly Reviews*, 6(3), 98–107. DOI: 10.31014/aior.1992.06.03.523

Weber, M. (1978). Ethnic groups. In Roth, G., & Wittich, C. (Eds.), *Economy and Society: an outline of interpretative sociology, 1, (II), Berkele: Univ. Of California press, 385-398*. DOI: 10.1007/978-1-349-26403-2_2

Welch, I. (2000). Herding among security analysts. *Journal of Financial Economics*, 58(3), 369–396. DOI: 10.1016/S0304-405X(00)00076-3

Weller, C., Kleer, R., & Piller, F. T. (2015). Economic implications of 3D printing: Market structure models in light of additive manufacturing revisited. *International Journal of Production Economics*, 164, 43–56. DOI: 10.1016/j.ijpe.2015.02.020

Whig, P., Kouser, I. S., Bhatia, A. B., Nadikattu, I. R. R., & Alkali, Y. J. (2024). 6 IoT Industrial. *Wireless Communication Technologies: Roles, Responsibilities, and Impact of IoT, 6G, and Blockchain Practices*, 101.

Wohlers Associates. (2023, May 31). *Wohlers Report (2023)*. Wohlers Associates. https://wohlersassociates.com/product/wr2023/

Work-Related fatalities up nearly six percent in 2022. (n.d.). American Society of Safety Professionals. https://www.assp.org/news-and-articles/work-related-fatalities-up-nearly-six-percent-in-2022

World Bank. (2020). *World development report 2020: The changing nature of work*. World Bank Group., DOI: 10.1596/978-1-4648-1457-0

World Bank. (2023). Food-Security-Update 2023 https://thedocs.worldbank.org/en/doc/40ebbf38f5a6b68bfc11e5273e1405d4-0090012022/related/Food-Security-Update-XCVI-November-30-23.pdf. Retrieved on 29th May 2024.

Xia, H., Weng, J., Boubaker, S., Zhang, Z., & Jasimuddin, S. M. (2024). Cross-influence ofinformation and risk effects on the IPO market: Exploring risk disclosure with a machine learning approach. *Annals of Operations Research*, 334(1), 761–797. DOI: 10.1007/s10479-022-05012-8 PMID: 36312208

Xie, J., Wang, J., & Yang, L. (2018). Reference group perspective on individual investors'herdbehavior: The effects of self-esteem and trait anxiety. *Psychologia*, 61(1), 1–25. DOI: 10.2117/psysoc.2019-A003

Yadav, S. (2024). Transformative frontiers: A comprehensive review of emerging technologies in modern healthcare. *Cureus*, 16(3). Advance online publication. DOI: 10.7759/cureus.56538 PMID: 38646390

Yang, W. R., & Chen, Y. L. (2015). The response of dynamic herd behavior to domestic and us market factors: Evidence from the greater China stock markets. *Emerging Markets Finance and Trade, 51*(sup1), S18-S41.https://doi.org/DOI: 10.1080/1540496X.2014.998884

Yang, W. R. (2011). Herding with costly information and signal extraction. *International Review of Economics & Finance*, 20(4), 624–632. DOI: 10.1016/j.iref.2010.12.004

Yang, W., Yang, C., Yang, B., & Feng, G. (2022). Time-Varying Research on Investors' Trading Psychology Rational and Irrational Market Sentiment Based on the Perspective of 5G Networks and Information Economics. *Wireless Communications and Mobile Computing*, 23(2), 675–689. DOI: 10.1155/2022/3594213

Yang, X., Zhang, Y., Chen, X., Huang, L., & Qiu, X. (2024). Limitations and Management of Dynamic Navigation System for Locating Calcified Canals Failure. *Journal of Endodontics*, 50(1), 96–105. Advance online publication. DOI: 10.1016/j.joen.2023.10.010 PMID: 37890613

Yan, Y. (2024). Research on optimal path planning technology for vehicle positioning and navigation system. *Applied Mathematics and Nonlinear Sciences*, 9(1), 20230397. Advance online publication. DOI: 10.2478/amns.2023.1.00397

Yazdi, M. (2024). Digital Twins and Virtual Prototyping for Industrial Systems. In *Advances in Computational Mathematics for Industrial System Reliability and Maintainability* (pp. 155–168). Springer Nature Switzerland. DOI: 10.1007/978-3-031-53514-7_9

Yousaf, I., & Yarovaya, L. (2022). Herding behavior in conventional cryptocurrency market, non-fungible tokens, and DeFi assets. *Finance Research Letters*, 50, 103299. DOI: 10.1016/j.frl.2022.103299

Youssef, M. (2022). What drives herding behavior in the cryptocurrency market? *Journal of Behavioral Finance*, 23(2), 230–239. DOI: 10.1080/15427560.2020.1867142

Youssef, M., & Waked, S. S. (2022). Herding behavior in the cryptocurrency market during COVID-19 pandemic: The role of media coverage. *The North American Journal of Economics and Finance*, 62, 101752. DOI: 10.1016/j.najef.2022.101752

Yunus, M., & Sijabat, F. N. (2021). A review on blue ocean strategy effect on competitive advantage and firm performance. *Academy of Strategic Management Journal*, 20(1), 1–10.

Yusuf, S. (2001). *The East Asian miracle: Economic growth and public policy*. Oxford University Press.

Zeng, D. Z. (2015). *Global value chains: What are the benefits and why do they matter?* World Bank Group., DOI: 10.1596/978-1-4648-0395-5

Zhang, D., Ge, Y., Stein, A., & Zhang, W. (2021). Ranking of VGI contributor reputation using an evaluation-based weighted pagerank. *Transactions in GIS*, 25(3), 1439–1459. Advance online publication. DOI: 10.1111/tgis.12735

Zhang, X., Singh, S., Li, J., & Shao, X. (2024). Exploring the effects of value co-creation strategies in event services on attendees' citizenship behaviors: The roles of customer empowerment and psychological ownership. *Journal of Retailing and Consumer Services*, 76, 103619. DOI: 10.1016/j.jretconser.2023.103619

Zhang, Y., Love, D. J., Krogmeier, J. V., Anderson, C. R., Heath, R. W., & Buckmaster, D. R. (2021). Challenges and Opportunities of Future Rural Wireless Communications. *IEEE Communications Magazine*, 59(12), 16–22. Advance online publication. DOI: 10.1109/MCOM.001.2100280

Zheng, D., Li, H., & Zhu, X. (2015). Herding behavior in institutional investors: Evidence from China's stock market. *Journal of Multinational Financial Management*, 32, 59–76. DOI: 10.1016/j.mulfin.2015.09.001

Zheng, Z., Tang, K., Liu, Y., & Guo, J. M. (2021). Gender and herding. *Journal of Empirical Finance*, 64, 379–400. DOI: 10.1016/j.jempfin.2021.10.005

Zhong, L. X., Xu, W. J., Ren, F., & Shi, Y. D. (2013). Coupled effects of market impact and asymmetric sensitivity in financial markets. *Physica A*, 392(9), 2139–2149. DOI: 10.1016/j.physa.2013.01.030

Zhou, L., Miller, J., Vezza, J., Mayster, M., Raffay, M., Justice, Q., Al Tamimi, Z., Hansotte, G., Sunkara, L. D., & Bernat, J. (2024). Additive Manufacturing: A Comprehensive Review. *Sensors (Basel)*, 24(9), 2668. DOI: 10.3390/s24092668 PMID: 38732776

Zhou, R. T., & Lai, R. N. (2009). Herding and information-based trading. *Journal of Empirical Finance*, 16(3), 388–393. DOI: 10.1016/j.jempfin.2009.01.004

Zou, G., Cheng, Q., Chen, W., & Meng, J. G. (2020). What causes the IPO underpricing? New evidence from China's SME market. *Applied Economics*, 52(23), 2493–2507. DOI: 10.1080/00036846.2019.1693017

Zschirnt, E., Ruedin D., (2016) Ethnic Discrimination in Hiring Decisions: A Meta-Analysis of Correspondence Tests 1990–2015. *Journal of Ethnic and Migration Studites*, 1–19.

About the Contributors

Erum Shaikh has a PhD from the Institute of Business Administration, University of Sindh, Jamshoro, Pakistan. She is an assistant professor and head of the Department of Business Administration at Shaheed Benazir Bhutto University, Sanghar Campus. Her research interests are Corporate Social Responsibility, Finance, Entrepreneurship, Sustainability, Corporate Governance, Management and Entrepreneurial Finance. She has authored over 40 publications (research papers, conference papers and book chapters) in top-notch research journals. She has edited seven books and is the editor of five research journals. She has wide experience in teaching and administration and has served more than ten years in academics. She has organized and participated in several research conferences and workshops as a keynote speaker, session Chair and guest speaker. She is a good teacher, researcher, speaker and trainer.

Abdul Samad Dahri holds PhD degree in Human Resource Management (HRM) awarded in 2019 at Universiti Utara Malaysia, Malaysia. He endeavours research in HRM prospects in different fields of life. His research profile includes many national and international research publications and conferences. Hands-on data screening and analysis through SPSS and Smart-PLS. He strongly believes in the ability to fulfill or to deliver as per the commitment. Dr. Abdul Samad have blended 4 years of academia and 6 years of industry experience. He has unique mix of teaching and supervising experience for research projects, research reports, and thesis of students from graduate to postgraduate level. He is currently serving as an Assistant Professor, Director ORIC, member of academic accreditation team, and academic advisor to the variety of management sciences programs at Shaheed Benazir Bhutto University, Pakistan.

***

Munir Ahmad is a seasoned professional in the realm of Spatial Data Infrastructure (SDI), Geo-Information Productions, Information Systems, and Information Governance, boasting over 25 years of dedicated experience in the field. With a PhD in Computer Science, Dr. Ahmad's expertise spans Spatial Data Production, Management, Processing, Analysis, Visualization, and Quality Control. Throughout his career, Dr. Ahmad has been deeply involved in the development and deployment of SDI systems specially in the context of Pakistan, leveraging his proficiency in Spatial Database Design, Web, Mobile & Desktop GIS, and Geo Web Services Architecture. His contributions to Volunteered Geographic Information (VGI) and Open Source Geoportal & Metadata Portal have significantly enriched the geospatial community. As a trainer and researcher, Dr. Ahmad has authored over 50 publications, advancing the industry's knowledge base and fostering innovation in Geo-Tech, Data Governance, and Information Infrastructure, and Emerging Technologies. His commitment to Research and Development (R&D) is evident in his role as a dedicated educator and mentor in the field.

Luigi Alieri is a Professor at the University of Salerno, Italy.

Atanu Bhattacharya has Started the career in Front Office with Radisson Hotels in 2010 and served till the position of Lobby Manager. Joined the academics in 2014 and has been in association with some reputed colleges all over India such as Golden Regency Institute, AIMS College of Hotel Management, Regal College of Hotel Management & Tourism, Om Sterling Global University and is currently working as Head of the Department, Medhavi Skills University. He has 13 International Research Papers under his belt. He has also secured publishing authority for 6 Indian Patents under Intellectual Property Rights.

Mohsen Brahmi is affiliated to the University of Sfax.

Houssem Chemingui, Ph.D., is a dedicated academic researcher and educator specializing in Information Systems. With a keen interest in Business Process Management, Requirements Engineering, and Software Product Lines, he brings a wealth of knowledge and expertise to his teaching and research endeavors. Houssem obtained his Ph.D. in Computer Sciences from the University of Paris 1 Panthéon Sorbonne in 2021, following a Research Master in Computer Science from Manar University, Tunisia, in 2014, and a Bachelor's Degree in Computer Science Applied to Business Management from Carthage University, Tunisia, in 2012. His teaching interests span Process and Data Mining, Management of Information Systems, Data Analysis, and Web Development. Houssem's courses, at both the Master and Bachelor levels, cover a range of topics including Information Systems Management, Software Engineering, Web Development, Database Management, and Programming

Languages such as Python. With a commitment to excellence in both research and education, Houssem is dedicated to shaping the next generation of IT professionals.

Trupti Dandekar Humnekar is a distinguished professional with over 15 years of experience spanning industry, academia, and research. She is currently working as Associate Professor at Jain (Deemed to be) University. Dr. Humnekar has established herself as a thought leader and innovator, contributing significantly to her field through numerous national and international publications. Her extensive expertise reflects a deep commitment to advancing knowledge and fostering development within her discipline.

Salman Hameed has extensive experience in production and manufacturing and has developed strong people management skills through his passion for learning and implementing new strategies. He holds an MS in HR and is pursuing a Ph.D. on the impact of employee values on organizational sustainability. He is also experienced in HSE with international certification in OHSAS 18000 and has a PDG in Psychology. Mr. Salman is an advocate for sustainability and has given talks on the topic, as well as championing the idea of sustainability on social platforms. His multi-dimensional experience enables him to understand and impart value-based solutions to process owners in their work.

Ahsan Ahmed Jaleel is an Assistant Professor at the Qasim Ibrahim school of Business at Villa College, Maldives. He holds a Doctor of Philosophy in Mathematics from Monash University, a Master of Science in Mathematics from the University of Adelaide, and a Bachelor of Science in Mathematics, Computing, and Statistics from Goldsmiths, University of London. Part of his research is dedicated to building mathematical models in various aspects of business studies, with a particular emphasis on consumer behavior. His scholarly pursuits aim to unravel the complexities of how individuals make purchasing decisions and how these psychological processes can be effectively modelled. In addition to his work on consumer behavior, he is recently focused on gamified and simulation-based learning. He is the lead researcher on the project titled "Effectiveness of Gamification for the 10 Second Generation," a research initiative funded by Villa College. Dr. Ahsan combines his robust mathematical background with his passion for understanding human behavior, contributing valuable insights to the fields of business studies and educational methodologies

Archana K, Department of Management, Sambhram Academy of Management Studies, Bangalore

Muhammad Khan is an accomplished professional in the field of business administration, holding a Master's degree in Business Administration with a specialization in International Management from Ballarat University, Australia. His academic journey has provided him with a profound understanding of international business practices, leadership, and management strategies. Throughout his career, Muhammad Khan has garnered extensive experience as a Program Director and Coordinator, skillfully overseeing and developing academic programs to align with industry trends and meet student needs. Currently, he serves as a Senior Lecturer and MBA Program Coordinator in the Qasim Ibrahim school of Business at Villa College in the Maldives, where he continues to impart his knowledge and expertise to the next generation of business leaders.

Deepika Krishnan is doctor at Symbiosis School of Banking and Finance, Symbiosis International (Deemed University), Pune, India-412115.

Maida Maqsood did MS in English from Government College Women University, Sialkot. Throughout her academic journey, she has achieved notable successes that have strengthened her foundation in literature, education and linguistics. Her Master's research reflects her dedication to exploring critical themes in literature with the use of linguistics style. Additionally, her active participation in different conferences and seminars, such as The International Conference on Modern Trends in Applied Linguistics, and 7th ASNeT International Multidisciplinary Academic Conference 2024 (AIMAC 2024) highlight her commitment to staying updated with current trends in her field.

Ibtissem Missaoui is a Doctor at High Institute of Managment, University of Sousse.

Annamaria Nese is a Doctor at Department of Economics and Statistics, University of Salerno

Nitin Poddar is a distinguished service expert with an impressive career spanning 14 years in both industry and academics. Holds an MBA in Marketing from IEC University and a degree in Hotel Management from Banarsidas Chandiwala Institute of Hotel Management and Catering Technology, New Delhi. Began his career with the ITC group in Front Office Operations. His career trajectory includes significant roles with Fitness First India Pvt. Ltd. and Co-Incept Hospitality Pvt. Ltd., where he served as Training Head and General Manager (Operations). Prior to joining the ITM group of Institutions, he was the Associate Director at AAFT School of Hospitality and Tourism & School of Health and Wellness. His expertise lies in Food & Beverage (F&B) Service, Front Office Operations, and Sales & Marketing.

Alok Prasad as 26 years experience in Teaching (Amity University Noida, IP University Delhi, UPTU Lucknow) and Training Hospitality Industry 6 years experience in Hotel Industry (Jaypee Group, Oberoi Group)

Natasha Saqib is currently working as Sr. Assistant Professor at the Department of Management Studies, University of Kashmir, India. She received her B.Sc. (Hon.) Industrial Chemistry from University of Kashmir, MBA from Islamic university of Science and Technology and Ph.D. from University of Kashmir, India. Dr. Natasha has more than 13 years of experience in academia. She has several research publications in internationally acclaimed journals like International Journal of Emerging Markets, Online Information Review, Journal of Entrepreneurship in Emerging Economies, Young Consumers, Journal of Tourism Analysis, International Journal of Innovation Science, Asia Pacific Journal of Innovation and Entrepreneurship, Management and Labour studies and PSU Research Review, among others.

Deepa Saxena completed graduation in Science from Rani Durgavati University, Jabalpur in the year 1999 and afterwards have pursued MBA in Marketing and HR from Guru Ghasidas University, Bilaspur in the year 2001. Completed PhD in Advertising on the topic, 'Ethical issues in Advertising in Vindhya Region', from Awadhesh Pratap Singh University, Rewa in the year 2010. Currently working as Guest Faculty in the Department of Business Administration, Awadhesh Pratap Singh University, Rewa (MP).

Muhammad Nawaz Tunio, an accomplished scholar in Entrepreneurship, Management, and Policy, brings much experience and expertise to the academic arena. With a Ph.D. in Entrepreneurship, Innovation, and Economic Development from Alpen Adria University, Klagenfurt, Austria, Dr. Tunio has established himself as a leading authority in his field. Currently serving as an Assistant Professor at the Department of Business Administration, University of Sufism and Modern Sciences, Bhitshah, Pakistan, he has also held positions at esteemed institutions such as Greenwich University and Mohammad Ali Jinnah University. Dr. Tunio's research interests encompass many topics, including Entrepreneurship, Innovation, Economic Development, Youth Development, CSR, and Qualitative Methods. His scholarly contributions extend far beyond the confines of academia, with numerous research articles published in top-tier journals and prestigious book chapters with reputable publishers. With an impressive research profile boasting over 1000 citations, an H-Index of 18, and an i10-index of 31, Dr. Tunio's work has made a significant impact in the academic community. His consultancy experience includes projects.

Index

www.ingramcontent.com/pod-product-compliance
Lightning Source LLC
LaVergne TN
LVHW081330021026
849161LV00008BA/1926
* 9 7 9 8 3 6 9 3 5 7 2 3 1 *